ALAN RO[...]

Good Camp[...]

Britain and Ire[...]

Contents

Published by: **DENEWAY GUIDES & TRAVEL LTD**
Chesil Lodge, West Bexington, Dorchester, Dorset DT2 9DG
Tel: (01308) 897809 Fax: (01308) 898017

Printed by: BPC Wheatons, Exeter
Covers: Jayne Homer - Maps: Charles Broughton
Cover photograph is of Wave Crest, Co. Kerry, Ireland by George Boyce

Sales: **Derek Searle Associates**
The Coach House, Cippenham Lodge
Cippenham Lane, Slough SL1 5AN
Tel: (01753) 539295 Fax: (01753) 551863

Distribution: **Bookpoint Ltd**
39 Milton Park
Abingdon, Oxon OX14 4TD
Tel: (01235) 835001 Fax: (01235) 861038

© **Deneway Guides & Travel Ltd 1995**
ISBN: 0 901586 74 9 ISSN: 0963-1135

Foreword

"While there may be plenty of site guides to choose from, there aren't any more accurate or trustworthy than the Alan Rogers Good Camps Guide series" - not our words, but those of travel writer Ian Waller when reviewing site guides in Caravan Plus magazine earlier this year. He went on to nominate our Britain & Ireland Guide `Best Buy' amongst all the most popular site guides!

So what is it that makes our Guides so special? The answer essentially is our **selective** approach, whereby we inspect, select and then write our own fully descriptive, honest report on every park we feature. This approach was introduced by Alan Rogers himself when he started the Guides nearly thirty years ago and when Alan retired we continued with the same philosophy. You can find plenty of guides which feature far more parks than ours, but you'll have a problem finding a guide which gives you anywhere near as much objective information or detail about each park as we do.

During the year, as usual, we have undertaken our extensive monitoring reviews of our featured parks. Some previously featured parks have been removed from the 1996 edition following our Assessors' reports for several reasons - falling standards, poor maintenance, overcrowding, increased emphasis on holiday homes as distinct from touring pitches or too many rallies in high season, being typical examples. We have also continued our search for additional parks and are happy to feature over 40 new ones in this edition.

We are very pleased also to have been able to extend our section on Ireland even more, thanks to the peace initiative and the assistance of Rosemary and George Boyce, who joined our small team of assessors and have been undertaking a thorough review of parks in both Northern Ireland and the Republic. This extended commitment to Ireland has been reinforced through our new co-operative initiative with Irish Ferries whereby our readers will be able to enjoy substantial savings on their services during 1996 - **full details of these arrangements are given on the vouchers in this guide.**

Once again we wish all our readers a thoroughly enjoyable Camping and Caravanning New Year, hopefully favoured by another fine summer!

Lois Edwards MA, FTS
Clive Edwards BEd, FTS
Sue Smart   Directors

The Alan Rogers' Philosophy

Our philosophy has been always to feature a selection of good quality, well maintained and efficiently run parks, irrespective of size and/or the range of facilities offered, and to provide sufficient objective information for readers to use as a basis for making their own choice of park. The information provided is designed to provide an insight into what a park is really like, as well as factual information about its facilities, etc. Our criteria for selection are based on the *quality* of the park and its facilities, rather than just the number or range of facilities provided. We are particularly concerned about the quality of the *park itself* and its *pitches*, the *sanitary facilities* and the `hospitality'. Unless these features, which every park has, meet our quality standards it will not even be considered for inclusion. Of course, many parks have other facilities in addition to these, such as restaurants, pools, etc. and where these are provided, they too must conform to our quality standards.

Every park featured in our Guides is, of course, known to us personally and is only included after a rigorous initial inspection by one of our small team of Site Assessors. All parks are chosen on merit alone - we do not charge parks to be in one of our Guides. We also carry out regular (unannounced!) monitoring visits to parks featured in the Guides to ensure that standards are being maintained after its initial selection. Of course, we do occasionally get caught out, usually by events beyond our control such as an unexpected change of management, so we do appreciate the invaluable feedback we receive from our readers which enables us to follow up such changes, etc. with the minimum of delay - we provide a special Readers Report form in the Guide for just this purpose (see page 180).

Over the years we have responded to readers' requests to provide additional information. In recent years, we have given more `tourist destination' information, more about pubs, restaurants and local public transport and more about facilities for motorcaravans, particularly the large `American motorhome' type.

In this edition we have included whether payment can be made by credit card. Lack of space precludes us giving details about exactly which of the many different credit cards, debit cards, charge cards etc., are accepted. Since 1993 we have significantly increased the amount of space devoted to this type of information and as a result of the generally much improved provision of sanitary facilities over the years, we have somewhat reduced the amount of detail provided in that respect. To a large extent the improvement in sanitary facilities has been influenced by the Graded Holiday Parks scheme (featuring the Quality Tick logo), operated by the British Holiday Homes and Parks Association, the National Caravan Council and the National Tourist Boards.

The Guide is arranged geographically - for England we have used the 11 official Tourist Board Regions as a basis for dividing the country into manageable sections. These regions, and the counties within each, are identified at the start of each section with a small location map. For Scotland, Wales, the Irish Republic and Northern Ireland we have simply used tourist region or county boundaries. The maps and index on pages 184 to 192 form the basis on which to identify both the approximate location of parks regionally and by county, and also the page number on which the appropriate Site Report is to be found. Unless stated otherwise, sites featured in our Guide accept all types of unit, but if you have something exceptional (e.g. a very large American motorhome or large twin-axle caravan), it is worth checking with the park first, to avoid disappointment on arrival.

For 1996 we have introduced a grid system for our maps, whereby each grid square is identified by co-ordinates in the form of two letters - one on the horizontal axis, and a different one on the vertical axis. In the index, therefore, each park is identified by two letters, indicating the map grid square in which it is located, followed by a number which identifies the actual site location within that square. We hope this will make it easier and quicker to identify the location of parks in unfamiliar areas.

An example of an entry, with explanatory notes, is shown overleaf.

How to use the 1996 Discount Voucher !

The Discount Card/Vouchers are in three parts:

Part 1   should be retained and must not be removed from the Guide. You should complete it by adding your name, address and signature. This part includes the printed Card Number, and should be shown to those parks indicating special offers for our readers as identified by an Alan Rogers' logo in the Guide.

Part 2   should be completed by adding your name, address, the card number as shown in part 1, and your signature. This part may then be used to claim your discount(s) for travel, breakdown, caravan or motorcaravan insurance.

Part 3   should be completed by adding your name, address, the card number as shown in Part 1, and your signature. This part may then be used to claim your FERRY DISCOUNT, as directed.

Note that the Discount Cards are valid from **1 January - 31 December 1996 only**

Alan Rogers' Travel Club - arrangements for 1996

For some years we have operated a readers' club, known as the Alan Rogers Travel Club, which has provided members with a range of benefits in the form of discounted travel, breakdown insurance and a range of 'special offers' at some of our featured parks. With effect from 1 January 1996 however, we have decided to discontinue operating our Travel Club as a separate entity, and to make the various benefits available to ALL our readers. In other words, the benefits of Travel Club membership, apart from the newsletter, are now included in the price of our Guides. The 1996 editions of our other annual Guides include similar vouchers - the France Guide providing reductions for caravanners and motor-caravanners on most BRITTANY FERRIES services to France, and the Europe Guide reductions for campers, caravanners and motorcaravanners for early booking on all P&O EUROPEAN FERRIES services.

Campsite Reports

Example of an entry:

---

number   park name, nearest village, town
These details should identify the park's location to within a mile or so on any medium scale map - finer details are given in the directions section at the foot of the main report.

summary line

main text
*A general description of the park in which we try to give an idea of the general features of the park - its size, its situation, its strengths and weaknesses, the quality and adequacy of the toilet block, special amenities and any special local attractions. Some things may be assumed unless the report states otherwise: that the toilet block has free hot showers, hot water in washbasins, mirrors, some razor points and chemical toilet disposal, and that dogs are accepted on leads. Throughout the reports the word 'site' is used in the sense of park or campsite itself, not your individual place on the park, which we have called a 'pitch'. Practically all our parks now have electrical connections to some pitches and we include details of the amperage available. We try to tell you if the park does **not** take any particular type of normal touring unit - caravans, motorcaravans and tents - however, if you have an unusual unit (e.g. American motorhome, commercial vehicle or motorcycle) it is advisable to check with the park first to make sure that there are no special restrictions.*

Charges:
Open:
Address:
Tel/Fax:
Reservations:

General administrative detail is given in the right hand column. - see below.

Directions:
*Given last, separated from the main text in order that they may be read and assimilated more easily by a navigator en route. It is possible that a few may have changed due to road improvement schemes, etc. since we visited the park. If this has happened we trust that any delay caused is or was of only minor proportions. The 6-figure **Ordnance Survey Grid Reference** (O.S.GR:) point is provided by the park for those wishing to locate a site by this means.*

General information: is grouped under the headings of charges, opening dates, address, telephone and reservation policy. Please note that the opening dates are those advised to us during the early autumn of the previous year - park operators can, and sometimes do, alter these dates before the start of the following season - often for good reasons - so if you intend to visit a park shortly after its published opening date, or shortly before its closing date, it really is wise to check that it will actually be open at the time required. Similarly some parks operate a restricted service during the low season, only opening some of their facilities (e.g. swimming pools) during the main season - where we know about this, and have the relevant dates, we indicate it, but if you are at all doubtful again it is wise to check.

Charges are the latest provided by the parks. In those few cases where the 1995 or 1996 prices are not given, we try to give a general guide. The pricing structures vary considerably and we try to be as uniform and succinct as possible in what is included since some parks have a simple tariff, while others have a vast complex of possibilities. The same is true of reservations and what is written cannot wholly replace the official park tariff and reservation form. Disabled readers are also advised to telephone the park of their choice before turning up to ensure that facilities are appropriate to their particular needs.

We note an ever increasing number of 'special' pitches under a variety of fancy names (e.g. Executive, Panorama, Super). These provide a range of extra facilities such as waste water disposal, TV and phone connections, patios, etc. and they are often booked up well in advance. We would suggest that readers interested is such pitches should contact the park concerned to check exactly what is provided and to pre-book if that is what they want.

KENT

1 Hawthorn Farm Caravan and Camping Park, Martin Mill, nr. Dover

Large, relaxed park with excellent facilities, close to Dover, useful for ferries.

Hawthorn Farm, set in 27 acres, is an extensive park taking 224 touring units of any type on several large meadows which could accommodate far more, plus 157 privately owned caravan holiday homes in their own areas. Campers not requiring electricity choose their own spot, most staying near the two toilet blocks leaving the farthest fields to those liking solitude. A special area is reserved for motorcycle campers. There are 100 large places with electricity (16A) marked by half hedges in groups of 6 either side of tarmac roadways. The sanitary blocks are modern and of excellent quality with free hot water to washbasins, set in flat surfaces, and roomy pre-set showers with seat and screen. Good washing-up sinks in each block - mostly covered. Launderette. Shop. Pub near. This is a well run, relaxed park with plenty of room and mature hedging and trees making an attractive environment. A torch would be useful.. Being only 4 miles from Dover docks, it is a very useful one for those using the ferries and is popular with continental visitors. Close to the sea at St Margaret's Bay, it is a fairly quiet situation apart from some rail noise. Gates close at 10 pm. - cards are available. A member of the Best of British group.

Directions: Park is north of A258 road (Dover-Deal), with signs to park and Martin Mill you turn off, about 4 miles from Dover. O.S.GR: TR341464.

Charges 1995:
-- Per adult £2.75 - £3.50; child (10-16 yrs) £1.50 - £2.00; pitch £2.75 - £3.50; hiker or biker less £2.00; dog £1.00; awning £1.50; electricity £1.80.
-- Less 10% for over 4 days booked.d.
Open:
1 March - 31 October or mid-December by arrangement.
Address:
Martin Mill, Dover, Kent CT15 5LA.
Tel:
Dover (01304) 852658.
FAX: (01227) 740585.
Reservations:
Contact park.

2 Broadhembury Holiday Park, Ashford

Small, pleasant touring park with some holiday homes, near to Folkestone and ferries.

In quiet countryside just outside Ashford, this well landscaped, sheltered park takes 55 touring units of any type, plus 25 caravan holiday homes, all on level, neatly cut grass and backing onto hedges. The central areas are left free, except where areas edging the roadway are used for transit stays. Of the total, 40 have electrical connections (16A). The park is friendly and popular and often becomes full in the main season, with a good proportion of continental visitors, so reservation is advisable. The single small toilet block is kept very clean and has free hot water to washbasins with shelf, mirror, and showers. Alongside are partially covered dishwashing sinks with hot and cold water. Small laundry room. The well stocked small shop also has comprehensive tourist information. TV room. Games room with table tennis and pool. Children's playground (grass or wood-chip bases) and play field away from the touring area but overlooked by the shop and reception. Public phone. Dog exercise field. Excellent security arrangements: gates are closed at 11 pm. in high season, coded exit. For those who want a trip to France, the new International railway terminal is at Ashford (Paris in 2 hours) - take your passport. A member of the Best of British group

Directions: From junction 10 on the M20 take the A2070 road. After 2 miles follow the sign for Kingsnorth. Turn left at 2nd crossroads in Kingsnorth village. O.S.GR: TR010382.

Charges 1995:
-- Per unit incl. 2 persons £8.00 - £10.50; extra adult £2.00; child (5-16 yrs) £1.50; extra car £2.00; dog £1.00; electricity £1.50;
-- Less 10% outside July/Aug. for bookings of 4 days or more.
-- VAT included.
Open:
All year.
Address:
Steeds Lane, Kingsnorth, Ashford, Kent TN26 1NQ.
Tel:
(01233) 620859.
FAX: (01233) 733261.
Reservations:
Made with £5 per night deposit (min. 3 nights at Easter or Spr. B.H.)

3 Pine Lodge Touring Caravan Park, Bearsted, nr. Maidstone

Newly established park near main London - Folkestone - Dover M20 motorway.

Set in the heart of Kent, near Leeds Castle and central for the historical and scenic attractions of this county, this recently opened park now has a new, purpose built reception/sanitary block. On a slight slope, the rectangular field is surrounded by rolling hills, farmland and trees. A gravel, one-way road system circles the site with pitches set against hedges around the perimeter and with a figure of eight in the centre and picnic areas. Trees have been planted across the park but these at present are for decoration and will take a while to grow large enough to provide shade. Of the 100 pitches, 85 have electricity (10A), there are water points around and a fenced central refuse, chemical disposal and waste water area. Good access from the A20 main road but there might be some traffic noise on pitches near the entrance. This is where the new, good sanitary facilities are situated. These include vanity style washbasins (free hot water), metered showers (token required), good laundry and washing up facilities. Basic supplies and gas exchange are available from reception which also has a range of tourist information. Local shops are 1 mile (Bearsted) or 3½ miles (Maidstone). The park is very convenient for events staged at Leeds Castle and is a good overnight stop between London and the channel ports. Small children's play area in a corner of the site, well away from the entrance. No dogs admitted.

Charges 1995:
-- Per unit incl. 2 adults £7.50; extra adult £1.50; child (3-14 yrs) 50p; electricity £1.50; tent, m/cycle incl. 1 person £4.00, 2 persons £5.00; hiker or cyclist's tent incl. 1 person £3.00, 2 persons £4.00 -- Min. charge £7.50.
Open:
All year.
Address:
A20 Ashford Road, Bearsted, Maidstone, Kent ME17 1XH.
Tel:
Maidstone (01622) 730018.
Reservations:
Contact park.

Directions: From junction 8 on M20, at A20 roundabout, turn towards Bearsted and Maidstone and park is about 1 mile on the left. O.S.GR: TQ808548.

PINE LODGE
TOURING PARK

Pretty grassed site of 7 acres. Large easy access with overnight parking area. New trees and shrubs; bordered by fields with woods to rear. Leeds Castle 1 mile. Very central for touring Kent; ideal stop for continental ports and Channel Tunnel. New centrally heated shower/toilet block. Dishwashing room; laundry room. Calor gas exchange. Shop. Chemical disposal; motorhome discharge point. Electric hook-ups. Play area. Open all year. Sorry - no dogs.

A20 Ashford Road, Hollingbourne, Maidstone, Kent ME17 1XH Tel: (01622) 730018

4 Manston Caravan and Camping Park, nr. Ramsgate

Pleasant, spacious, quiet park near Thanet resorts and only 3 miles from Sally terminal.

This 10 acre, flat park, quite close to RAF Manston airfield and the Spitfire Memorial Museum (little flying across the park), is very centrally situated for visits to the north Kent resorts, being 2 or 3 miles from Margate, Broadstairs or Ramsgate. There is a nice, open atmosphere to the touring part with plenty of room for the 100 touring units of any type for which it is licensed. There are 41 marked places with electricity (5A) for tourers, some taken up on a seasonal basis. Other pitches are not marked and campers find their own space. The total provision is spread over three hedged areas with extra areas for recreation, dog exercise and for 46 privately owned caravan holiday homes. The modern toilet block is of good quality and about right for size with washbasins spaced out and set in flat surfaces, with hot water, mirror and shelf, and large, fully controllable hot showers on payment. 2 partially enclosed washing-up sinks with hot water on meter. Washing machine and dryer. Small shop open twice a day. Large children's adventure play area on grass with safety mats. Public phone. The park is run personally by the friendly proprietors. Useful for the Ramsgate ferry - you can arrive at any time but for busy periods it is best to book and pay in advance.

Charges 1995:
-- Per small tent incl. 2 persons, no car £4.00 - £5.00; tent, caravan or motor caravan (4 persons) £5.50 - £10.00; awning £1.00 - £1.50; extra person £1.00; electricity £1.80; dog 80p.
-- VAT included.
Open:
Easter/1 April - end Oct.
Address:
Manston Court Road, Manston, Ramsgate, Kent CT12 5AU.
Tel:
(01843) 823442.
Reservations:
Any length with £10 deposit.

Directions: From west via M2/A229 or Canterbury/A28 follow Ramsgate signs on A253. Left after 1½ miles on B2048, right to B2190 and B2050 to Manston, cross airfield then left at camping sign. O.S.GR: TR346667

5 Black Horse Farm Caravan and Camping Park, Densole, nr. Folkestone

Well organised park near Channel Ports and Tunnel.

This neat, tidy and attractive 6 acre park, no longer a working farm, is situated amidst farming country in the village of Densole on the Downs just 4 miles north of Folkestone, 8 northeast of Dover and 11 south of Canterbury. This makes it ideal for a night stop travelling to or from the continent, or a base for visiting the many attractions of this part of southeast England. Accessed directly from the A260, the gravelled entrance road leads past reception towards the Top field which has neat, level grass, paved or gravel pitches, clearly numbered and with electricity, past hedging to the Middle area, then to the Bottom field with an open aspect and mostly level pitches. Half this area is given over to a play field, half to a wooded area - very pleasant. In total there are 45 pitches, 22 with electricity. There could be some road noise in the Top field. The crowning glory of the park is the carefully thought out and well constructed toilet block below reception. This has washbasins set in flat surfaces, two in private cabins, good sized shower compartments, a baby room and en-suite facilities for the disabled, laundry and washing-up facilities, all with free hot water and heated in cool weather. Opposite the entrance is a general store and newsagent and within 100 m. are a pub and filling station. Sports centre with pool (3 miles), golf (3 miles), horse riding (1 mile) and other nearby interests include the Tunnel Exhibition Centre, Battle of Britain Museum, Butterfly Centre, Canterbury Cathedral, Dover Castle to name just a few. Day trips to France can be made by Sea-Cat (Folkestone), tunnel, ferry or hovercraft (Dover). The friendly reception staff will advise and supply details. With reasonable charges, booking is necessary at peak times and B.Hs. Only one dog per unit accepted.

Charges 1995: -- Per person (6 yrs or above) £1.50; child (up to 5 yrs) 80p; caravan, tent, trailer tent, car, motorcycle (each) £1.75; motorcaravan £3.50; awning £1.00; dog 60p; electricity £1.50 (summer) - £1.75 (winter). **Open:** All year. **Address:** 385 Canterbury Road, Densole, Folkestone, Kent CT18 7BG. **Tel:** (01303) 892665. **Reservations:** Any length with 20% deposit except B.Hs min. 3 days and £10 deposit.

Directions: Directly by the A260 Folkestone - Canterbury road, 2 miles north of junction with A20. Follow signs for Canterbury. O.S.GR: TR211418.

6 Yew Tree Caravan Park, Petham, nr. Canterbury

Tranquil country site with excellent pool.

Yew Tree Park, a small site, is located in the heart of the Kent countryside overlooking the Chartham Downs. Just 5 miles south of Canterbury and 8 miles north of the M20, it is ideally placed either to explore the delights of the ancient city or the many attractions of eastern and coastal Kent. Its nearness to the channel ports also makes it useful for a night stop on the way to, or on return from, the continent. If catching a late evening ferry you may remain on site after 12 noon for a small payment. Apart from the peaceful environment, the main feature of the park is the very good, 60 x 30 ft. pool which is surrounded by 13 caravan holiday homes, but is available to all campers. There are 45 pitches for tourers, 12 with electricity, marked on level grass either side of the entrance road, the remainder unmarked on a rather attractive, sloping area which is left natural with trees and bushes creating cosy little recesses in which to pitch. The main brick sanitary block behind reception has two washbasins (warm water from a single tap), two toilets and two showers (on payment) for both sexes with two more toilets on the edge of the camping area. Facilities could be under pressure at busy times. Clothes and dishwashing facilities are in another small room, plus a washing machine, dryer and iron. Basic food items are available at reception and two pubs with restaurants, one at park entrance (Tandoori) and another in the village a one mile stroll away. The neat, tidy, well cared for park, which the resident proprietors, Derek and Dee Zanders, have created makes an excellent base away from the hurly-burly of life where you can enjoy the rural scenery and also have the opportunity for walking, fishing, riding, visiting local places of interest or for cross-Channel excursions. Tourist information.

Charges 1995: -- First two adults £3.00 - £3.20; extra adult £2.00 - £2.20; child 2-11 yrs 75 - 85p, 12-16 £2.00 - £2.20; caravan £2.00 - £3.00; motorcaravan £1.00 - £2.00; tent free - 80p; electricity (deposit required) £1.50. -- Low season discounts for senior citizens, more than 3 nights. **Open:** March - September. **Address:** Stonestreet, Petham, Kent CT4 5PL. **Tel:** (01227) 700306. **Reservations:** Made for min. 2 days with deposit of £5 per night.

Directions: Park is on the B2068 Canterbury-Folkestone road. From the south, take exit 11 from the M20. From Canterbury, ignore signs to Petham and Waltham on B2068 and continue towards Folkestone. From either direction, turn into road beside the Chequers Inn, turn left into park and follow road to owners' house/reception. O.S.GR: TR138507.

7 Tanner Farm Touring Caravan and Camping Park, Marden

Quality park in quiet, spacious, rural setting.

Recently developed as part of a family working farm, Tanner Farm has rapidly received recognition as a top class park. This is the heart of the Weald of Kent with orchards, hop gardens, lovely countryside and delightful small villages. The owners are much concerned with conserving the natural beauty of the environment and visitors are welcome to walk around the farm and see the Shire horses at work. The park extends over 15 acres, part of which is level and part a gentle slope. The grass meadowland has been semi landscaped by planting saplings, etc. which units back onto as the owners do not wish to regiment pitches into rows. Places are numbered but not marked giving plenty of space between units and large open areas which give a pleasant and easy atmosphere. There are 100 electrical hookups, 1 all service pitch and 6 with hardstanding. The park is a member of the Caravan Club's 'managed under contract' scheme although non-members are also very welcome. The farm drive links the park with the B2079 and a group of refurbished oast houses (kept as listed heritage buildings), with a duck pond in front, along with rare pigs and piglets, pygmy goats, lambs, etc. make a focal point. The traditional farm building on the right at the entrance houses a small shop (limited stock and opening hours in winter) and reception. The new sanitary block in the centre of the caravan and camping area is centrally heated, tiled and given a most pleasant appearance with interior flower arrangements, hanging baskets and flower beds. There is free hot water in the washbasins (rather close together), which have mirrors and shaver points, in the showers and in the washing up sinks. Purpose built facilities for the disabled and a small launderette. Small children's play area with swings, an adventure climbing frame. Dogs accepted on leads with paths for exercise. There is good lighting around the park, but a torch may be advisable. The friendly management will advise on local attractions, shops and pubs. There is a high concentration of National Trust attractions in the area (Sissinghurst, Scotney Castle, Bodiam Castle), horse riding and golf are available within 6 miles, leisure centres and sailing facilities near and good shopping facilities at Maidstone and Tunbridge Wells. Note: only one car per pitch permitted.

Charges 1995:
-- Per pitch £3.00; adult £2.50 - £3.50; child £1.10 - £1.20; 2-man tent plus car (incl.) £6.50, plus bicycles £5.00.
-- Credit cards accepted.
Open: All year.
Address: Goudhurst Road, Marden, Kent TN12 9ND.
Tel: Maidstone (01622) 832399.
FAX: (01622) 832472.
Reservations: Made with deposit £5 up to 3 nights; £10 over 3 nights.

Directions: Just south of Marden on B2079 Goudhurst-Marden road, park is well signed. From south take B2079 at Flimwell on A21 Hastings- London road, from north leave the A229 Maidstone-Cranbrook road at Linton. O.S.GR: TQ744188.

8 Canterbury Camping and Caravanning Club Site, Canterbury

Ideal site for touring northern Kent or as a stop-over for the ferry or the Tunnel.

Just off the A257 Sandwich road, about 1½ miles from the centre of Canterbury, this site is an ideal base for exploring Canterbury and the north Kent coast, as well as being a good stop-over to and from the Dover ferries, and the Folkestone Tunnel terminal. There are 210 pitches, 56 with electric hook-ups, and except at the very height of the season, you are likely to find a pitch, although not necessarily with electricity. All the pitches are on well kept grass with hundreds of saplings planted. Some pitches do slope so blocks are advised. There is a good sized overnight area for late arrivals which can be reached even when the barriers are down. There are two modern toilet blocks but, surprisingly, only one chemical disposal point adjacent to the main toilet block; as a result you could be faced with walk of several hundred yards to empty your toilet. The main toilet block also has a laundry room, a room for dishwashing and outside vegetable preparation area. Not far from the second toilet block is a motorcaravan service area. Reception stocks a small range of essential foods, milk and newspapers with an excellent tourist information room next door. Not far from the reception is a children's play area with the equipment on bark chippings. Although the site is next to the busy A257 there is minimal noise from the traffic.

Charges 1995:
-- Per adult £3.15 - £3.50, acc. to season; child £1.20 - £1.35; non-member pitch fee £3.00; electricity £1.70; visitor £1.00 per car or adult couple.
Open: All year.
Address: Bekesbourne Lane, Canterbury, Kent CT3 4AB.
Tel: (01227) 463216 (No calls after 8 pm).
Reservations: Are accepted - contact the wardens.

Directions: From the A2 take the Canterbury exit and follow signs for Sandwich - A257. After passing the Howe military barracks turn right into Bekesbourne Lane opposite the golf course. O.S. GR: TR173575.

9 Thriftwood Caravan and Camping Park, Wrotham Hill, nr. Stansted

Pleasant park in beautiful woodland setting, easily accessed from M20/M26.

Thriftwood is delightfully situated in 20 acres of natural woodland. Pitches connected by gravel roadways, some terraced on a gentle slope, occupy half the park according to season and the atmosphere is relaxed and informal with a minimum of rules. Campers choose their own spots and tall trees give good shade in all parts. Despite being within easy reach of London, the Channel ports, stately homes, beautiful gardens and picturesque villages, the park is quiet and secluded with lovely walks possible. Used extensively by continental visitors, it is open for 11 months of the year and is under personal supervision of the resident owners who strive to maintain and extend the garden atmosphere. Electrical connections are available on 102 of the 150 pitches. An interesting feature is the provision of two specially constructed covered areas with gas stoves (gas on meter) for backpacking campers, also a special barbecue area with picnic tables, etc. There are 10 pitches for caravan holiday homes with 3 for hire. The single toilet block has free hot water in the washbasins and washing sinks and on payment in the showers (20p). Extra toilets are in a separate section. There is a family shower room, baby bath and a toilet for the disabled. Small well stocked shop at reception. Shops, pubs and restaurants nearby. Children's playground. Motorcaravan service point. Laundry room with washing machine, dryer and iron. Freezer for campers' use. Possibly some road noise.

Directions: On A20 near M26 exit 2A (but no named camping sign) and signed from the A20. O.S.GR: TQ598608.

Charges 1995:
-- Per unit incl. 2 persons £7.75 - £10.30; extra adult £1.00 - £1.75; child (5-16 yrs) free - £1.25; awning free - £1.50; extra small tent £1.50 - £2.00; extra car £1.00; electricity £1.80; hiker/cyclists (2 persons) £5.60 - £8.00.
-- Less 10% for over 7 days.
-- VAT included.
-- Credit cards accepted.
Open:
All year except Feb.
Address:
Plaxdale Green Road, Stansted, nr Wrotham, Kent TN15 7PB.
Tel:
(01732) 822261.
Reservations:
Made with £10 non-returnable deposit.

10 Horam Manor Touring Park, Horam, nr Eastbourne

Secluded rural park with excellent sanitary block.

In the heart of the Sussex countryside, the touring park is part of but under separate management from, Horam Manor, a small country craft centre which has a farm museum, nature trail, forge and well known Merrydown Winery (entry not included in park charges). The 90 pitches, 46 with electricity, are on two open meadows joined by a tarmac/gravel access road. The field nearest reception has an undulating surface but the second field is flatter but gently sloping. Pitches are of generous size, those with electricity being numbered and marked, the rest not. Both areas are ringed with a variety of mainly tall trees. The whole park, back from the main Eastbourne-Tunbridge Wells road, is a haven of peace and tranquillity. The modern, well built sanitary block at the entrance to the larger field has free hot water in the washbasins (set in flat surfaces), showers, laundry and washing up sinks. The block is said to be cleaned four times daily. A family room (access by key from reception) has shower, washbasin and toilet and is suitable for the disabled. Washing machine. No shop but the village is close, with supermarkets in Heathfield, 3 miles. Two good inns within walking distance and the Barn cafe at the Farm Centre serves drinks and snacks (10 am. - 5 pm). The Craft Centre to the side of the site has some interesting exhibits, farm machinery, riding stables and a small blacksmith's forge. The nature trail has walks ranging from ½ -1½ hours in length (written guide available) and the Merrydown Winery arranges tours of the factory and tastings.

Directions: Entry to the park is signed at the recreation ground at the southern edge of the village. O.S.GR: TQ577169.

Charges 1996:
-- Per unit incl. 2 adults and 2 children (under 18 yrs) £10.00; extra adult £3.50; extra child 75p; electricity £1.65; extended awning £2.50; dogs (max 2) free.
-- VAT included.
Open:
1 March - 31 October.
Address:
Horam, nr. Heathfield, E. Sussex TN21 0YD.
Tel:
(01435) 813662.
Reservations:
Telephone or write to park.

HORAM MANOR
Touring Park

Horam, Nr Heathfield
East Sussex TN21 0YD

Tel: 01435 813662

In the beautiful Weald of Sussex, an area of outstanding natural beauty

- ❖ 90 Pitches
- ❖ Free hot water & showers
- ❖ Gently sloping site
- ❖ Electric hook-ups
- ❖ Mother & toddler shower room

- ❖ Nature trails
- ❖ Riding
- ❖ Fishing
- ❖ Merrydown Winery
- ❖ Farm Museum

- ❖ Ashdown Forest
- ❖ Historic Houses
- ❖ Motor Museum
- ❖ Drusillas Zoo
- *and many other attractions nearby*

- ❖ Brighton
- ❖ Hastings
- ❖ Lewes
- ❖ Tunbridge Wells
- ❖ Eastbourne
- *all within 15 miles*

11 Woodland View Touring Park, Horam, nr. Eastbourne

Small, rural park on the edge of the Sussex Weald and Horam village.

Woodland View is ideally situated for exploring the coastal resorts and inland rural areas of East Sussex. Established in 1990, it is a pretty, family run park approached through the family agricultural fencing business, for just 25 units in 3 acres. Bordered by tall trees, the numbered pitches of some 100 sq.m. are on open, gently sloping grassland, in regular rows marked out by young saplings; 16 have electrical connections. Two small sanitary blocks (one for each sex) have a rustic air, being well constructed in wood. Each contains 2 toilets, 2 washbasins and 2 showers. Hot water is free in the basins, which are set in flat units, and in the dishwashing sinks and on payment in the showers. Washing machine, dryer and iron. Small chalet for wet weather use with free freezer, fridge and tourist information. Small children's playground with boat and play house! Public phone. Local shops and pub/restaurants nearby. Calor gas available. Dogs or pets not allowed. The park is near the Cuckoo Trail for cycling and walking.

Directions: Park is in Horebeech Lane at south end of the village. The turning from the A267 is signed ½ mile from this main road. O.S.GR: TQ575173.

Charges 1996:
-- Per unit incl. 2 persons £7.00; extra person (over 5) £1.00; pup tent £1.00; electricity £1.50; visitor £1.00 or £3.00 per car.
-- VAT included.
Open:
1 April -- 31 October.
Address:
Horebeech Lane, Horam, East Sussex, TN21 0HR.
Tel:
(01435) 813597.
FAX: (01435) 812750.
Reservations:
Precise dates with 25% deposit and £5 fee.

12 Raylands Caravan Park, Southwater, nr. Horsham

Quiet, tranquil, spacious park with excellent facilities in rural environment.

Peace, quiet and an air of excellence greet you as you enter this pleasant, reasonably priced park (owned by Roundstone Caravans at Southwater), deep in the heart of the Sussex countryside. Beautifully maintained and thoughtfully landscaped, Raylands is very modern and well organised. The 65 caravan holiday homes occupy an area of their own and touring units use marked, numbered pitches on flat grass meadows separated into smaller areas by trees and hard access roads. There are some hardstandings for caravans and motorcaravans and 50 of the 65 places available for tourists have electrical connections. The park manager seems to have engendered a friendly atmosphere and is willing to advise on the very numerous attractions the locality has to offer. London and Brighton are easily reached by rail from nearby Horsham and the region abounds with places of historical, cultural and sporting interests. The clubhouse (open from Easter) has snacks and good value full meals at weekends with a special bar/dining room for non-smokers and a new children's games room with pool, table tennis, video games and TV. An adults games room has pool, darts and a small library. The single toilet block is centrally situated and is a modern building of good quality with free hot water in the basins and hot showers on payment. The dishwashing point is under cover and has free hot water in the sinks. Laundry room. Separate en-suite facility for the disabled. There is no shop on site but a supermarket and other shops are under 2 miles distant. Public telephone. Large field for children's ball games, tennis court, a swimming pool 3 miles away and fishing nearby. Large dog exercise field complete with seats at the far end.

Charges 1996:
-- Per pitch £8.00; extra person 50p; hiker or cyclist tent, 1 person £5.75.
Open:
1 March - 31 October.
Address:
Jackells Lane, Southwater, Sussex. RH13 7HD.
Tel:
(01403) 730218.
Reservations:
Essential for busy times with deposit if electricity is required.

Directions: Leave A24 Worthing-London road for Southwater and follow signs for approx. 2 miles on narrow lanes to park. O.S.GR: TQ170265.

13 Wicks Farm Caravan Park, West Wittering, nr. Chichester

Peaceful rural park with good facilities for motorcaravans and tents.

Set in a rural situation about 1½ miles inland from the inlet to Chichester harbour, this peaceful park, most of which is taken up with caravans of the holiday home type only used by their owners, is surrounded by trees which provide a windbreak in this low lying area. Only motorcaravans and tents are accepted and these pitches are in a separate section to the side of the main part. However, just as much care is taken over this as the main part with the units parked in rows on a flat meadow. The whole park has been thoughtfully landscaped with a wide variety of trees and plants and is well maintained. This is a popular area with tourists, many from abroad, with sporting, historic and cultural interests nearby. The single sanitary block is of reasonable quality, fully tiled and, unusually, carpeted with industrial type carpets which are regularly washed. Cleaning is said to be carried out four times daily in high season. There is free hot water in the washbasins which are set in vanity units and the showers have hot water on payment (also for clothes and dish washing). Being for the sole use of touring units (the holiday homes are fully plumbed) the provision should be quite adequate for the 40 touring pitches, 26 of which have electricity connections - fridges may be hired. Washing machines, dryers and irons are provided. There is a playground and a field for ball games, separated from the camping area by tall trees. Pub with real ales and good food 300 yds. A member of the partners' family look after the park and run the small shop which has a good supply of basic food stuffs and a comprehensive range of camping accessories. A friendly and peaceful park.

Charges 1995:
-- Per unit incl. up to 4 persons £7.50 - £9.25; extra person or car 50p; walkers or cyclists (2 persons) £5.00; electricity £1.00.
-- Less 10% for 7 nights or more.
-- Electric fridges £5 per week.
-- VAT included.
Open:
15 March - October.
Address:
Redlands Lane, West Wittering, Chichester, W. Sussex PO2O 8QD.
Tel:
Birdham (01243) 513116.
FAX: (01243) 511296.
Reservations:
Made for min 4 nights with £6 deposit.

Directions: Park is north of West Wittering just off the B2179 Chichester - West Wittering road. From the Chichester bypass take A286 West Wittering exit. O.S.GR: SZ796995.

 Alan Rogers' discount 50p p/night off total bill

14 White Rose Touring Park, Wick, nr. Littlehampton

Small, well organised park close to West Sussex seaside resorts.

Situated about midway between the imposing castle at Arundel and the beaches of Littlehampton, White Rose makes an excellent base from which to enjoy the many attractions of this popular district. Water sports centres, race courses, beaches, historical and cultural interests, downland walks and the resorts of Bognor and Brighton are within easy reach. The flat grassy meadow is surrounded by trees and divided into two areas. The first part has pitches on either side of concrete access roads which are semi-hedged with electrical (10A), hook-ups and shared water and waste water connections. The second area includes 14 super pitches (each having mains hook-up, fresh, waste water and sewer connections, TV aerial socket and night light), full sized pitches with no electricity, plus special pitches for small tents and small motorcaravans with a maximum of 3 persons at a special price. With just 13 static units and 144 pitches available for tourists (60 electrical connections) the emphasis is on touring visitors and the friendly director, who manages the park, gives helpful advice on the attractions the neighbourhood offers. This is a neat, tidy and very pleasant park. The central toilet block, recently refurbished, is fully tiled with free hot water in basins set in flat units and showers with hot water controlled by pushbutton taps. Two washrooms for the disabled may also be used as family rooms (key from reception). No restaurant but a path leads from the site to the local pub which serves food. Reception has a few basic supplies with a supermarket ¼ mile away. Special dog walking area and a well equipped central play area for children.

Directions: Take A284 Littlehampton road from A27 just to the east of Arundel station, pass the camp site behind the pub at this junction and park is signed along on the left. O.S.GR: TQ026604.

Charges 1995:
-- Per pitch incl. unit, car and up to 6 people: super pitch £13.60, pitch with electricity £11.60, no services £9.70; mini pitch (incl. 3 persons) £6.75; extra person £2.50; extra car or trailed boat £3.00.
-- Reductions for 1 week or 1 month.
Open:
All year except 16 Jan - 14 Mar.
Address:
Mill Lane, Wick, W. Sussex BN17 7PH
Tel:
Littlehampton (01903) 716176.
FAX: (01903) 732671.
Reservations:
Made with deposit of 1 nights fee p/week reserved.

15 Chichester Camping, Southbourne, nr. Chichester

Small, well kept family touring park near Hampshire/Sussex coast.

This is a neat park, just to the west of Chichester and north of Bosham harbour. Formerly an orchard, it is rectangular in shape with 60 pitches on flat, well mown lawns on either side of gravel roads. Situated on the main A259 road, although the new A27 bypass takes most of the through traffic, there may be some traffic noise in some parts (not busy at night). Opposite the park are orchards through which paths lead to the seashore and the location is ideal for touring this part of the south coast or inland. The well designed, brick built sanitary block is of really first class quality. Fully tiled and heated in cool weather, there is free hot water in the washbasins set in flat units, showers and sinks, with facilities for the disabled. Dogs are accepted on leads. No ball games or children's bicycles permitted on the park. There are shops, restaurants and pubs within easy walking distance in the nearby village and the park is on a main bus route.

Directions: Park is on main A259 Chichester - Havant road at Southbourne, 750 yds. past Chichester Caravans on the right hand side. O.S.GR: SU7790.

Charges 1995:
-- Per unit (any type), all incl. £8.00 - £10.00.
-- Motorcaravans up to 5.9 metres.
-- Teenage groups or commercial vehicles not admitted.
-- Credit cards accepted.
Open:
Mid February - end October.
Address:
Main Road, Southbourne, Hanmpshire PO10 8JH.
Tel:
(01243) 373202.
Reservations:
Made with £10 deposit.

 Alan Rogers' discount Ask at park for details

Remember - to claim your discount you will need to show your 1996 discount card

Southern Tourist Board

40 Chamberlayne Road, Eastleigh, Hampshire SO50 5JH
Tel: (01703) 620006. Fax: (01703) 620010

East Dorset, Hampshire, Berkshire, Buckinghamshire, Oxfordshire
Isle of Wight, South Wiltshire

1996 Events: Weymouth Int. Beach Kite Festival, 5-6 May: Royal Windsor Horse Show, 8-12 May: Southern Counties Craft and Design Show, Farnham, 17-19 May: Portsmouth Navy Days, 25-27 May: Bournemouth Musicmakers Festival, 22 June-6 July: Cowes Week, 3-10 Aug: International Firework Festival. Weymouth, 5,12,21,26 Aug: Farnborough International Air Show, 2-6 Sept: Bournemouth International Boat Show, 14-22 Sept.

16 Fishery Creek Caravan and Camping Park, Hayling Island

Friendly, family run park adjoining a tidal waterway of Chichester harbour.

This attractively situated park offers 165 numbered pitches, 120 of which have electrical connections. Some of the central pitches are separated by fences with climbing roses, others around the perimeter lie alongside the creek. There is direct access to a slipway (no charge) suitable for small craft and to a footpath which leads to the south beach (5 mins walk). The modern toilet block has vanity style basins with mirrors and hand dryer. There are separate shower blocks for men and women, of oldish construction and basic design. Washing up sinks are under cover, with free hot water throughout. The on site shop, with a microwave for campers' use, is combined with the reception area. Also within this area, is a small games room with pool, fruit machines and TV. Behind the toilet block is a fenced children's play area with climbing frame and goal posts. Pubs, restaurants and shops are within easy walking distance and a bus service to Havant leaves from the top of the road, also a service to the ferry across to Southsea.

Directions: From A27 follow Hayling Island signs on A3023 and cross bridge onto island. Proceed to large roundabout and turn left to Mengham. Go through town, turn left opposite Hayling Motors, left after 500 yds into Fishery Lane and park is at the end. O.S.GR: SU734985.

Charges 1995: -- Per unit incl. 2 persons £6.00 - £8.50; extra adult £1.00; child (4-12 yrs) 50p; awning £1.30; dog £1.50; extra car or boat £1.50; electricity £1.80. -- VAT included.
Open: March - 15 October.
Address: Fishery Creek Lane, Hayling Island, Hampshire PO11 9NR.
Tel: (01705) 462164. FAX: as phone.
Reservations: Made with deposit (£15) and fee (£1.50).

17 Southsea Caravan Park, Southsea, nr Portsmouth

Touring park close to beach, town and ferry terminals.

At the eastern end of Southsea seafront, this is a tidily arranged 12 acre site suitable for a stop en-route for ferries from Portsmouth. There are 188 touring pitches, of which some 166 are clearly marked out and with electricity. There are 40 of these with hardstanding and 22 pitches reserved for tents with 45 caravan holiday homes for hire. The terrain is level with direct access to a pebbly beach with good views over the Solent towards the Isle of Wight. The two good, clean toilet blocks, with coded locks, are fully tiled with free hot water to showers and washbasins. Sections also have hair dryers. Facilities include a small, free outdoor heated swimming pool and paddling pool, a children's playground and a family bar and restaurant with takeaway and waitress service in evenings. A new bar opens onto a patio area with tables and chairs. There is entertainment at Easter and peak season and activities such as skating, bowling, skittles and pitch and putt nearby. On site are a launderette, shop, TV/video and games rooms and a barbecue area. Bicycles and fishing rods for hire. Water ski-ing centre nearby at Langstone Harbour. Public telephones.

Directions: From M27/A27/A3(M) take southbound A2030 signed Southsea and Eastney. After about 3 miles turn left onto A288 and follow signs for park and Langstone Marina. O.S.GR: SZ678990.

Charges 1995: -- Per pitch incl. 2 adults, 3 children and electricity £8.50 - £13.50; extra adult £2.00; extra child (under 16 yrs) £1.00; pet £1.50. -- Senior citizens discount (50p). -- VAT included. -- Credit cards accepted.
Open: All year.
Address: Melville Rd, Southsea, Hampshire PO4 9TB
Tel: (01705) 735070. FAX: (01705) 821302.
Reservations: Deposit £20 per week per pitch. Contact park.

18 Hollands Wood Camping and Caravanning Site, Brockenhurst

Spacious, level Forestry Commission site in the heart of the New Forest.

Hollands Wood is a large 168 acre, 600 pitch secluded site in a natural woodland setting (mainly oak) with an abundance of wild-life, including the famous New Forest ponies. The site is arranged informally with unmarked pitches but it is stipulated that there must be at least 20 ft between each unit. There are **no** electrical connections and possible traffic noise from the A337 which runs alongside one boundary. Two large modern toilet blocks (and a third smaller/older one) have free hot showers, hot and cold water to washbasins (not in private cubicles) free hairdryer, razor points, 2 laundry rooms, 6 water points, a chemical toilet disposal point, and facilities for the disabled. No shop or restaurant, though a mobile shop selling essentials visits each morning, twice daily in high season; however the site is only about half a mile from Brockenhurst village, with shops, trains and buses. Night security. Public telephones. It can get very busy and we have now included the small Ashurst site as an alternative.

Charges 1996:
-- Per standard unit £7.20 - £10.80.
-- Credit cards accepted
Open:
26 March - 20 October.
Address/Tel:
For reservations (necessary for B.H.s and peak times) and information: see address in advertisement.

Directions: Entrance to the site is on the east side of the A337 Lyndhurst - Lymington road, half a mile north of Brockenhurst. O.S.GR: SU303038.

---

19 Ashurst Forestry Commission Site, Ashurst, nr. Lyndhurst

Attractive Forestry Commission site on the fringe of the New Forest

A smaller site than Hollands Wood (23 acres), Ashurst is set in a mixture of oak woodland and open grassland and heathland. Of the 280 pitches, 180 have been gravelled to provide semi-hardstanding; otherwise you pitch where you like, applying the 20 ft. rule. Electrical connections are planned. There may be some noise from the adjacent railway line - the station is just five minutes walk away. The single central sanitary block is somewhat spartan, but provides everything necessary, including hairdryers, a well equipped unit for the disabled and good laundry room, and it appears to be well maintained. Within easy access of all pitches are 8 water points and 3 chemical disposal points. Reception is run by the very helpful wardens and a mobile shop calls daily. There is a 'late arrivals' area and separate car-parking area for those arriving or returning after the gate has closed (11.30 pm). A nearby pub is accessible by footpath across an adjacent field and shops and local buses are within a five minute walk. Guided forest walks and Activity Walks for children are available during the main season. Bicycle hire. Dogs are only allowed after 20 Sept. when other sites have closed.

Charges 1996:
-- Per standard unit £6.20 - £9.80.
-- Credit cards accepted
Open:
26 March - 30 October.
Address/Tel:
For reservations (necessary for B.H.s and peak times) and information: see address in advertisement.

Directions: Site is 2 miles east of Lyndhurst, set back from the A35 road (Southampton - Bournemouth). O.S.GR: SU332102.

20 Camping International incorporating Redcote Holiday Park, St Leonards, nr. Ringwood

Well kept, lively, family managed touring park with small heated pool, close to New Forest.

On entry this park has a neat, compact appearance and closer inspection of the facilities confirms that everything is in fact orderly, clean, and well cared for. The flat, grassy terrain is divided into two parts. The first, which is the original Camping International, comprises 80 numbered pitches, quite close together, all with electricity and 30 with gravelled area for awnings. This is the more lively part with a central bar, pool and children's adventure play area, shop, reception and tourist information. The second part, formerly Redcote, is the quieter area taking 125 units on a flat, grassy meadow with some hardstanding. A children's games room and new, fully fenced ball game area are to one side. Both parts have fully equipped sanitary facilities with hot showers on payment. The block in the second part is larger and more functional with plenty of toilets including one for mother and child. Both have facilities for babies, covered dishwashing facilities (H&C) and laundry rooms. The pub, 'The Old Trout', has a pleasant licensed bar, family room and a patio overlooking the children's play area and pool. Hot food and takeaway are available at most times in high season. Games room with 3 pool tables, table tennis, amusement machines. TV room. Public telephones. Shop with camping accessories. There is plenty to do on the park, however, this is an excellent touring area with the New Forest, Bournemouth, Beaulieu, etc. all within easy reach. Essentially a park for families, it is very popular, particularly with visitors from the continent, so reservation is advisable for July/Aug. On pitches near the main A31 there may be some traffic noise.

Charges 1995:
-- Per pitch incl. 1 car and 2 persons £7.00 - £10.40; extra person (over 3 years) £1.20 - £1.40; 2-man tent or motorvan £6.10 - £8.00; awning, extra car £1.20 - £1.60; dog £1.10 - £1.40; electricity £2.00.
-- 10% discount for stays of over 10 days or for OAPs if booked in advance.
-- VAT included.
-- Credit cards accepted.
Open:
March - October incl.
Address:
229 Ringwood Road, St Leonards, Ringwood, Hampshire BH24 2SD.
Tel:
(01202) 872817.
FAX: (01202) 861292.
Reservations:
Made with £20 deposit and £3 fee (min. 5 days in high season).

Directions: Park is off main A31 road to south at second roundabout travelling west from Ringwood (3 miles). Turn off at camp signs. O.S.GR: SU106024.

 Alan Rogers' discount
Less 10% in low season

Camping International

The New Forest with its quaint villages set in unspoilt open country and full of wild life. Bournemouth with its shops and entertainments. Dorset & Hants coast and country. 60+ places of interest to visit in good or bad weather.

STATISTICALLY THE BEST WEATHER IN THE U.K.

Enjoy all this whilst staying at one of the most popular parks in the area. Designed for the more discerning camper/caravanner who demands superior continental standards along with all of the facilities.

CAMPING INTERNATIONAL HOLIDAY PARK
229 Ringwood Rd., St. Leonard's, Ringwood, Hants BH24 2SD
Telephone (01202) 872817
Fax (01202) 861292

HAMPSHIRE

21 Shorefield Country Park (Lytton Lawn), Lymington

Modern, self-contained touring park with access to Leisure Complex, near Milford on Sea.

Lytton Lawn is the touring arm of Shorefield Country Park, a holiday home park and leisure centre. Situated 2½ miles from Shorefield itself, campers and caravanners staying at Lytton Lawn are entitled to free membership of the Leisure Club. The comprehensive facilities at Shorefield are of a very good standard and are free (except tennis). They comprise a very attractive indoor pool, solarium, sauna, spa bath and steam room, dance studios and two all weather tennis courts, open all year with fully trained attendants. Outdoor pools and crazy golf May to Sept. Restaurants include a bistro and there is a range of entertainment and activity programmes, fitness classes and treatments (Easter-Oct), all well managed and organised. A minibus operates between Lytton Lawn and Shorefield on Fri. and Sat. nights in the latter half of July and in August.

Lytton Lawn provides 126 spacious pitches, including 43 'super' type pitches (hardstanding, electricity, pitch light, satellite TV, water and waste water outlet) in a hedged field area. This section, with its heated toilet block, is open for a longer season (March - 5 Jan). The rest of the pitches, all with electricity (tenters note), are in the adjoining, but separate, gently sloping field, edged with mature trees and hedges and with a further toilet block. Tarmac access roads throughout. Both purpose built, the modern toilet blocks are fully tiled and well fitted, with free hot water, vanity style basins, showers with dressing area, laundry room and chemical disposal in each block. Baby changing facilities in one block. Simple shop (limited opening out of main season), with supermarket and takeaway at Shorefield. Children's play frame, field with goal posts. Separate field for dog walks. Village pub 10 minutes walk. Barbecues allowed. Public phone. The New Forest, the Isle of Wight, Bournemouth, Southampton and the beach at Milford on Sea are all near, as are golf, fishing, riding, sailing and windsurfing facilities.

Directions: From the M27 follow signs for Lyndhurst and Lymington on the A337. Continue towards New Milton and Lytton Lawn is signed at Everton, Shorefield is signed at Downton. O.S.GR: SZ293937.

Charges 1995:
-- Per `super' pitch incl. all persons, electricity, water, drainage and TV connection £9.00 - £20.00; basic pitch incl. electricity £8.00 - £18.00; pup tent or awning £1.00; dog £2.00.
-- Less 50% Mon - Thurs in certain periods.
-- Min. weekly charge at busy times.
-- Credit cards accepted.
-- VAT included.
Open:
1 March - 5 January.
Address:
Shorefield Road, Downton, Lymington, Hampshire SO41 0LH.
Tel:
(01590) 642513, FAX: (01590) 645610.
Reservations:
Made with deposit and cancellation insurance - contact park for details.

see advertisement opposite

22 Bashley Park, New Milton

Pleasant park with large section for caravans or motorcaravans, with pools and evening entertainment.

A well run park with a large number of privately owned holiday homes (400 including 80 for hire), Bashley Park also has a very sizeable tourist section and can now take 420 touring units (tents, trailer tents and pup tents are not accepted). Spread over three flat meadows plus a woodland area, pitches are all individual ones with electricity, marked but not separated. Ground sheets must be lifted daily, no awnings are allowed in the woodland area and reservations are required for peak times. The four toilet blocks, one central to each area, are well constructed, fully tiled with modern fittings. Free hot water throughout, vanity style washbasins and push-button, pre-set showers (no dividers, but shower head is set fairly low). Set in pleasant park-like surroundings not far from beaches, Bournemouth and the New Forest, the site has a good clubhouse with excellent facilities overlooking an 18 m. circular outdoor swimming pool (heated mid-May - mid-Sept) and 18 m. children's paddling pool, a sensible size and fun with its geysers and beach effect. An indoor pool complex houses a water flume, sauna, spa bath, steam room and sunbeds. There are evening entertainments (and children's entertainment) in the club with live or taped music Spr. B.H. - mid-Sept; it has a ballroom, large lounges and bars, restaurant, simple hot food takeaway all day, TV room. Also a video arcade and games room with 2 full-size snooker tables, plus 3 pool tables spread among other rooms. Well equipped children's play area. Nine hole, `par 3' golf course on site and 3 tennis courts. Children's playground. Self-service shop (mid-May to end Sept). Launderette. Up to 6 American motorhomes accepted (40 ft. max). One dog or pet is allowed per unit. A popular park with lots going on, part of the Hoburne group.

Directions: Park is on B3055 road ¼ mile east of crossroads with B3058 in Bashley village. O.S.GR: SZ246969.

Charges 1996:
-- Per unit incl. all persons and electricity £8.50 - £20.00; pet £2.00.
-- Weekly rates available.
-- VAT included.
-- Credit cards accepted.
Open:
2 March - end October.
Address:
Sway Road, New Milton, Hampshire BH25 5QR.
Tel:
New Milton (01425) 612340.
FAX: (01425) 612602.
Reservations:
Any length: 1-6 nights with payment in full at booking; 7+ nights, £50 p/w. deposit, balance 3 weeks before arrival.

see advertisement on inside back cover

Best of both worlds

The New Forest

Superb Pool

★ Sandford in Dorset & Mullion in South Cornwall

★ Areas of Outstanding Natural Beauty

★ All Weather Facilities

★ Heated Indoor and Outdoor Pools

★ Level well drained pitches

★ Electric Hook Ups

★ FREE Live Entertainment

★ FREE Childrens "90's Gang"

★ FREE Teen" Allstars" Club

★ Restaurants, Takeaways Supermarkets & Launderettes

★ Everything for the PERFECT family Holiday

★ Luxury Holiday Homes, Lodges and Bungalows

★ *NEW "SUPERPITCHES" at Sandford*

WESTSTAR
HOLIDAY ★ PARKS

Pull up to the Perfect Pitch

RING NOW! for your FREE Colour Brochure (quote R1)

Sandford (01202) 631 600
Mullion (01326) 240 000

Very Special Places!

at Oakdene

🌲 A Holiday Park that all the family will love, offering a wealth of things to see and do, with excitement and all-weather fun for the kids and perfect relaxation for mum & dad.

🌲 The Village is situated in 55 acres of beautiful forest, just 9 miles from Bournemouth's safe Blue Flag beaches, bustling shopping centre and entertainment's complex making an ideal base for your holiday.

🌲 With 2 superb heated pools, indoor & outdoor, our own 'Forest Edge' riding stables, Children's adventure playground, licensed clubhouse incorporating teens disco, solarium, mini gym & sauna. You'll be spoilt for choice.

🌲 Some pitches have plug in mains electric & water and with easy access to modern service blocks. Pre-booking service available.

🌲 On site cafeteria and takeaway, general store and laundrette for your day to day requirements.

(some facilities only available at peak times)

ROSE AWARD CARAVAN HOLIDAY PARK 1996

RAC Approved

24hrs FREEPHONE
0500 202216 ASK FOR EXT 21

Also static Holiday Homes for sale, ask for details

✂ -

For more details call 01202 875422 or complete coupon & send to: Village Holidays, Oakdene, St Leonards, Ringwood, Hampshire BH24 2RZ.

Mr/Mrs/Miss: _____ Address: _____

_____ Postcode: _____

Ref: AR

23 Village Holidays at Oakdene, St. Leonards, nr. Ringwood

Large park with 2 swimming pools and evening entertainment.

Whether this park will suit you will depend on what you are looking for. It has amenities on a holiday park scale - for daytime there are both indoor and outdoor swimming pools, both heated and of fair size, sauna, solarium and gym, riding stables, adventure playground and bike hire. There is much organised sport, competitions, etc. in season. For evenings there are large bars open late, with dancing and entertainment in the big clubhouse (also food bar and takeaway), children's disco and separate 'pub'. Most amenities are available from Easter to end Oct. The park has 100 caravan holiday homes to let, plus over 100 privately owned, and 435 touring pitches. These are all numbered and marked in some way so there should be no overcrowding, however the park could be very busy at peak times with facilities stretched. Touring pitches are on flat or slightly sloping grass (which can get bare in summer) divided by access roads, 360 with electricity (long leads needed in some cases) and a number with water and drainaway. Though not perhaps an upmarket park, the proprietors have made improvements both to the less attractive corners of the terrain and also to the sanitary facilities, where two new blocks have made both the supply and quality better. Practical rather than luxurious, they have free hot water in the basins and controllable hot showers with dividers and shelves. Supermarket and launderette.

Charges 1995:
-- Per unit with all persons £5.00 - £15.00 (standard pitch) or £7.00 - £17.00 (serviced pitch); extra car £3.00; awning £1.00; pet £2.00.
-- VAT included.
-- Credit cards accepted.
Open:
February - December.
Address:
St. Leonards,
Ringwood, Hampshire
BH24 2RZ.
Tel:
(01202) 875422.
FAX: (01202) 894152.
Reservations:
Min. 3 nights; full amount plus £6 fee.

Directions: Park access leads off the main A31 westbound carriageway about 2½ miles west of Ringwood. O.S. GR: SU101016.

Alan Rogers' discount
Less 10% outside school holidays

see advertisement opposite

24 New Forest Country Holidays, Godshill, Fordingbridge

Large New Forest touring park with some holiday caravans and indoor pool, open all year.

This is a very well run, 120 acre park, formerly known as the Sandy Balls Holiday Centre, with a wide range of leisure facilities developed around a 'village' centre. Open all year, it covers an extensive area which includes terrain of different types: light woodland with 150 caravan and chalet holiday homes, and some tent field areas with unmarked pitches, tourist units for the most part on open meadows, and some parts including woodland not used for camping. They include over 200 all service pitches (with electricity (16A), water, drainaway and TV) on concrete or gravel with gravel hardstanding for awnings. There are four spacious, airy modern toilet blocks with under floor heating plus one of portacabin type which remains as overflow - they should be adequate for peak season. One block has a bath in each section and all have cubicled washbasins. Hot water is free and showers are pre-mixed. Toilets for the disabled and baby facilities in at least two blocks. The central area is pleasantly laid out and designed to fit the forest surroundings. A large indoor pool (66 x 30 ft.) and an outdoor pool are heated and free all season (high season sessions timed according to demand). Well equipped fitness gym, jacuzzi spa bath, steam room, toning tables, sauna, solarium and dance studios. New, comprehensive supermarket, takeaway and pub with family room, patio and entertainment in season. Games room with pool and table tennis, children's adventure playground and two other playgrounds. Bicycle hire, archery, orienteering, clay modelling tuition for children. An attractive, thatched restaurant offers that special meal at affordable prices with vegetarian options. River fishing on permit, riding near. Excellent launderette plus washing machines in three toilet blocks. Tourist information. Gift shop. Public telephones. This park provides all-round family entertainment, with river bathing, woodland leisure trail where animals and birds can be observed in their natural surroundings, as well as the New Forest on your doorstep, and even wild life workshops for children. American motorhomes accepted in low seasons.

Charges 1995:
-- Standard pitch £9.00 - £12.00; all service pitch £11.50 - £14.00, both acc. to season; adult £1.50 - £2.00; child (5-16 yrs) 50p; awning free - £1.00; car free - 50p; dog 50p - £1.00.
-- 50% reduction for mid week nights outside main season.
-- VAT included.
-- Credit cards accepted.
Open:
All year.
Address:
Sandy Balls Estate,
Godshill, Fordingbridge,
Hants SP6 2JY.
Tel:
Fordingbridge (01425) 653042.
FAX: (01425) 653067.
Reservations:
Made with deposit (£15 per week/part week) + £3 compulsory cancellation insurance and booking fee (non-returnable).

Directions: Park is northwest off the B3078 (Fordingbridge-Cadnam) road just west of Godshill village, 1½ miles east of Fordingbridge. O.S.GR: SU168147.

ISLE OF WIGHT

25 Adgestone Camping Park, nr. Sandown

Well run touring park with swimming pool, popular with families.

Nestling at the foot of Brading Down, near the Adgestone Vineyard and with pleasant views across the valley, Adgestone provides a relaxed holiday atmosphere for families, complementing the attractions of nearby beaches and amenities at Sandown and Shanklin. About 200 pitches (100 sq.m. and 170 with 10A electricity) are divided into groups by tidy fences, growing hedges and many attractive, ornamental young trees. A further 26 pitches have been added on the banks of the small River Yar at the foot of the site, together with a pleasant river walk (no dogs). At one end of the park, around part of a small playing area, pitching is more flexible for ridge tents and a 28-day field, with new hedges and electric hook-ups, can accommodate more. There are no static holiday caravans. Two, low, neat sanitary blocks offer very clean facilities with free hot water to controllable showers and well appointed washbasins (some private cabins). Three family shower rooms, baby bathrooms, dishwashing sinks, full facilities for the disabled and refurbished laundry. Coin operated irons and hairdryers. Amenities include floodlit swimming and paddling pools, heated from mid-May, but open earlier for brave swimmers, with a sheltered, grass sun bathing area. Well stocked, licensed shop (with wide range of camping and caravan accessories - in fact the island's main stockist). Good value takeaway (limited opening before May). Two sturdy children's adventure playgrounds (grass based) with Tudor playhouse for small ones. 2 public telephones, post box and tourist information. Ice pack and battery charging services. Good sized, hedged dog exercise field - dogs allowed on lead. River fishing. Barbecues allowed (fishing rods and barbecues for hire). Access to walks and bridleways on Downs behind park. One mile to bus route and pub - taxi service available.

Directions: Park is signed only from the A3055 at Lake (a place) between Shanklin and Sandown. Leave A3055 just west of railway bridge, by Manor House pub. 1 mile to park. O.S.GR: SZ590855.

Charges 1995:
-- Per adult £3.00 - £4.90; child (3-15 yrs) £1.50 - £2.45; dog £1.30; electricity £1.85; extra car £1.00; pup tent or awning free.
-- Off peak concessions for the over 50s.
-- Ferry packages available - park will help get best deal.
-- Good behaviour deposit required for young persons.
-- VAT included.
Open:
Easter - end September.
Address:
Adgestone,
nr. Sandown, I.O.W.
PO36 0HL.
Tel:
Sandown (01983) 403432 or 403989.
FAX: (01983) 404955.
Reservations:
Deposit £4 per night booked; balance payable on arrival.

26 The Orchards Holiday Caravan Park, Newbridge, nr. Yarmouth

Peaceful, family park in quieter western part of island with well kept touring area and swimming pool.

A select park, in a quiet village situation, The Orchards combines 61 holiday caravans (in a separate area) with a neat, well kept touring area. Run personally by the proprietor as a quiet, friendly, family park without evening entertainment, it provides a pleasant, comfortable base from which to explore and is about 4 miles from the beaches and from Yarmouth, in the west of the island. There is a medium sized, heated swimming pool and child's pool open mid-May to mid-Sept. About 175 marked pitches are arranged on gently sloping meadow, broken up by attractive trees, mature hedges and fences; 140 have electricity, 7 with hardstanding and 14 with semi-hardstanding for car and jockey wheel. The park is part of the Caravan Club's `managed under contract' scheme, although non-members are also very welcome, and is a member of the Best of British group.

Sanitary facilities are provided by two modern, and one older block, which together should be an ample provision. Hot water is free for the washbasins (some with shelf, others set in flat surfaces and a few in private cabins), for the controllable hot showers (many refurbished) and for dishwashing. There are also baths for children on payment and toilet facilities for the disabled (a hardstanding pitch close by can be reserved if requested). Free irons, hairdryers and vacuum cleaners are thoughtfully provided, with full laundry facilities. Ice pack and battery charging services. Large reception with useful tourist information. Well stocked shop and takeaway service (limited opening April and late Sept. and Oct). Dog walk area. A meetings room (up to 50 persons) is suitable for small rallies. Children's play equipment, pool, TV and amusements rooms complete the facilities. Walks from park. Three pubs within 2½ miles and membership available for village social club. Coarse fishing. Golfing and walking holidays available.

Directions: Park is in Newbridge village, signed north from B3401 (Yarmouth - Newport) road. O.S.GR: SZ412878.

Charges 1995:
-- Per pitch £1.10; adult £2.60 - £4.15; child £1.25 - £2.55, both acc. to season; awning free; pup tent £1.00; electricity (10A) £1.90; dog £1.00; extra car £1.00; no pitch fee for hikers or cyclists.
-- Packages incl. ferry travel available - ring site for best deal.
-- VAT included.
-- Credit cards accepted.

Open:
30 March - 31 October.

Address:
Newbridge, Yarmouth, I.O.W. PO41 0TS.

Tel:
(01983) 531331 or 531350.

FAX: (01983) 531666.

Reservations:
Made for min. 5 days with £20 p.w. deposit.

Alan Rogers' discount

Less 5% if no other discounts being claimed or ferry package

□ Special ferry inclusive package holidays

□ Excellent toilet, shower and laundrette facilities

□ Outdoor heated swimming and paddling pools

□ Superb self service shop with off-licence

□ Take-away food bar

□ Electric hook up

□ Private coarse fishing

□ Small rallies welcome

The Orchards Holiday Caravan & Camping Park

The only Caravan Club Appointed site on the Isle of Wight

Dial-a-brochure now on (01983) 531331

Write to: Malcolm J. Peplow, The Orchards, Newbridge, Yarmouth, Isle of Wight, PO41 0TS

27 Southland Camping Park, Newchurch, nr. Sandown

Quiet, family run touring park 3 miles from popular resorts.

This well kept park, formerly part of a plant nursery business, is now owned by Viv and Vanessa McGuinness. It is a sheltered, flat, well drained site enhanced by many attractive shrubs and trees in the peaceful country setting of the Arreton valley, where they hold the August National Garlic festival. The 100 marked pitches, all with electricity and some with water points also, are pleasantly arranged in a level, main field - about 40 round the perimeter, with generous spacing, the others in rows along the middle separated into groups by growing hedges. A modern building houses reception and the shop, with tourist information. A single toilet block has washbasins with shelf, mirror, hairdryers, adjustable hot showers, all with free hot water; family bathroom on payment, baby bath and vanity units. A rustic building houses laundry and dishwashing sinks and there are plentiful water points. A quiet park, there is a children's play area but no other on-site activities. Sandown and Shanklin are 3 miles, the beach at Lake, 2½ miles. A main bus route stops at the top of the road, 2 pubs are within walking distance and the village of Newchurch and craft village are near. Direct access to walks and bridleways from the park.

Directions: Park is signed from A3055/6 Newport-Sandown road, southeast of Arreton. O.S.GR: SZ557847.

Charges 1995:
-- Per adult £2.50 - £3.50; child (up to 15 yrs) £1.00 - £1.50; pitch £1.00; electricity £1.75; dog 80p; extra car 90p.
-- Package deals - Vanessa will help you get the best ferry deal.
-- VAT included.
-- Credit cards accepted.
Open:
Easter - mid October.
Address:
Newchurch, Sandown, I.O.W. PO36 0LZ.
Tel:
(01983) 865385.
FAX: (01983) 867663.
Reservations:
Any length with £15 deposit per pitch, per week (or part week).

Alan Rogers' discount 10% off site fees

SOUTHLAND CAMPING PARK

NEWCHURCH
Nr. SANDOWN
ISLE OF WIGHT
PO36 0LZ
Tel: (01983) 865385
Fax: (01983) 867663

This secluded, sheltered camping park set on the outskirts of the small rural village of Newchurch, offers level and well-drained meadowland - of special benefit to the early and late season camper. Access is good. Off the beaten track but within reach of some of the finest beaches and places of interest. The modern, purpose-built service block has excellent facilities. Individually marked pitches are well spaced, all with electrical hook-up points. 10 or 16 amp.

Booking is recommended. Write or telephone for details.

Special Package offers available including Return Ferry fares.

OPEN EASTER TO OCT. NO STATIC CARAVANS

CAMPSITE OF THE YEAR '97 - '98

APPROVED

28 Ninham Country Holidays, Shanklin

Touring site on spacious grassland, in rural location but close to coastal resorts.

Just outside Shanklin, the approach to Ninham is through a residential area and past a lively holiday park but eventually one reaches open countryside and a quiet wooded valley with lakes and nature reserves. Family owned and run, Ninham has direct access to miles of pretty footpaths and bridleways. The quiet park has pitches for about 130 units (60 with electricity) on sloping meadows. Trees are maturing to provide shelter but at present the fields are rather open. There are just three holiday caravans in one corner. The single, elderly toilet block is not particularly large or luxurious but is quite acceptable with free hot water to basins and showers. The farmhouse is by a small lake and a converted building houses a laundry room, 2 baby-care cubicles, hair-care room, ample dishwashing sinks, information section and public phone. A new reception and shop, providing only basics, is at the site entrance. Attractive, sheltered, heated outdoor pool with child's pool and patio area. Barbecue area in the orchard. Adventure play area and a younger child's area, petanque and coarse fishing. Ice pack service. Care with pets is necessary because of water fowl and wild life. Note: one field is let to the C&C Club, managed by resident wardens, with a beautiful view, an elderly, but well maintained toilet block, good dishwashing facilities and a simple play area.

Directions: Access road leads off A3056 (Sandown-Newport) road on edge of built up area. O.S.GR: SZ572825.

Charges guide:
-- Per adult £3.50 - £4.60, acc. to season; child (2-14 yrs) £1.75 - £2.25, under 2 yrs free - £1.00; electricity (10A) £1.65.
-- Discounts for senior citizens in low season.
-- Ferry packages.
-- VAT included.
Open:
Easter - 30 September
Address:
Shanklin, I.O.W. PO37 7PL.
Tel:
(01983) 864243.
FAX: (01983) 868881.
Reservations:
Any length with £10 per week deposit.

29 Appuldurcombe Garden Caravan Park, Wroxall, nr. Ventnor

Pleasant park with heated pool and other amenities, with some holiday caravans.

This well kept little park would be a pleasant spot for your stay on the Isle of Wight. Quietly situated in a village, it is a little back from the sea - Ventnor beach 2½ miles and Shanklin 3 - with distant views and good walks nearby. It has a good, sheltered, heated swimming pool (60 x 25 ft.), with underwater floodlighting, (open Spring B.H.) and an attractive bar and lounge, with dance floor, beside the pool, where there are evening entertainments nightly at Spr. B.H. and the school holiday period, otherwise on limited nights. It is therefore quite a lively park - there are also 40 holiday caravans for hire in the attractive, old walled garden and two 8-bed flats. The 100 marked touring pitches, 40 with electricity, are arranged on either side of gravel access roads on a flat grassy meadow. A further field with a pond is available for recreation and a pretty little stream flows past the reception block. Two small sanitary blocks provide free hot water for the washbasins, set in flat surfaces and for the dishwashing sinks. Showers are on payment. Facilities for the disabled. Shop and kiosk by the pool in season. TV room. Pitch and putt plus children's play equipment. The park can be peaceful and quiet in early and late season, whilst being busily active in high season, when reservation is advisable.

Charges guide:
-- Per adult £2.00 - £3.25 acc. to season; child (3-13 yrs) £1.00 - £1.85; pitch £1.00 - £2.00; dog £2.00 per week; electricity £1.50.
-- Weekly packages and ferry bookings.
-- VAT included.
Open:
1 March - end October.
Address:
Wroxall, nr. Ventnor, I.O.W. PO38 3EP.
Tel:
(01983) 852597.
Reservations:
Any length with £25 refundable deposit and £1 fee.

Directions: From the A3020 Newport-Sandown road turn onto A3020 Shanklin road, following this through Godshill to Whiteley Bank roundabout and turn right for Wroxhall. Continue for 1 mile past the Donkey Sanctuary and park is off to the right in the village - watch for sign. O.S.GR: SZ548803.

see advert in previous colour section

30 Hoburne Park, Christchurch

Well kept holiday and touring park with many amenities for caravans, motorcaravans and trailer tents only, with holiday homes section.

Conveniently situated for Bournemouth or the New Forest, this is a well kept and tidy site with a range of good quality amenities. There are 285 level, grass touring pitches (for caravans, motorcaravans and trailer tents only), all with 16A electricity and some with individual water supply and hardstanding, in three separated hedged areas. The amenities include an outdoor pool, with both paved and grass sunbathing areas, children's pool and an attractive indoor leisure pool with sauna, spa bath, solarium and steam rooms. We are most impressed with the number of life guards on duty and the attendance to safety here and at other Hoburne parks. A large reception area, restaurant, takeaway, well furnished bar with terrace, video games room and snooker room form part of the indoor complex area. A large adventure play area with play castle is near this main complex together with hard court tennis and crazy golf and there is an organised programme of entertainment for adults and children in the season. A well stocked shop and launderette complete the facilities.

The sanitary facilities are modern and include free hot showers in blocks central to each field area, with additional facilities attached to the main building. Mother and baby room with bath in one block and nappy changing unit in the pool area. Many large sites have a somewhat frenzied atmosphere in the high season. This one can be busy but the atmosphere is pleasantly quiet and relaxed. No tents or pup tents are permitted. Dogs and pets not accepted. American motorhomes accepted in limited numbers up to 30 ft. A well managed park, the flag flier of the Hoburne group.

Charges 1996:
-- Per unit, incl. electricity and awning (up to 3 x 9m.) £8.50 - £20.00, acc. to season.
-- Weekly rates and special weekend breaks.
-- VAT included.
-- Credit cards accepted.
Open:
March - October.
Address:
Hoburne Lane, Christchurch, Dorset BH23 4HU.
Tel:
Christchurch (01425) 273379.
FAX: (01425) 270705.
Reservations:
Made with payment in full (6 days or less) or £50 deposit; min. periods 4 nights for B.H.s, 7 nights mid July - end Aug.

Directions: Park is signed (left) from roundabout roughly 2 miles east of Christchurch on the A337. From Lyndhurst, travel south on A35 to the junction with A337 - turn left onto A337 then left again at the first roundabout. O.S.GR: SZ169928.

see advertisement on inside back cover

Other parks in the Hoburne Group are:
Bashley Park (22), Grange Court (66), Twitchen Park (108), Blue Anchor (114) and Cotswold (163).

31 Mount Pleasant Touring Park, Christchurch, nr. Bournemouth

Neat tidy park in woodland setting, within 3 miles of Bournemouth centre.

Although situated between Bournemouth airport and the A338 dual-carriageway, this is a surprisingly pretty, 'rural' park. The pine trees, wild life and the welcome make up for any noise. Pitches are on mostly level, sandy grass with circular connecting tarmac roads, neatly fenced and interspersed with pine trees and rhododendron bushes. In total there are 175 pitches for all types of units, 87 of them marked and with 10A electricity. Two purpose built, modern toilet blocks are well maintained and fully tiled, with vanity style washbasins with free hot water (some washbasins are in cubicles). Pre-set, well equipped showers at present cost 20p but the meters are due to be removed. Toddler room and separate, fully equipped units for the disabled. A good basic shop and information area are in reception and a mobile takeaway, open all season, is very popular for breakfasts! Fenced adventure play area and direct access to the forest for dog walking, etc. Bournemouth is around 10 minutes away by car (depending on the traffic) and a Tesco hypermarket, 7 minutes. Dry ski centre within ½ mile with bars and restaurants. The nearest bus service is 2 miles. Barbecues are allowed.

Directions: From the A338 Ringwood-Bournemouth road, take thr B3073 road in the direction of Hurn airport. Follow camp signs at first mini roundabout onto Matchams Lane. O.S.GR: SZ129987.

Charges 1995:
-- Per unit incl. up to 2 persons £5.50 - £10.00; small tent £4.50 - £8.50; extra person (over 4 yrs) £1.00 - £1.50; awning £1.00 - £2.00; extra car, boat or trailer £1.50 - £2.00; dog £1.00; electricity (6A) £1.70.
-- Credit cards accepted.
Open:
1 March - 31 October.
Address:
Matchams Lane, Hurn, Christchurch, Dorset BH23 6AW.
Tel:
(01202) 475474.
Reservations:
Accepted only for weekly bookings, with £30 deposit.

32 Sandford Caravan Park, Holton Heath, nr. Poole

Pleasant, well run park with many first-class amenities near popular coastal areas; holiday caravans and large touring section.

Sandford Park has a large permanent section with 75 residential caravans and 160 hire units. However, the touring sections can accommodate 450 units of any type, mainly on individual pitches, on level grass with mature hedging in the main area. All have 16A electrical connections. Early booking is advisable. The main toilet block in the touring area is of good quality providing facilities for the disabled and a baby room. It is supplemented by the former main block and subsidiary units in the touring and static areas (one a bath block). Free hot water in the washbasins, set vanity-style in flat surfaces, and in the pre-set showers. Plenty of water points around. No dogs or pets permitted in the touring section. Sandford Park, now under new ownership, is a large, busy holiday park with a wide range of entertainment. The luxurious clubhouse (open May - Oct) is very spacious and tastefully designed. It manages to cater for different tastes and age groups - two ballrooms for dancing and entertainment (one mainly for children) but both with a nightly programme over a long season. Teenage dancing room. There is a variety of bars, restaurants and simple hot meals elsewhere. The outdoor swimming pool, 25 m. long, heated mid May-mid Sept. and supervised, and a very large play pool (0-2 ft.) with a sandy beach - ideal for children - are attractively situated with a snack bar and terraced area. Solarium. Large supermarket and other shops, including a well stocked camping accessory shop (open mornings only until May). Large launderette. Ladies' hairdresser. TV lounges. Many activities include riding stables and pony rides, children's playground, 2 tennis courts, table tennis, 2 short mat bowling greens (outdoor) and a large crazy golf course. Public phones.

Directions: Park is just west off the A351 (Wareham - Poole) road at Holton Heath. O.S.GR: SY940913.

Charges 1995:
-- Per pitch free - £5.40; adult £3.85; child (3-14 yrs) £1.25 - £2.25; extra car free - 50p; awning free; electricity £2.00; boat and trailer £1.50 - £1.75; visitor £3.75.
-- Club membership included.
-- VAT included.
-- Credit cards accepted.
Open:
April - October.
Address:
Holton Heath, nr. Poole, Dorset BH16 6JZ
Tel:
Lytchett Minster (01202) 631600.
Reservations:
Early booking advisable (min. 3 days) - write to park or contact Weststar Holidays on (01392) 447447.

see advert in previous colour section

33 Merley Court Touring Park, Wimborne Minster

Family run park with excellent amenities and heated outdoor pool.

Only 4 miles from Poole and 8 from Bournemouth, this well planned and pleasantly landscaped park has 160 pitches on flat grass, all numbered and marked by lines on the ground. All have electricity (16A) and 11 are all-service with hardstanding, water, TV aerial socket and waste water drainage. Motor caravan disposal point provided. No static caravans. The park has developed the adjoining 5 acres of woodland to provide some attractive tent pitches, walks (including a marked dog walk), badminton area and children's wooden play frames (sand base). The three toilet blocks are of good quality with free hot water in the washbasins, covered dishwashing sinks, two with pre-set showers. Room for the disabled and for babies. Hair dryers and make-up area for ladies. On site is a heated swimming pool (30 x 20 ft) with children's section open 19/5-10/9. Also hot food takeaway with reasonable prices. All-weather tennis court, free quality crazy golf, pitch and putt, outdoor table tennis and a games room with pool tables. Excellent children's playground on sand base. Some weekly children's and adult entertainment in high season. 2 public phones. Winter storage available. A large, well appointed indoor games room and a family room have been added adjoining the club complex with lounge bar, where meals are available (limited hours low and mid seasons). The complex is exceptionally well furnished and the family room opens out onto a spacious and attractive sheltered patio, which leads through to the paved, walled pool area. No dogs permitted in high season (15/7-2/9). Merley Bird Gardens and Merley House Model Museum are adjacent. A member of the Best of British group.

Directions: Park is signed at an exit from the A31/A349 roundabout on the Wimborne bypass. O.S.GR: ST008984.

Charges 1995:
-- Standard pitch (caravan, small tent or motorcaravan - no awning) £1.50 - £5.00, select pitch £2.50 - £6.00, all service pitch £4.00 - £7.50; adult £2.20 - £2.60; child (3-13 yrs) £1.20 - £1.60; electricity (16A) £1.80; dog £1.00; extra car/boat £1.00.
-- Min. 7 nights Easter, Spr B.H. & high season.
-- VAT included.
Open:
All year except 8 Jan - 28 Feb.
Address:
Merley, Wimborne, Dorset BH21 3AA.
Tel:
(01202) 881488.
Reservations:
Made with deposit (£30 p/w) and £2 fee, balance more than 28 days beforehand.

34 Manor Farm Caravan Park, Wareham

Small, rural park near the Purbecks.

Family owned and carefully run, this park is sited in a hedged, level field with a small stream on one edge. It provides 40 level, well spaced pitches, some seasonal, with 30 (16A) electrical connections. The toilet block (operated on a key system) is at the top of the field and is timber clad but modern inside providing all necessary facilities. Hot water is available but showers are metered. There is a toilet for the disabled in the men's room. Sink for washing-up and one for laundry with spin dryer (all metered). An original recycling point is to be found next door for rubbish. A well stocked, small shop is opened at certain hours. Ice pack service. Sturdy children's play unit. Pub in East Stoke village, Wool is 2 miles with a pub and shops. Wareham and Swanage are near. Dogs are accepted at the discretion of the owner. Public telephone..

Directions: From Wareham take A352 in the direction of Weymouth. Turn left on B3070. At the first crossroads, signed East Stoke, turn right, and right again at second crossroads signed to park which is on the left. O.S.GR: SY872867.

Charges 1995:
-- Per unit incl. 2 persons £5.00 - £6.50; extra person (over 2 yrs) 50p - 75p; awning £1.00 - £1.50; large tent, extra car, boat or trailer £2.00; electricity £2.00.
Open:
Easter - 30 September.
Address:
1 Manor Farm Cottage, East Stoke, Wareham.
Tel:
(01929) 462870.
Reservations:
Made with £15 deposit.

23

Springfield Chamba~ 881719 8 73202

35 Wilksworth Farm Caravan Park, Wimborne Minster

Spacious, quiet park with heated outdoor pool, for families.

Wilksworth Farm has a lovely rural situation just outside Wimborne and around 10 miles from the beaches between Poole and Bournemouth. With its duck pond at the entrance, it is a quiet, well designed park on good quality ground with fairly level grass and some views. It takes 65 caravans (awning groundsheets up in daytime) and 25 tents mainly on grass but with some hardstandings. Some 68 pitches have electricity, 6 water and drainaway also. Also 77 privately owned and self contained holiday homes (2 for hire). Reservation is advisable for July/Aug. and B.Hs. The central toilet block, converted from an original farm barn, is of good quality and is well maintained; it should be ample for these numbers. It has free hot water in the showers and washbasins set in vanity-type flat surfaces, in recessed alcoves. Toilet facilities for the disabled and baby changing point, 3 covered, outside washing-up sinks and a laundry room. Amenities include a heated 40 x 20 ft. swimming pool (unsupervised, but fenced and gated) with small children's pool with paved surround, shop (limited hours), barbecue, BMX track and full and half size tennis courts. Football ground and excellent, safe children's adventure section. Dog exercise paddock. Games room with table tennis, pool, some games machines, etc. Public phone. Freezer for ice packs. A fish and chip van calls certain nights in the main season. Golf and riding 3 miles and Tower Park Leisure Centre is 6 miles. Several restaurants are close.

Directions: Park is 1 mile north of Wimborne, west off the B3078 road to Cranborne. O.S.GR: SU010019.

Charges 1996:
-- Per pitch incl. 2 adults £6.00 - £10.00, acc. to season; child (3-16 yrs) £1.00 July, Aug. & Spring B.H - other times one free with each adult; electricity £2.00; dog £1.00; extra adult £2.00; boat or extra car £1.00.
-- VAT included.
Open:
March -- October incl.
Address:
Cranborne Road, Wimborne, Dorset BH21 4HW.
Tel:
(01202) 885467.
Reservations:
Made with payment in full or £20 per week deposit (min. 5 days at B.Hs).

36 Whitemead Caravan Park, Wool, nr. Wareham

Pleasant, small, family run park between Dorchester and Wareham.

Whitemead is a fairly small, unpretentious park for all units run personally by Mr McCullagh. In a quiet situation, with no on-site evening activities, but within walking distance of the village facilities, it has 95 numbered pitches on flat grass sloping gently north and orchard-like in parts, very natural, with open views over the Frome Valley water meadows. They are well spaced out and mostly back onto hedges or fences; 35 electrical connections for tourers and no static caravans. The park is 4½ miles from the nearest beach at Lulworth and is handily placed for many attractions in this part of Dorset (train services and limited bus service close). The single, spacious, light toilet block provides free hot water both in the washbasins, set in flat surfaces, and the pre-set hot showers (with adjustable flow in ladies) and a baby room which doubles as a facility for the disabled. Small shop (limited hours), doubling as reception. Information room. Microwave (coin operated). Washing machine, spin and tumble dryer. Small children's playground with sand or grass base and small adventure area for older children. Public phone. Fish and chip van calls some nights in season.

Directions: Turn off main A352 on eastern edge of Wool, just north of level crossing, onto East Burton road. Site is 300m. on right. O.S.GR: SY841871.

Charges 1995:
-- Per pitch £4.00 - £7.00, acc. to season; person (over 5 yrs) 50p; awning 50p - £1.00; one man tent less £1.00; extra car or boat £1.00; electricity £1.50.
-- VAT included.
Open:
1 April - 31 October.
Address:
East Burton Rd, Wool, Dorset BH20 6HG.
Tel:
(01929) 462241.
Reservations:
Made with £5 deposit, any length except Spr. B.H. (4 nights min).

𝕎hitemead Caravan Park

East Burton Road, Wool, Dorset BH20 6HG
Telephone: Binden Abbey (01929) 462241

A very attractive personally run site especially noted for its friendly and helpful service and atmosphere. It is divided into 4 sections each with individual charm. The toilet block is of a high standard and exceptionally clean with facilities for disabled persons. There is a well-stocked shop. Wool is a good centre for many beaches, interesting and beautiful countryside and picturesque villages of the "Thomas Hardy" Novels. Early summer is usually warmer and drier here!

37 The Inside Park, nr. Blandford Forum

Small, family run, rural park ideal for touring Dorset.

The Inside Park is set in the grounds of an 18th century country house (which burned down in 1941). Family owned and carefully managed alongside a dairy and arable farm, it is a must for those interested in local history or arboriculture and is a haven for wild life and birds. The reception/toilet block and games room block are respectively the coach house and stables of the old house. The 9-acre camping field, a little distant, lies in a sheltered, gently sloping dry valley containing superb tree specimens - notably Cedars, with walnuts in one part. Under a Cedar of Lebanon is a dog graveyard dating back to the early 1700's. In total there are 120 spacious pitches, 68 with electricity (10A). Six acres adjoining are the old pleasure gardens of the house where campers can walk and exercise dogs in the former garden, now mostly overgrown and providing what must be one of the largest children's campsite adventure-lands in the UK. The toilet block, recently extended, houses comfortably sized showers (pre-set, push button type with curtain splash back), washbasins (some cubicles in ladies) and toilets, all with free hot water and non-slip tiled floors. A room for use by the disabled and mothers and babies has been added, plus new dishwashing sinks. A laundry room is in the same block. Spacious games room with video games, etc. and an information section. Safe based children's adventure play area, complete with trampoline, and a shop with basics (farm milk available) and camping provisions (open limited periods out of main season). Pony rides in high season and organised farm tours. Public telephone. No access to the park allowed after 10.30 pm. (separate late arrivals area and car park). Day kennelling facilities for dogs. The market town of Blandford with its new leisure and swimming centre is 2 miles and the area is excellent for walking and cycling.

Charges 1995:
-- Per pitch £2.50 - £3.50, acc. to season; adult £2.25 - £2.75; child (5-16) free - 80p; dog 50p - 80p; electricity £1.75.
-- Credit cards accepted.
Open: Easter - 31 October.
Address Blandford Forum, Dorset DT11 0HG.
Tel: Blandford (01258) 453719.
FAX: (01258) 454026.
Reservations: Made with £10 deposit (min. 4 nights 15 July - 3 Sept).

Alan Rogers' discount
50p p/night discount

Directions: Park is about 1½ miles southwest of Blandford and is signed from the roundabout at the junction of the A354 and A350 roads. If approaching from the Shaftesbury direction, do not go into Blandford but follow the bypass to the last roundabout and follow camp signs. O.S.GR: ST864045.

38 Wareham Forest Tourist Park, nr. Wareham

see advert in previous colour section

Well run park in forest setting with swimming pool.

A tranquil, spacious park in an unspoiled corner of Dorset, this park has been developed to high standards by the present owners, comparing favourably with European sites. Attractively set in Wareham Forest, providing a choice of open field or wooded location, there are 200 level marked pitches, of which over 180 have electrical connections, some with hardstanding. There are also some luxury pitches on hardstanding with water, drainage, TV aerial, dustbin and light. A snack bar/restaurant (open main season) looks out over a patio-terrace onto the free, open-air swimming pool, which can be heated (60 x 20 ft open all day in peak season), with a surrounding, grassed sunbathing area. Games room with video machines. Two well maintained toilet blocks are spacious and of a good standard and, unusually for Britain, have some washbasins in private cabins (adjustable showers on payment). Facilities for the disabled, mother and toddlers room. Laundry rooms. Shop with off-licence (limited hours outside main season). Children's adventure play area on sand and grass. Motorcaravan service point. Forest walks. Well situated to explore the Dorset coast and Thomas Hardy country. All year storage facilities, long or short term. Resident wardens on site.

Directions: Park is north of Wareham between Wareham and Bere Regis, located off the A35 road. O.S.GR: SY899903.

Charges 1995:
-- Per pitch £2.50 - £6.80; adult £1.60 - £2.70; child (2-14 yrs) £1.00 - £1.60; awning, boat, trailer, extra car 50p - £1.00; extra tent 50p - £2.00; dog 50p - £1.00; electricity £1.90. -- Discount for OAPs in low season.
-- VAT included.
Open:
All year.
Address:
North Trigon, Wareham, Dorset BH20 7NZ.
Tel:
(01929) 551393.
Reservations:
Made with £25 deposit Contact park for details.

WAREHAM FOREST TOURIST PARK
Resident owners Peter and Pam Savage

Enjoy the peace and tranquillity of Wareham Forest, developed to the highest standards and comparable with the best in Europe

HEATED SWIMMING POOL ✦ CHILDREN'S POOL ✦ Fully serviced pitches
✦ Children's adventure playground ✦ Indoor games room ✦ Shop ✦ Off Sales ✦ Snackbar
✦ Takeaway foods ✦ Disabled facilities ✦ Discount rates for S/Cits early and late season
All year Storage Facilities ✦ Direct access to forest walks

WAREHAM FOREST TOURIST PARK

Situated mid-way between Wareham and Bere Regis (off A35), an ideal base for exploring this unspoilt corner of Dorset, with over 60 miles of coastline offering sandy beaches and sheltered coves.

OPEN ALL YEAR

For further details and free coloured brochure write or phone:
Peter & Pam Savage, Wareham Forest Tourist Park, North Trigon,
Wareham, Dorset BH20 7NZ. **Tel: Wareham (01929) 551393**

---

39 Moreton Glade Touring Park, Moreton, nr. Dorchester

Family run, neat, well kept park in popular holiday area.

On nearly level ground, surrounded on three sides by mature woodland, this purpose built, well organised and efficiently run park is handy for touring Dorset and there are good safe beaches at Weymouth, 10 miles away. It can take 154 units on pitches which are a little bit regimented but well marked; 106 with electricity and some hardstandings. Two identical, heated, good, modern toilet blocks are well maintained, with hand and hair dryers, and perfectly adequate. All hot water is free, and in the showers is controllable. Each block has a well appointed shower/washroom/toilet for the disabled (highly rated by campers) and a dishwashing room. Refuse disposal, water and chemical toilet disposal facilities are neatly fenced on concrete bases. Small shop (7.30-12 am. and 2-8 pm.) with basic provisions and camping stocks, takeaway service (certain nights and lunch times), laundry room, an attractive, safe children's play area, dog exercise area in woodland and 2 public phones. There is an hotel next to the park entrance and Moreton station (halt) is across the road for regular train services to Poole/Bournemouth or Dorchester/Weymouth. A leisure centre with dry ski slope and pool is a short drive away. **continued overleaf**

Charges 1995:
-- Per unit incl. 2 persons £4.50 - £8.00; extra person (over 4 yrs) £1.00 - £1.50; awning, extra pup tent £1.00 - £1.50; extra car, boat, trailer, dog £1.00 - £1.50; electricity £1.60; hiker + tent £3.50 - £6.50.
-- Senior citizens 50p off in low season (if booked).
-- VAT included.
Open:
All year except 6 Jan -15 March.

39 Moreton Glade Touring Park, Moreton, nr. Dorchester (continued)

Directions: Park is east off the B3390 (Bere Regis - Weymouth) road, just north of the level crossing at Crossways and adjacent the Frampton Arms Hotel. O.S.GR: SY782892.

Alan Rogers' discount
5 nights for the price of four in low season

Address: Station Road (B3390), Moreton, Dorchester, Dorset DT2 8BB.
Tel: (01305) 853801.
Reservations: Any length, £10 per pitch.

40 Rowlands Wait Touring Park, Bere Regis

Pretty, rural site with good facilities.

Recommended by readers, we arrived on a spring morning to find that this site had changed hands and was now owned by Bernard and Linda Hammick and their two young children, who were keen to welcome us. Attractively situated, the park has direct access to the heathland and views across to Bere Regis and Woodbury Hill. It provides various areas, some better situated for camping, with mature trees and very natural - the wild flowers and birds were impressive. The lawn and terraced areas are more level for caravans and are nearer to the central toilet block. This is purpose built and well equipped, with free hot water, except for the showers. Laundry room and covered dishwashing area. Plans to add a baby changing room and some provision for the disabled are in hand. A shop cum reception provides milk, papers and basic essentials. The village, a 10 minute walk, has shops, a pub, etc. plus a bus service for Dorchester and Poole. A new play area for little ones with miniature assault course and castle is well placed next to reception. Bike hire and fishing can be arranged. Bernard tells us that his slogan is 'Make us your first call, not your last resort' and they are well situated for just that. We wish them well and await your comments.

Directions: South of Bere Regis, just off the road to Wool, well signed from the A35/A31 roundabout. O.S.GR: SY842933.

Charges 1995:
-- Per unit incl. 2 persons £5.30 - £8.30, acc. to season; adult £1.35 - £1.85; child (under 16 yrs) 85p; awning or small tent £1.00; electricity £1.80; dog 60p; extra car, boat or trailer £1.00.
Open:
16 March - 31 October.
Address:
Rye Hill, Bere Regis, Dorset BH20 7LP.
Tel:
(01929) 471958.
Reservations:
Made with £15 deposit per week.

41 East Fleet Farm Touring Park, Chickerell, Weymouth

Genuine touring park, attractively situated on the coast by the Fleet.

Developed within the confines of a 300-acre working dairy and arable farm, this is a rural touring park with no caravan holiday homes or other statics. It is situated by the shores of the Fleet, a lagoon renowned for its wildlife (no motor or sailing boats allowed). The site is on gently sloping grassland, with hardcore roadways, leading to the shores of the Fleet, beyond which is the famous Chesil Bank and the sea. The busy resort of Weymouth, with safe bathing beaches and many watersports facilities is only 3 miles away. There are 210 pitches of which 84 are marked and have electricity (10A). Trees and shrubs are growing and will, in time, provide shade and add to the attractiveness as the site matures. The central sanitary block is built in natural stone and provides adequate rather than luxurious facilities, including flush WCs, washbasins with hot and cold water, coin operated hot showers, electric shaver points, hairdryers, continental-style washing-up facilities and a launderette. There is a shop for groceries, bread, newspapers, gas, etc, a public telephone and a children's play area. Bus service from the top of the lane leading to park (½ mile). Nearest pub about 1 mile. A torch may be useful.

Directions: Park is signed from the B3157 Weymouth - Bridport road, approx. 3 miles west of Weymouth. The narrow approach road is by the army camp on the southern side of the B3157. O.S.GR: SY639798.

See advertisement overleaf

Charges 1995:
-- Per pitch incl. 1 or 2 adults £4.50 - £8.50; extra adult 50p - £1.00, child (5-14 yrs) 25p - 50p; dog 25p - 50p; awning free - £1.25; extra car or large boat 25p = 50p; electricity £1.50 - £1.85.
-- VAT included.
Open:
Mid March - end October.
Address:
Chickerell, Weymouth, Dorset DT3 4DW.
Tel:
(01305) 785768.
Reservations:
Write with £10 deposit.

27

DORSET

42 Binghams Farm Touring Caravan Park, Melplash, nr. Bridport

Small, new, purpose built park in rural Brit Valley location, open all year.

Binghams has a pleasant situation 2 miles from the market town of Bridport, with views seaward towards West Bay and inland across Beaminster Downs and Pilsdon Hill. Frank and Sue Beazer have provided 40 individual pitches with 10A electricity, nicely landscaped with shrubs and trees growing between the pitches. These are linked by a gravel road with a central recreation and play area which is partly screened. Five hardstandings are available and a tenting area is to one side. There is a slight slope in one area. The toilet block, a small shop, the reception and a games room (with table tennis and pool) have been sympathetically converted from the original farm buildings. The toilet blocks, with under floor heating for winter use and free hot water, provide well fitted, tiled, curtained showers, vanity style washbasins, hairdryers and a separate, fully equipped room for the less able with ramped access. Laundry room. Entrance to the site is neatly tarmaced and the resident peacocks and chickens provide interest for children. A path is provided to the river which links with the main footpath for Bridport (20 mins). Limited bus service on the main road. The Brit Valley is an unspoilt area of West Dorset with an ancient heritage and coastal West Bay is only a couple of miles.

Directions: At the main roundabout on the A35 on the east side of Bridport take the A3066 in the direction of Beaminster. Watch for site entrance after approx. 2 miles on the left. O.S.GR: SY482963.

Chares 1995: -- Per pitch £4.00 - £5.50, acc. to season; adult £1.50 - £2.00; child (3-16 yrs) 75p - £1.00; dog 50p - £1.00; electricity £2.00 - £1.50. -- VAT included. **Open:** All year. **Address:** Melplash, nr. Bridport, Dorset DT6 3TT. **Tel:** (01308) 488234. **Reservations:** Made with £20 deposit and £2 fee.

Alan Rogers' discount 50p p/night discount

See Editorial Report on previous page

28

DORSET

43 Freshwater Beach Holiday Park, Burton Bradstock, nr. Bridport

Busy holiday and touring park with direct access to private beach.

Parks with direct access to a beach are rare in Britain and this one has the added advantage of being in beautiful coastal countryside in West Dorset. It is an ideal situation to explore the 'Hidden County' and the resort of Weymouth (17 miles away). This lively park is next to the sea and pebbly beach, sheltered from the wind by pebble banks. Approached by a fairly steep access road, the park itself is on level ground. The 425 touring pitches, over 200 with 10A electricity (with more connections planned) are on an open, undulating grass field. Additionally there are 11 serviced pitches with hardstanding. Tent pitches are unmarked. There are many caravan holiday homes for hire.

This is a holiday park type of site with an extensive range of facilities which include a licensed restaurant with interesting menu, and two bars with evening entertainment in season. Also good value supermarket and other shops, launderette, takeaway, heated and supervised outdoor swimming pool and children's pool, adventure play area, pets corner and pony trekking (park's own stables). A golf course is adjacent and there is a footpath to the attractive village of Burton Bradstock. Sanitary facilities, including a new block on the touring field, are quite acceptable, rather than luxurious as, being a busy beach park, they receive very heavy use in high season with consequent wear and tear. However, cleaning and maintenance seem good and both blocks have free hot water, facilities for the handicapped and a baby changing room. Laundry and washing up sinks. The overall impression is of a large, busy holiday park with a friendly reception and atmosphere.

Directions: Park is immediately west of the village of Burton Bradstock, on the Weymouth - Bridport coast road (B3157). O.S.GR: SY980898.

Charges 1995:
-- Per unit incl. 4 persons £6.50 - £13.00, acc. to season; small tent or motorvan incl. 2 persons £4.50 - £7.50; extra person £1.00 - £1.50; awning £1.50; dog £2.50; extra car or boat £1.00 - £1.50; electricity £1.25.
-- VAT included.
-- Credit cards accepted.
Open:
15 March - 10 Nov.
Address:
Burton Bradstock, Bridport, Dorset DT6 4PT.
Tel:
(01308) 897317.
FAX: (01308) 897336.
Reservations:
Made for min. 1 week with £10 deposit p/week, plus £1 fee. Short break reservations - ring for details.

see advert in next colour section

44 Monkton Wylde Farm Touring Caravan Park, nr Charmouth

Small, relaxed, family run park attached to a working farm.

This is a recently developed park, opened in 1991 by Simon and Joanna Kewley, in countryside as part of a working sheep farm. The 6 acre park offers 60 numbered pitches on gently sloping grass, 20 of which have been levelled as part of a continuing improvement programme. Over 24 pitches have 16A electrical connections. The sanitary block is modern and it was extremely clean when we visited. It has a family room with shower and baby changing facilities, which is also accessible by wheel chair, individual showers which are very spacious with free hot water and vanity style washbasins. Small laundry with washing machine and tumble dryer and under cover washing up facilities. Beautiful countryside surrounds the park and there is an abundance of mature trees around the perimeter providing shade and plenty of space between the pitches giving a feeling of spaciousness. On site facilities are limited but a separate field has been turned into a children's play area, with a good area for ball games. Basic items may be obtained from the farm opposite the park (ie. milk, bread, newspapers). There is no reception as such - a small wooden hut is situated near the entrance where information is available regarding pitch vacancies and so forth and the owners are never far away. A gate system is operated and it is locked at 11 pm. (except in high season). A separate paddock along the lane has been set aside as a dog walk. There are shops within a mile and Charmouth and Lyme Regis are only 3 miles away (buses leave from just along the road to both towns).

Directions: Park is signed on the A35 between Charmouth and Axminster, approx. 1½ miles west of Charmouth. Turn right at 'Greenway Head' and park is 600 yds on the left. (Do not go to Monkton Wylde hamlet - the road is very steep). O.S.GR: SY329966.

Charges 1995:
-- Per unit £1.00 - £3.00, acc. to season; adult £2.25; child (5-16 yrs) free - 90p; electricity £1.35 - £1.65; dog free - 50p; no extra charge for awnings, 2nd car, boats or visitors.
-- VAT included.
Open:
Easter - end October.
Address:
Monkton Wylde Farm, Charmouth, Dorset DT6 6DB.
Tel:
(01297) 34525.
Reservations:
Made with deposit of £2 per night (eg £14 per week).

45 Golden Cap Holiday Park, Chideock, nr. Bridport

Beachside touring park with holiday caravans in a rural situation.

Golden Cap, named after the adjacent high cliff top which overlooks Lyme Bay, is only 150 yards from a shingle beach at Seatown. The park is arranged over several fields on the valley floor, sloping down gently towards the sea. It is in two main areas, having once been two parks, each separated into fields with views around and providing 150 tourist pitches, 104 with electricity and 28 with hardstandings with drainaway, electricity and gravelled awning area, which are individually fenced. There are 190 caravan holiday homes in their own areas. American motorhomes are not accepted. The main toilet block is modern and of very good quality, with free hot water in the washbasins and spacious shower cubicles (some with toilet and washbasin), good facilities for the disabled and a baby room. There are three other smaller blocks around the park. Laundry room. Useful shop, also takeaway, caravan sales information and tourist information rooms. A pub with food service is close. The most attractive indoor swimming pool at Highlands End (under the same ownership) 3 miles away, is available for campers. Public telephone. Beaches, sea fishing, riding, fossil hunting and good walks are near. A member of the Best of British group.

Directions: Turn off A35 road at Chideock, (a bigger village with shops and restaurants) 3 miles west of Bridport, at sign to Seatown opposite church. Park is less than 1 mile down narrow lane. O.S.GR: SY423919.

Charges 1995:
-- Per unit incl. 2 persons, awning and car £7.50 - £10.75; electricity £1.50; extra adult £2.50, child (3-17 yrs) £1.25; dog £1.00; extra car £1.00.
-- VAT included.
-- Credit cards accepted.
Open:
22 March - 3 November.
Address:
Park: Seatown, Chideock, nr. Bridport; Booking: West Dorset Leisure Holidays, Eype, Bridport, Dorset DT6 6AR.
Tel:
Park: (01297) 489341; bookings: (01308) 422139.
FAX: (01308) 425672.
Reservations:
Essential in high season and made with £20 deposit (1 week min. in high season).

46 Highlands End Farm Holiday Park, Eype, nr. Bridport

Well kept park on cliffs by sea, with holiday caravan and touring sections.

On slightly sloping ground with superb views, both coastal and inland, Highlands End is quietly situated on the Dorset coastline. A path in front of the park runs along the cliff top and then leads down to a shingle beach a little further along. There are 160 caravan holiday homes which are mostly privately occupied but a number are for letting. The 122 touring pitches are in two areas nearest to the sea - one has to travel through the holiday homes to reach them. All have electricity available (10A) and 45 also offer water, drainaway and a gravel awning area. A further area is used for tents in high season. The two toilet blocks plus a good new separate shower block near the tourist sections, are well kept like the rest of the park. Free hot water to the washbasins, some in cubicles with toilets, the pre-set showers, and the covered washing-up sinks. Laundry room, facilities for the disabled and baby room. Water points around. A modern, attractive building houses a good sized lounge bar, family room and games room (open Spr. B.H.-late Sept.) and there is an excellent air-conditioned indoor heated swimming pool with attendant (20 x 9 m.), a fitness room, sun beds and games room. New tennis court. Children's adventure playground. Well stocked shop. Public phones. An efficiently run park and a member of the Best of British group.

Directions: Follow Bridport bypass on A35 around the town and park is signed to south (Eype turning), down narrow lane. O.S.GR: SY452914.

Charges 1995:
-- Per unit incl. 2 persons and awning £7.50 - £10.75; electricity £1.50; extra adult £2.50, child (3-17 yrs) £1.25; dog £1.00; extra car £1.00.
-- VAT included.
-- Credit cards accepted.
Open:
22 March - 3 November.
Address:
West Dorset Leisure Holidays, Eype, Bridport, Dorset DT6 6AR.
Tel:
(01308) 422139.
FAX: (01308) 425672.
Reservations:
Essential in high season and made with £20 deposit (min. 7 days in high season).

47 Wood Farm Caravan Park, Charmouth, nr. Lyme Regis

Attractive family run park for all touring units, with indoor pool.

Wood Farm is a very well kept park on the western side of Charmouth beside the A35 (some road noise may be expected), and only a mile or two from Lyme Regis and its beaches. Part of the Caravan Club's `managed under contract' scheme (non-members are also very welcome) and a member of the Best of British group. On sloping, well landscaped ground, it has open views across the countryside. There are 216 pitches of which 180 are neat, all-weather pitches with hardstanding, electricity (10A) and TV connections, and provision for awnings. One grassy terraced field takes about 25 tents. American motorhomes not accepted. Four toilet blocks give an ample provision and provide free hot water to the washbasins and pre-set hot showers. All visitors to the park are offered temporary membership to the on-site heated indoor swimming pool (27 x 54 ft.) on payment of £1.45 per session. There is a snooker room, family games room and a tennis court. Other amenities include a laundry room, a new shop, and a children's play field (equipment on safety surface). A fish and chip van calls 2-4 times a week (acc. to seaon). Dogs are accepted and there is a good dog walk. A small coarse fishing lake (carp, rudd, roach and tench) is now available adjacemt to the park - day and weekly tickets available (NRA licence required, also available from park). Mobile homes to rent. Golf course 1 mile, beaches and shops ¾ and 2 miles.

Directions: Park is ½ mile west of Charmouth village with access near the new roundabout at the junction of the A35 with the A3052 (Lyme Regis) road. O.S.GR: SY356940.

Charges 1995:
-- Per unit incl. side awning £2.00 - £4.00; adult £3.00 - £3.50; child (5-16 yrs) £1.10 - £1.20; electricity (10A) £1.75; dog, extra car, trailer or pup tent £1.00.
-- Special senior citizens low season discounts.
-- VAT included.
Open:
29 March - 3 November.
Address:
Axminster Road, Charmouth, Dorset DT6 6BT
Tel:
(01297) 560697
Reservations:
Made with £25 deposit per week/part week (non-returnable), min. 5 nights in high season, 3 nights other times.

48 Oakdown Touring and Holiday Park, Weston, Sidmouth

Well kept and environmentally conscious park with good pitches.

Oakdown is in attractive countryside with easy access from the A3052, near to unspoilt Devon villages. The small resort of Sidmouth is 3 miles away and the cathedral city of Exeter only 18 miles. The park is very well kept and has been landscaped, with many flowers and young trees planted (in fact 64 named varieties). It provides 120 individual pitches on flat grass, divided mostly into groves each bearing the name of a tree. Reached by concrete access roads, all pitches are separated by young trees, which are providing privacy as they grow. There are 26 pitches with water, drainage and electricity and a further 82 with electricity only (10 or 16A). The central amenity block provides good, fully tiled sanitary facilities which include controllable showers, washbasins set in flat surfaces (one private cabin for ladies) and sinks for dishwashing, all with free hot water. Hairdryers, razor points and 2 family bathrooms (coin operated entry with bath, shower, toilet and washbasin), laundry facilities and free use of a freezer. The centrally heated block also provides extra unisex facilities. Games and TV rooms. Well stocked shop (Spr. B.H.-mid-Sept) and well equipped, grass based children's play area including play castle. Public phones. A Field Trail leads through the countryside to the nearby Donkey Sanctuary and one can walk further to the sea. Secure caravan storage facilities. Park is lit at night. Wardens on site. No cycling, skateboards or kites permitted. New holiday park, `Oak Grove', with 46 holiday homes, some for hire is south of the touring park.

Directions: Turn off A3052 road to south 2½ miles east of junction with A375 road and park is on left. O.S.GR: SY167902.

Charges 1995:
-- Per unit incl. 2 persons: standard pitch £6.55 - £10.00, electricity £1.90; super pitch (incl. full services) £11.80 - £15.20; extra person (5 yrs and over) £1.55; dog 70p - £1.00; awning £1.55; porch awning 85p.
-- Less 70p for senior citizens in low season.
-- VAT included.
Open: 1 April - 31 October.
Address: Weston, Sidmouth, Devon EX10 0PH.
Tel: (01297) 680387.
FAX: (01395) 513731.
Reservations: Made with £20 deposit, min. 3 days at B.Hs.

49 Andrewshayes Caravan Park, Dalwood, nr. Axminster

Rural park adjoining working farm, with outdoor pool.

Andrewshayes is 6 miles from the sea at Seaton and 8 from Lyme Regis. It has a pleasant, small, heated swimming pool (50 x 25 ft.), open Spr. B.H - mid Sept. and one can also watch the milking on the adjoining farm. Surrounded by trees, one field, sloping in parts, takes about 60 units on numbered pitches most with electrical connections. The other area offers a further 30 pitches for longer stays only, each with hardstanding, electricity, water and drainage. Also 80 holiday caravans, either for hire or privately owned, in a separate area, plus a rally field with its own small sanitary block. An excellent, well designed toilet block has free hot water in the washbasins set in flat surfaces (with hand and hair dryers) and in the spacious showers. Family rooms (3) provided in the ladies, plus facilities for the disabled. Sinks for dishes and clothes are under cover, with free hot water. Well stocked shop with off-licence (mid-May - Sept). Large games room. Snack bar with conservatory overlooking the pool and takeaway service. Laundry room. Information centre. TV room. Children's play area. Public phone.

Directions: Park is 150 yds off A35 road, 3 miles west of Axminster, close to Little Chef restaurant. O.S.GR: SY247987.

Charges 1995:
-- Per pitch + 2 adults £8.00 - £9.50; extra person (over 2) £1.00; awning £1.50; dog 50p; electricity £1.50.
-- Less 10% outside 29/5-11/9.
-- Credit cards accepted.
Open: Easter -- end October.
Address: Dalwood, Axminster, Devon EX13 7DY.
Tel/Fax: (01404) 831225.
Reservations: Any period with £10 deposit.

50 Forest Glade Int. Caravan and Camping Park, nr. Cullompton

Country park with small swiming pool and some holiday homes.

Forest Glade is set well away from busy roads, deep in the wooded Devon countryside. The home of the Welland family, it provides 80 touring pitches. Touring caravans must book in advance (by phone is acceptable). There are 35 pitches which accommodate hire caravans and some seasonal tourers. Touring units go mainly on one flat meadow, mostly backing on to woods and hedges, with some hardstandings, also a rally field. There are 68 electrical connections (10/5A). The single toilet block is well kept, clean and heated in cold weather. It has free hot water in vanity style washbasins (two in cubicles for ladies), new hot showers and washing-up sinks. Small laundry. Unit for disabled. Because of its situation, this is a peaceful park without evening activities but there is a small indoor heated swimming pool, with paddling pool and a patio area outside, and an all weather tennis court. There is a safe-based adventure playground, volleyball and a games room with table tennis, video games and pool table. Shop, tourist information and takeaway food service. Woodland walks. Public phone. Motorcaravan service point. A member of the Best of British group.

Directions: Park is 5½ miles from M5 exit 28. Take the A373 for 3 miles, then turn left at camp sign towards Sheldon. Park is on left after approx. 2½ miles. This access is **not** suitable for touring caravans due to a steep hill - phone park for alternative route details. O.S.GR: ST101073.

Charges 1996:
-- Per unit incl. 2 adults £5.50 - £10.50; extra adult £1.60; child (5-9) 80p; student (10 yrs - end of study) £1.60; backpacker or cyclist £2.50 per person; dog 50p; electricity £1.75.
-- VAT included.
Open:
Mid-March - early Nov.
Address:
Cullompton, Devon EX15 2DT.
Tel:
(01404) 841381.
FAX: (01404) 841593.
Reservations:
Any length with deposit (£4 per day or £20 per wk, £15 B.H. w/ends).

FREE INDOOR HEATED SWIMMING POOL

A small country estate surrounded by forest in which deer roam.
LARGE FLAT, SHELTERED CAMPING/TOURING PITCHES – MODERN FACILITIES BUILDING. LUXURY 2/6 BERTH FULL SERVICE HOLIDAY HOMES ALSO SELF CONTAINED FLAT FOR 2 PERSONS.
Shop, Take Away Food, Adventure Play Area, Electric Hook-up Points, Games Room, Tennis Court, Forest Walks. Riding, Gliding and Fishing are nearby. Freedom for the children – peace for the adults. Central for touring the South West. Easy access to coast and moors.
Motor caravans welcome – Facilities for the disabled.
Dogs welcome. Tourers please book in advance.
FREE COLOUR BROCHURE
FOREST GLADE COUNTRY HOLIDAY PARK (CG)
CULLOMPTON DEVON EX15 2DT. TEL: 01404 841381 (Evenings to 9pm)

Country Holiday Park

51 Minnows Camping and Caravan Park, Sampford Peverell, nr. Tiverton

Small, neat, rural park close to M5 motorway, with pleasant views.

The Minnows is an attractive, compact park with views across the Devon countryside, separated from the Grand Western canal by hedging, yet easily accessible from the M5. Part of the Caravan Club's 'managed under contract' scheme, non-members are also very welcome. Open for 11 months of the year, 40 level, semi-terraced, grass pitches provide for all units. Accessed by a gravelled, circular roadway, there are 31 with electricity (16A) and 20 all weather pitches, of which 3 are fully serviced for motorhomes. The heated toilet block is well maintained with modern facilities, constant hot water, facilities for disabled, covered dishwashing sinks and one for laundry. Service wash or tumble dry. Small, safe based children's play area. Bicycle hire. The village of Sampford Peverell, with pub and general store, is a ½ mile walk via the tow path. Tiverton Parkway (BR) is 1½ miles. Pay phone. Golf driving range near. Coarse fishing permits (from 1 June) from reception. No powered boats allowed but a horse drawn barge makes trips on the winding 11 miles of the canal.

Directions: Leave M5 junction 27 on A361 signed Tiverton. After 600 yds take first exit signed Sampford Peverell. After 200 yds right at roundabout and cross bridge over A361 to second roundabout. Straight on and park is ahead. O.S.GR: ST042148.

Charges 1996:
-- Per unit £2.00; small tent and car £1.00; adult £2.50 - £3.00; child £1.10; electricity £2.00; extra car or trailer £1.00; walker or cyclist £2.50 - £3.00 per person; dog and awning free (no groundsheets).
-- Less in low season for bookings 7 days or over.
Open:
All year except Feb.
Address:
Sampford Peverell, nr. Tiverton EX16 9LD.
Tel:
(01884) 821770.
Reservations:
Made with £5 deposit.

 Alan Rogers' discount £1 off pitch fee

52 Kennford International Caravan Park, Kennford, nr. Exeter

Good touring park near historic city, on a main route to the southwest.

Within easy reach of the cathedral city of Exeter for shopping or sightseeing and only 5 miles from the sea at Starcross, this well run park is attractive for longer stays, although it is also most conveniently situated for travellers to and from South Devon and Cornwall. It is situated right beside the main A38 near the end of the M5 motorway (so a little road noise should be expected) and takes up to 120 units of any type on individual pitches separated by a pleasant mix of bushes and trees with open, rural views. There are 106 electrical connections and 16 hardstandings for caravans. On a few pitches connection to mains drainage is possible. The two toilet blocks, quite attractive in appearance with wooden cladding, are of good quality and should be an ample provision. They provide washbasins with shelf, mirror and including 17 individual cabins for ladies with WC also, free controllable hot showers and 2 baths on payment (but free for the disabled). There are also family shower units with external access. Covered washing-up sinks. Well equipped laundry room. Shop (high season). Small bar and tropical style family lounge with snack bar and takeaway in high season. Patio with open fire. Public phone. Children's play equipment on grass and dog exercise field. Children's riding stables, Powderham Castle, Riverside leisure centre and Bird Sanctuary close. A member of the Best of British group.

Directions: From north follow Torbay/Plymouth signs from M5 and take exit for Kennford services and park (signed from both sides of dual carriageway). O.S.GR: SX911856.

Alan Rogers' discount
Less £1p/night

see advertisement on page 48.

Charges 1996:
-- Per unit incl. 2 persons £8.50, trailer tent or large tent £10.00; extra person (over 5 yrs) £1.50; awning or small tent £1.50; dog £1.00; electricity £2.20.
-- Less 10% for stays of over 10 days.
-- VAT included.
-- Credit cards accepted.
Open:
All year.
(Reduced facilities mid-Sept - March).
Address:
Kennford, nr. Exeter, Devon EX6 7YN.
Tel:
(01392) 833046.
FAX: as phone.
Reservations:
Made for any length with £15 deposit.

53 Cofton Country Holiday Park, Starcross, nr. Dawlish

Large touring park with swimming pool and bar and beautiful country views.

About 1½ miles from a sandy beach at Dawlish Warren this popular, family site takes some 450 touring units on a variety of fields and meadows. The smaller, more mature fields, including a pleasant old orchard for tents only, are well terraced. While terraces have now been constructed on most of the slopes of the larger, more open fields, there are still some quite steep slopes to climb. There are over 200 electrical connections. One area has 62 park-owned holiday homes, including a special one for disabled visitors, to hire and there are 5 attractive holiday cottages (available all year). A well designed, central complex is decorated with flowers and hanging baskets and houses reception, a shop and off-licence (5/4-29/9)and a bar lounge, the `Cofton Swan', where simple bar meals are usually available. A family room and bar are on the first floor of this building and there is an outdoor terrace. Some light entertainment in season. The adjacent kidney-shaped heated pool (overall length 100 ft. open from Spr. B.H.), with paddling pool and slide, has lots of grassy space for sun bathing. Other facilities include a fish and chip shop, 2 launderettes and a games room (busy in high season). A small, but good, adventure playground is in an elevated position overlooking the swimming pools and there is further children's play equipment in two areas - one being modern, the other older and with some concrete bases. Coarse fishing (£15 per rod for 7 days) is available in two lakes on the park and there is a woodland trail towards Dawlish Warren. Sanitary facilities consist of three blocks, one on each side of the road dividing the park for the touring pitches and the third near the holiday home area. The newest, at the top of the larger fields is first rate, with laundry and facilities for the disabled. The blocks have free hot water throughout, well equipped and controllable showers, basins set in rows in flat surfaces with 2 in cubicles, hair dryers, and dishwashing facilities under cover. Public phones. Post box. Ice pack hire service.

Directions: Access to the park is off the A379 about 3 miles north of Dawlish. O.S.GR: SX968798.

Charges 1996:
-- Per unit incl. 2 persons £5.00 - £9.50; awning or child's tent 80p - £1.75; extra adult 80p - £1.75; child (2-13 yrs) 80p - £1.50; boat, dog or extra car 80p - £1.50; electricity £1.80.
-- Discounts for Senior Citizens advance bookings outside July/Aug.
-- VAT included.
-- Credit cards accepted.
Open:
April - end-October.
Address:
Starcross, nr. Dawlish, Devon EX6 8RP.
Tel:
(01626) 890111.
FAX: (01626) 891572.
Reservations:
Made for 7 nights min. (Sat to Sat only in high season) with £15 deposit.

54 Lady's Mile Touring and Camping Park, Dawlish

Spacious, family touring park under a mile from the beach, with indoor and outdoor pools.

A large, open park, Lady's Mile has extensive grassy fields in addition to the main, landscaped camping area which is arranged in broad terraces. In July and August caravans and tents normally go in separate sections, at other times they are grouped together in the main part. The park has 486 pitches, mostly marked by lines but with nothing between them, almost all with electrical connections. It is under a mile from a good sandy beach at Dawlish Warren with parking facilities, and also has its own good sized, free swimming pool with 100 ft. slide, children's pool and a paved surround (open mid-May-early Sept. with lifeguard). A large indoor pool (20 x 10 m.) with separate paddling pool will open at Easter 1996 In spite of its size, the park is fully booked over a long season, with reservation necessary.

There are four toilet blocks, of various ages and styles, well spaced around the main areas of the park. They are of a fair standard, with free hot water and, with an additional shower block (with some basins also), there should be an adequate provision overall. Facilities for the disabled and 4 family bathrooms (50p). Dishwashing sinks are under cover with free hot water. Two launderettes. Mini market and takeaway. A new, attractive bar complex with food available also has a spacious games room below with pool tables and video games. Sloping field for recreation, ideal for kite flying and good, fenced children's adventure playground with safe, sand surface. Dog walk. Public phones and post box.

Charges 1995:
-- Per unit incl. 2 adults £5.20 - £9.50; awning or child's tent 80p - £1.80; extra adult 80p - £1.80; child (2-14 yrs) 80p - £1.50; boat, dog or extra car 80p - £1.80; electricity £1.90.
-- Discount for OAPs.
-- VAT included.
Open:
Mid-March - mid-Nov.
Address:
Dawlish, Devon
EX7 0LX.
Tel:
(01626) 863411.
FAX: (01626) 888689.
Reservations:
Made for Sat to Sat only in peak seasons, with £15 deposit.

Directions: Park is 1 mile north of Dawlish with access off the A379 (Exeter - Teignmouth) road. O.S. GR: SX968786.

SOUTH DEVON

55 Finlake Leisure Park, Chudleigh

Large, lively park, with entertainment complex and leisure facilities.

This extensive park, situated on the edge of Dartmoor, has been purpose built as a modern touring park and leisure complex. Approached by a long, sweeping drive, with views up to the moor, the park is on well landscaped, undulating ground surrounded by woodland. There are around 400 flat, numbered pitches in two main areas, with some terrracing on the higher parts. The pitches in the area around the central complex may well be affected by noise from the bars, etc. - for a quieter place, ask for a pitch further away (Lakeside or Deer Park). The pitches are of varying size, all with hardstanding and electric point (10A), 56 with water also. A separate, enclosed field is retained for tents and there is a special area for dog owners, with dog walks available. Six modern toilet blocks set around the park are pine clad and of good quality. They have washbasins set in flat surfaces and pre-set hot showers on payment, a bathroom for ladies, suitable toilet/washrooms for the disabled and washing-up sinks outside, under cover. With additional 'portaloos' for busy times, the provision should be quite acceptable, although the block near the pools receives heavy use.

Also open to the public, the park offers extensive leisure activities including a 9-hole pitch and putt course, two fishing lakes, fitness track, tennis courts and walks in the woodland around the 130-acre park with pony riding 100 m. from the entrance. The modern, attractively designed, central complex provides no less than three bars around a pool terrace, with one specifically for children with soft drinks, snacks and games. There is a lively, free organised entertainment programme over a long season and food is available in the bars with takeaway also (Easter-Oct, plus Xmas and New Year). The indoor and outdoor pools (with slide) are supervised in season but are also easily observed from the bar areas and terrace. Supermarket (limited opening early and late season). Launderette, with ironing room. 41 luxury log cabins, well hidden in woodland, for hire.

Directions: Park is signed on A38 dual carriageway; take exit for Chudleigh Knighton, Kingsteignton, Teign Valley. O.S.GR: SX850778.

Charges 1995:
-- Per unit incl. up to 4 persons, with electricity £7.50 - £16.00, with water also £9.00 - £17.50; trailer tent or tent without electricity £5.50 - £11.50; extra person over 5 yrs, car, boat, awning or dog, all £1.50.
-- Min. stay 4 nights at Easter.
-- VAT included.
-- Credit cards accepted.
Open:
All year except 5 Jan - 16 Feb.
Address:
Chudleigh, Devon TQ13 0EJ.
Tel:
(01626) 853833.
FAX: (01626) 854031.
Reservations:
Made with 25% deposit, balance 28 days before arrival.

see advert in next colour section

56 Holmans Wood Caravan and Camping Park, Chudleigh

Neat, attractive touring park adjacent to main Exeter - Plymouth road.

Close to the main A38 Exeter - Plymouth road, with easy access, this attractive, peaceful park makes a sheltered base for touring south Devon and Dartmoor or a comfortable overnight stop. The hedged park is arranged on well kept grass surrounding a shallow, filled in quarry, the floor of which makes a safe, grassy play area for children. Many attractive trees have been planted and the park is decorated with flowers. In two main areas, the 144 levelled pitches, most with electrical hook-ups, are accessed by tarmac roadways. There are 51 with hardstanding and electricity, TV aerial hook up, water and drainage, with grassy areas for tents. The park is divided into areas for those with or without dogs (wooded exercise area provided). The single toilet block is of good quality with washbasins set in flat surfaces, roomy, fully controllable free hot showers, a dishwashing room, laundry room and facilities for babies and the disabled. The reception building at the entrance also houses a small shop. Adventure play equipment for children, badminton and tennis nets and an extra meadow for recreation. Tourist information and advice. Public telephone. This is a pleasant, well run park and with no other on-site amenities would suit couples or families who prefer a peaceful stay.

Directions: Signed from the A38 Plymouth road. From Exeter, ½ mile after the racecourse and just after a garage, take Chudleigh exit and park is immediately on the left. From Plymouth, turn off A38 for Chudleigh/Teign Valley, then right for Chudleigh. Continue through town and park is 1 mile. O.S.GR: SX882811.

Charges 1995:
-- Per unit incl. 2 persons £5.70 - £7.70, acc. to season, deluxe pitch £6.95 - £8.95; extra adult £1.50 - £2.00; child (4-14 yrs) £1.20 - £1.50; awning/child's tent £1.50; extra car/boat £1.00; dog 75p; electricity £1.75.
-- VAT included.
Open:
Easter - mid October.
Address:
Chudleigh, Devon TQ12 5TX.
Tel:
(01626) 853785.
Reservations:
Any length, £20 deposit.

37

57 The River Dart Country Park, Ashburton

Good quality touring site in a country park near Dartmoor, with many outdoor activities for families.

With its mature park and woodland, this interesting and unusual park could appeal to many, particularly those with children. Close to Dartmoor, in the beautiful Dart valley, it is part of a large country estate. The park is open to the general public on payment and features a variety of unusual adventure play equipment, streams and lake with raft, for swimming and inflatables, pony riding, fly fishing and marked nature and forest trails - all free to campers except riding and fishing. It can become busy at weekends and school holidays and reservation is strongly recommended. Also arranged (in the school holidays) are supervised courses in caving, canoeing, archery, climbing, etc.

The camping and caravanning area is in open parkland, surrounded by woodland and is mainly on a slight slope. There are some 120 individual pitches of very reasonable size, marked by lines on the grass with about 80 electrical connections. The toilet block for campers is of good quality and adequate in size for the numbers. Free hot water in the washbasins (with flat surface, hook and mirror), in the good hot showers and in the 7 washing-up sinks. Hair dryers. Launderette. Shop (all season). Restaurant and adjoining snackbar with takeaway (July/Aug). Small, heated swimming pool (from Easter), tennis courts. Bar (July/Aug, plus Easter and B.Hs) with TV and games room with pool and amusement machines. Some self catering accommodation for rent. The entire estate is kept very clean and tidy. Dogs (up to 2 per pitch) are allowed on leads. American motorhomes are only accepted in dry periods (no hardstanding).

Directions: Signed from the A38, the park is about 2 miles west of Ashburton, on the road to Two Bridges. O.S.GR: SX734701.

Charges 1995:
-- Per adult £3.65 - £5.10; child (over 5 yrs) £2.85 - £3.80, acc. to season; electricity £1.70.
-- VAT included.
-- Credit cards accepted
Open:
Easter - 30 September.
Address:
Holne Park, Ashburton, Devon TQ13 7NP.
Tel:
Ashburton (01364) 652511.
Reservations:
Low or mid season, any length with £3 fee; high season, £15 deposit plus £3 fee for 7 days or less; £30 + £3 for longer.

**Alan Rogers'
discount**
Less 10%
outside July,
August & Spring B.H.

58 Ashburton Caravan Park, Ashburton

Small secluded park for tents and motorcaravans only.

The 4 acres of Ashburton Park nestle in a hidden valley below Dartmoor, bordered by mature woodland. The Ashburn, a shallow stream with rocky pools, evenly divides and screens the 2 acres of holiday homes from the 2 acre camping area. Sheltered and south facing, the park is a tranquil retreat but for the energetic a ½ mile 'steep' uphill walk brings you to the moor or 1½ miles by Devon lanes to Ashburton village. There are 35 level or gently sloping pitches, 4 with electric connections (16A), either side of a tarmac road which culminates in a small field area.

First class, purpose built sanitary facilities provide free hot showers and vanity basins in cabins for ladies. Washing machine and tumble dryer are coin operated but a spin-dryer and iron are provided free. The unit also contains a pay phone. The shop cum reception provides for basic food supplies (end May - early Sept, 8.30-9.30 am and 5-6 pm), freezer pack service, tourist information, maps and walks and a daily weather report. Each visitor receives a copy of the 'Dartmoor Visitor', the information paper supplied by Dartmoor National Park - the site is actually within the boundaries of the Park. Shops, banks, post office and small heated swimming pool and pubs, etc. are in Ashburton, with limited bus services to Newton Abbot, Exeter or Plymouth. Discover the cult of letter boxing on Dartmoor (maps on loan with walks shown). Popular with continental visitors - French and German spoken. Dogs (limited breeds only) are welcome if exercised off the park. Torches useful. A well maintained tranquil park for nature lovers.

Directions: In the centre of Ashburton turn northwest into North Street. As built up area thins out bear right before bridge following signs for 'Waterleat' (tent symbol) for approx. 1½ miles. Park is on the left. O.S.GR: SX752721.

Charges 1996:
-- Per unit incl. 2 persons £7.00 - £9.00; extra person (over 1 yr) £1.50 - £2.25; dog 70p; electricity £1.25.
Open:
Easter - 30 September.
Address:
Waterleat, Ashburton, Devon TQ13 7HU
Tel:
(01364) 652552.
Reservations:
Made for min. 3 nights with £15 deposit.

59 Ross Park, Ipplepen, nr. Newton Abbot

Interesting, family run park - a plant lover's delight!

The keen horticulturists who own this park have developed a most attractive park using a wide range of flowers, flowering shrubs and trees, mostly raised by themselves. You may select fresh herbs to use from the small beds on the park and an impressive, heated conservatory sitting area houses yet more named plants. Connected to the conservatory is the `New Barn' providing a lounge, gallery bar (open certain evenings) and restaurant with á la carte menu or bar snacks. The touring area, with good views (but possibly some wind) across the fruit fields towards Dartmoor, provides 100 pitches, 80 with electricity. They are divided into groups by growing shrubs or hedges and 60 pitches are hardened ones, some extra large. The modern, unusual sanitary facilities open from under a veranda style roof, with 6 en-suite cubicles, heated in cool weather, and separate additional toilet and shower facilities. Free hot water throughout, shaver points and hairdryers are provided. Laundry room with dishwashing sinks, free iron, freezer and battery charging facilities. A four acre park area for recreation has been developed with unusual ornamental shrubs, bowling and croquet greens and an adventure play area on bark for older children. Dogs are welcome with a variety of walks in fields and orchards and a purpose built dog shower with hot water and grooming facilities. Golf course adjacent (9 hole, par 36). Tourist information chalet, shop and games room. A conservation area with information on wild flowers and butterflies, and beautiful views completes the environmentally considered amenities. Facilities may be limited in winter (Jan/Feb).

Charges 1995:
-- Per unit incl. 2 persons £6.50 - £9.60, acc. to season; extra person over 3 yrs £1.50; electricity (10A) £1.70 - £2.00.
-- Discounts for repeat stays.
-- Special Xmas and New Year breaks.
-- VAT included.
Open: All year.
Address: Park Hill Farm, Ipplepen, Newton Abbot, Devon TQ12 5TT.
Tel: Ipplepen (01803) 812983.
Reservations: Made with £20 deposit.

Directions: From A381 Newton Abbot - Totnes road, the park is signed towards Woodland at the Park Hill crossroads and BP filling station. O.S.GR: SX845671.

OUR SITE IS SPECIALLY DESIGNED FOR WINTER USE
Tarmac & Stone Roads - 60 Hard Standings - Night Lights on site - Showers, Toilets Heated
Excellent Indoor Heated Facilities - Lounge, Tropical Conservatory
Bowls - Croquet - Snooker - Golf Course Adjacent - Christmas & New Year a Specialty
Devon is renowned for its mild winter climate, excellent hostelries and eating houses.
OR ARE YOU LOOKING FOR PEACE AND TRANQUILITY ON THE PRETTIEST PARK IN DEVON AT THE PEAK OF THE SEASON?
In either case ring Ross Park on 01803-812983 - Phone now!

60 Parker's Farm Holidays, nr. Ashburton

Touring site on working farm at the foot of Dartmoor, close to A38 road.

Although well situated with fine views towards the moor, Parker's Farm is perhaps not impressive on first arrival with the trappings of a working farm all around. Closer inspection, however, reveals a unique chance to experience Devon country life at first hand. Not only can visitors smell, feel and take part in the workings of a farm, but now they can taste it too! The Parker family have now added a family bar (open from Whitsun) and games room and the building and theme are in context with their 'country life' programme, including a play area for children with authentic hay wagon and made-safe farm implements similar to those scattered around the site and animal pens. The bar area will provide entertainment during the season and fills the gap created by the closure of the local pub. Farm walks are tremendously popular and Mrs Parker takes along all those interested at feeding times to help with the animals. Cottages and site owned holiday caravans are also available for hire. The touring pitches, with electrical connections available, are situated directly above the farm buildings on a gently sloping, well mown field which has been terraced to give broad, flat groups of pitches, all with good views. Young trees and hedges have been planted. The shower and toilet block serving this area is modern and clean, tiled throughout and provides adequate facilities with free hot water. Family shower room and baby bathroom. Dishwashing and laundry facilities are provided and a small shop is located next to reception (open from Whitsun). Dogs are welcome on leads with 400 acres for walks! Public phone. American motorhomes accepted by prior arrangement. Holiday homes and barn conversion cottages for hire. Parkers Farm will suit those who don't seek the sophisticated amenities of more developed parks and a warm welcome awaits.

Charges 1995:
-- Per unit incl. 2 persons £4.00 - £7.50; backpacker tent £3.50 - £6.00; extra adult £1.10; child (3-15 yrs) 90p; awning £1.10; pup tent £1.00; electricity £1.70; dog 50p.
-- VAT included.
Open:
Easter - 31 October.
Address:
Higher Mead Farm, Ashburton, Newton Abbot, Devon TQ13 7LJ.
Tel:
Ashburton (01364) 652598.
FAX: (01364) 654004.
Reservations:
Made with £10 deposit

Alan Rogers' discount
Ask for details at the park

Directions: From Exeter on A38, 26 miles from Plymouth, turn left at Alston Cross signed 'Woodland Denbury ¼ mile'. Site is ½ mile. O.S.GR: SX757702.

61 Lemonford Caravan Park, Bickington, nr. Newton Abbot

Pretty, family run park on edge of Dartmoor.

Lemonford has the look and atmosphere of the 'cultivated' caravan park. Well mown grass and trimmed, smart hedges bordered by the pretty Lemon River (more of a brook), create the tranquil, attractive atmosphere the owners work hard to maintain. The buzzards, which are depicted in the site logo, rest on the small hill behind the site and can be seen circling overhead on most days. Despite its quite close proximity to the main road, this is a peaceful and relaxing site for all ages and families on the southern edge of the National Park, some 3 miles from both Ashburton and Newton Abbot. There are now 70 touring pitches (42 with 10A electricity) on well kept, level grass and grouped in four areas according to whether they are to be used by families, couples or individuals. Some holiday homes for hire are in a separate area. The single, modern sanitary block is tiled and has free, roomy, preset hot showers and free hairdryers. Free hot water is also provided to the washbasins (some in private cabins for ladies) and to the dishwashing area which is under cover. Developments continue with a new reception area and shop and improved laundry facilities. Ice pack service. Children's play area. Public phone. Dog exercise area. Chalet with tourist information. Well located for excursions, the site also provides discount vouchers for many nearby tourist attractions. Two good pubs are within walking distance and there is a leisure pool in Newton Abbot.

Charges 1995:
-- Per unit incl. 2 persons £6.00 - £8.00; extra person £1.50; child (3-15) £1.10; awning £1.00; electricity £1.60; extra small tent, car or boat £1.00; dog 70p.
-- VAT included.
Open:
Easter -- end September.
Address:
Bickington, Newton Abbot, Devon TQ12 6JR.
Tel:
Bickington (01626) 821242.
Reservations:
Made with £15 deposit (min. 4 nights Jul/Aug).

Directions: Turn off A38 Exeter-Plymouth road at A382 (Drumbridges) exit signed Newton Abbot, Bovey Tracey, Mortonhampstead. At roundabout take third exit to Bickington. Pass Toby Jug Inn in the village and park is on left at the bottom of the hill. O.S.GR: SX793723.

PARKERS FARM HOLIDAYS

Level Touring Site.
Self-Catering Holidays
on a Working Farm in
Beautiful South Devon.
**HIGHER MEAD FARM
ASHBURTON, NEWTON ABBOT
SOUTH DEVON TQ13 7LJ. Tel 01364 652598**

62 Dornafield, Two Mile Oak, Newton Abbot

Family run, spacious, rural touring park with new luxury pitches.

A quiet, superbly appointed and well maintained park, Dornafield is an idyllic retreat for those who prefer small, family run parks a little away from the coast and without evening activities. A member of the Caravan Club's 'managed under contract' scheme, members and non-members are all made very welcome. In a sheltered situation away from main roads, the entrance leads into the courtyard of a charming old farmhouse where outbuildings have been sympathetically converted into reception, shop and games room (the old milking parlour). Well tended flowers and shrubs decorate the park. The original part, the Butter Meadow and the Orchard, offers 75 individual, numbered pitches on flat grass, separated by grassy ridges and in some places, wild rose hedges. Of good size, all have electricity (10A). Awning ground sheets must be lifted every day and tents repitched for stays in excess of a week. The attractively designed, modern toilet block serving these pitches is very good. It has washbasins (2 in cabins) set in vanity units and showers, all with free hot water, with a babies' section and make-up area in the ladies'. Good unit for the disabled. All is kept spotlessly clean. Laundry room and 4 washing-up sinks under cover with a microwave. A further 60 extra large, luxury pitches in Blackrock Copse have electricity, water, drainage and TV connections, all cleverly concealed and with 32 hardstandings. The temporary sanitary facilities for this area are well designed and maintained with a separate wooden chalet for dishwashing with a microwave. Again many flowers and shrubs have been planted including herbs - very useful when barbecuing. Two woodland play areas with adventure play equipment and a Wendy house. Games room with table tennis, TV and all-weather hard tennis court. Pub with meals ½ mile. Dog exercise area. All year storage facilities.

Directions: Park is northwest of the A381 (Newton Abbot - Totnes) road. Leave A381 at Two Mile Oak Inn, opposite a garage, and turn left at the crossroads after about ½ mile. Park entrance is on the right. O.S.GR: SX848683.

Charges 1996:
-- Per pitch £1.50 - £4.50; adult £2.50 - £3.50; child (5-16 yrs) £1.10 - £1.20; awning free - 90p; pup tent or porch awning free - 45p; tents over 100 sq.ft. charged awning rate; electricity (10A) £1.25 (£2.00 before 1/4); extra car or trailer £1.00; dog 60p.
-- VAT included.
Open:
23 March - 31 October.
Address:
Two Mile Oak, Newton Abbot, Devon TQ12 6DD.
Tel:
Ipplepen (01803) 812732.
Reservations:
Any length, with deposit: £10 p.w. low season, £25 p.w. high season.

DORNAFIELD

Superb facilities for the truly discerning caravanner.
Our brochure is only a phone call away - 01803 812732

**Two Mile Oak
Newton Abbot, Devon**

41

63 Woodlands Leisure Park, Blackawton, nr. Dartmouth

Well planned touring site forming part of family run, countryside leisure park

Woodlands has been sympathetically developed from farm and woodland to form a popular leisure park, open to the public and appealing to all ages. Children (and many energetic parents too!) are entertained for hours by a variety of imaginative adventure play equipment hidden amongst the trees, farm animals, birds and boats, while those more peacefully inclined can follow woodland walks around the attractive ponds. There is plenty of play equipment for younger children too, including a new indoor play barn with a circus theme. Campers at the attached touring park are admitted free of charge.

The camping and caravan site which overlooks the woods, takes 80 units on a sloping, grassy field which has been fully terraced to provide groups of five flat, spacious pitches, all with electrical connections and a shared water tap and drain. A larger area at the top of the site is reserved for tents. The rather open nature of the site will be broken up as hedges and young trees mature. A central, modern toilet block is well maintained and kept very clean. It has free hot water in controllable showers and washbasins (with dividers but no private cabins, except for the disabled), and also for the 5 dishwashing sinks. Hot water in the good family bathroom is on payment. Laundry room with just one washing machine, spin-dryer, tumble dryer and iron. Hair dryers. Freezer for ice packs. The leisure park cafe, with an outdoor rose terrace, provides good value meals and cream teas, with entertainment (music, Morris men etc.) at busy times, and a takeaway food service for campers. The opening hours of the cafe and adjoining gift shop, where a few basic food supplies are kept, vary according to season and demand. Dogs are permitted on short leads and an exercise area is provided. A popular park, reservation is advisable. The charming town of Dartmouth and the South Hams beaches are near.

Directions: From the A38 at Buckfastleigh, take the A384 to Totnes. Before the town turn right onto the A381 Kingsbridge road. After Halwell turn left at Totnes Cross garage, on the A3122 to Dartmouth. Park is on the right after 2½ miles. O.S.GR: SX813522.

Charges 1995:
-- Per unit, incl. 2 persons £5.75 - £9.90, acc. to season; electricity £1.95; extra adult £2.50, child (2-14) £1.95; awning or extra pup-tent £2.50; large tent or trailer tent (120 sq.ft. plus) £2.00 extra; backpack tent (hikers and cyclists only) £5.50 - £7.50; extra car, boat or trailer £1.00; one dog free, other £1.25.
-- min. charge for 2 nights or less £15.
-- VAT included.
Open:
15 March - 15 October.
Address:
Blackawton, Totnes, Devon TQ9 7DQ.
Tel:
(01803) 712598.
FAX: (01803) 712680.
Reservations:
Accepted for min. 3 nights with £25 deposit, except July/Aug. when min. 7 days and £35 deposit. Balance on arrival.

64 Beverley Holidays, Paignton

Popular Torbay park with many facilities and evening entertainment.

Beverley Park is a holiday centre, attractively sited with views over Torbay, with swimming pools and a large dance hall, with bars and entertainments, etc. - all attractively furnished and run in an efficient and orderly manner. The holiday caravan park has 205 caravan holiday homes, mainly around the central complex. There are 194 touring pitches, all reasonably sheltered, mainly in the lower areas of the park, some on slightly sloping ground. All pitches can take awnings and have electrical connections, 11 have hardstanding. The park has a long season and for caravans, reservations are essential. American motorhomes are accepted (max. 20 ft). There are toilet blocks among the holiday homes not too far from the touring pitches and a new one in the camping field. They are good, particularly the newer one and although they receive heavy use and need regular attention, they are well maintained. Free hot water in basins and showers, baths on payment and a unit for the disabled. Water points around park and a range of recycling bins. Large general shop and secondary shop. Express diner, garden bar and takeaway service. Dance hall with bars - entertainment at Easter and from mid-May. Heated outdoor swimming pool, children's pool and indoor pool, all supervised. The Oasis fitness centre provides a steam room, jacuzzi, sunbed, excellent fitness room, swimming lessons, etc. Tennis court. Children's playground. Laundry. Amusement centre with pool, table tennis and amusement machines. No dogs are taken. The park is in the heart of Torbay, with some sea views, and sandy beaches less than a mile away.

Directions: Park is south of Paignton in Goodrington Road between the A379 coast road and B3203 ring road and is well signed on both. O.S.GR: SX882584.

Charges 1995:
-- Per unit incl. 2 persons: caravan £6.50 - £12.50; tent or motorcaravan £6.50 - £11.00; electricity incl. for caravans, + £1.50 for tents or motorcaravans; extra adult £2.50, child (4-14 yrs) £1.50; awning £1.50; extra pup tent £2.00.
-- VAT included.
-- Credit cards accepted.
Open:
Easter -- 31 October.
Address:
Goodrington Road, Paignton, Devon TQ4 7JE.
Tel:
(01803) 843887.
FAX: (01803) 845427.
Reservations:
Made with £20 deposit (min. 7 days mid-July - beg. Sept).

65 Ramslade Touring Park, Stoke Gabriel, Paignton

Well kept, quiet park in attractive rural location, 3 miles from sea.

Personally run by the owners, Ramslade is a smaller, rural park and provides a quiet, peaceful alternative to the larger holiday parks in and around Paignton itself. A member of the Caravan Club's 'managed under contract' scheme, non-members are also very welcome. The attractively landscaped park takes 135 touring units of all types. Pitches are neatly arranged in two areas which are planted with attractive young trees. The larger area slopes towards the centre of the park but has been gently terraced and most pitches are level or very slightly sloping. Tarmac access roads give good access and all but two pitches have electricak hook-ups. There are 28 'all-service' pitches with shared picnic tables, hardstandings for large motorhomes and a drive on service area for motor-caravans. No groundsheets allowed in awnings and inner tents to be lifted daily. A range of recycling bins is provided. A renovated lime kiln, lit at night, provides ideal places for barbecues (raised ones only). The well maintained central toilet block is heated for cooler weather. Hot water is free for the washbasins, with two private cabins for each sex, and for the plentiful showers. Make-up area for ladies. Hair dryers. A baby bathroom and washing-up sinks (free hot water) are in a covered area at the rear of the block. Facilities for the disabled, laundry room with microwave and a super luxury, family bathroom (£2 charge) complete the facilities. Small shop for essentials (open on request in quiet times). TV room. Games room with pool and table tennis. Play area set away from the pitches, plus a small, central area for younger children next to an attractive splash pool with fountain feature and jacuzzi which is walled with locking gate and a paved area for parents to relax or sunbathe. Weather station with daily forecasts. No dogs or pets accepted in the peak six weeks. Indoor and outdoor caravan storage available with servicing. A quality park.

Charges 1995:
-- Per unit incl. 2 persons and awning, acc. to season: standard pitch £7.50 - £10.00; electric pitch £8.75 - £11.25; all service pitch £9.25 - £13.15; extra adult £3.00 - £3.50; child (5-16 yrs) £1.10 - £1.20; extra car or boat £1.00.
-- VAT included.
Open:
23 March - 2 November.
Address:
Stoke Road, Stoke Gabriel, Paignton, Devon TQ9 6QB.
Tel:
(01803) 782575.
FAX: (01803) 782828.
Reservations:
Recommended for July/Aug. and school holidays. Any length stay, £10 deposit, balance appreciated 1 month before arrival.

Directions: Park is south of the A385 (Paignton-Totnes) road and is well signed. Turn off the A385 to south alongside the Parkers Arms Pub (½ mile west of the Paignton ring road), then follow road for 1½ miles. O.S.GR: SX857583.

66 Grange Court Holiday Centre, Paignton

Busy holiday caravan park with good entertainment facilities; touring sections for caravans only.

Situated to the south of central Paignton, with a short walk to the sea and some views of Torbay, Grange Court's major interest is the complex of 500 holiday homes (with letting service) which totally dominate the site. However there are also 157 touring pitches (no tents) in two sections, each with its own resident wardens. One, probably the quieter of the two, is on flat grass by the entrance, with 2 fairly standard toilet blocks (washbasins with free hot water, shelf and mirror, and free pre-set hot showers with pushbutton). The other is on higher ground with some views at the top of the park with the site shops close by. It is on a gentle slope, with a single, but larger, tiled block of better quality. The individual pitches are of reasonable size, though with some variation, and all have electricity. The park can become full for most of July/Aug. and B.H.s. For those who like entertainment, the central complex is the park's best feature, with a good sized free heated swimming pool (80 x 40 ft. open 6/5-16/9). A new indoor pool complex with flume, spa bath, sauna, steam room and sun bed is due to open during the 1996 season. The clubhouse has a large bar lounge and separate room with dance floor - entertainment is organised almost nightly from Spr.B.H. to end Sept. and at Easter. Supermarket and other shops, takeaway and fast food bar (all Easter-Oct). Games rooms with 2 pool tables and one full size snooker table, and an amusement arcade, playground and large adventure play area (on bark). Large launderette. Range of recycling bins. Up to 30 American motorhomes accepted (30 ft. max). No dogs or pets are accepted. Reception is busy, but efficient. Part of the Hoburne group.

Charges 1996:
-- Per unit £7.25 - £17.50, incl. electricity and awning, acc. to season (no tents, trailer tents or pup tents allowed).
-- VAT included.
-- Credit cards accepted.
Open:
All year except 15 Jan -15 Feb.
Address:
Goodrington, Paignton, Devon TQ4 7JP.
Tel:
(01803) 558010.
FAX: (01803) 663336.
Reservations:
For 1-6 nights, full payment in advance; for 7 nights and over, £50 deposit per week (min. 7 days in Jul/Aug and B.H. weeks).

Directions: Park is signed (not the normal camp site signs) from outer Paignton ring road. Turn off Goodrington Road into Grange Road. 150 yds from A379 coast road at signs for camp and Marine Park. O.S.GR: SX890585.

67 Galmpton Park, Galmpton, nr. Brixham

Quiet, neat touring park with wonderful views over the River Dart estuary.

Within a few miles of the lively amenities of Torbay, Galmpton Park lies peacefully just outside the village of Galmpton, overlooking the beautiful Dart estuary just upstream of Dartmouth and Kingswear. About 120 unmarked pitches are arranged on a wide sweep of grassy meadow, each place with its own view of the river. Situated on the hillside, some parts have quite a slope, but there are flatter areas (the owners will advise and assist). There are 60 electrical connections. American motorhomes not accepted. A central, substantial looking sanitary block provides clean facilities which have been upgraded by the current owners. There are washbasins in flat surfaces with mirrors, with three private cabins, free hot showers, baby bath and hair care areas. A dishwashing room (free hot water) and a laundry room are to one end of the block. A small shop is located at the entrance to the park and there is play equipment for children. Dogs (max. 2 per unit) are accepted only outside the school summer holidays with an exercise area provided. Galmpton is a quiet and simple park (with the gates closed at night) in a most picturesque setting, within easy reach of all the attractions of South Devon.

Charges 1995:
-- Per unit incl. 2 persons and awning £6.50 - £9.50; tent or motorcaravan £5.50 - £8.50; extra adult £1.00 - £2.00; extra child 50p - £1.00; electricity £1.60; extra pup tent, car, van or boat £1.00; dog (off peak only) 50p.
-- VAT included.
Open:
Easter - mid-October.
Address:
Greenaway Road, Galmpton. Brixham, Devon TQ5 0EP.
Tel:
(01803) 842066 or 844405.
Reservations:
Accepted for min. 7 days in peak season, 4 days at other times.

Directions: Take the A380 Paignton ring road towards Brixham until the junction with the Paignton - Brixham coast road. Turn right towards Brixham, then second right into Manor Vale Road. Continue through the village, past the school and site is 100 yds on the right. O.S.GR: SX885558.

68 Slapton Camping and Caravanning Club Site, Slapton, nr. Kingsbridge

Well kept site overlooking the sea and freshwater Slapton Ley nature reserve; caravans limited.

Slapton is a charming village with tiny lanes and cottages, a shop and two historic pubs, one dominated by the ruined tower of an old, collegiate monastery. The village is about ½ mile inland from the shingle beach of Slapton Sands and the freshwater Ley which is administered as a nature reserve by the Field Studies Council. The Camping and Caravanning Club site is situated on the road which leads from the Sands, on a well kept meadow overlooking the bay - the sea views are panoramic from most areas of the site, with shelter provided by some large bushes and the surrounding hedge. There are 115 grass pitches, some with a slight slope and electrical connections are available on half the site. Motorcaravans, trailer tents and tents are accepted without problems but the planners will only permit 8 caravans (make sure to check with the warden on pitch availability). The modern toilet block is central and kept very clean, providing toilets, washbasins, all in private cabins, and good hot showers (free). Dishwashing facilities and chemical disposal. Other than a small children's play area, there are no other on-site facilities but the village is a pleasant stroll (don't take the car into the narrow lanes!) and the milk lady calls daily with bread, eggs, etc. The Field Studies Centre arranges guided walks and short study courses on a wide variety of interests and can issue fishing permits for the Ley (perch and pike, of legendary size, in the summer months). Beach fishing is also popular. This area was used for rehearsals for the Second World War Normandy landings, when the whole population was evacuated. The quaint port of Dartmouth is 7 miles, Kingsbridge 6 miles and there is a variety of beaches and coves around the beautiful South Hams coastline, all within easy reach.

Charges 1995:
-- Per adult £3.15 - £3.50, acc. to season; child £1.20 - £1.35; non-member pitch fee £3.00; electricity £1.50; visitor 95p per car or adult couple.
Open:
27 March - 6 Nov.
Address:
Middle Grounds, Slapton, Kingsbridge, Devon TQ7 1QW.
Tel:
(01548) 580538.
(No calls after 8 pm.)
Reservations:
Are made - contact the wardens.

Directions: From the A38 Exeter - Plymouth road, take the A384 to Totnes. Just before the town, turn right on the A381 to Kingsbridge, then the A379 through Stokenham and Torcross to Slapton Sands. Half way along the beach road turn left to Slapton village and the site is 200 yds on the right. **Note:** Do not use the very narrow Five Mile Lane from the A381 which is signposted Slapton, just after a filling station, 6 miles from Kingsbridge. O.S.GR: SX825456.

69 Harford Bridge Holiday Park, Peter Tavy, nr. Tavistock

Attractive, mature park on west Dartmoor with river boundary; holiday caravans and chalets to let.

The present owners continue to improve this quiet, rural park which lies inside the Dartmoor National Park and which has a charming stretch of the River Tavy as one long boundary of the touring area. The 16½ acre park provides 120 touring pitches on a level grassy meadow with some shade from mature trees and others recently planted; 40 pitches have electrical hook-ups and 12 have `multi services'. Out of season or by booking you may get one of the delightful spots bordering the river. Holiday caravans and chalets are also available for hire, neatly landscaped in their own discrete area.

The single toilet block is older in style but is kept perfectly clean, well decorated and properly maintained. Hot water is free throughout. The facilities include hand and hair dryers (free), baby bathroom, a good launderette and drying room, freezer pack facility and chemical disposal point. At the entrance to the park a central grassy area is left free for barbeques, bands and other recreation and is overlooked by the site shop which is well stocked and reasonably priced. While the river will inevitably mesmerise the youngsters, there is also a recreation area and an adventure playground on a hilly tree knoll, with bark bases. Games room with table tennis and separate TV room. Tennis court. Fishing (by licence). Communal barbecue area. Well behaved dogs are accepted and a 4 acre exercise field is provided. Situated right on the edge of the moor, this park is ideal for a restful or energetic holiday in glorious countryside, or as a centre for touring.

Directions: Turn off A386 just south of Mary Tavy village, 2 miles north of Tavistock, towards Harford Bridge. O.S.GR: SX504768.

Charges 1996:
-- Per unit, incl. 2 persons £6.00 - £9.00; extra adult £1.70 - £2.20; child 70p - £1.30; dog 80p; electricity £2.00; awning 90p; extra car 50p.
-- Less 10% for stays over 7 days (not electricity or fishing).
-- VAT included.
Open:
Mid-March - mid November.
Address:
Peter Tavy, Tavistock, Devon PL19 9LS.
Tel:
(01822) 810349.
FAX: (01822) 810028.
Reservations:
Made for any length with first night's fees.

Alan Rogers'
discount
Less 50p
per night

70 Higher Longford Farm, Moorshop, nr. Tavistock

Small, family run park, ideal for staying on Dartmoor.

Situated within the National Park boundaries, this small park has views up to the higher slopes of the moor. Formerly a farm, the site has a sheltered touring field where 40 level pitches are arranged on either side of a ring road, two smaller touring areas for 12 units and a seasonal camping field. Facilities include 49 electrical hook-ups and an area of hardstanding for poor weather. There is a further area adjacent containing residential caravans and chalets for hire. The main toilet block is alongside the touring field and there are further facilities in the reception area in the old farmyard and in a new block beside the main house. These provide roomy showers, smallish washbasins with one private cabin for ladies, hand and hair dryers, laundry and dish washing, all with plentiful, free hot water. Clothes drying facilities are provided - important after a wet tramp over the moor! The new block has facilities for the disabled.

Within the 14th century farmhouse, a small shop offers, not only standard lines, but also fresh farm produce. It adjoins a pleasant, small bar and restaurant with open fire and TV, where takeaway or full meals are offered (all March-Oct). A spacious conservatory is available for sitting in poor weather. Dogs are welcome but must be kept under strict control (exercise field provided). This enables the site to keep rabbits, goats, guinea pigs, many birds and even lambs (in season) - an unending delight to youngsters. Higher Longford is an ideal centre for touring Dartmoor, either by car, on foot, or astride a local pony. The site is sometimes used by groups of youngsters for trips onto the moor. Game or coarse fishing can be arranged and Tavistock golf course is almost next door.

Directions: Park is clearly signed from the B3357, 2 miles from Tavistock. O.S.GR: SX520747.

Charges 1995:
-- Per unit, incl. 2 persons £6.50 - £8.00; electricity £1.50 - £1.75; extra person 50p - 75p; extra car 50p - 75p.
Open:
All year.
Address:
Moorshop, Tavistock, Devon PL19 9LQ.
Tel:
Tavistock (01822) 613360.
Reservations:
Are made with £5 deposit.

Alan Rogers'
discount
Less £1
per stay

71 Clifford Bridge Park, Clifford, nr. Drewsteignton

Riverside touring park in beautiful, country location within the Dartmoor National Park.

This 8 acre park is in a really rural setting on the edge of the National Park and 3 miles from the nearest village with any facilities. In a wooded valley, on the banks of the River Teign, it can only be approached on narrow lanes (single track for the last mile), so is a site for staying a while with plenty to do for those who like country pursuits. Fingle Bridge is 3½ miles and Castle Drogo 5 miles. It is licensed for 24 touring vans and 40 tents. Pitches are of a good size on a flat grassy meadow, mainly around the perimeters of the park, some backing onto the river, with 3 hardstandings and 19 electrical connections. Plenty of grassy space is left free and there is a free swimming pool (54 x 24 ft. open 4/5-1/9, heated from Spr. B.H). Three holiday homes and two lodges for rent. The toilet block is not large or modern but is satisfactory and kept clean, with free hot water in smallish washbasins and showers. Hand and hair dryers. A `portacabin' provides additional facilities in high season. Dishwashing sinks are outside, under cover. Farm outbuildings house a shop (4/5-1/9), games room with pool, amusement machine and tourist information, and a small launderette. Excellent walks from the site. Fishing available on permit. Golf near. Public phone.

Directions: To avoid much single-track road approach via the A30, turning off 11 miles west of Exeter to Cheriton Bishop. Left there (at Old Thatch Inn), 2 miles to crossroads where right for Clifford Bridge, 1 mile of single track, over crossroads and bridge and left to park. O.S.GR: SX782897.

Charges 1995:
-- Per unit incl. 2 persons £6.85 - £9.95; small motorvan £5.95 - £9.20; backpacker or cyclist £2.40 - £3.70 pp; extra person £1.80; child 4-16 yrs free - £1.45; awning £1.30; dog £any car 50p; electricity £1.40.
-- Discounts available.
-- VAT included.
Open:
Easter -- 30 September
Address:
Clifford, Drewsteignton, Devon, EX6 6QE.
Tel:
(01647) 24226.
Reservations:
Advisable for school holidays; any length with £20 deposit.

OS Ref: SX782897

CLIFFORD BRIDGE Park

AA 3 pennant   RAC Appointed

A small and level, family run, picturesque country estate within the Dartmoor National Park surrounded by woodland and bordered by the River Teign. Pitches for tents (40) and touring or

motor caravans (24) - set in eight acres of outstanding natural beauty.
HEATED SWIMMING POOL. Small shop. Electric hook-ups. Flush toilets and free showers.
Fly fishing on site. Golf at Moretonhampstead.
Three holiday caravans for hire.

Magnificent walks along woodland tracks start from the Park - walk upstream through the Teign Gorge to Fingle Bridge or Castle Drogo (N.T.) downstream through Dunsford nature reserve.

Write or phone for colour brochure

Nr. Drewsteignton, Devon EX6 6QE
Tel: Cheriton Bishop (01647) 24226

72 Dartmoor View Caravan Park, Whiddon Down, nr. Okehampton

Small, developing park on north Dartmoor touring route.

This small park is well situated, just off the main A30 road which marks the northern edge of Dartmoor. With new and enthusiastic owners who continue to develop the park, it would be suitable for overnight stops on the way further west or as a base to explore Devon and Cornwall. Easily accessible, it offers 75 touring pitches, 34 with electricity including 10 with full services, around a flat grass meadow with stone access roads. Trees have been planted to break up the rather open nature of the field; 30 caravan holiday homes, 15 for hire, are arranged around the park. The brick-built toilet block is modern and kept clean, with free hot water in pushbutton showers, washbasins and dishwashing sinks. Laundry equipment and rotary dryers. First aid room. A friendly park, there is a cosy bar with a family area and barbecue nights on Saturday evenings. Shop, games/TV room with tourist information and a takeaway service including breakfast in high season. Good quality children's play equipment and a heated swimming pool (10 x 5 m.) with child's pool, fenced with paved surrounds and open Whitsun-end Sept. Bicycle hire. Telephone. Small exercise area for dogs.

Directions: From the Merrymeet roundabout, on the A30 dual-carriageway, take the Whiddon Down road. Park is ½ mile on the right. O.S.GR: SX685928.

Charges 1996:
-- Per unit, incl. 2 persons £5.80 - £8.10; extra adult £1.80; child (3-12 yrs) £1.50; dog 50p; electricity £2.00; all service pitch £3.30.
-- VAT included.
-- Credit cards accepted.
Open:
March - November.
Address:
Whiddon Down, Okehampton EX20 2QL
Tel:
(01647) 231545.
FAX: (01647) 231654.
Reservations:
Any length, with deposit of £4 p/night.

See editorial report for Kennford International on page 34

73 Riverside Caravan Park, Plymouth

Good sized touring park with heated pool, close to main routes and city.

Riverside is well placed for those using the car ferries or en-route to Cornwall and is also pleasantly situated for touring Dartmoor and south Devon. Although under 4 miles from the city centre, its location on the banks of the River Plym in a wooded valley is a quiet one. Attractive shrubs and trees, flower beds, well kept grass and tarmac roads give a neat, park-like appearance. Over 230 units are taken on flat, numbered pitches, including 97 with electricity and hardstandings. There are 65 pitches reserved for tents and a large, hard area for late arrivals. In the centre of the park arranged around a patio are a lounge bar (fully open from July with nightly entertainment), coffee bar and restaurant with takeaway (6-10 pm), games and TV rooms and a play area. A free, sheltered and heated swimming pool (60 x 30 ft.), with children's paddling pool, is open Spr. B.H.-mid-Sept. The two sanitary blocks are of different construction and have been modernised and decorated somewhat haphazardly. Both have free hot water in the washbasins (some in private cabins for ladies in one block), showers and dishwashing sinks. Hair and hand dryers, shaver points. Laundry facilities plus irons on loan. Shop at entrance open to all (Spr. B.H. - mid-Sept). Public phones and post box. Fishing and riverside walks up to Dartmoor.

Directions: From the A38 dual-carriageway from Exeter, take the Marsh Mill exit (the first signed to Plymouth city centre). Follow good camp site signs to third exit, turning left after a few yards. O.S.GR: SX518576.

Charges 1995:
-- Per pitch £4.00 - £10.25; adult £2.50 - £3.00; child (3-16) £1.10 - £1.25; electricity £2.00 - £1.75; awning 75p - £1.10; dog, extra car or boat £1.00.
-- Discounts for the over 50s in low season.
-- VAT included.
Open:
All year.
Address:
Longbridge Road, Marshmills, Plymouth, Devon PL6 8LD.
Tel:
(01752) 344122.
Reservations:
Deposit £15 per week.

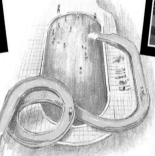

STOWFORD FARM MEADOWS
Touring Caravan and Camping Park
COMBE MARTIN : ILFRACOMBE : DEVON : EX34 0PW : TEL: 01271 882476

North DEVON
England's green & pleasant land

Situated on a farm in Beautiful
Devon Countryside, only a short
distance from the coast with it's
superb choice of 5 local beaches;
and on the fringe of Exmoor
National Park.

Great Facilities · 3 Bars · Shop ·
Take-Away & Carvery · Indoor
Swimming Pool · Pitch & Putt ·
Snooker · Games Room · Crazy
Golf · Nature Walks · Horse Riding ·
Undercover Mini Zoo · Large Play
Area · Kiddies Kars ·
Phone for a FREE Colour Brochure

Nestling in a beautiful wooded valley

Secluded from the world

AWARD WINNING PARK
Hidden Valley

Coast and Country Touring and Camping Park

MOST IMPROVED PARK IN ENGLAND 1994 ● CALOR CARAVAN PARK AWARDS
PRACTICAL CARAVAN TOP 100 PARKS '92/3/4/5/6 ● ALAN ROGERS GOOD CAMPS GUIDE
AA AWARD FOR EXCELLENCE ATTRACTIVE ENVIRONMENT '92/3/4/5/6

Where wild ducks often join our tame ones on the lake. Herons seem to appear from nowhere, fishing for their breakfast. Buzzards glide gracefully overhead. Kingfishers, squirrels and wild deer have all been seen at Hidden Valley. Only a few minutes drive to our famous golden coast or Exmoor's National Park.

Sheltered level pitches. Hardstandings and grass. Reduced rates for over 50s. Free TV hook-ups to all pitches.

● Shop ● Lounge/Restaurant ● Modern toilet blocks with disabled, baby and laundry facilities
● Free hot water ● Electric hook-ups ● Children's play area ● Dog walk ● Woodland walks

For details: MRS SUSAN TUCKER, HIDDEN VALLEY TOURING & CAMPING PARK,
ILFRACOMBE, NORTH DEVON EX34 8NU
Situated on the A361.

    Tel: 01271 813837

Newquay Holiday Park
C O R N W A L L

JUST WHAT YOU'RE LOOKING FOR !

If you want a high quality Holiday Park in a beautiful country setting yet only 3 miles from some of the finest beaches in Cornwall then Newquay Holiday Park is just what you're looking for...

EXCELLENT FACILITIES

You'll find all the high standard facilities you would expect from an AA five pennant holiday park.

- *Free electric hook-ups**
- *Children Free** • *Free showers* • *Launderette*
- *Self-service shop* • *Takeaway foods*

* At selected times, see our brochure for details

GREAT FAMILY VALUE

Great value holidays and so much to enjoy...

- *Free childrens club* • *Free 3 heated swimming pools & 200ft waterslide* • *Free nightly entertainment for all the family* • *Amusements* • *Snooker & pool*
- *Crazy golf* • *Pitch & putt* • *Children's playgrounds*
- *Recreation field* • *Golf course adjacent*

PERFECT LOCATION

A beautiful scenic park ideally situated for exploring the magical county of Cornwall...

- *Superb holiday caravans are also available*

01637 871111 *(ext: 3)*

3 Newquay Holiday Park, Newquay, Cornwall TR8 4HS

Fabulous Family Fun !

74 Polborder House Caravan and Camping Park, Looe

Small, neat touring park just back from sea with good views, personally run by the owners.

Polborder House may appeal to those who prefer a quiet, well kept little family site to the larger ones with many on-site activities. It has good countryside views and is basically a well tended grass on which some 31 touring units can be accommodated. Pitches are marked with some hedging being planted and there are 28 electrical connections (13A). The sanitary block is very well kept, of ample size for the park and provides free hot water in vanity style washbasins with curtained hot showers on payment. There is a baby room with washing and changing facilities, a laundry room (H&C) with washing machine, spin and tumble dryers and iron, and 3 covered sinks outside for dishwashing (free hot water). A toilet unit for the disabled has a ramped approach. Seaton is 2 miles, Looe 2½ and the nearest beach 20-25 minutes walk from a gate in the corner of the park. Shop for basics, including off licence and tourist information and public phone but no other special amenities. The owners live on the park and there are five caravan holiday homes for hire.

Charges 1996:
-- Per unit incl. 2 persons £6.00 - £8.00, acc.to season; extra person £1.50 - £2.00; child over 4 75p - £1.00; awning £1.00; dog 50p; electricity £1.75.
-- Less 10% for senior citizens.
-- VAT included.
Open:
Easter/31 March - 31 October.
Address:
St. Martins-by-Looe, Cornwall PL13 1QR.
Tel:
Looe (01503) 240265.
Reservations:
Any period, £10 deposit.

Directions: Park is ¾ mile south of B3253; turn 2 miles east of Looe and follow signs to park, Monkey Sanctuary and Seaton at junctions. O.S.GR: SX283555.

75 Whitsand Bay Holiday Park, Millbrook, nr. Torpoint

Self-contained, developing, family holiday park with magnificent views, for all units.

The Rame peninsular, or 'Cornwall's forgotten corner', provides a unique setting for this unusual park, which was converted from a gun battery built in 1890 for defence from the sea - hence the marvellous views. Approaching the park along the cliff tops is deceiving, as the moatway and gun emplacements completely hide what is, in essence, a self-contained village, with even a chapel/reading room. Holiday homes and chalets (to let) blend into the fort's structure. The 120 marked touring pitches are carefully terraced and tiered (quite steeply in places) into four areas and a rally field to give views landwards across to Plymouth, the Tamar estuary, Dartmoor and Exmoor. With tarmac access roads, they vary in size and 60 have electrical hook-ups (16A). Torches would be useful at night. Two toilet blocks, well placed between the fields, have been refurbished and provide large, metered showers (no dividers), vanity style washbasins (H&C), razor points and hairdryers. Ramps are provided so use by the disabled is possible. Washing up sinks (H&C) under cover and chemical disposal points. The laundry room is part of the Quartermaster's store, the rest of which has been used to develop the Battery Club (a 'real' pub), providing a cosy bar open to the public, with family area, evening bar food and dance hall with nightly entertainment during high season. Opposite, beside the well stocked shop, is the pool area, which is walled and paved to provide a sunbathing terrace. It is overlooked by the 'Café Bar', open all day in season, with a dining area. Sauna and sunbed. Games room with TV. Children's play area (never mind the tunnels linking the gun batteries!). All facilities are open in the main season - outside this opening is flexible. A steep 200 ft. cliff path provides access to Whitsand Bay (10 mins down, 20 mins up and not suitable for very small children or the infirm - other beaches are nearby). Dogs accepted by prior arrangement. The Battery is a designated ancient monument and the area is one of 'outstanding natural beauty', so it is unspoilt, ideal for fishing and walking, yet only 8 miles from Plymouth. The owners live on site - rather like having the Squire in attendance - therefore the welcome and security are good.

Charges 1995:
-- Per pitch £6.50 - £11.50, acc. to season; electricity (16A) £2.00.
-- Club membership £1 per adult for entire stay.
-- VAT included.
-- Credit cards accepted.
Open:
Easter/1 April - end Oct.
Address:
Millbrook, Torpoint, Cornwall PL10 1JZ.
Tel:
Plymouth (01752) 822597.
FAX: (01752) 823444.
Reservations:
Made with £10 deposit per week.

Directions: Using the Torpoint ferry, follow signs for Antony on disembarking (3 miles). Take left fork marked Millbrook (B3247) and continue for 2 miles to T-junction. Turn left for Whitsand Bay, then after less than 400 yds turn right and follow road overlooking the bay for 2 miles. Signs for park on left. O.S.GR: SX417506.

76 Treble B Holiday Centre, nr. Looe

Large touring park near sea with full facilities and swimming pool.

Although it is really a large touring park for all types of unit, with some 30 completely self-contained letting caravan holiday homes, Treble B has installations and amenities rather similar to a small holiday camp with evening entertainment. The camping grounds consist of three spacious fields, some slightly sloping taking, in all, 570 touring units of any type (276 electrical connections - 16A). Pitches are in rows on marker lines and you find your own. It can be crowded in peak season but at other times there should be plenty of room. On site are a medium-sized swimming pool and children's pool. The site is between the two picturesque fishing villages of Looe and Polperro. The nearest beach, of sand and rock, is 1½ miles away at Talland. The site has four toilet blocks, some quite large, which seem well maintained and, with about 90 toilets when all are open, should be ample and has free hot water. Some washing-up sinks in blocks. Large self-service shop (open from late May). The extended clubhouse has a ballroom, large bar, disco room, 3 TV rooms and a full restaurant (Whitsun-mid Sept). Takeaway. Large launderette. Crazy golf. Games room. Public phone. Dog exercise area.

Directions: Park entrance is on the north side of the A387, 2 miles west of Looe. O.S.GR: SX228536.

Charges 1996:
-- Per unit incl. 2 persons £6.80 - £10.00; extra adult £1.50 - £3.00; child (3-15 yrs) 75p - £1.50; electricity £1.80; dog free.
-- Special offers - contact park.
-- Credit cards accepted.
-- VAT included.
Open:
30 April - end Sept.
Address:
Looe, Cornwall PL13 2JS.
Tel:
Looe (01503) 262425.
FAX: as phone.
Reservations:
Any length with £20 deposit. Essential for July/Aug.

77 Killigarth Manor Holiday Estate, Polperro, nr. Looe

Busy park for all units with much on site entertainment and with holiday caravans to hire.

A substantial part of Killigarth Estate is occupied by caravan holiday homes but a separate part is allocated to touring units providing 202 marked, level or gently sloping grass pitches. They are approached by a tree lined driveway and 73 electric hook-ups 16A) are provided with strategically placed bins and water points. One large, modern, spacious toilet block has pre-set hot showers (no dividers), vanity style basins, dryers, soap and hairdryers and some under cover washing up facilities. This is a supplemented by 'portaloo' facilities. Unit for the disabled. Very well equipped laundry. The heart of the park is the Talland Suite - a large bar, entertainment hall with bar, family room, takeaway and bar snacks, heated indoor pool and sun terrace with beautiful views. A children's playground beside the pool (plus additional one in the camping area) and well stocked mini-market, information room, amusement arcade and games and TV rooms complete the provision. Early evening 'young entertainment' is provided and followed later by discos or groups. A programme showing family films and cartoons is repeated fortnightly. Skittle alley. Crazy golf. The park is popular with families with children of all ages and there is much to do in the area.

Charges 1995:
-- Per pitch £2.80 - £5.00; adult £2.50; child (3-16 yrs) £1.00; electricity £1.75.
-- VAT included.
Open:
Easter - 1 October.
Address:
Polperro, Looe, Cornwall PL13 2JQ.
Tel:
(01503) 72216 or 72409.
Reservations:
Are made (Sat. - Sat. in main season) with £25 deposit.

Directions: From Looe take A387 towards Polperro. After 3½ miles, fork left just past a bus shelter and phone box at sign. Site is ¼ mile. O.S.GR: SX213519.

Killigarth Manor Holiday Estate

POLPERRO near LOOE, CORNWALL

A delightful Family run Holiday Estate set in beautiful countryside, close to picturesque Polperro and Talland Bay.

Luxurious new facilities for Tents and Tourers, Toilets, Showers, Wash-Basins, Hairdryers, Razor points. Electric Hookups available.

Illustrated brochure from Mr. P. MARKS

KILLIGARTH MANOR HOLIDAY ESTATE
POLPERRO, LOOE, CORNWALL PL13 2JQ
TELEPHONE: 01503 272216

Heated Indoor Swimming Pool, Adventure Play Areas. Bar, Club/Ballroom with Entertainment. Restaurant, Take-away, Launderette, Ironing room and Shop. (Free Club membership).

The family run holiday park
– for your family!

CARAVAN OR TENT INCLUDING 2 PERSONS FROM £8.50 PER NIGHT

RAC APPOINTED
EXCELLENT
AA
MEMBER
AWARDS FOR EXCELLENCE
SPORTS AND RECREATIONAL FACILITIES
1994-5
AA

78 Powderham Castle Caravan Park, Lanlivery, nr. Lostwithiel

Tranquil, sheltered family touring park well situated for exploring Cornwall.

This is a most pleasant, peaceful park with plenty of 'green' space and a natural, uncommercialised atmosphere which has been enhanced by careful planting of trees and shrubs to form a series of linked paddocks with a small stream running through. The nearest beach at Par is 4 miles. The park's numbered pitches take 38 private caravan holiday homes in a separate field and 75 touring units, spread round the perimeter of the paddocks, each with 10-15 pitches (groundsheets to be lifted alternate days). There are 75 electrical connections (5/10A) for tourers and 7 hardstandings. Dustbin and water points around the park are hidden by trees and bushes. The central, heated toilet block is good with free hot water in basins, hot showers on payment, curtained cubicles in ladies, hairdryers and a family washroom with shower, basin, WC, etc. Separate dishwashing area with 5 sinks (free hot water). Laundry room. Badminton court. Games room with table tennis, pool. TV room. Superb, large children's activity play area on grass in one of the hedged paddocks with paddling pool. Putting green. Milkman calls with bread, eggs, pasties, etc. Seasonal pitches and caravan storage available. Telephone. Boat moorings nearby, boats and canoes for hire. Village pub is within walking distance. Two golf courses, fresh and sea fishing, indoor tennis courts (Bodmin) and a swimming pool are close. There are several good local restaurants.

Charges 1996:
-- Per unit £3.40 - £4.40; person £1.50 - £2.10; child (3-16 yrs) 50p - £1.00; electricity £1.75; awnings, extra small tent, car free.
-- No single sex groups
-- VAT included.
Open:
Easter/1 April - 31 Oct.
Address:
Lanlivery, Cornwall PL30 5BU.
Tel:
(01208) 872277
Reservations:
Made with £10 deposit.

 Alan Rogers' discount
Less 10% all season

Directions: Approach road leads off A390 1½ miles southwest of Lostwithiel signed 'Lanlivery, Luxulyan'. No other approach advised. O.S.GR: SX083592.

79 Carlyon Bay Caravan and Camping Park, Bethesda, Carlyon Bay

Spacious, tranquil, family owned park, 5 minutes walk from busy sandy beach.

Open meadows edged by mature woodland provide a beautiful holiday setting with a blue flag beach 5 minutes walk from the top gate at this park. The original farm buildings have been converted and added to, providing an attractive centre to the park, also home for the owners, with a certain individuality of design which is very pleasing, particularly in the three toilet blocks. These have pre-set hot showers (curtains, shelves and hooks provided), vanity style washbasins (H&C), hairdryers and a baby area. The latest block, rather plush with modern tiking, includes en-suite basins and toilets, extra family showers and hair washing and make up facilities - very smart. Dishwashing sinks with hot water are under cover. Fully equipped laundry room (hot water metered) with free irons and a well hidden chemical disposal point. The 180 pitches in 5 areas are spacious, allowing for a family meadow, a dog free meadow, and an area for couples, etc. All are on flat or gently sloping grass, unmarked except for the 104 electric pitches (10 or 5A). There is even a 'discreet' area, well screened and hidden, for naturists. The only official naturist beach in Cornwall, Polgaver Bay, at the far end of Carlyon Bay can be reached by walking over the cliff tops. The kidney shaped, heated pool (Easter-Sept) with children's paddling pool, is walled and paved for sunbathing and is part of the central area, along with a canopied entertainment area, TV lounge, crazy golf, table tennis, pool table and barbecue area. There is a covered 'Country Kitchen' takeaway (June-Aug), two children's play areas and crazy golf. Socially the park provides family entertainment in high season but those who wish for more can choose between the Cornish Leisure World complex on the beach, with its pool, bars and discos, or the social club near the entrance to the park which welcomes campers. For the more active, there is also a golf course opposite the entrance (concessionary rates available) and the coastal footpath passes near. All Cornwall's attractions are within touring distance. 2 holiday caravans and 1 chalet for rent.

Charges 1995:
-- Per unit incl. 2 persons and car £6.00 - £12.00, acc. to season (motorcaravan deduct £1.00, hikers tent without car less £2.00); extra adult £2.00 - £3.00; child (3-15 yrs incl.) £1.00 - £2.00; awning or small pup tent free - £1.00; dog £1.00; extra car free - £1.00; electricity £2.00.
-- Max. charge £20.00 per unit/night.
-- VAT included.
-- Credit cards accepted.
Open:
April - October.
Address:
Bethesda, Carlyon Bay, St. Austell, Cornwall PL25 3RE.
Tel:
(01726) 812735.
Reservations:
Made with £30 deposit and £2 fee.

Directions: Approaching from the Plymouth direction on the A390, pass Lostwithiel and 1 mile after the village of St. Blazey, turn left at the roundabout beside the Britannia Inn. After 400 yds turn right on an uneven road and right again at site sign. O.S.GR: SX078520.

80 Pentewan Sands Holiday Park, Mevagissey

Beachside touring park with large individual pitches and pool; some hire caravans and chalets.

Pentewan Sands is a popular park with an ideal position right beside a wide sandy beach offering safe bathing, with direct flat access and no roads to cross. A busy park with lots going on, there are 460 individual touring pitches, 298 with electrical connections, and 95 caravan holiday homes for hire. The pitches are of reasonable size on sandy ground with nothing between them, and are marked by frontage stones, mostly in rows adjoining access roads. There is carefully monitored public access to the beach through the park. A good sized free heated swimming pool about 72 x 26 ft, with small children's pool (supervised), is adjacent to the Clubhouse. Open all season, the Clubhouse contains two licensed bar lounges upstairs and a further one downstairs opening on to the pool area, open all day and serving a variety of good value food. A full entertainment programme and a children's club are organised and there is a small water sports centre on the beach and an adventure playground. The three main toilet blocks are rather utilitarian, receiving heavy use in peak season. There is free hot water in nearly all washbasins, many in vanity style, a few for ladies in private cabins, free hot showers, 2 bathrooms and baby room. Facilities for the disabled, well equipped laundry room and washing up sinks. Large, general self-service shop (open Easter - late Sept). Bistro, bar meals and fast food on site (genuine Thai restaurant with takeaway close by). Freezer service for ice packs. Battery charging service. Public phones. Sailing club adjoining with membership available for campers. Scuba diving, windsurfing courses, etc. Slipway. All weather tennis court area (with 5 compact courts). Mevagissey, with its throngs of tourists, is 2 miles. Dogs are not accepted.

Charges 1995:
-- Per unit incl. 2 adults £5.00 - £12.25; extra adult £1.00 - £2.85; child (5-15 yrs) 60p - £1.75; extra small tent or car £1.00; boat and trailer £1.50; electricity (10A) £2.00.
-- VAT included.
Open:
Easter/1 April - 31 Oct.
Address:
Pentewan, nr. St. Austell, Cornwall PL26 6BT.
Tel:
(01726) 843485.
FAX: (01726) 844142.
Reservations:
Made Sat - Sat or Wed - Wed with one week's payment in advance, £2 booking fee and compulsory cancellation insurance (£2.50 - £5).

Directions: From St. Austell ring road take B3273 for Mevagissey. Park is 3½ miles, where the road meets the sea. O.S.GR: SX018468.

 Alan Rogers' discount Less 50p per pitch per night

81 Penhaven Touring Park, Pentewan, Mevagissey

Family owned touring park with swimming pool, one mile from sandy beach.

For those who prefer the quiet life and don't wish direct access to the beach, Penhaven is a grassy, level 13 acre valley park. Part of the Caravan Club's 'managed under contract' scheme, non-members are also very welcome. Bordered by the river bank, woods and roads, it provides 105 good sized, marked pitches, 72 with electricity (10A) and 5 with hardstanding. The park comprises three fields. The North field is used by the Caravan Club for rallies with a small `portaloo' on one side, the South field is part children's ball game area, part caravan storage and part a tenting area for 35 tents on a 28 day licence (torches are necessary here). All the facilities are in the Middle field - these include a heated pool (40 x 20 ft. open mid-May-Sept. and unsupervised) with paved sunbathing surround, fenced play area for small children on sand and grass, reception and self service shop (open 9 am. - lunchtime and on demand) with a separate takeaway unit only in high season. The tiled toilet block is heated and provides for each sex, 9 washbasins (a little cramped), with hooks and shelves, 8 toilets and 2 free showers. This provision is now supplemented by 4 family shower rooms and 6 extra showers (no dividers or shelves) for the main season. Chemical toilet disposal points. Washing-up units (H&C), partly covered and laundry facilities. The park is well situated for exploring Cornwall and a 20 minute walk along the river bank takes you to the village of Pentewan and the beach. Dogs are welcome if kept on lead and exercised off the site. Late arrivals area with toilet facilities. American motorhomes welcome. Restaurant within walking distance at London Apprentice. Bus or coastal path to Mevagissey.

Charges 1995:
-- Per unit incl. 2 persons £9.00 - £16.00, acc. to season; tent incl. 2 persons £8.00 - £11.60; extra adult £3.00 - £3.50; child (5-17 yrs) £1.25; extra car, boat/trailer £1.00; electricity (10A) £1.75; dog 50p.
-- VAT included.
-- Credit cards accepted.
Open:
Easter/1 April - 31 October.
Address:
Pentewan, St Austell, Cornwall PL26 6DL.
Tel:
Mevagissey (01726) 843687.
FAX: (01726) 843870.
Reservations:
Made for min. 3 days with £20 deposit per week.

Directions: From St. Austell on the A390, take the B3273 to Mevagissey and park is on left, 1 mile from London Apprentice before the village of Pentewan. O.S.GR: SX008481.

82 Sea View International, Gorran, nr. Mevagissey

First class, family owned, quality park with landscaped pool area and near safe beaches.

You are immediately struck by the beautiful flower displays and well trimmed appearance of Sea View which has a deserved reputation for consistent quality and attention to detail. Dominated by 'The Dodman' Cornish headland providing marvellous views, with environmentally safe beaches, coves and harbours nearby (the nearest beach is within walking distance), it is a magical area steeped in mystery, tradition and folklore. Taking some 165 units overall, Sea View has four neatly cut grass meadows, one solely for holiday letting caravans, two for mixed units and one large play field. Pitches are individually numbered on flat grass, over 140 with electricity (16A), and 47 'premium' pitches (with electricity, water, waste gulleys and extra taps for plug in systems) backing onto Cornish hedges and 5 hardstandings. It is a reasonably sheltered, quiet and orderly park, family run for families, with good views but without evening activities, and it is very popular, so reservation for main season is necessary. The separate shower and toilet blocks, both of excellent quality, are centrally positioned and well equipped and maintained. They provide large, free hot showers, baths on payment, vanity style washbasins (2 cubicles for ladies, 1 for men), facilities for the disabled, hair dryers, baby bath and changing areas (in both ladies' and men's), 13 covered washing-up sinks and freezers for ice. The park has a free swimming pool (68 x 30 ft.) heated mid May - mid Sept, terraced and beautifully landscaped, with paddling pool, paved areas for sun loungers and pool-side games. Launderette. General shop. Simple takeaway service (5-8 pm, Whitsun - first week in Sept). The excellent large play field area at the top of the park provides plenty of room for leisure activities with 3 grass tennis courts, 3 badminton courts, volleyball, basketball, football, putting green, table tennis, crazy golf and adventure play area, all sheltered by a small pine wood. Games room (video machine). **continued overleaf**

Charges 1996:
-- Per unit incl. 2 persons and awning £6.00 - £14.90; child (2-15) £1.70; extra adult £2.50 - £3.50; pup tent (outside 17/7-27/8) £1.00; electricity £2.00; dog (limited breeds and numbers) £1.00 - £2.00; extra car £1.00; special facility pitch £3.00.
-- VAT included.
-- Credit cards accepted.
Open:
1 April - 30 September.
Address:
Boswinger, Gorran, St. Austell, Cornwall PL26 6LL.
Tel:
Mevagissey (01726) 843425.
FAX: (01726) 843358.
Reservations:
Min 7 nights, w/e - w/e, 27/7-1/9. other times, any length, with £25 deposit and £2 booking fee.

82 Sea View International continued

Table tennis. Barbecue area including covered log fire. Motorcaravan service station. Dog exercise field. Public phones. A member of the Best of British group. One of the few UK parks used by Eurocamp.

Directions: From St. Austell take B3273 towards Mevagissey; 1 mile before Mevagissey village turn right at Gorran sign and continue towards Gorran for 5 miles. Fork right at camp sign and follow signs to park. O.S.GR: SW991412.

83 Tretheake Manor Tourist Park, Veryan

Rural, spacious, family touring park close to the sea.

Quietly situated about 1½ miles back from the sea between Mevagissey and St. Mawes, the site consists of a large meadow, mainly on a slight slope and broken up by small copse of trees and bushes, which takes up to 175 touring units. On part of the site - around the perimeter or adjoining the roads - there are some individual numbered pitches which are used for reservations. Over the rest of the field siting is left to campers. There are 77 electrical connections for caravans, 19 pitches with water also and 10 fully serviced with water, electricity and drainage. Outside the peak weeks there is usually some room but reservation is advisable in high season. A varied selection of sandy beaches is within 2-8 miles. The toilet block is of good quality, well maintained and heated in low season. It has washbasins in flat surfaces of vanity type with free hot water, some private washing cabins for ladies, free hot showers (pushbutton) and hand and hair dryers. 6 covered, lit washing-up sinks (H&C). Water points around. Launderette. Well stocked shop with microwave and freezer pack facilities. Coarse fishing lake (16-22 rods). TV room and games room with pool, table tennis. Good children's playground. Public phone. Information room. Pub food can be excellent value in Cornwall and there are several good ones within the Roseland Peninsular. A good value site.

Directions: Turn off A3078 to southeast 2 miles south of Tregony on St. Mawes road, keep right, then second left to site. O.S.GR: SW933413.

Charges 1995:
-- Per unit incl. 2 adults £5.00 - £7.50; child (under 3) free; child (3-16 yrs) £1.20; extra adult £2.00; electricity £1.60, plus water £2.00, plus drainage £2.50
-- Senior citizens less 10% outside 2/7-2/9.
-- VAT included.
Open:
Easter/1 April - October.
Address:
Veryan, nr. Truro, Cornwall TR2 5PP.
Tel:
Veryan (01872) 501658.
FAX: as phone.
Reservations:
Made with £15 deposit p/week or part.

84 Trethem Mill Touring Park, St Just-in-Roseland, nr. St Mawes

Rural family park on the Roseland Peninsula.

Situated 3 miles from the quaint village of St Mawes, in an area of outstanding natural beauty, Trethem is owned and managed by the Akeroyd family who continue to work hard to provide good facilities on the 11 acre park, with 80 pitches for all units on gently sloping grass with an oval connecting tarmac road. Some level pitches are at the entrance and there are 40 (16A) electric hook-ups. An extra lower field, bordering the woodland is brought into use in the main season. A tree planting scheme is underway in another field to provide nature walks and a smaller, naturally hedged field is equipped as the children's play area. Games room and a TV room. Facilities in one block to the side of the park consist of reception, a well stocked shop, laundry room, babies changing room, tourist information and the sanitary units which are neatly tiled with all modern facilities and kept neat and clean. They can be heated and all hot water is free. Indoor tiled washing up area. Windsurfer and mountain bike hire. Freezer for ice packs (free). Public telephone.

Directions: From Tregony follow the A3078 to St Mawes. Approx. 2 miles after passing through Trewithian, watch for camping sign. O.S.GR: SW862364.

Charges 1996:
-- Per unit incl. 2 adults £5.50 - £8.50; per person, hiker or cyclist £3.00 - £3.50; extra adult £1.50 - £2.50; child (4-16) £1.00 - £2.00; electricity £1.80; dog 50p; extra car 50p; extra small tent 50p.
-- Credit cards accepted.
Open:
1 April/Easter - 31 Oct.
Address:
St Just-in-Roseland, nr. St Mawes, Truro, Cornwall TR2 5JF.
Tel:
(01872) 580504.
Reservations:
Made with £15 deposit.

85 Maen Valley Holiday Park, Falmouth

Long established park in sheltered valley with a relaxed atmosphere.

We have long wanted to find a suitable site in the Falmouth area and it seems that Maen Valley fits the bill. In a south facing, sheltered valley, with two beaches within a mile, a range of activities (and courses) nearby, from sailing, windsurfing, fishing and diving to tennis coaching, with access to the coastal path for walking and with many well known Cornish gardens near by, one can be active or just relax on the park. A clear Cornish stream runs through the park, at one part adapted to form a children's paddling pool, and the sheltering mature woods provide walks. A club, open evenings and also lunch times at weekends, provides for social life and food if required. Crazy golf and skittles. There is a number of privately owned permanent holiday homes and 70 caravan holiday homes to let, as well as 80 plus places for touring units, mostly informally arranged on sloping hedged fields, 60 with electrical hook-ups. A separate level area with views at the top of the park near the second entrance is useful for caravans and motorhomes. The toilet facilities are average providing free hot showers with folding seat and curtain, washbasins (H&C), with a small additional unit in top area. Laundry facilities, no separate dishwashing sinks except in the top area. Reception, shop open 8.30-11am. and 4-7 pm. Local pub in the village, Falmouth 5-10 minutes by car or a 25 minute walk.

Directions: From Truro, follow signs for Falmouth on A39 until you reach the roundabout on the outskirts. Turn right, signed Maenporth and industrial estates (on Bickland Water Road). Watch for signs and park is on the right. The first turning leads to the bottom of the valley and reception and is rather narrow and steep. The second entrance may be easier for caravans. O.S.GR: SW789311.

Charges 1995:
-- Per adult £3.00 - £5.00; child (3-16 yrs) £1.00 - £2.00; dog £10.00 per week; electricity £1.70.
Open:
Easter - 31 October.
Address:
Falmouth, Cornwall TR11 5BJ.
Tel:
Falmouth (01326 312190.
FAX: (01326) 211120.
Reservations:
Made with £20 deposit.

86 Calloose Caravan Park, Leedstown, Hayle

Friendly rural touring park with swimming pool and a few holiday caravans.

This park is quietly situated in an inland valley, about 4 miles from Hayle, with an extra ½ mile to the beaches beyond, 9 to St. Ives on the north coast and 6 to Helston and Praa Sands on the south. Attractively landscaped with almost a tropical feel, units are personally sited. The terrain is mainly flat but is dry, with two slightly raised areas on terraces. There are 120 tourist pitches (99 with electricity, 8 with water and 14 gravelled hardstandings) with individual markers, and 17 caravan holiday homes which are let. In the main meadows, pitches are arranged round the perimeter with free space in the middle. Both toilet blocks have been refurbished and they provide washbasins in cubicles, free hot showers, a family shower room, baby room, a unit for the disabled and washing up sinks under cover. A heated swimming pool (40 x 20 ft. open from early May) with separate paddling pool, is neatly landscaped with sunbathing terrace and access for the disabled. Well stocked shop. Large recreation block with themed bar and family room adjoining, with bar meals daily in the main season, takeaway service and organised family entertainment most evenings in the main season. Weekly barbecues. TV lounge. Pool table. Games room with skittle alley. All-weather tennis court. Crazy golf, floodlit. Table tennis. Sun loungers and mountain bikes for hire and extensive local information in reception. Adventure playground. Laundry room. First aid room. Public phones. The village is within walking distance. A popular park, enthusiastically run by Phil Gardner and his wife, the owners, Booking is essential.

Charges 1995:
-- Per unit incl. 2 persons £5.50 - £8.50, acc. to season; extra person (over 3 yrs) 75p - £1.75; pup tent 75p - £1.00; dog 75p - £2.00; electricity (10A) £2.00.
-- VAT included.
-- Credit cards accepted.
Open:
1 April - 28 September.
Address:
Leedstown, Hayle, Cornwall TR27 5ET.
Tel:
Hayle (01736) 850431.
FAX: as phone.
Reservations:
With deposit - £15 per pitch (5 days min) balance on arrival.

Directions: From crossroads of the B3280 and B3302 roads in Leedstown take B3302 towards Hayle. First right, then left on the ½ mile access road to park. O.S.GR: SW605350.

87 River Valley Caravan Park, Relubbus, Penzance

Quiet touring park for caravans and a few tents, east of Penzance.

A spacious park aiming to provide a quiet relaxing holiday, this one is set in a pleasant river valley. It is quite strictly run, with special rules relating to groundsheet use and repitching for long stays to keep the grass in as optimum a condition for as long as possible. Its main feature is perhaps the spaciousness - it takes only 90 trailer or motorcaravans spread over an area which would hold many more, and limited tents. Pitches are mainly around the perimeters of small meadows or clearings, most with electrical connections (15A), some hard-standings and special sections for families, couples, tents, dogs, etc. There are three good quality, tiled toilet blocks which are large enough, clean and well maintained. Hot water is free in the basins, showers (with an original pulley system to keep clothes dry!) and the 10 washing-up sinks. Hand dryers. A few private cabins for ladies and a special make-up room with hair dryers. Laundry room. Baby bath. Water points around the park. Motor caravan service point (fresh water top up and waste wter empying). Trout fishing free on site. Walks. Shop (closed from Oct). Public phone. No children's playground, but lots of very tame ducks on the river. Working windmill and waterwheel. St Michael's Mount is only 3 miles away and can be reached by footpath. A member of the Best of British group.

Charges 1996:
-- Per pitch (incl. vehicle) £3.00; adult £1.80 - £2.20; child 50p - £1.10; awning/pup tent 60p - 80p; dog 70p - £1.30; electricity 95p - £1.50; extra vehicle £1.00.
-- Min. charge 2 adults per vehicle; large motorvans add £1.00.
-- VAT not included.
-- Credit cards accepted.
Open:
All year except 6 Jan-4 March.
Address:
Relubbus, Penzance, Cornwall TR20 9ER.
Tel:
Penzance (01736) 763398
Reservations:
Any period with deposit (£10) and fee (£1).

Alan Rogers' discount
Less £1 per unit provided no other discount taken.

Directions: Park approach leads off the B3280 at east end of Relubbus village, northeast of Marazion. O.S.GR: SW566320.

88 Cardinney Camping Park, Crows an Wra, Penzance

Well kept, personally run small park near Lands End beauty spots.

Perfectly situated for visiting the famous Lands End beauty spots and tourist attractions, Cardinney is also within easy driving distance of small Cornish beaches and coves. The level field is semi-divided into three camping areas and is neatly kept with some landscaping. The facilities are limited compared to many of the more sophisticated sites in Devon and Cornwall, consisting of one block of 3 metered showers and 6 mirrored washbasins for each sex. Razor points, hair dryers and baby cubicle are also available. The block is situated adjacent to the 105 marked pitches, of which 50 have electrical connections (10A) and 17 hardstanding. The combined café and shop acts as a social point providing breakfasts and takeaway food at most times. Children's playground and games room with TV, pool table and video games. Good laundry facilities and dishwashing sinks with hot water. Coastal, cliff top walks nearby, also the Minnack Open Air Theatre.

Directions: Park is signed at Crows an Wra on main Penzance - Lands End A30 road. O.S.GR: SW426285.

Charges 1995:
-- Per unit incl. 2 adults £5.50 - £6.50; extra adult £1.50; child (0-14 yrs) 75p; extra car, tent or awning 50p; electricity £1.50; pets free.
Open:
1 April -- 31 October.
Address:
Main A30, Crows an Wra, nr. Lands End, Cornwall TR19 6HJ.
Tel:
Penzance (01736) 810880.
Reservations:
Made with £5 deposit.

89 Polmanter Farm Tourist Park, Halestown, nr. St. Ives

Family owned farm park with pool, in the hills behind St. Ives.

Polmanter is a good example of a sympathetic conversion of a farm from agricultural to leisure use and the Osborne family have developed the park well. The converted farm buildings provide a cosy bar lounge with bar meals available (good value) and overlooking the swimming pool, toddlers pool and sunbathing area, with an upstairs games room with pool and table tennis. Occasional entertainment is organised in season. The 240 tourist pitches (no statics) are well spaced in three large fields with 6 hardstandings and 140 electric hook-ups (16A). The park now has 85 deluxe pitches with electricity, water, waste water and cable TV connections. The toilet blocks vary - as the park has grown, so extra blocks have been added. There are now four and the latest is modern and good but still incorporates the ideas of the first block, which include a wall cupboard for clothes in each shower to keep them dry. Showers are free. Hair dryers. Extra dishwashing sinks in the new block and good laundry provision including free irons. There are two full size tennis courts, a children's play area with large wooden climbing frame on a sand base and a sports field. Well stocked, self service shop and takeaway facility also (bar, shop and pool Whitsun - mid Sept). Used by Eurocamp. It is a busy park with a happy atmosphere within 1½ miles of St. Ives - a footpath leads from the park (20 mins. downhill) or there is a bus service from the park in high season hourly, 10 am. - midnight. Golf and fishing nearby. Dogs accepted on leads (but not on the St. Ives beaches in high season) with a large exercise field provided.

Directions: Take the B3074 to St. Ives from the A30 and then first left at a mini-roundabout taking `Holiday Route' to St. Ives (Halestown). Turn right at the Halestown Inn then first left. O.S.GR: SW509392.

Charges 1995:
-- Per unit incl. car and awning £4.50 - £10.00, acc. to season; extra adult £1.75 - £2.50; child (3-15 yrs) £1.00 - £1.75; electricity (16A) £1.00 - £2.00; deluxe pitch £2.00 - £4.00; dog 50p; extra car 50p.
-- VAT included.
-- Credit cards accepted.
Open:
Easter - 31 October (full facilities to 10 Sept).
Address:
Halestown, St. Ives, Cornwall TR26 3LX.
Tel:
St. Ives (01736) 795640.
FAX: as phone.
Reservations:
Made with £20 deposit and £1 fee. For 21/7-25/8 only: multiples of 7 nights with arrival on Fri, Sat or Sunday.

All the parks in this guide are inspected regularly by our team
of experienced site assessors, but we welcome your opinion too.
- See Readers Report on page 180 -

90 Ayr Holiday Park, St. Ives

Family owned park with holiday homes within walking distance of St. Ives, with superb views.

On first arrival Ayr Park seems to be all caravan holiday homes but behind them is a series of naturally sloping fields with marvellous views over St. Ives Bay and Porthmeor beach providing 40 touring pitches. Level, hardcore, terraced areas also provide places for motorhomes and vans with 35 (16A) electrical connections. The toilet block has been nicely modernised and is well maintained with free, hot, controllable showers (some accessed direct from the outside and some with toilet), hot water to washbasins, vanity style, hairdryer and 3 under cover dishwashing sinks with hot water. Good laundry facilities. With the extra field for tents open in July and August, the facilities could be a little hard-pressed, but were coping well when we visited in August. A small café, attractively done out in pine, is open from June for simple meals and a shop provides essentials. St. Ives centre and supermarkets are within easy walking distance, also the new Tate Gallery. Children's play area and football field. Direct access to the coastal footpath. One dog per pitch, up to medium size, is permitted but it is advisable to contact the park as dogs are not allowed on St. Ives beaches in high season.

Directions: 300 yds after leaving the A30 turn left at a mini-roundabout following signs for St. Ives for heavy vehicles and day visitors which, after approx. 2 miles, joins the B3311 and then the B3306 about 1 mile from St. Ives (an octagonal building will be on your left). Still heading for St. Ives turn left at a mini-roundabout following camping signs through residential areas. Park entrance is 600 yds at Ayr Terrace. O.S.GR: SW515388.

Charges 1995:
-- Per adult £1.85 - £3.00; child (5 to under 16 yrs) £1.00 - £1.55; caravan or tent £3.30 - £5.90; car £1.10; motorcaravan £3.90 - £6.00; large tent (120 sq.ft. plus) £3.60 - £7.75; hiker's tent incl. 2 persons £5.50 - £8.75; awning £1.60 - £3.10; m/cycle £1.10; dog £1.00; electricity £2.00. -- VAT included.

Open:
Easter/1 April - 31 October.

Address:
Higher Ayr, St. Ives, Cornwall TR26 1EJ.

Tel:
St. Ives (01736) 795855. FAX: (01736) 798797.

Reservations:
Made with £25 deposit.

91 Trevalgan Family Camping Park, St. Ives

Friendly, smallish, `countrified' park.

We already have two very different sites in the St Ives area and Trevalgan is different yet again, based on a working farm on the cliffs 1½ miles west of St Ives. Providing 120 clearly marked pitches in a level stone walled field, the pitches vary in size as the park is very popular with walkers. A purpose built toilet block has curtained washbasins, controllable hot showers with seat and curtain, plus rooms for babies, laundry and washing up, and even a hot drinks machine. Amenities include reception with a small shop for basics and a 'farm house kitchen' with takeaway for breakfast or evening food with some outside tables only. Games field, children's play area and farm pets corner with baby chickens, two donkeys, etc. A games room in an original barn has table tennis, pool, fruit machines and a comfortable upstairs TV room. There is access to the coastal path and to a cove below the cliff and it is a 25 minutes walk to St Ives. Bus service at top of road. With bicycle hire, tractor rides and a farm trail, it is, in all, quite an original type of park.

Directions: Approach park down a narrow Cornish lane from the B3306 St Ives - Land's End road, following sign. O.S.GR: SW490400.

Charges 1995:
-- Per adult £2.50 - £4.00; child 3-14 yrs £1.50 - £3.00, under 3 yrs £1.00; electricity £2.00. -- Min. fee in high season £8.00.

Open:
1 May - end September.

Address:
Trevalgan Farm, St Ives, Cornwall TR26 3BJ.

Tel:
(01736) 796433.

Reservations:
Contact park - made for Sat.- Sat. only 9/7-20/8 for electricity.

Liskey Touring Park

EXCELLENT

A small, peaceful, all-touring park for the discriminating visitor seeking a quiet, relaxing holiday. Just 68 pitches with banks of colourful shrubs & trees creating a garden-like setting...

... & lots of space for children with a large adventure playground, playbarn, 1 acre games field & a tiny tots play area.

Enthusiastic caravanners themselves, Jill & Nigel Parkins, the owners, extend a warm welcome. For details please ring:

Truro (01872) 560274
Greenbottom, Truro, Cornwall TR4 8QN

92 Liskey Touring Park, nr. Truro

Quiet, family run park conveniently situated for visiting western Cornwall.

The entrance to Liskey is wide with room to manoeuvre, pleasantly landscaped with rockeries and flowers. The gently sloping tarmac road passes the TV room/small library, which also contains tourist information, to the reception office cum shop. The shop provides necessary groceries with off licence (open Spr. B.H. - end Sept), also a takeaway service (June-Sept). The main, slightly sloping camping area, with views across the countryside, has been thoughtfully landscaped to provide 53 levelled, well spaced pitches, including 43 with 10A electric hook-ups and 7 'all-service' pitches. There is a feeling of spaciousness and shrubs and flowers give an attractive aspect. The central toilet block is very clean and well maintained and is equipped with free hot water, some cubicled basins, showers and hand and free hair dryers. It has been extended to provide a further 4 unisex showers and a family bathroom with bath (70p). Well equipped laundry room, 4 under cover dishwashing sinks and recycling bins. Continuing up and past reception is a further field with a rural aspect, for 15 units beside the 'under 5s' fenced play area with Wendy house, slide, etc. Adventure play area, play field for older children with nets for volleyball and basketball, and a play barn providing an under cover children's meeting place with table tennis and further play equipment on bark chippings. No bikes, skateboards or roller skates are allowed. Barbecue areas. Free house with real ale and good food within 600 yds. Tickets for a coarse fishing lake available at reception. Dogs accepted but on a **short** lead at all times.

Directions: From A30 take A390 to Truro. At next roundabout turn right (signed Threemilestone) and, immediately at mini-roundabout, right again towards Chacewater. Park is 600 yds on right past Leverton Place. O.S.GR: SW756463.

Charges 1996:
-- Per unit incl. 2 persons £5.20 - £8.50; hikers/cyclists £2.20 - £2.50 per person; extra adult £2.20 - £2.50, teenager (13-17 yrs) £1.50 - £1.80, child (3-12 yrs) £1.20 - £1.50; 1st dog free - £1.00, extra dog £1.00; electricity £1.50; tent power unit incl. electricity £2.30.
Open:
1 April - 28 September.
Address:
Greenbottom, Truro, Cornwall TR4 8QN.
Tel:
Truro (01872) 560274. FAX: as phone.
Reservations:
Made with £2 deposit (£3 in high season) per night booked or payment in full if less than 5 days.

How to use the 1996 Discount Voucher !

The Discount Card/Vouchers are in three parts:

Part 1 should be retained and must not be removed from the Guide. You should complete it by adding your name, address and signature. This part includes the printed Card Number and should be shown to those parks indicating special offers for our readers.

Part 2 should be completed by adding your name, address, the card number as shown in part 1, and your signature. This part may then be used to claim your discount(s) for travel, breakdown, caravan or motorcaravan insurance.

Part 3 complete by adding your name, address, the card number as shown in Part 1, and your signature. This part may then be used to claim your FERRY DISCOUNT, as directed.

Note that the Discount Cards are valid from **1 January - 31 December 1996 only**

93 Penrose Farm Touring Park, Goonhavern, nr. Truro

Pleasant family park in popular area.

This sheltered park in the village of Goonhavern provides 100 marked pitches in four level, hedged, grass fields. Of these 62 are provided with 16A electricity and 4 have hardstanding. The enthusiastic owners, Colin and Joanne Stobbs, have refurbished the toilet block, providing light, clean facilities with vanity style washbasins, hot showers with curtain, stool, etc. and under cover, lit washing up facilities (H&C) and fully equipped laundry room. All are very well maintained and cheerful, with flowers and pot plants. For children, a new, well equipped adventure playground and a pets area have been developed (6 guinea pigs, 2 rabbits and 4 miniature goats are now in residence!), plus an aviary for the adults. A shop, telephone and tourist information at reception complete the facilities. Work continues with improvments to the roadways, pitch spacing and drainage, and general landscaping, which will combine to improve the overall appearance of the park. Perranporth beach is 2½ miles and all the amenities of the village, ie. post office, shops, pubs and craft centre, are within walking distance. A neat, well run, good value park.

Charges 1995:
-- Per unit incl 2 persons £4.00 - £8.00; extra person (6 yrs and over) 50p - £1.50; awning free - £1.00; extra car free - £1.00; electricity £2.00.
-- VAT included.
-- Credit cards accepted.
Open:
1 April - 31 October.
Address:
Goonhavern, nr. Truro, Cornwall TR4 9QF.
Tel:
(01872) 573185.
Reservations:
Made with £20 deposit.

Directions: Take A30 past Bodmin and Indian Queens. Just before wind farm take B3285 to Perranporth. Park is on left entering Goonhavern. O.S.GR: SW790535.

Alan Rogers' discount
Less 10% in low season

Penrose Farm
TOURING PARK
Goonhavern, Nr Truro, Cornwall TR4 9QF   Tel: 01872 573185

★ Quiet family park - no club / no bar
★ Just 2½ miles from Perranporth's famous beach
★ Excellent centre for touring Cornwall ★ Level and sheltered ★ Animal centre
★ Adventure play area ★ Free hot water ★ Shop & laundry ★ Dogs welcomed
From £4 to £8 per night - Please ring for Brochure

94 Chacewater Camping and Caravan Park, Chacewater, Truro

Small, quiet country touring park between Truro and Redruth.

This little park, a few miles back from the sea in a quiet situation, may appeal to those who prefer a quieter type of site without evening activities. Formed from a series of hedged meadows, there is provision for 50 units (of any type), well spaced around the edges. Care is taken in placing families, with a special field for dog owners and a separate area for the park's 13 caravan holiday homes (to let). Some hardstandings will be available from 1996 and there are 29 electrical connections (10A). The central toilet block has been refurbished and is light and airy with open style washbasins (H&C), controllable, free hot showers, hairdryers for ladies and, to complete the provision, two very useful en-suite family shower rooms. Washing up and laundry rooms. The rest of the facilities have been converted from old farm buildings and are attractively situated in a small courtyard to one end of the park. They comprise a TV room and lounge, games room/children's room and shop (Spr. B.H. to mid Sept) and reception. Children's play field. Dogs are accepted by arrangement. The village is close (Truro 4 miles) and a good choice of beaches is within 5-10 miles.

Charges 1995:
-- Per unit incl. 2 persons £6.00 - £8.50; small tent £5.00 - £7.50; extra person £1.50; child (2-12 yrs) £1.00; electricity £1.35; dog free - £1.00.
-- Discounts for advance bookings.
-- VAT included.
-- Credit cards accepted.
Open:
1 May - 30 September.
Address:
Cox Hill, Chacewater, Truro TR4 8LY.
Tel:
St. Day (01209) 820762.
Reservations:
Any length, £10 deposit, balance on arrival.

Directions: Park can be approached either from A390 road or from the A30. Park is ½ mile west of village - follow signs. O.S.GR: SW742439.

Alan Rogers' discount
10% discount

95 Leverton Place Caravan Park, Truro

Neat, well kept park with swimming pool and other amenities, just west of Truro.

About 6 miles from the northern coast of Cornwall and not much more from the southern, Leverton Place has been well designed and laid out along continental lines and is now part of the Caravan Club 'managed under contract' scheme although non-members are very welcome. The pitches are attractively arranged in groups in a series of secluded bays with neat, well drained lawns divided up by access roads, hedges and shrubs. There is provision for 110 touring units of any type with 7 chalets and 15 caravans to let. Pitches are marked, 80 with electrical connections (10A) and 30 with hardstanding. There are four toilet blocks serving the touring section, a central one providing 15 individual en-suite shower rooms, heated in winter, one of which has been specifically designed for the disabled. Otherwise it is a good, well maintained provision with two excellent dishwashing and laundry kitchens. The newest block near reception has a 'state of the art' chemical toilet and boot washing facility. An attractive walled patio area, complete with palm trees, provides a 58 ft. long pool (heated over a long period, but not for Easter), a paddling pool, lounge bar and bistro (mid May - mid Sept) with terraced sitting out area overlooking the pool. The bar opens each evening and perhaps at other times, but is sufficient distance from the pitch areas so as not to be intrusive. New self service shop open all day beside reception. Two children's playgrounds and two games rooms, both with pool, one with table tennis. First-aid room. Bicycles, roller skates and skate boards not allowed. Two well stocked fishing lakes are 5 minutes walk away. A park of quality, worth consideration.

Charges 1995:
-- Per pitch 22 July-28 Aug. £7.50, otherwise £1.00; adult £3.00 - £3.50; child (5-17 yrs) £1.10 - £1.20; dog free - £1.00; electricity £1.25- £2.00; extra car or trailer (in excess of 2 units) £1.00.
-- VAT included.
-- Credit cards accepted.
Open:
All year.
Address:
Truro, Cornwall TR4 8QW.
Tel:
Truro (01872) 560462.
FAX: (01872) 560668.
Reservations:
Made with deposit of £20 per week or part for high season, £5 at other times.

Directions: Park is 3 miles west of Truro, signed from the A390 road ½ mile from village of Threemilestone on the road to Chacewater. O.S.GR: SW770451.

96 Silverbow Park, Goonhavern, nr. Perranporth

Select, spacious, well kept park with swimming pool 2½ miles back from sea.

Silverbow has been developed by the Taylor family over 25 years and they are justifiably proud of their efforts. Hard work, planting and landscaping has provided a beautiful 14 acre park which now takes part in the well known 'Gardens Scheme'. The owners believe Silverbow is a way of life and staying is an experience - they have certainly created a relaxed and tranquil atmosphere. The park has 90 tourist pitches which are all of good size and include 62 `super' pitches in a newly developed area, with electricity, water and drainaway, which are even larger. Many are on a slight slope with some attractive views. There is much free space not used for camping, including an excellent sports area with 2 all weather and 2 grass tennis courts, with free coaching in season, 3 outdoor badminton courts, short mat bowls, a children's adventure playground on sand and a general play field, as well as wild meadow and wooded areas ideal for walks. An attractive, kidney shaped, heated swimming pool and small paddling pool (open mid-May - mid-Sept) sheltered by high surrounding garden walls is a real tropical sun trap.

There are 15 park owned high quality leisure homes in a separate part. The park is 2½ miles from the long sandy beach at Perranporth (30 mins. walk away from traffic) and 6 miles from Newquay. Three toilet blocks, all of excellent quality with private cabins for each sex, fully controllable free hot showers, 4 family shower/toilet rooms, 2 of which are accessible for wheelchairs, and one bath on payment for each sex. 6 enclosed washing-up sinks by touring field. Laundry room. Room for reading or quiet games. Recycling bins. Free freezer service. Shop (mid May-mid Sept). Pub within walking distance. Concessionary green fees are available at Perranporth golf club. Gliding, riding and fishing are nearby. Mountain biking from the park (but no bikes on site).

Directions: Entrance is directly off the main A3075 road, ½ mile south of Goonhavern. O.S.GR: SW781531.

Charges 1995:
-- Per unit incl 2 adults £5.50 - £12.00; extra person 2-13 yrs or over 50 yrs £1.50 - £2.60, 13-50 yrs £2.80 - £4.80; dog free - £1.50; fully serviced pitch incl. electricity £2.00 - £2.50, pitch with electricity only £1.50 - £1.80. -- VAT included.
Open:
1 May - mid-October.
Address:
Goonhavern, nr Truro, Cornwall TR4 9NX.
Tel:
Truro (01872) 572347.
Reservations:
Made with £20 p/week deposit (Sat. - Sat. only 10/7-28/8).

97 Newperran Tourist Park, Rejerrah, nr. Newquay

Large capacity touring-only park, with swimming pool.

This is a level park in rural Cornish countryside and on high ground making it quite open but also giving excellent views of the coast and surrounding district. Although it has its own manager, it is under the same family direction and ownership as Trevella Park, with the same sort of standards and is also a member of the Best of British group. Newperran is a little further back from the sea, but only 2½ miles from Perranporth beach, and there is a free heated swimming pool on site. Those who prefer traditional camping to a holiday camp atmosphere should appreciate this park. This is not to say that it is without facilities; it certainly has its full share of amenities, but it is a quiet park used mainly by families and with few evening activities. It consists of a number of flat, well drained, hedged meadows, all divided into 250 individual pitches; some fields have larger and reservable plots, with more free space in the middle. There are about 100 (13A) electrical connections. The anitary facilities consist of four clean, permanent blocks with free hot water in basins (some in cabins) and hot showers. There are two bathrooms, hair drying and dressing room, a unit for the disabled, washing up sinks and a launderette. Good self-service shop. Cafe with hot snacks to eat there or take away. Games room with table tennis, pool. TV room with some children's video shows. Adventure playground. Crazy golf. Children's room and activity programme in season. Free fishing at Trevella. Goonhavern village is within walking distance with pubs and post office.

Charges 1996:
-- Per caravan or tent £5.95 - £9.20;
motorcaravan £5.40 - £8.40.
-- VAT included.
-- Credit cards accepted.
Open:
Mid-May - mid-Sept.
Address:
Rejerrah, Newquay, Cornwall TR8 5QJ.
Tel:
(01872) 572407.
(1/10-1/5: (01637) 830308).
FAX: (01872) 571254.
Reservations:
Advisable in high season (ie. for electricity); £20 p/w deposit and £2 fee.

Directions: Turn off A3075 to west at camp sign 7 miles south of Newquay and just north of Goonhavern village. O.S.GR: SW794546.

98 Trevella Camping and Caravan Park, Crantock, Newquay

Orderly touring park close to sea, with swimming pool and fishing lakes, for families and couples only, with some letting caravans.

One of the best known and most respected of Cornish parks with its colourful flowerbeds and a regular winner of a 'Newquay in Bloom' award, Trevella is also one of the first to fill up and has a longer season than most. Well organised, the pitches are in a number of adjoining meadows, most of which are on a slight slope. Of the 350 pitches for touring units (any type), some 200 can be reserved and these are marked-out individual ones; elsewhere pitches are in rows but not marked. Over 100 electrical connections (10A) with 28 hardstandings. A small, free heated swimming pool with sunbathing area is centrally positioned, open like the shop, etc. from Easter - October, weather permitting. The nearest beach is ½ mile on foot, 1 mile by car and Newquay is 2 miles. There are pubs and restaurants at Crantock, 1 mile. During the peak season a nurse calls every morning. Trevella is essentially a quiet family touring park with an accent on orderliness and cleanliness; on-site evening activities are limited. The sanitary installations are kept very clean, and the three blocks provide sufficient coverage with individual basins with shelf, in private cabins for ladies, and free hot water to basins, plentiful washing-up sinks and controllable hot showers. Hair drying and dressing room, baby room and launderette. Well stocked supermarket. Post box and telephone. Hot dishes and snacks to take away or eat there, open late. TV room. Crazy golf. Large adventure playground and separate play and sports area. Free access to three fishing lakes, two on site (permits from reception); some fishing instruction and wildlife talks for youngsters in season. Minibus service to Newquay and Crantock. A member of the Best of British group.

Charges 1996:
-- Per caravan or tent £5.95 - £9.80;
motorcaravan £5.40 - £9.00.
-- VAT included.
Open:
Easter -- 31 October.
Address:
Crantock, Newquay, Cornwall TR8 5EW.
Tel:
Crantock (01637) 830308 (24 hr).
FAX: (01872) 571254.
Reservations:
Made with £20 deposit and £2 booking fee (16/7-27/8: Fri/Fri or Sat/Sat only).

Directions: To avoid Newquay leave A30 or A392 at Indian Queens, straight over crossroads with A39 and A3058, left at A3075 junction and first right at camp sign. O.S.GR: SW802598.

CORNWALL

99 Trevornick Holiday Park, Holywell Bay, Newquay

Large, busy, modern, family park for all units near sandy beach, with wide-ranging amenities.

Trevornick has been sympathetically converted from a working farm and has grown to provide caravanners and campers (no holiday caravans) with over 600 grass pitches (270 with electricity) in five level fields and two terraced areas (few trees, but some good views), providing `all singing, all dancing' facilities for family holidays in a rural setting. The four toilet blocks of standard modern design provide washbasins in vanity style, toilets, coin operated showers including a family shower room, baby bath and dishwashing and laundry facilities. The farm buildings provide an attractive setting for the farm club (open from Spr. B.H.) with licensed facilities and food, children's rooms, games room, video/TV with multi screen, cafeteria, chip bar and takeaway. Outside barbecue area and much entertainment in season including a weekly disco and barbecue. Activities include a good sized pool with slide, sauna and solarium, tennis courts, 2 adventure playgrounds, crazy golf and indoor adventure play area (supervised for 2-8 yr olds at a small charge). Dogs are accepted in one field only with a walk provided. A good sized `farm shop' and stables providing pony trekking remind one of the park's background. The rest of the development has provided an 18 hole golf course, pitch and putt, a small, quiet club with bar meals and lovely views out to sea, Holywell leisure `fun' park next door (site `fun pass' gives reduced rates) and recently much improved coarse fishing with 3 lakes. The sandy beach is 5 minutes by car or 20 minutes walk through the sand dunes past the Holywell. The park now offers 50 Eurotents to hire.

Charges 1995:
-- Per adult £3.15 - £5.00; child (3-14 yrs) free - £2.85; car free - 80p; electricity £2.50; dog free - £1.50.
-- Families and couples only.
-- VAT included.
-- Credit cards accepted.
Open: Easter - 30 September.
Address: Holywell Bay, Newquay, Cornwall TR8 5PW.
Tel: Newquay (01637) 830531.
Reservations: Made with £20 deposit per week (Sat. to Sat. only July/Aug).

Directions: From A3075 approach to Newquay - Perranporth road, turn towards Cubert and Holywell Bay. Park is through Cubert, on right. O.S.GR: SW776586.

100 Newquay Holiday Park, Newquay

Park with swimming pools and other amenities near town.

This park lies on a terraced hillside only just outside the town, some 2 miles from the beaches and town centre. The main feature of the site is an attractively laid out group of three heated swimming pools with giant waterslide (lifeguards in attendance) and surrounding sunbathing areas. Mainly a touring park, it has some 360 marked pitches for any type of unit in a series of hedged fields, although some fields are just for caravans and some for tents, plus 112 caravan holiday homes which are let. Most pitches are individual ones marked out by lines on ground but with nothing between them. There are 64 electric points for caravans, 24 for tents, plus 10 special pitches with hardstanding, water and drainaways. The sanitary installations include two good-sized, modern blocks with washbasins set in flat surfaces with free hot water and fairly basic free hot showers with pre-mixed hot water which runs automatically for 4 minutes and stops. Baby bath. Covered external washing-up sinks with hot water.

There is entertainment each night with live music, discos etc. in the site's Fiesta Club which also has a bar. TV lounge and games room with pool tables. Well stocked self-service shop. Takeaway food bar. Full launderette. Pitch and putt course. Crazy golf. Good children's playground. Amusement arcade. Bus service to Newquay from site. No dogs or pets taken.

Directions: Park is east of Newquay on A3059 road 1 mile east of junction with A392. O.S.GR: SW853626.

Charges 1995:
-- Per person £2.80 - £4.95; child free - £3.40; vehicle 75p; electricity free - £2.50 (16A); star pitch supplement £3.50.
-- VAT included.
-- Credit cards accepted.
Open:
May - mid September.
Address:
Newquay,
Cornwall TR8 4HS.
Tel:
(01637) 871111.
FAX: (01637) 850818.
Reservations:
Advisable for main season and made with £20 deposit (peak weeks Sat. - Sat. only).

see advert in previous colour section

101 Dennis Cove Camping, Padstow

Unusual site overlooking the Camel estuary and within walking distance of Padstow, mainly for tents.

Don't be put off by the narrow, Cornish lane approach - the views are marvellous from every pitch. However, it is only a small site and may appeal more to those with small dinghies and inflatables. The Camel Trail cycle path from Bodmin to Padstow passes through the site between the forefront field and the rest of the site and provides easy walking access to Padstow (10 mins). This field takes about 21 tents and has a fairly steep slipway, mainly for board sailors and small dinghies. A main slipway is in the town. The site has 4 moorings of its own. Behind is the restaurant and 25 m. swimming pool (open 2-5 pm.) with plenty of surrounding grassy areas. It is very natural and informal. This part of the site is open to the public. The restaurant with small bar provides home cooked food throughout the day from Whitsun to early Sept. and has lovely views from the terrace. The pool has changing rooms, a lifeguard on duty when open (every day in school holidays, weekends only at other times, Whitsun-early Sept).

The toilet facilities are above this area and are of older construction but clean and well maintained. There are 3 individual cubicles for ladies and two new family rooms have been added. Showers are metered, 3 of a good standard, others more simple. Dishwashing sinks are under cover with free hot water and there is a laundry room. Behind this are 5 places for caravans and 43 tenting pitches (12 suitable for motorcaravans but blocks useful) on gently sloping grass with a central, gravelled road leading to another more steeply sloping tenting field with fantastic views and room for ball games. A torch is necessary. This is very much a family concern and is ideally situated to enjoy the busy atmosphere of Padstow or to take the ferry to Rock and laze on the sandy beaches or learn to windsurf.

Directions: Park is signed right just before entering Padstow on the A389 road. Turn right at the next crossroads, following small Cornish lane to site. O.S.GR: SW916738.

Charges 1995:
-- Per pitch incl. 2 persons and car £6.85 - £9.60; hiker £3.55 - £4.55; extra adult £1.85 - £2.60; child (3-16 yrs) 95p - £1.35; extra car £1.80 - £2.00; dog 95p - £1.35; dinghy or large inflatable £1.30 - £1.90 or sailboard, canoes using foreshore and slipway 80p - £1.40; mooring £2.45 - £3.10.
-- VAT included.
Open:
Easter - 30 September.
Address:
Padstow, Cornwall PL28 8DR.
Tel:
(01841) 532349.
Reservations:
Made with £20 deposit and essential for caravans.

67

102 The Colliford Tavern Campsite, Bodmin Moor, nr. St. Neot

Small, quiet family run park in mid-Cornwall.

The main feature at Colliford is the tavern with five en-suite rooms to let, bar, dining room, etc, all attractively furnished and landscaped. Real ale is served and a range of home cooked food, including vegetarian dishes, is provided which seems to present good value. The camping area, however, has been kept very natural with the grass kept short by the rabbits and sheltered from the moor by tall pine woods. The main field provides 40 fairly level grass pitches (watch for rabbit holes), with 15 electric hook-ups (16A), backing on to the pine trees. The smaller, lower area is nearer to all the facilities therefore may not be so quiet. The modern, pine fitted toilet block is well equipped and carefully maintained with free hot water, baby room, unit for the disabled (no shower), laundry sink and spin dryer, 2 washing up sinks and a good chemical toilet facility. There is a separate reception area but no shop - the milkman carries basics. The park is next to Colliford Lake Park and, with easy access from the A30, it is ideally situated to visit the north or south coasts or for simply walking, fly fishing or birdwatching and relaxing in the bar at night.

Directions: Approaching on the A30 travelling south, pass the Jamaica Inn on the right and site is signed a further 1-1½ miles on the left. Follow for ½ mile and site is signed beside Colliford Lake Park. O.S.GR: SX168730.

Charges 1996:
-- Per unit incl. 1 adult £4.25 - £5.00, 2 adults £6.50 - £9.00; extra adult £2.00 - £2.50; child (2-14 yrs) £1.25 - £1.75; electricity £1.75; dog 50p.
-- Less 10% for bookings over 3 nights.
-- VAT included.
Open: Easter/1 April - 31 Oct.
Address: Colliford Lake, Bodmin Moor, nr. St. Neots, Liskeard, Cornwall PL14 6PZ.
Tel: (01208) 821335.
Reservations: Recommended for high season - contact park.

Small, secluded & family-run
COLLIFORD TAVERN
"An oasis on Bodmin Moor"
The perfect place to relax and ideal for exploring Cornwall.
Booking essential for high season

BROCHURE & ENQUIRIES:
(01208) 821335

 English Tourist Board COMMENDED   RAC
RAC ** INN   GRADED EXCELLENT

103 Southleigh Manor Naturist Holiday Club, St. Columb Major

Welcoming family naturist site in the mature grounds of a large house with pool.

For those who have ventured to try the naturist sites in our French guide and who also may appreciate that special ambience at home, we are happy to feature Southleigh. The respect that the naturist has for the environment and for fellow beings provides a very special, caring atmosphere and this can be truly experienced on this site. The 50 pitches have been developed in the south facing, sheltered, lawned garden and orchard with mature trees. There are 2 hard-standings and 34 electrical connections (5/10A). 8 touring vans to let. The purpose built toilet block has identical, well equipped, unisex units at each end, well maintained, with a laundry room in the middle. Small shop - bread, milk, papers and tourist information. A sun room and leisure suite including sauna, spa bath and exercise equipment, are in the house. The open air swimming pool is heated and therefore useable all season. Boules, croquet (in the walled garden), volleyball, minigolf and children's play area with tree house. You'll be encouraged to get involved with barbeques, social evenings and the opportunity to enjoy Cornwall's naturist beaches and many tourist attractions, which combine to provide a relaxed holiday atmosphere. Dogs permitted on leads.

Directions: From north A30 (Bodmin - Truro) road, after going under railway bridge, first right (A3059 St Mawgan/St Columb) and site is 3 miles. From A39, take A3059 at Newquay/St Columb roundabout. O.S.GR: SW904622.

Charges 1995:
-- Per unit £3.75 - £4.75; person £2.10 - £2.20; child (under 14) 95p - £1.15; awning £1.55 - £1.65; supplement for tents over 120 sq.ft. £1.55 - £1.65; extra pup tent £1.00; electricity £1.60; dog 90p.
-- Club membership £2.50 per couple/family.
-- VAT included.
Open: Easter/1 April - 30 Sept.
Address: St. Columb Major, Cornwall TR9 6HY.
Tel: (01637) 880938.
Reservations: Made with £25 deposit.

104 Lakefield Caravan Park, Camelford

Small working farm park where children can really become involved at feeding time.
With only 30 pitches, well spaced and in sight of the small lake and its feathered inhabitants, it is no wonder that the owners, Maureen and Dennis Perring, know all the campers, especially the children - particularly as the children's help is welcome both at morning and evening feed-ups. All the farm animals have names and respond to the children who help with bottle feeding and grooming. The rabbits, etc. are ideal for the little ones to handle. The pitches are all on level grass with 24 electric hook-ups (10A). The toilet block is clean and bright, providing the shelves, hooks, stools etc. which make life easier. The ladies' has lost two of its washbasins for a washing machine and dryer. Washing up sinks are outside, but under cover. Hot water is free except in showers where it is metered. The white-washed shop/reception, converted from one of the old farm barns and including a fascinating picture gallery, is open all day and all season which impressed us for such a small site and it provides all necessary basics. Half a dozen picnic tables dotted about the site, a children's play area on grass, a separate dog walking field (dogs accepted despite all the animals) and a pay phone complete the facilities. This is a park where you must not mind dirty feet - it is all part of the ambience - or the presence of Cornwall's first wind farm watching over the site. When the children tire of the animals there is a little boat for messing about on the lake (with a grown up in attendance), pony rides (50p) and the occasional sports day and a trampoline. After that, Tintagel, Boscastle, Bodmin Moor and the many beaches and coves of the north Cornwall coast wait to be explored.

Charges 1996:
-- Per unit incl. 2 adults £4.00 - £7.00, acc. to season; small hikers tent £4.00; extra adult or child 5 yrs or over 50p; dog, awning or extra car 50p; electricity £1.50.
Open:
1 April - 31 October.
Address:
Lower Pendavey Farm, Camelford, Cornwall PL32 9TX.
Tel:
Camelford (01840) 213279.
Reservations:
Made with £5 deposit per week.

Directions: Follow the B3266 north from Camelford. Park is accessed directly from this road on the left just before the turning for Tintagel. Park is clearly signed. O.S.GR: SX097852.

105 Budemeadows Touring Holiday Park, Poundstock, nr. Bude

Touring park with swimming pool, south of Bude, 1 mile from beach.
As this park is very close to the A39 through road, only about a mile from the sandy surfing beaches at Widemouth Bay and 3 miles from Bude with all its amenities, it is suitable both for holidays and also for overnight or short stays if there is space. It is pleasantly situated with some panoramic views and two extensive well kept meadows which are flat or slightly sloping. Some 100 units of any type are taken and there is plenty of room for these numbers. Pitches are marked and hedges have been planted and there are 52 electrical connections (10A) and 26 hardstandings. There is a heated swimming pool and toddlers pool with patio and grass sunbathing area. The pine toilet block is of good quality with free hot water in all the washbasins, good controllable showers and the 6 washing-up sinks under cover; 6 private cabins for ladies with basin and WC. There are 3 family shower units, a family bathroom, free of charge to disabled visitors and a baby bathing and changing room. Washing machine, dryer and iron. Shop (open Spr. B.H.-end Sept). Large adventure playground. Picnic tables and brick built barbeques provided. Mobile 'Catch a Snack' van calls evenings. Public phone. TV and games room with skittle alley, pool table, darts and board games. Large scale chess set and outdoor table tennis. Bicycle hire. Holiday chalet for rent. The owners live on site.

Charges 1995:
-- Per adult £3.30 - £4.50, acc. to season; child (5-14 yrs) £1.65 - £2.25; dog 40p - 80p; electricity £1.75.
-- Pitch and awning included.
-- VAT included.
Open:
All year.
Address:
Poundstock, Bude, Cornwall EX23 0NA.
Tel:
(01288) 361646.
Reservations:
Made with £20 deposit p/week.

Directions: Park entrance is from a layby to the east off the A39 road just north of a turning to Widemouth Bay. O.S.GR: SS216017.

106 Wooda Farm Caravan and Camping Park, Bude

Spacious, relaxed, family run farm park with views of sea and countryside.

This well organised and cared for park on a working farm is situated 1¾ miles from the sandy, surfing beaches of Bude, in peaceful farmland with plenty of open spaces. The 160 pitches, spread over 4 meadows, are on level or gently sloping grass, 100 with electricity (10A) and 24 fully serviced with hedging dividers, 5 with hardstanding. There are some holiday letting units beside the shop and reception at the entrance. Three well maintained toilet blocks with free hot water provide fully tiled showers with seat and hooks, washbasins in vanity style with hand dryer, 6 under cover washing up sinks (H&C), a unit suitable for the disabled and a baby room with small bath. Laundry with 2 washing machines, 2 tumbler dryers, sinks with metered water and iron and board.

A comprehensive range of facilities are provided from Spr. B.H. These include a self-service shop with off-licence (8.30-8.30 in main season) and licensed restaurant, with takeaway menu. There is a children's play area in a separate field on grass, with plenty of room for ball games, a 9 hole 'fun' golf course (clubs provided), and a woodland walk with added attractions for the children. There is also a small farm museum and friendly farm animals. Children (and adults) are also welcome to assist at feeding time! Pony rides, pony trekking, archery and clay pigeon shooting with tuition are provided according to season and demand. Coarse fishing is also available in a 1½ acre lake (permits from reception). Dogs are accepted (not certain breeds) with a large dog exercise field. Public phone. The local village inn is only 5 mins. walk. There is also much to do in the area - the Leisure Centre and Splash Pool in Bude itself, sandy beaches and coastal walks, Tintagel with King Arthur's Castle and Clovelly are nearby.

Directions: Park is north of Bude at Poughill; turn off A39 road on north side of Stratton on minor road for Coombe Valley, following camp signs at junctions. O.S.GR: SS225080.

Charges 1996:
-- Per unit incl. 2 persons £4.50 - £9.00; extra adult £1.00 - £1.50; child (3-16 yrs) 50p - £1.00; awning/pup tent £1.00 - £1.20; dog free - £1.00; electricity £1.70; fully serviced pitch (incl. electricity) plus £3.00 - £4.00.
-- VAT included.
-- Credit cards accepted.

Open:
Easter/1 April - 31 October.

Address:
Poughill, Bude, Cornwall EX23 9HJ

Tel:
(01288) 352069.
FAX: (01288) 355258.

Reservations:
Made with £20 deposit.

Alan Rogers' discount
Less 10% p/n outside July/Aug.

107 Easewell Farm Holiday Park, Mortehoe, nr. Woolacombe

Family run park on working sheep farm, with own golf course.

Easewell Farm is set in the rolling hills leading down to the sandy beaches of Woolacombe Bay. It is (despite its title) a more traditional touring park than its near neighbour Twitchen Park, with a friendly welcome from the resident owners. Unusually, it has the added attraction of its own 9-hole golf course (reduced fees for campers). There are lovely views across the headlands to the sea from the larger, sloping, more open field or more shelter in two smaller, lower fields, where pitches are marked on terraces. One back field offers 18 hardstandings, and of the total of 200 pitches, electricity (15A) is available on 80. A central sanitary block provides washbasins in rows, with mirror, shaver points, hairdryers, good, free hot showers and baby changing unit. The facilities are good but readers report a little lack of attention to maintenance and cleaning at peak times. Dishwashing sinks (H&C) are under cover outside and there is a launderette. Other amenities, arranged around the farmhouse, include a shop, takeaway food kitchen and an attractive bar which has been extended to provide a patio area overlooking a pond, a restaurant (open to the public) and an area for entertainment. Small, indoor, heated swimming pool (unsupervised) adjacent. All amenities open from Spr.B.H. Playground, games room and TV room. One dog per pitch is permitted with an exercise field provided. Good walks locally.

Directions: From Barnstaple, take A361 Ilfracombe road through Braunton. Turn left at Mullacott Cross roundabout on B3343 to Woolacombe, turning right after 2-3 miles to Mortehoe. Park is on right before the village. O.S.GR: SS465455.

Charges 1996:
-- Per caravan, incl. 4 persons, electricity and awning £8.50 - £13.50, acc. to season; tent incl. 4 persons £6.00 - £11.00; extra person £1.00; child (under 5 yrs) 50p; extra car £1.00; electricity £1.50; awning or extra pup tent free.
-- VAT included.
-- Credit cards accepted.
Open:
Easter - 31 October.
Address:
Mortehoe, Woolacombe N. Devon EX34 7EH.
Tel:
Woolacombe (01271) 870225.
Reservations:
Made with £20 deposit per week booked.

108 Twitchen Park, Mortehoe, nr. Woolacombe

Holiday park with areas for tourers and tents, with extensive family entertainment programme.

Set in the grounds of an attractive Edwardian country house, Twitchen Park's main concern lies in holiday caravans and flats. However it also provides some 50 marked pitches for tourers and sloping fields for all types of unit. These are at the top of the park, with some views over the rolling hills to the sea. The formal touring pitches, all with hardstanding and electricity, are arranged around an oval access road in a hedged area. Behind are the two rather open, unmarked fields and a further rally field. These fields are sloping but blocks are thoughtfully provided (stored in neat wooden boxes next to the water points); 27 electrical connections (15A). There are two sanitary blocks of a fair standard. Built on a sloping field, the larger block is of an unusual design with different levels and rather narrow corridors. It provides free, pre-set, hot showers (rather small), washbasins in rows and WCs. The smaller block has just washbasins and toilets. Baby changing unit. Dishwashing facilities are under cover outside each block with laundry facilities in each also, plus a good modern launderette at the central complex. The touring areas are cared for by helpful wardens who keep the blocks very clean. American motorhomes accepted (up to 30 ft.) A smart, modern entertainment complex incorporates a licensed club and family lounge with snacks, a restaurant, an adults only bar, a teenage disco room, and cartoon lounge, together with games rooms for table tennis, pool, snooker and arcade games. Entertainment is provided for both adults and children, during the day and in the evenings. Outside is a swimming pool (heated mid-May - mid-Sept) and paddling pool and free swimming lessons are offered in high season. Here too is a shop and takeaway food facilities. An excellent children's adventure play area (on bark), a putting green and a games field complete the facilities, which would make this park very popular for families with children. If they became bored, there are always the excellent beaches nearby! No dogs or pets are permitted.

Directions: From Barnstaple take A361 road towards Ilfracombe and through Braunton. Turn left at Mullacott Cross roundabout towards Woolacombe and then right towards Mortehoe. Park is on left before village. O.S.GR: SS466456.

Charges 1996:
-- Per touring pitch, incl. electricity, awning and up to 6 persons £8.25 - £16.00; tent pitch (no electricity available) £7.25 - £13.50; extra person 50p.
-- Reductions for stays of 7 or 14 days booked in advance.
-- VAT included.
-- Credit cards accepted.
Open:
1 April/Easter - end Oct.
Address:
Mortehoe, Woolacombe, N. Devon EX34 7ES.
Tel:
(01271) 870476.
FAX: (01271) 870498.
Reservations:
Made with £50 deposit for tourers, payment in full for tent pitches. Min. period at Easter, May Day B.H. 7 days days, Spr. B.H. 7 days and mid July and Aug, 7 days from Sat. to Sat.

109 Stowford Farm Meadows, Combe Martin, nr. Ilfracombe

Pleasant family run farm park set in North Devon meadow land.

Stowford Farm dates from the 15th century and is set in 450 acres of rolling countryside all of which is available for recreation and walking. This large touring park has been developed in the fields and farm buildings surrounding the attractive old farm house. There are 570 pitches on four slightly sloping meadows for all types of unit. They are unseparated but are all numbered and marked. Most have electrical connections (10A) and there are well placed water points. The four identical toilet blocks are kept clean and provide good, functional facilities with free hot water to the washbasins, which are in rows and set in flat surfaces, and to the dishwashing sinks. Showers are on payment. Each block has laundry facilities including irons and boards.

The old farm buildings have been converted into a well stocked shop (including holiday and camping accessories) and a takeaway service with a restaurant area. Limited in size by planning regulations, these facilities may be crowded in high season. The original stables have become the Old Stable Bars, refurbished recently to a high standard and entertainment in high season includes barn dances, discos, karaoke and other musical evenings. A barn houses a good, 70 x 30 ft. swimming pool (heated Easter - end-Sept) at a small charge (50p) and the park has its own riding stables. Other activities available include an 18-hole pitch and putt golf course, games room (with pool tables, table tennis and amusement machines), snooker room, crazy golf, bicycle hire, `kiddies kar' track and a large children's play area. Children will also be entertained by the under cover mini-zoo (Petorama) where they can handle many sorts of animals (on payment). Dogs are welcome in one section and there is a dog exercise area. Public phone and tourist information available at reception. American motor-homes are accepted (but not converted buses or coaches). Summer parking and winter storage available. During low season some facilities may not be available (eg. shop and pool close end Sept). Stowford Farm Meadows provides plenty to keep families occupied without leaving the park, but is also a friendly, countryside base for exploring the North Devon coast and Exmoor. The park has negotiated a series of discount offers for local attractions.

Charges 1995:
-- Per unit and car incl. up to 4 persons £3.95 - £8.85; extra person (over 5 yrs) free - £2.20; awning free - £2.10; extra car or small tent £1.50; dog 30p - 80p; electricity £1.00 - £1.50.
-- Reduced fees for over-50s in low/mid-season.
-- VAT included.
-- Credit cards accepted.

Open:
Easter - end October.

Address:
Combe Martin, Ilfracombe, N. Devon EX34 0PW.

Tel:
(01271) 882476.
FAX: (01271) 883053.

Reservations:
Any length, deposit £2 per night, £12 per week, £20 per fortnight. Balance due 28 days before arrival.

see advert in previous colour section also

Directions: From Barnstaple take the A39 towards Lynton. After 1 mile turn left onto the B3230. Turn right at garage onto A3123 and park is 1½ miles on the right. O.S.GR: SS560427.

110 Hidden Valley Touring and Camping Park, West Down, Ilfracombe

Delightful, small, family run park in countryside near Ilfracombe.

Aptly named, this award winning park has been carefully developed by the owners in keeping with its lovely setting. In the valley beside a small stream and lake (with ducks), it is most attractive and is also convenient for several resorts, beaches and the surrounding countryside. The original part of the park offers some 75 level pitches of good size on three sheltered terraces. All have hardstanding and 73 have electricity (16A) and free TV connections, with a water point between each pitch. Park rules require that ground sheets be positioned on hardened areas. Kingfisher Meadow, a little way from the main facilities and reached by an unsurfaced road, provides a further 60 pitches entirely on grass (so suitable for campers with tents) of which 50 have electrical connections. Two modern sanitary blocks, one in each part, are tiled and have non-slip floors. They provide free hot showers, washbasins, hand and hairdryers (free), WCs, baby changing room, laundry facilities including washing machine, dryer and iron, and dishwashing sinks under cover, plus an en-suite WC/shower for the disabled. These facilities are supplemented in the original area by extra neat 'portacabin' facilities.

There are good children's adventure play areas with wooden equipment and safe bark surface, a dog exercise field, a small shop with off license, takeaway and a lounge bar and restaurant serving a range of home cooked meals in attractive surroundings and also a games room. This is essentially a park for those seeking good quality facilities in very attractive, natural surroundings, without too many man-made distractions - apart from some slight traffic noise during the day time. It provides a really peaceful setting in beautiful surroundings.

Directions: Park is on the A361 Barnstaple - Ilfracombe road, 3½ miles after Braunton. O.S.GR: SS499408.

Charges 1995:
-- Per caravan, motorcaravan or trailer tent incl. up to 3 persons, all acc. to season £3.50 - £9.00; tent £3.50 - £8.00; extra adult 50p - £1.00; child (5-15 yrs) 50p; extra car/boat 50p - £1.00; dog free - £1.00; awning free - £1.25; electricity (16A) £1.50.
-- VAT included.
Open:
15 March - 5 November.
Address:
West Down, Ilfracombe, N. Devon EX34 8NU.
Tel:
(01271) 813837.
Reservations:
Accepted with £25 deposit.

see advert in previous colour section

111 Zeacombe House Caravan Park, East Anstey, nr. Tiverton

Delightful, smallish park on edge of Exmoor.

Zeacombe House is owned by Mr and Mrs Cumming but 'franchised' to the Caravan Club and run to club rules, however it very much has their stamp on it. In a beautiful, rural situation on the southern edge of Exmoor, the beech and leylandi hedging slightly restrict the views but give a sheltered, comfortable feel to the park. One large and one smaller field provide mostly level, neat grass pitches for 60 caravans or motorhomes and space for 5-6 tents. Electricity (15A) is available for 56, mainly around the edge and they are connected by a gravel roadway. Pitches are not allocated - the choice is made from those available. The toilet block is to one side, near the entrance and provides vanity style basins, plus one in a cubicle for ladies, and hot showers (20p, 4 in total), neat and clean when inspected. Fully equipped laundry room, free hot water to both laundry and washing up sinks (partly covered). Facilities for emptying motorhomes and for chemical toilets. The reception cum shop backs onto Mrs Cumming's kitchen from whence fresh bread rolls, scones and pasties emerge (delecious!) - in fact a range of hot meals are prepared (booked by 3 pm. for 6.30 - 8.30 pm. with a daily special) to take and eat in the caravan, which are excellent and good value. A wealth of local information is on hand and we were generally impressed with the help Mr and Mrs Cumming will provide on where to go and what to do. A small caravan and camping accessory shop could also be very useful.

Directions: Park is best approached from the A361 North Devon link road (exit 27 from the M5), 7 miles northwest of Tiverton, turning right signed Knowstone. Do not go into Knowstone but follow East Anstey signs and park is on left just before you reach the B3327 (the old A361). O.S.GR: SS862241.

Charges 1995:
-- Per unit incl. 2 persons £6.00 - £7.00; extra person £2.50 - £3.00; child £1.10; electricity £1.25 - £2.00, acc. to season.
Open:
March (2nd w/end) - 31 October.
Address:
Blackerton Cross, East Anstey, Tiverton, Devon EX16 9JU.
Tel:
(01398) 341279.
FAX: as phone.
Reservations:
Contact park.

112 Greenacres Touring Caravan Park, Bratton Fleming, nr. Barnstaple

Newly developed, neat, quiet, small park on edge of Exmoor.

Now in its third season, Greenacres has been purpose designed as a diversification from the farm, which is operated separately. Drive through the farmyard to the park (clearly signed), but you need to go back and call at the farm to book in - as yet there is no separate reception. There are 30 good sized pitches, well drained, with connecting gravel paths to the road. In theory you can get to your van, tent or awning without stepping on the grass; 18 electric hook- ups (16A). The top side is level with some views, the lower part is next to beech woods. semi-terraced to provide 5 hardstandings and 3 newly hedged places. The toilet block, in the centre of the semi-horseshoe layout of pitches, is well designed. It has vanity style basins with plenty of room, showers (20p) and an en-suite room for the disabled which doubles as a baby room. Laundry room, with spin dryer, iron and board, and dishwashing room, both with free hot water. Chemical toilet disposal. An area for children with net and swings is separated by a Devon bank from the 2 acre dog field. West of Exmoor, the park is suitable for the coast at Ilfracombe and Combe Martin, or for exploring the moor.

Directions: From North Devon link road (M5 exit 27) turn north onto A399 at South Molton for 9-10 miles past sign to Exmoor Steam Centre. Left at Stowford Cross towards Exmoor Bird Gardens. Park is on left. O.S.GR: SS658403.

Charges 1995:
-- Per car and caravan, incl. 2 persons £3.50 - £6.00; motorcaravan £3.50 - £5.50; extra person £50p - £1.00; child (under 5 yrs) free; awning free - £1.00; dog free; electricity £1.50.
-- VAT included.
Open:
1 April - end October.
Address:
Bratton Fleming, Barnstaple, Devon EX31 4SG.
Tel:
(01598) 763334.
Reservations:
Contact park.

113 Minehead and Exmoor Caravan Park, Minehead

Attractive small park, close to Minehead and Exmoor.

Very conveniently situated in a rural setting on the edge of Exmoor, yet only a mile from the resort of Minehead, this is a small, family run park providing some 50 level pitches of reasonable size, 32 of which have electricity. The park is arranged in four small bays, separated by mature trees and hedges and terraced down to a small stream, each with around 8 pitches, and one slightly larger field. Apart from being very attractive the hedges and trees help to screen the site from the main road running past the entrance, although some traffic noise is still evident - apparently the traffic dies down during the evening, so should not present a serious problem. There are few facilities on the park but it is close to the town with shops, restaurant and a pool within 1 mile. The sanitary facilities, in one main block, are good with hot showers (20p payment), washbasins with H&C, hand-dryers, dishwashing under cover (20p) and facilities for the disabled.

Directions: Park is by the A39 Minehead-Porlock road. 1 mile west of the town. O.S.GR: SS950457.

Charges 1996:
-- Per adult £4.00; child (over 3 yrs) £2.00; awning £1.00; electricity £1.50.
Open:
1 March - 31 October.
Address:
Porlock Road, Minehead, Somerset TA24 8SN.
Tel:
(01643) 703074.
Reservations:
Made for any length, details with SAE.

114 Blue Anchor Park, Blue Anchor, nr. Minehead

Beachside site, for caravans and motorcaravans only, with views across the Bristol Channel.

Although mainly a holiday park, with a large number of caravan holiday homes, Blue Anchor nevertheless offers good facilities for tourers (no tents), providing 103 level touring pitches. All have 16A electricity and are virtually in a separate touring area. Facilities on the park include a good size indoor swimming pool, crazy golf, a small supermarket/shop and an excellent and attractive children's play area. Its situation, directly across the small road from the beach, is unusual and gives some beautiful views across the Bristol Channel to South Wales. Dunster Castle, Exmoor, Minehead and the West Somerset Steam Railway are close. Sanitary facilities include large, free hot showers with push-button, vanity style washbasins and two launderettes, in a single, modern block serving just the touring area. There are both restaurants and takeaway food facilities within easy walking distance. No dogs are accepted. American motorhomes accepted (max. 36 ft). Part of the Hoburne group.

Directions: From M5 junction 25, take A358 signed Minehead. After approx. 12 miles turn left onto A39 at Williton. After 4 miles turn right onto B3191 at Carhampton signed Blue Anchor. Park is 1½ miles on right. O.S.GR: ST025434.

Charges 1996:
-- Per unit, incl. up to 6 persons, electricity and awning £6.25 - £12.50; extra person 50p; extra pup tent £1.50.
-- Credit cards accepted.
Open:
25 February - 28 Oct.
Address:
Minehead TA24 6JT.
Tel:
(01643) 821360.
FAX: (01643) 821572.
Reservations:
Contact park.

see advertisement on inside back cover

115 The Isle of Avalon Touring Caravan Park, Glastonbury

Well planned, modern park with excellent facilities, 10 mins walk from centre of Glastonbury.

The design and layout of this park compares very favourably with top European sites and we are quite impressed. Developed on flat, grassy ground, the park has been landscaped to provide 70 individual pitches, well spaced out and connected by hard roads. They have hardstanding with adjacent grass for awning and electrical points. A further 50 tenting spaces are on the adjoining, level field. Water and refuse points are well spaced around and attractively surrounded by trees and shrubs. All units are personally seen to their pitches. A single, excellent, tiled toilet block is purpose built and designed to avoid condensation. It provides large, controllable hot showers, basins in cubicles for women and excellent units for the disabled (plus ramps to the shop and reception). It is a good provision, well maintained. Large laundry room and dishwashing area. Chemical toilet and motorcaravan disposal point. American motorhomes are welcome. A well stocked shop and reception with tourist information has been built at the entrance with a well cared for, attractive and spacious feel with beautiful hanging baskets. There is generally a friendly, welcoming atmosphere. The top area of the tenting field is left clear as a playing field for children and parents. Glastonbury centre (including a good fish and chip shop) and Abbey are ½ mile walk, and there are indoor and outdoor swimming pools within 2 miles. Millfield School with its summer activity programme is close. The nearby town of Street is famous for its shoes and 'Clarke's Village' development with 22 factory outlets for well known high street names.

Charges 1995:
-- Per unit £4.30 - £5.30; hiker or car with small tent £3.10 - £4.10; adult £1.60; child (3-14 yrs) £1.10; awning or small tent £1.30; electricity £1.60; dog 50p; extra car 60p.
-- VAT included.
Open:
All year.
Address:
Godney Road,
Glastonbury, Somerset
BA6 9AF.
Tel:
Glastonbury (01458)
833618.
Reservations:
Any length with £5 deposit.

Directions: Park is on west side of town in Godney Road off the B3151. O.S.GR: ST495397.

The Isle of Avalon Touring Caravan Park

Godney Road, Glastonbury, Somerset. BA6 9AF.
Please Write or Telephone for Brochure (Tel: 01458 833618)

The Park, which is open all year round, offers a modern architecturally designed service building, with a high standard of cleanliness. All individual level placements have a hard standing, grass area and electric hook-up facility, with provision for tenting on an all grass area. For Guests' convenience, there is also a well stocked shop with off licence and Reception Office with useful information for touring the area.

Located in the heart of Somerset, this Family run Park within sight of the 520 Foot Tor, is 15 minutes walk from the unique historic town of Glastonbury and famous Abbey Ruins. An ideal base for "Discovering Somerset" — We look forward to meeting you.

ANWB (Dutch)
ADAC (German)

RAC
APPOINTED

AA

English and West Country Tourist Board Members

SOMERSET

116 Mendip Heights Camping and Caravan Park, Priddy, nr. Wells

Peaceful, family run park in an area of outstanding natural beauty.

Situated a mile from the village of Priddy in open country among the Mendip Hills, this park caters mainly for families and couples seeking peace and quiet. Priddy is strategically placed for exploring this part of Somerset, with Wells, Wookey Hole, Cheddar, Glastonbury, Bath, Bristol and Weston-super-Mare all within 20 miles. The site has 90 pitches, some with electrical connections and a few hardstandings, situated in two slightly sloping fields bordered by trees. The sanitary block is well equipped, with hot showers (on payment), washbasins, razor points, hairdryers for ladies, dishwashing facilities and a laundry room with washing machine, dryer and ironing facilities. The building itself is utilitarian rather than luxurious but was very clean when inspected in early September. There is a well stocked site shop (open all season) selling groceries, calor/camping gaz, etc. and an off-licence (no bar - three pubs in the village). There are no on-site activities but free guided walks are provided via the Mendip Hill Rangers and outdoor activities, such as canoeing, caving, mountain biking, etc. can be arranged from the site.

Charges 1995:
-- Per adult £2.95; child (3-15 yrs) £1.50; electricity £1.50.
-- No charge for awning or dog.
Open:
1 April -- 31 October.
Address:
Townsend, Priddy, nr. Wells, Somerset BA5 3BP.
Tel:
Wells (01749) 870241.
Reservations:
Made with £5 deposit.

Directions: From the M5 use exit 21 for Weston-super-Mare and take A371 to Banwell. Turn left along A368 to B3134, turn right along B3134 to B3135 and turn right; after 2 miles turn left at camp sign. From the M4 westbound leave at exit 18 and follow A46 to Bath, then A4 towards Bristol. Take A39 for Wells and turn right at Green Ore traffic lights along the B3135; after 5 miles turn left at camp sign. From Shepton Mallet, follow A37 north to junction of B3135 and turn left. Continue along B3135 to traffic lights at Green Ore. Continue straight on and after 5 miles turn left at camp sign. O.S.GR: ST522518.

117 Quantock Orchard Caravan Park, Crowcombe, nr. Williton

Small, attractive park with heated pool, in rural setting.

Nestling at the foot of the Quantocks, this small but friendly park is located in quiet countryside, close to the many attractions of this area. The hills and Crowcombe station on the West Somerset Steam Railway are a short walk and the Brendon and Exmoor hills, Minehead, Dunster Castle and Taunton are all within 10-15 miles. The park, managed by the owners Mr and Mrs Biggs, comprises two gently sloping fields with surrounding mature hedgerows. Old apple trees, recently planted trees and shrubs and flower beds form an attractive mix. Pitches for 50 touring caravans and 20 tents are of variable size, either side of gravelled access roads. There are 20 hardstandings and 55 electrical points, including 2 fully serviced pitches. Picnic tables are provided in the central space with an open barbecue.

The single, clean, insulated, heated sanitary block is of the pine and tile type. Hot water is free to washbasins (3 in cabins for ladies); controllable showers, with good screens, are free. Other facilities include a large, well equipped family bathroom, dishwashing room with microwave, laundry and mother and baby room. The park does offers a games room, Sky TV and a good, safe based children's play area (closed 9 pm.), although there is not much space on the park for children to run around. Heated swimming pool, walled and with paved sunbathing area (40 x 20 ft. open May-Sept) - children must be accompanied by an adult. Mountain bike hire. Visiting fish and chip van (twice weekly in summer). Well stocked shop with tourist information also. Caravan storage.

Charges 1995:
-- Per unit incl. 2 adults and children under 3 yrs £6.90 - £9.25; medium or small tent £6.90 - £8.00; extra adult £1.80; child 3-5 yrs 65p, 5-16 yrs £1.25; children's pup tent with caravan £1.00; electricity £1.65 - £1.80; backpacker or cyclist £3.30 - £4.40 per person.
-- Winter weekend special rates.
-- VAT included.
Open:
All year.
Address:
Flaxpool, Crowcombe, Taunton, Somerset TA4 4AW.
Tel:
Crowcombe (01984) 618618.
Reservations:
Made with £10 per week deposit, per booking

Directions: Park is west off A358 road (Taunton - Minehead), about 1 mile south of Crowcombe village. O.S.GR: ST140363.

118 Broadway House Holiday Caravan and Camping Park, Cheddar

Family owned park with some holiday caravans and activities for all ages, beside Cheddar Gorge.
An interesting and individual park offering a range of facilities on continental lines, Broadway has been developed by the family owners with T.L.C. over a period of 30 years. On a gently sloping area at the foot of the Mendips, the park takes 250 touring units of all types. From the entrance, after the neat caravan holiday home area, a series of touring areas graduates upwards, culminating in a tent and overflow rally field. The central access avenue is lined by trees with the groups of pitches on either side marked by ranch style fencing and landscaped with trees and shrubs and interesting `bygones'. There are 150 pitches with electrical connections and 10 with water and drainage. The main, gently sloping tent field is clearly marked out near the pool.
The large, purpose built, tiled toilet block at the start of the touring area has a good provision of showers, with seat and hooks, vanity style washbasins and some private cabins. Extra facilities, newly refurbished with bathroom (coin operated) and a unit for the disabled are available near reception, and a `portaloo' unit in the top tenting field. Facilities include a babies room, coin operated hairdryers, washing up sinks and a new, well equipped launderette. There is a heated pool (60 x 25 ft.) and children's pool (Easter - early Oct.) with grass sun-bathing area and shade from silver birches, but a sun bed is also available! The range of activities now organised from the park includes abseiling, canoeing, hill-walking, archery, shooting, caving, mountain biking (these are also available for hire), windsurfing can be arranged and there is a dry ski slope nearby. On site is an adventure playground, football field, indoor table tennis, barbecue area, target golf, boules pitch, skateboard ramp, croquet, games/ amusements room, family room and large screen TV and tourist information room. There is a dog exercise field and two animal enclosures with a variety of interesting animals and `Sonny' the parrot may talk to you. There is also a shop with an extensive range of goods and a bar/lounge (open Easter, May Day, then Whitsun - end-Sept). Motorcaravan service point. This is really a park to be experienced - there is always something to see from the moment you turn in the gates. Everything is well signposted.

Charges 1995:
-- Per adult £2.00 -
£3.00; child (3-14 yrs)
50p - £1.50; pitch free -
£4.00, acc. to season
and unit; premier pitch
(incl. 3 services) £2.00;
electricity £1.50;
awning, pup tent or
extra car free - £1.00;
dog 50p.
-- Special discounts for
O.A.P.s.
-- VAT included.
-- Credit cards accepted
with 5% charge.
Open:
1 March - 30 November.
Address:
Cheddar, Somerset
BS27 3DB.
Tel:
Cheddar (01934)
742610.
Reservations:
Advisable in high
season, with £3 deposit
per night. Sat. - Sat.
preferred for Spr. B.H.
and 20/7-31/8 and
essential for electric
pitches.

Directions: Park entrance is very close to junction of A371 and B3135 on northwest side of Cheddar. O.S.GR: ST449547.

VOTED
CAMPSITE OF
THE YEAR SW
ENGLAND 1990/91

QUANTOCK ORCHARD CARAVAN PARK
in the beautiful Quantock hills
The small, clean and friendly Park for Touring Caravans & Camping
Situated at the foot of the glorious Quantock hills, this small family-run Park is close to Exmoor
and the coast in the perfect location for touring Somerset and North Devon.
Our full range of facilities include:
Immaculate timber and tiled washing facilities and showers (AA award winners for cleanliness 1990, 93, 94, 95)
Large en-suite bathroom - Full laundry facilities - Dishwashing room with microwave (free use) - Beautiful heated swimming pool
Good children's play area - Games room/TV - level individual pitches, most with hook-up, some on hardstanding
Tastefully landscaped - plenty of flowers - level tent paddock
Quality without quantity - in a designated area of outstanding natural beauty
Dogs welcome on leads. Riding. Fishing. Steam Railway. Good Pub Food - all nearby. OPEN ALL YEAR
Send s.a.e. for colour brochure and price guide to
Mr & Mrs E C Biggs
QUANTOCK ORCHARD CARAVAN PARK, Crowcombe, Taunton, Somerset TA4 4AW
Tel: (01984) 618618

AND CAMPING
AND WALKING
MAGAZINE

AA

119 Southfork Caravan Park, Parrett Works, nr. Martock

Personally run park in pretty surroundings.

Don't be put off by the address, you will not find Dallas characters or an industrial site. Mr and Mrs Metcalfe own and run this excellent, modern, but small site (30 pitches on grass with gravel access road, 18 with electricity hook-ups) just outside the lovely village of Martock. This orderly, quiet park is on 2 acres of flat, tree lined meadow situated by the River Parrett - fishing licences available. All the expected facilities are close to the entrance. Most things are available, including an RAC approved Caravan Repair Centre (not open Xmas and New Year). The heated toilet block has free hot water to basins and showers. Laundry room. Children's play area. Shop with off licence. Despite the rural setting, the A303 trunk road is just ten minutes away. This area of South Somerset contains so much of interest, including historic houses and sites, the Fleet Air Arm Museum and Cricket St Thomas Country Park. As the owners live on the premises, the well drained park is open all year. Two caravans for hire. Dogs must be on leads, with a walk provided.

Directions: From the A303 between Ilchester and Ilminster take signs for South Petherton and Martock; signs for the park are on the road between the two villages. O.S.GR: ST447187.

Charges 1995:
-- Per unit inc. 2 persons £7.00; extra person £1.00, child under 5 free; awning £1.00; dog 50p; electricity £1.50.
Open:
All year.
Address:
Parrett Works, Martock. TA12 6AE.
Tel:
(01935) 825661.
FAX: (01935) 825122.
Reservations:
Advisable for B.Hs. and peak season and made with deposit.

120 Newbridge Caravan Park, Bath

Good, purpose-designed touring park for caravans and motorhomes only.

Ownership of this 4 acre park has passed from Bath City Council to the Marina on the adjacent River Avon and it has been much improved and updated. Efficiently and attractively laid out with concrete hardstandings, only caravans and motorcaravans are taken (no tents) and all 88 pitches have electricity (16A). These are well spaced out in a regular way with made-up access roads and the whole park has a neat appearance with many shrubs and trees planted. Awnings or child's tents are possible beside some pitches. However, not all the hardstandings in the newly developed area will hold a car as well as a caravan so, when necessary, extra hardstanding is allocated. The two heated toilet blocks, with free hot water in basins and showers, provide an ample supply, with vanity units in individual washing cubicles. Unit for the disabled. Plenty of dustbin and water tap units. Laundry room. Shop. Public phone (card type - buy on site). Shops nearby and children's play park next door. `Park and Ride' bus to city centre on opposite side of road. This is a very useful park for summer and winter with all the facilities of Bath (and Bristol) nearby. For the active there is now a cycleway along the old railway line to Bristol.

Directions: Park is within Bath city limits, north of the Avon just off A4 Bath - Bristol road, about 1½ miles from city centre. Best approach is from direction of Bristol on A4 to city limits, where park is signed. O.S.GR: ST720655.

Charges 1996:
-- Per pitch £6.50; adult £1.75; child 75p; electricity £1.50; awning £1.50; extra car £1.00; dog 50p.
-- Special winter rate £9.50 all inclusive.
-- VAT included.
Open:
All year.
Address:
Brassmill Lane, Bath, Avon BA1 3JT.
Tel:
Bath (01225) 428778.
Reservations:
Any length with one nights fee as deposit (non-returnable).

121 Piccadilly Caravan Park, Lacock, Chippenham

Attractive, small, quiet park, family owned and run.

Piccadilly is set in open countryside close to several attractions in northern Wessex, notably Longleat, Bath, Salisbury Plain, Stourhead, and Lacock itself. The park is neat and tidy and the landscaped shrubs and trees are beginning to mature, giving the impression of three separate areas. There are 43 well spaced, clearly marked pitches, 11 of which have hardstanding. Electrical connections (10A) are available on 34 pitches. The one toilet block is exceptionally well maintained with free controllable hot showers in large cubicles, with excellent drop seat, and washbasins with ample shelving, hooks and mirrors; one shaving socket. It should be adequate in size for peak period use. Dishwashing area within the block with 4 sinks. Laundry room. Public phone. Dog exercise walks from park. Limited Calor and Gaz supplies. Papers and milk can be ordered. No other on-site facilities save a small, bark-based children's playground and large, grassed ball play area. Bus service from Lacock village to Chippenham.

Charges 1996:
-- Per pitch £7.00;
electricity £1.50.
-- VAT included.
Open:
April (or Easter) -
October.
Address:
Lacock, Chippenham,
Wiltshire SN15 2LP.
Tel:
Lacock (01249)
730260.
Reservations:
Any length; deposit of
1 nights fee.

Directions: Park is signed west off A350 Chippenham-Melksham road (turn to Gastard) by Lacock village. 300 yds. to park. O.S.GR: ST911682.

122 Alderbury Caravan and Camping Park, Whaddon, nr. Salisbury

New touring park, convenient for visiting Salisbury and the New Forest.

Located at one end of Alderbury/Whaddon village, this newly developed park is on level ground, with a gravel access road to the 40 numbered pitches; 18 have access to electricity (10A). The park has some mature trees for shade, plus younger trees, shrubs and flowers. The park is not lit so torches would be useful. The centrally located toilet block is practical, clean and well maintained. It provides hot showers in cubicles with curtain and seat, washbasins set in vanity units, WCs, a separate unit for the disabled and a dishwashing sink also in a separate room. Hot water is free throughout. Water taps are evenly distributed around the park, and there is a chemical disposal point. The village shop and post office, a pub serving meals, public phone and a bus stop (hourly services to Salisbury, Southampton and Romsey) are within easy level walking distance of the entrance. Some road noise, most noticeable at the far end of the park.

Charges 1995:
-- Per unit incl. 2 adults
£6.50; extra adult £2.00;
child (under 14 yrs)
£1.00; awning £1.00;
electricity £1.50.
-- VAT included.
Open:
All year.
Address:
Southampton Road,
Whaddon, Salisbury,
Wiltshire SP5 3HB.
Tel:
Salisbury (01722)
710125.
Reservations:
Write or phone park for
details.

Directions: From Salisbury take A36 towards Southampton and after 3 miles (at far end of dual carriageway), turn left to Alderbury and Whaddon, right, over bridge, and left for park entrance. From Southampton on A36 towards Salisbury, go past A27 (Romsey) junction and over Pepperbox Hill. At end of downhill straight, left on slip road marked Alderbury, park is signed. O.S.GR: SU198263.

123 Oxford Camping International, Oxford

Modern touring park on outskirts of city.

Just off the ring road, close to residential streets, this site is opposite a `park and ride' car park with a good bus service to the city centre 1½ miles away. Obviously, because of its position, the site also attracts backpackers and cyclists from many countries and can be very busy. Some road and rail noise. It has about 100 numbered pitches on flat grass either side of a peripheral access road, plus room for 30 tents. Over 80 electrical connections (10A). The modern, central toilet block is of good size; washbasins with shelf, mirror, hot showers on payment (20p); free hair dryers. Laundry room. Licensed shop. Dishwashing sinks (H&C). Telephone and post box. Within walking distance are a pub serving hot meals and a range of shops. Gates closed 11 pm. (parking outside).

Charges 1996:
-- Per unit incl. 2 adults
£7.60; ridge tent £2.50,
plus car £1.75; adult
£1.50; child (under 14
yrs) 85p; electricity
(10A) £1.90.
-- VAT included.
-- Credit cards accepted.
Open:
All year.
Address:
426 Abingdon Road,
Oxford OX1 4XN.
Tel:
Oxford (01865) 246551
FAX: (01865) 240145.
Reservations:
Not normally necessary
but may be accepted
with £5 deposit.

Directions: Park is behind Touchwood Camping shop - look for the Murco sign on petrol station forecourt (12 ft. wide entrance). Best approach from southern ring road (site is signed). From east, leave ring road at A4144 junction, toward city; first left and park is on right after 50 m. From other directions take A34 to junction with southern ring road, turn onto the latter, then first left and camp is on left just before junction with A4144, well signed. O.S.GR: SP518038.

124 Lincoln Farm Park, Standlake, nr. Witney

Attractive, family run park with indoor pool, in quiet sheltered rural location.

Set amongst semi-mature trees in the pretty Oxfordshire village of Standlake, this park has been attractively landscaped taking 61 units in two flat, hedged, grass fields, both with illuminated, gravelled perimeter access roadways. Neat and tidy, all pitches are marked and of good size, 51 have electricity (10A) and there are 5 hedged, grass super pitches with gravel area for awnings and satellite TV connections also. Four new ones with full hardstanding have been added with the facility for sewage disposal. There are also a few hardstanding pitches with electricity suitable for motorhomes (Note: only environmentally friendly groundsheets allowed). The park is part of the Caravan Club's 'managed under contract' scheme, but all visitors are made very welcome, and it is a member of the Best of British group. The pine clad toilet block is a little compact but clean and well appointed with free hot water to washbasins (2 cabins and 2 free standing), showers and good outside, but covered, dishwashing sinks. The controllable showers are in small rooms with curtained screen, stool, hooks, rack, mirror and, for the ladies, a small washbasin. Laundry room. Baby room. Amenities include a small shop with basic supplies (all season), public telephone, putting green, children's playground (bark chipping base) and, in the tenting field, a campers kitchen. In addition, the park has an indoor leisure centre comprising a heated pool (30 x 15 ft.), spa pool and sauna developed in an old barn at the rear of reception. This can be used either during open sessions (£1.50 per adult, 75p per child) or by private hire (£2.50 per adult, £1.00 all children, with min. £10 per hour). Post Office and pub/restaurants 300 yds. Oxford and the Cotswolds are close.

Charges 1996:
-- Per unit incl. 2 persons £9.50 - £11.00, plus 2 children £11.50 - £13.50; extra adult £2.00; child (5-16 yrs) £1.00; full awning (no groundsheets) £1.00, porch awning 50p; electricity (10A) £2.00; super pitch (excl. electricity) £4.00; dog 50p; extra pup tent, car, day visitor £1.00.
-- Special B.H. and low season offers.
-- VAT included.
-- Credit cards accepted.
Open:
1 March - 30 October.
Address:
High Street, Standlake, nr. Witney, Oxon OX8 7RH.
Tel:
Oxford (01865) 300239.
Reservations:
Made with £10 non-returnable deposit.

Directions: Take the A415 Witney-Abingdon road and turn into Standlake High Street by garage; park is 300 yds on the right. O.S.GR: SP396029.

125 Cotswold View Caravan and Camping Site, Charlbury

Family run site in rural location with good facilities.

Cotswold View is an interesting example of successful farm diversification providing a spacious, purpose designed site side-by-side with a small working farm of 54 acres (7 are set aside for the site). Visitors are welcome to meet the animals (ask for Simon and observe Rabbit City and its occupants), book a meal at the farm kitchen (also takeaways) and use the newly developed forest or farm trails on the farm land or local bridleways and footpaths.

Hedges and trees have grown to give the camping area a more mature, green look and wide, gravelled or tarmac roadways give easy access to 90 level, grassy pitches on a gently sloping site. At present this allows for 64 caravans and 26 tents, with 75 electrical connections (10A). Good provision of water taps and waste disposal points. The single, tiled toilet block has been purpose built from Cotswold stone providing (plus music!) a complete separate unit for the disabled, showers with curtain and stool, 4 basins in cabins, 2 in the open, shaver points, long mirror, H&C water and a bath (50p). Vegetable preparation room and dishwashing under cover (free hot water). Laundry room and freezer for ice packs. The small reception block doubles as a shop providing all basic provisions and off licence and if not manned, is accessible by bell. Good central play area on grass hidden by trees. Dog walks. Hard tennis court. Bicycle hire. Tourist information room. American motorhomes accepted if booked in advance. A well run park, ideal for exploring the Cotswolds area, Oxford and Stratford on Avon, with a warm welcome from the owners. B&B available at the farm and self catering farm bungalows (with facilities for disabled). Farmhouse meals may be booked in advance - menu at the shop, even breakfast if booked the night before.

Charges 1995:
-- Per unit incl. 2 persons £8.50 - £9.50; extra adult £1.75; child (5-16 yrs) £1.00; electricity £1.75.
-- VAT included.
Open:
Easter/1 April - 31 October.
Address:
Enstone Road, Charlbury, Oxon OX7 3JH.
Tel:
(01608) 810314.
Reservations:
Advisable for B.H.s and peak season.

Directions: From A44 Oxford - Stratford-on-Avon road, take the B4022 road to Charlbury, just south of Enstone. Park is 2 miles on left. O.S.GR: SP365210.

126 Diamond Farm Camping Park, Bletchingdon, Oxford

Small park with swimming pool, near Oxford.

This little park, set in countryside 8 miles north of Oxford, takes 37 units of any type on a flat, hedged field with pitches marked by sections of fencing. Most go around the perimeter and there are 26 electric hook ups (10A). The park is made all the more pleasant by the profusion of shrubs and flower baskets in and around the old farm buildings and the variety of trees and greenery planted. The small toilet block is of good quality and provides free hot water in individual basins with shelf and mirror, plus one private cabin for each sex, also in the nearby showers (4) and in outside washing-up sinks. Family bathroom with metered water. Laundry facilities. There is a small, deep, heated pool (40 x 20 ft.) open 9 am. - 7.30 pm. (1/5-15/9). Shop (1/4-30/9). Licensed bar (1/4-30/9) with full-sized billiards table (adults only), TV room and games room. Bar food is provided in the main season (1/6-31/8). An extra top field provides a children's play area with surrounding cycle track.

Directions: Park is on west of B4027 road 1 mile north of the A34 (Bicester - Oxford) road, just south of Bletchingdon. From the M40 use exit 9 and follow A34 in Oxford direction. O.S.GR: SP514168.

**Alan Rogers'
discount**
Low season: stay
7 nights, pay for 6

Charges 1996:
-- Per unit incl. 2 persons £7.00 - £9.00, acc.to season (Nov, Dec, Jan and Feb £5.00); extra person over 3 yrs £1.00 - £1.50; full awning £1.00; extra car £1.50; dog (max. 2) free; electricity £2.00.
-- VAT included.
Open:
All year.
Address:
Bletchingdon, Oxford OX5 3DR.
Tel:
(01869) 350909.
Reservations:
Any length with £10 deposit (min 3 nights at B.Hs with £10 per night deposit).

127 Wellington Country Park, Riseley, nr. Reading

Quiet, wooded touring site in popular country park.

The Wellington Country Park itself is open to all on payment of an entry fee (entry for campers included in pitch fee) and many visit it for a day out. It contains a boating and fishing lake, a large adventure playground and other activities for children, nature trails, fitness course, crazy golf, narrow-gauge railway, animal farm and a dairy museum. Riding centre adjacent. Within the Park, the camping site has about 60 numbered pitches, in small groups in woodland clearings. 43 electrical connections. It is a pleasant, very shady setting though very quiet at night with no evening activities of any sort. Some camp lighting. The site often has space but has much weekend trade and for arrival after 5.30 p.m. advance arrangements are necessary because of a locked gate (£5 deposit for gate key). There is a late arrivals field without sanitation in a different area. We like this park and what it has to offer, apart from the sanitary block which is of older construction and only just satisfactory. It has free hot water in all facilities, 3 showers in each section are pre-set and only have a short run-on; one (adjustable) has a toilet en-suite. New dishwashing sinks (6) and a new small laundry. Small shop for basics, some mobile traders visit at weekends and high season. Public phones near reception and at the sanitary block.

Directions: Park is signed at Riseley, off A32/A33 road between Reading and Basingstoke, and from M4. It is about 4 miles south of M4 exit 11 and 7 miles north of M3 exit no. 5. O.S. GR: SU727628.

Charges 1995:
-- Per unit incl. up to 2 adults and 2 children £10.00 for Fri, Sat. & B.H. Suns; £9.00 other nights; extra adult £1.25; child 75p; pup tent 75p; electricity £1.75.
-- Fee includes fishing permit for ONE person.
-- VAT included.
-- Off peak discounts for elderly and disabled.
Open:
1 March -- 31 October.
Address:
Riseley, nr. Reading, Berks RG7 1SP.
Tel:
(01734) 326444.
FAX: (01734) 326445.
Reservations:
Any length (min 2 nights July/Aug), £10 deposit to Caravanning Site Office.

128 Chertsey Camping and Caravanning Club Site, Chertsey

Splendidly located site on banks of the River Thames.

This is an old-established site (1926), a flag ship of the club, which is only a few minutes walk from the shops and amenities of Chertsey. Lovely flower displays greet you as you drive in - an indication of a well cared for site. There are 200 pitches in total (for all types of unit), 98 with 10A electricity and 19 with hardstanding. They are either in open, field-like areas, beside the river creek or in little nooks and corners, which avoids the regularity of some sites. Mature trees and plants create a pretty site, with views across the water and towards Chertsey bridge, although unfortunately there is some road noise and, depending on flight paths, aircraft noise. The main toilet block is centrally situated next to the Recreation hall (table tennis and snooker table). The other is at the entrance in the same building as reception and the shop. They are well equipped with free hot water, washbasins in cabins, hairdryers and laundry and dishwashing rooms. Separate facilities are approached via a ramp for the disabled. Special area available to hang clothes out. Good, under cover tourist information area next to reception, again suitable for the disabled. Children's play area on bark. Short dog walk areas. Shop (basics only) open 8-11 am. and 4-6 pm. The rail station for London is at Chertsey or Weybridge. Fishing is possible (NRA licence needed).

Charges 1995:
-- Per adult £3.75 -
£4.30, acc. to season;
child £1.40 - £1.45;
non-member pitch fee
£3.00; non-member
backpacker £5.00 -
£5.50; electricity £1.70.
Open:
All year.
Address:
Bridge Road, Chertsey,
Surrey KT16 8JX.
Tel:
(01932) 562405.
(No calls after 8 pm.)
Reservations:
Made for min. 3 nights -
contact the wardens.

Directions: Suggested: from M25 use junction 11. Turn left at roundabout in the direction of Shepperton and continue to second set of traffic lights. Turn right and right again at Texaco garage, just before Chertsey bridge. Opening is narrow - watch for club sign. O.S.GR: TQ052667.

129 Horsley Camping and Caravanning Club Site, East Horsley

Pretty site with small lake and good facilities.

London and all the sights are only 40 minutes away by train but Horsley is a delightful, quiet unspoilt site with a good duck and goose population. It provides 135 pitches, of which 47 have 10A electrical connections; 13 are all weather pitches (of which 7 have electricity). 17 of the pitches are around the lake, the rest further back in three hedged, grass fields with mostly level ground but some slope in places. There is a range of mature trees and a woodland dog walk area. Two purpose built, heated toilet blocks, one part of the entrance building which includes reception. Fittings and design are good, with free hot water, well equipped showers, hairdryers, some washbasins in cabins, Belfast sink and parent and child room with vanity style basin and wide surface area. Well designed facilities for the disabled. Recreation hall with TV, table tennis and darts, sometimes used for bingo. Children's play area. Basic provisions are available from reception. Shops and the station are 1 mile, pubs 1½-2 miles. Fishing is possible (NRA licence required). Resident wardens will make you comfortable.

Charges 1995:
-- Per adult £3.15 -
£3.50; child £1.20 -
£1.35; non-member
pitch fee £3.00;
non-member backpacker
£4.35 - £4.75; electricity
£1.70.
Open:
27 March - 6 November
Address:
Ockham Road North,
East Horsley, Surrey
KT24 6PE.
Tel:
(01483) 283273.
Reservations:
Contact the wardens.

Directions: 2½-3 miles from M3 junction 10 in the direction of Guildford, take first left on B2039 to East Horsley passing through Ockham. Site is on right - watch carefully for club sign. O.S.GR: TQ083552.

For travel further afield remember the other titles in the **ALAN ROGERS'** series

GOOD CAMPS GUIDE - FRANCE and GOOD CAMPS GUIDE - EUROPE

Available by mail order from the publishers - phone 01308 897809

London Tourist Board

26 Grosvenor Gardens, Victoria, London SW1W 0DU
Tel: (0171) 7303450

1996 Events: Ideal Home Exhibition, 14 Mar-8 Apr: Boat Race, 6 April: Chelsea Flower Show, 21-24 May: Stella Artois Tennis Championships, 10-16 June: Wimbledon Lawn Tennis Championships, 26 June-7 July: Henley Royal Regatta, 3-7 July: City of London Flower Show, 10-11 Sept: Horse of the Year Show, 2-6 Oct. Military: Beating Retreat, 5-6 June; Trooping the Colour, 15 June; Royal Tournament, 9-20 July.

130 Abbey Wood Caravan and Camping Site, Abbey Wood

Quiet Caravan Club touring site in S.E. London; no statics or lettings.

This is one of the nearest sites to London and it becomes very full and crowded in the summer months with campers of many nationalities. Reservations are made for all except tents and are advisable for July/August and B.Hs. Tent campers, for whom there is one special meadow, with cars parked separately, must take their chance. Stays are limited to a maximum of 14 days (7 days in peak weeks). Although within a built-up area, this grassy site is in a quiet and pleasant setting with many mature trees. Most parts, especially those for caravans, are sloping but most of the 380 pitches are levelled. In one area pitches are a little cramped. The site is run by the Caravan Club and there are reductions for their members. The three toilet blocks, all heated in cool weather, have free hot water in the individual basins (with shelf and mirror), controllable showers and washing-up sinks. There is not much on-site activity but nearly all those staying here want to visit London. There is a train service every 15 minutes from Abbey Wood station (5 mins walk) to either Charing Cross or Cannon Street. The site shop is well stocked and prides itself on having fresh bread every single day, much of it in continental style. Children's playground with sand base. Dogs are allowed on leads if exercised off the park. There is a car park at the entrance with electrical connections for late arrivals (after 10.30 pm.).

Directions: Southeast of London and east of Woolwich, the site is signed from the A2 (Dover - London) road (A221 exit - Danson). Follow camping signs north for about 3 miles (towards Plumstead). From the A206 (Plumstead High Street - Bostall Hill) turn right (north) into Basildon Road, first right into Macleod Road, right at roundabout onto Knee Hill, second right into Federation Road. Site is on left after about 100 yds. O.S.GR: TQ472785.

Charges 1995:
-- Caravans: per pitch £4.00 - £6.50; person £3.20 - £3.50; child £1.20; electricity £2.00 - £1.25; extra car £1.00.
-- Per tent plus car £5.50, with m/cycle, cycle or walker £2.00.
-- VAT included.
-- Caravan Club members pay less.
Open:
All year.
Address:
Federation Road, Abbey Wood, London SE2 0LS.
Tel:
0181-310-2233 (0800-2000 hrs).
Reservations:
Essential for Easter, Spring B.H. July/Aug with £5 deposit.

BEST PLACED FOR LONDON

Lee Valley Park, offers you a unique choice of camping sites for all tastes featuring high standards, modern facilities and a warm welcome.

FOR FREE COLOUR BROCHURE
TEL: 01992 700766
Lee Valley Park, PO Box 88, Enfield, Middlesex EN2 9HG

LEE VALLEY PARK

Lee Valley Leisure Complex
Edmonton, London N9 Tel: 0181-345 6666
One of Britain's largest leisure centres.

Lee Valley Campsite
Sewardstone, Chingford Tel: 0181-529 5689
Close to the M25 and Epping Forest. A splendid location with a warm welcome. Shop and children's play area.

Lee Valley Cycle Circuit
Leyton, London E10 Tel: 0181-534 6085
A small site set in 40 acres of open parkland only 4 miles from the City of London.

Lee Valley Caravan Park
Dobbs Weir, Hoddesdon, Herts. Tel: 01992 462090
Delightful riverside site with good fishing and walking. Shopping facilities and boating nearby.

See Editorial Reports on next page

131 Lee Valley Caravan Park, Dobbs Weir, Hoddesdon

Pleasant park north of London in Lee Valley Park.

Lee Valley Park, administered by the Lee Valley Regional Park Authority, covers 10,000 acres, stretching for 23 miles along the Lee valley from Ware to the edge of the east end of London. The Park has been developed into a leisure area with a wide variety of sporting and outdoor pursuits, including watersports, riding, golf and places of interest. Lee Valley Caravan Park, under the same management as Lee Valley Campsite (no. 132), is in the far north of the complex between the urban conurbations of Hoddesdon, Broxbourne and Nazeing. Half the site is taken up by caravan holiday homes and is quite separate from the touring section which consists of a large, open, well mown meadow with room for 100 units. 36 numbered pitches have electricity (5A) and, although there is no shade in the camping area, the site is surrounded by tall trees. It has a neat, tidy and well cared for appearance with a single sanitary block of good quality with free hot water in the washbasins, showers and sinks. There is a baby room and a laundry with washing machines, dryers and iron and facilities for the disabled. A swimming pool is 3 miles away and fishing is possible near the site. There is no shop on site but a free bus service to a superstore is offered three times a week and a bar/restaurant is some 100 yds from the entrance. Trains run from Hoddesdon (about 2 miles) to London with the journey taking about 30 minutes. Dobbs Weir industrial estate and garden centres are near but screened out by surrounding trees.

Charges 1996:
-- Per adult £4.40; child (under 16 yrs) £1.80; electricity £1.70.
-- Min. charge £6.05 (but not backpackers).
-- VAT included.
-- Credit cards accepted.
Open:
W/end before Easter - 31 October.
Address:
Charlton Meadows, Essex Road, Dobbs Weir, Hoddesdon, Hertfordshire EN11 0AS.
Tel:
(01992) 462090.
Reservations:
Made with £5 deposit - write to park for reservation form.

Directions: Take the Hoddesdon exit from the A10, turn left at second roundabout following signs for Dobbs Weir and park is on the right within 1 mile. O.S.GR: TL383082.

See advertisement on previous page

132 Lee Valley Campsite, Chingford, North London

Well run park conveniently placed for visits to the London area.

With easy access from the M25, and central London up to 1 hour away by public transport, this site provides an excellent base for visits to the capital. Quietly situated in the heart of the Lee valley (with many leisure facilities available) and close to Epping Forest, it can take up to 200 units of any type. Ten pitches where electricity is available are in effect spaced out by the connections but otherwise campers are left to site themselves leaving 6 m. between units. There are 12 pitches with hardstanding and electrical connections near reception. The ground is generally flat, broken in some places by bushes. Reception is open 8 am.-10 pm. The three toilet blocks, recently refurbished, are of good quality and quite adequate with free hot water to the washbasins and fully controllable showers and a few washing-up sinks. Laundry room. Small shop. Children's playground. Public phone. No other on-site amenities, but those staying here are usually out visiting London. A local bus stops by the site at fairly frequent intervals in season, but there is a good service every 20 minutes to Walthamstow underground station from a stop 500 yds away, or you can park at South Woodford or Chingford stations and go by train.

Charges 1995:
-- Per adult £4.75; child (under 16 yrs) £2.00; electricity £1.70.
-- Min charge £6.75, no charge for pitch.
-- VAT included.
Open:
25 March - 28 October.
Address:
Sewardstone Road, Chingford, London E4 7RA.
Tel:
0181-529-5689.
Reservations:
Any length up to 14 days with £5 deposit.

Directions: From M25 take exit 26 (Waltham Abbey) from where site is signed; take A112 road towards Chingford and the site is about 3 miles on right. It can also be approached on A112 from the North Circular Road. O.S.GR: TQ378970.

East Anglian Tourist Board

Toppesfield Hall, Hadleigh, Suffolk IP7 5DM
Tel: (01473) 822922

Norfolk, Suffolk, Cambridgeshire, Essex, Hertfordshire and Bedfordshire

This is a fascinating region which includes the Broads, the Isle of Ely,
Cambridge and Southend-on-Sea.

133 The Grange Country Park, East Bergholt, nr. Colchester

Pleasant well tended all year round park with heated pool and high season entertainment.

Set in the heart of Constable country, this neat 11 acre site offers 100 pitches, all with electrical connections (16A), 11 with hardstanding and now 15 'Executive' pitches which are fully serviced. 80 privately owned caravan holiday homes (8 only for hire). Pitches are on flat grass with mature trees and well lit, tarmac access roads and with separate areas for tents. A large range of facilities include a 60 x 30 ft. heated swimming pool with children's paddling pool (open Whitsun - 7 Sept, lifeguard during high season), with snacks available, and a sauna and solarium. There is also a free house bar and restaurant, entertainment in high season, games room, communal barbecue area and a small children's play area on grass and matting. Well stocked shop (open April-Sept, limited hours out of peak season). Three modern sanitary blocks with good, clean facilities have free hot water; also an en-suite unit for the disabled and 2 laundry rooms. Single groups and motorbikes are not accepted. Dogs are permitted (max. 2) and a dog walk and nature trail are available. Limited facilities available in winter. No one night bookings taken in high season. A member of the Best of British group.

Directions: Park is between Ipswich (8 miles) and Colchester (10 miles). Follow signs for East Bergholt from the A12 (4 miles). O.S.GR: TL097352.

Charges 1995:
-- Per unit incl. 2 persons £8.00 - £10.50; premier pitch £12.50 - £18.00; extra adult £1.50 - £2.00; child (3-14 yrs) £1.00 - £1.50; awning or pup tent free - £2.00; dog (max 2) 50p - £2.00; electricity (16A) £2.25 - £2.50.
Open:
All year except January.
Address:
East Bergholt,
Colchester CO7 6UX.
Tel:
(01206) 298567 or 912.
Reservations:
Made with deposit (£10) and fee (£2).

134 Low House Touring Caravan Centre, Foxhall, nr. Ipswich

Small tranquil touring park, open all year; tents accepted subject to space.

Set in 3½ acres, this beautiful garden site has 30 pitches, all with electrical connections (16A) and an abundance of trees, shrubs and flowers. In two sections, you drive through one field (the rally field) to reach the garden area - we understand from the owner that there are 90 different varieties of trees on site and an ornamental tree walk can be followed around the edge of the park. Pitches back onto trees offering plenty of shade and the opportunity to observe a range of wildlife, the rally field having a more open aspect. Tents are accepted only if space is available. There is no reception as such and guests are greeted by the friendly owner or warden. There is a small, modern, heated sanitary block with free hot water which is spotlessly clean. A washing machine is in the ladies section (no dishwashing sinks as yet). No shop but a supermarket is only 2 miles away (towards Ipswich) and an hourly bus service to Ipswich stops just outside the site. There is a small children's play area, set on grass, with the added attraction of a pets corner, with rabbits, guinea pigs and ornamental fowl. Public telephone. A torch would be useful. The enthusiastic and helpful owner, John Booth, has made arrangements for site residents to join the Civil Service club which is just 5 mins walk away with a bar, good value meal facilities and sports centre. There is also a pub in Bucklesham village, 1½ miles away and other good pubs nearby. The centre lies between Felixstowe (8 miles) and Ipswich (5 miles) and would be a useful stopover for the Felixstowe port.

Directions: Turn off A14 (was A45) Ipswich ring road (south) via slip road onto A1156 (signed Ipswich East). Follow road over the bridge which crosses over the A45 and almost immediately turn right (no sign). After ½ mile turn right again (signed Bucklesham) and site is on left after ¼ mile. O.S.GR: TM225423.

Charges 1996:
-- Per unit incl. 2 adults and children £6.50; extra adult (over 16 yrs) £2.00; awning no charge (but please lift groundsheets); electricity (16A) £1.50.
Open:
All year.
Address:
Foxhall, Ipswich,
Suffolk IP10 0AU.
Tel:
(01473) 659437.
FAX: as phone.
Reservations:
Advance booking advised - phone evenings after 6 pm.

Alan Rogers' discount
10% discount

135 Willowmere Camping Park, Little Cornard, nr. Sudbury

Small, quiet, well kept park in inland Suffolk.

This neat little park could be suitable for a weekend or as a touring base for inland Suffolk. It has just 45 numbered pitches (24 with 10A electricity) round the perimeter of a well tended flat grassy meadow plus a small area near the road used for overnight or overflow. The main touring area is set back and quiet. A pretty little pond (with fish) near the entrance has picnic benches set around it. There are also 9 residential units. The single toilet block is of good quality and well maintained, with free hot water in the washbasins set in flat surfaces and in the large controllable hot showers with seat. Washing up sinks with H&C. There are no other on-site amenities, apart from milk, cold drinks, etc. being kept but the village shops, etc. are ½ mile and good pubs are within walking distance.

Directions: Park is beside the B1508 road about 1½ miles southeast of Sudbury. O.S.GR: TL887390.

Charges 1995:
-- Per unit with 2 persons £8.00; extra person £1.00, under 14 free; electricity £1.00.
-- VAT included.
Open:
1 April - 30 September.
Address:
Little Cornard, Sudbury, Suffolk CO10 0NN.
Tel:
(01787) 375559.
Reservations:
Advisable peak seasons.

136 The Dower House Touring Park, Thetford Forest

Peaceful park in a woodland setting.

Situated in 20 acres of Britain's largest woodland forest on the Suffolk and Norfolk borders, the Dower House provides quiet woodland walks with an abundance of wildlife and is an ideal centre from which to explore Breckland. The present owners acquired the park some years ago and are continuing to work hard to update the facilities. There is provision for 60 tents and 100 vans on unmarked, level, open grass with some mature oaks, in four field areas surrounded by the forest, with the Dower House in the centre. Electrical hookups (10A) are available on three fields and wheel hardstandings on one. The field in front has a smallish swimming pool open from late May (only 1.1 m. deep) and a long slide (fenced) which are popular with children. The Dower House itself, as well as being the home of the owners, houses a bar, the `Travellers Rest' serving bar food (open selected nights in low season), TV and quiet rooms, and a takeaway. No games machines. A patio is used for special feature weekends. Separate licensed shop (daily in season, on request other times). There are two toilet blocks - a small, refurbished one near the entrance, and a larger one with free hot water in the row of washbasins. The showers (5 for each sex, 20p) are in a recently modernised, separate unit with facilities for the disabled and a baby room. Dishwashing room with lower sink for children or the disabled. Laundry room. Information room. Public phone. The Forestry Commission organizes walks to find out more about the forest (book through the District Office, Santon Downham, Brandon, Suffolk IP27 0TJ). Fishing near. Very large, open air Sunday market at Snetterton motor racing circuit (2-3 miles).

Charges 1995:
-- Per unit incl. 2 persons £6.75 - £8.25; extra adult £1.00 - £1.50; extra child (4-17 yrs) free - 65p; hikers or cyclists (2 persons) incl. tent £4.50 - £5.50; electricity £1.75 - £1.50; visitors £1.00 - £2.00; car; dog or awning free.
-- VAT included.
-- Credit cards accepted.
Open:
17 March - 31 October.
Address:
Thetford Forest, East Harling, Norfolk NR16 2SE.
Tel:
(01953) 717314.
FAX: (01953) 717843.
Reservations:
Accepted by phone; deposit of £10 required for electricity.

Directions: From A11 (Thetford-Norwich) road follow signs to East Harling and park. Turn right at church, right at T junction and park is on right. From A1066 Thetford-Garboldisham road follow signs for East Harling and park is on left after Forestry Commission site. O.S.GR: TL969853.

Alan Rogers' discount
Ask for details at the park

Enquiries to David or Karin
The Dower House Touring Park
Thetford Forest
East Harling
Norfolk
NR16 2SE
(01953) 717314

137 Clippesby Holidays, Clippesby, nr. Acle

Beautiful, self-contained, friendly, family park in the middle of the Broads.

A `gem' of a park, in the grounds of a private estate where one can wander at will, Clippesby offers the choice of pitching in shady secluded woodland or on more open parkland with mature colourful trees and shrubs on gently sloping lawns. All 100 pitches are well spaced and clearly numbered (70 have 10A electricity). Hardstanding is available in the car parking area. Three timbered toilet blocks are well placed, with free hot water in basins (some private cabins), 8 showers in total (could be a little pressured at peak times). Showers and hot water for washing up are charged (20p) - the park is not on mains services.

However, the real pleasure of Clippesby is not only the beautiful environment, but the friendly welcome from the family who live in the hall and the thoughtful provision of facilities planned with a degree of individualism not often found on British sites. You come on them unexpectedly; a sunken grass tennis court, a small swimming pool with mellowed flagstone patio area behind the hall, the timber adventure playground, putting and recreation greens and the mature garden area around the single storey hall. The Muskett Arms, with attractive and comfortable family bar and a sheltered courtyard outside, provides evening meals, music nights, barbecue evenings and other family entertainment, again individual in design. The craft shop, like a New England barn, has an unusual selection of handmade items, many in local wood. `Honey Bun's, by reception, comprises a shop to meet basic needs, a cafe for home-made breakfast, lunches, teas and takeaways, a gift shop, an exhibition of honey bees with observation hive, children's video shows, bric-a-brac area and equipment hire including board games. All fascinating and open 9 am.-5 pm. in main season.

Facilities also include a unit for the handicapped, washing machine and dryer and bicycle hire, but remember your torch and wellington boots - the environment is very natural and is deliberately kept that way. Reservations are advisable for peak periods and visitors return year after year. For those who want to take `granny', there are 23 cottages around the park for hire, all in keeping with the environment. Sunday evening services are held in the beautiful Saxon church on the estate. Children can roam at will, and in safety, and parents can unwind in this comfortable park, never mind all the attractions of the Broads and Great Yarmouth on your doorstep and only the peacocks to disturb you!

Directions: Park is signed off the B1152 road about a mile north of the junction with A1064 O.S. GR: TG423145.

Charges 1995:
-- Per unit incl. 2 persons £8.00 - £13.00, acc. to season; extra adult or visitor £1.00 - £1.50; child or student (over 3 yrs) 30p - 50p; awning £1.50; extra car £1.50 (on car park); small sleeping tent or boat trailer 75p; dog £1.00 - £1.50; electricity £2.00.
-- Short stay surcharge (£2) Spr. and Aug. B.Hs for stays less than 4 nights.
-- VAT included.
-- Credit cards accepted.
Open:
Easter - September.
Address:
Clippesby, Norfolk NR29 3BJ.
Tel:
Gt. Yarmouth (01493) 369367.
Reservations:
Made with deposit (£10 in low season, £20 per week in high season).

Alan Rogers' discount
£1 off a 2 night stay (max £7 per year)

CLIPPESBY HOLIDAYS

CLIPPESBY, NORFOLK, NR29 3BJ   **TEL: GT. YARMOUTH (01493) 369367**

IN BROADLANDS NATIONAL PARK

where tranquil waterways are a traditional haunt of fishermen, naturalists and sailors, and where the nearby golden sand beaches stretch for miles. Broadlands abounds in nature reserves and tourist attractions. Clippesby Holidays, a family-run, country park is winner of Best Family Park and Environmental awards. Ask for colour brochure!

138 Rose Farm Touring Park, Stepshort, nr. Belton

Neat, quiet site for touring units near Great Yarmouth.

There are many sites in the Great Yarmouth vicinity, mostly dominated by static holiday caravans and on site entertainment. Rose Farm is a smaller park for touring units with 80 pitches. Tents go in the open sloping field with neatly cut grass, and caravans along the former railway line, which is level, sheltered and quite pretty, with banks of natural vegetation. The tent field has 4 electric hook-ups and there are 24 for caravans (10A). A substantial, brick built toilet block has free hot water, except showers (30p), curtained washbasins for ladies, otherwise open, covered dishwashing and laundry sinks, washing machine and dryer and chemical toilet disposal. A further block in the caravan area is of the 'portaloo' type. Small shop. Fish and chip van. Games room and family room with 2 pool tables, amusement machine and TV. Separate reception with tourist information and a small children's play area outside. Rallies welcome Sept - March. Security barrier (key system). Beach at Gorlston (2 miles), fishing near. Local pubs within walking distance. Dogs or pets taken by arrangement.

Directions: From the Gt. Yarmouth bypass follow A143 in direction of Beccles. Take slip road at Bradwell and turn into New Road. Watch for sign with Belton and Burgh Castle together and park is just on the right. O.S.GR: TG488035.

Charges 1995:
-- Per unit incl. up to 4 persons £4.00 - £6.00; extra person 50p; extra car, large tent or awning £1.00; pet 50p; electricity £1.75 - £2.00;
Open:
All year.
Address:
Stepshort, Belton, Norfolk NR31 9JS.
Tel:
Gt. Yarmouth (01493) 780896.
FAX: as phone.
Reservations:
Made with £15 deposit per week; send S.A.E.

139 Two Mills Touring Park, North Walsham

Small, sheltered and secluded park but for adults only.

Two Mills, formerly Pampas Caravan Park, is situated in the bowl of a former quarry and is therefore a real sun trap, both secluded and sheltered. The park is neatly maintained with natural areas, varied trees, wild flowers and birds. It is a good centre to explore the North Norfolk coast, the Broads, or for visiting Norwich and a footpath from the park joins the Weavers Way. Including 4 'panorama' pitches (with patio area, water and waste water drainage), there are 59 level, marked, grassy pitches, all at least 10 m. wide and with electricity, 7 with hardstanding. A new, small, separate area for tents has been added. The central, very well maintained and heated toilet block has free hot water in the curtained showers and washbasins (some in cabins). New en-suite facilities for the disabled. Laundry and dishwashing rooms. Small shop with comprehensive tourist information. The town is 20 minute walk. Dogs accepted by arrangement (kennels and dog walk). Small community room with tea, coffee and TV. Public phone. Ice service. Adults only accepted.

Directions: Take Old Yarmouth road from North Walsham past police station and hospital; park is on left after 1 mile. Park is signed on the bypass south of North Walsham. O.S.GR: TG292287.

Charges 1996:
-- Per unit, incl. 2 persons £7.50 - £9.00; panorama pitch £85.00 - £99.00 per week; small tent incl. 1 person less £1.50; awning £1.00; electricity £1.85; extra person £2.00; dog 50p.
Open:
All year exc. 5/1-28/2.
Address:
Scarborough Hill, North Walsham, Norfolk NR28 9NA.
Tel:
(01692) 405829.
FAX: as phone.
Reservations:
Made with £10 deposit; balance on arrival.

 Alan Rogers' discount Ask for deatails at the park

140 Long Furlong Cottage Caravan Park, Wiveton, nr. Holt

Small, natural, all year park in pretty countryside near coast.

With just 34 touring pitches (24 with 10A electricity and one hardstanding) this is one of the smaller parks we feature - in this instance 'small is definitely beautiful'. The seemingly well drained pitches, all of good size, are on several flat grassy areas, screened by trees and bushes and partly separated by fruit trees. The insulated sanitary block is good, clean, with hot showers on payment (20p) and very adequate facilities. Dishwashing sinks and washing machine (pegs, basket and washing line), plus tourist information. A torch is useful. This is an idylic location for exploring this part of North Norfolk with its many attractions and activities, and is popular with bird watchers and walkers. A nearby pub offers bar snacks and there are many interesting restaurants in the area. The park is licenced to open all year but may close at times in the winter - phone first.

Directions: From A148 Fakenham-Cromer road, turn left at Sharrington towards Langham. Turn right after 2 miles at Blakeney sign and park is on right after Long Furlong House. Note: no caravan signs to follow. O.S.GR: TG02844146.

Charges 1995:
-- Per unit incl. 2 adults £4.00 - £7.00; electricity £2.00; awning 75p - £1.50; child (2-15 yrs) £1.00; extra adult £1.50.
Open:
All year, but phone first out of main season.
Address:
Wiveton, Holt, Norfolk NR25 7DD.
Tel:
(01263) 740833.
Reservations:
Advisable any time - with deposit £10 p/wk.

141 Kelling Heath Holiday Park, Weybourne, nr. Sheringham

Spacious, heathland park overlooking the North Norfolk coast.

Kelling Heath is a holiday park situated in a 250-acre estate in a designated area of outstanding natural beauty and the 300 caravan holiday homes (36 to let, the rest privately owned) and the 300 touring pitches blend easily into the part-wooded, part-open heathland. A wide range of on-site facilities, including a club complex, swimming pool and nature trail, provide activities for all ages. The touring area is quiet and peaceful, away from the facilities, on level grass amid pine trees and sandy open spaces. It has 200 marked pitches with electrical hookups (13A) and a further 100 unmarked. Three purpose built toilet blocks of brick and local stone serve the touring area and provide free pre-set hot showers, hot water in basins (a few in private cabins) and an excellent supply of toilets. There is also provision for the disabled, baby bath and in season, a nappy disposal service. 3 washing machines and 2 tumble dryers (irons also from reception with £20 deposit). The reception area in the centre of the park between the statics and the tourers is the hub of the facilities and is open to the public. 'The Forge' - the name for the complex comprising an entertainments bar, adults only bar, family room and pool area - provides a comprehensive range of entertainment and amusements for children all season. A newly created adventure playground is near and the nature trail starts and ends here. Other facilities include 2 hard tennis courts, a small outdoor, heated fun pool (main season only), sports field, play areas and a small lake for free fishing (permit holders only). Well stocked supermarket and takeaway. A range of information is available on places to visit and the North Norfolk Steam Railway has a halt within walking distance, giving access to Cromer.

Directions: Park is signed on A148 Holt-Cromer road between High Kelling and Bodham. On A149 Sheringham road turn right at church in Weybourne. O.S.GR: TG117418.

Charges 1995:
-- Per unit £6.95 -
£10.50; with electricity
£8.70 - £12.25; awning,
extra car or very large
tent free - £1.95; dog
£1.25 (max. 2).
-- Min. 4 days 21/7-2/9.
-- Credit cards accepted.
-- VAT included.
Open:
19 March - 31 October.
(Full facilities: Easter,
Mayday w/ends and
20/5-9/9).
Address:
Weybourne,
Sheringham,
Norfolk NR25 7HW.
Tel:
(01263) 708181.
Reservations: (01263)
588181.
Reservations:
Necessary for July/Aug.
on a weekly basis with
£15 deposit.

142 The Old Brick Kilns Caravan and Camping Park, nr. Fakenham

Tranquil, rural park on split levels.

This family run park, owned by Alan and Pam Greenhalgh, has been developed on the site of an old brick kiln resulting in land on varying levels. It provides areas of pitches (eg. the Dell, the Orchard) which have been well drained and grassed over. Banks around the park and trees provide shelter and there are new garden areas. A central fishing pond is the main feature, with a jetty for pond dipping. There are 60 pitches, all with electricity (10A) and semi hardstanding. Drinking water is supplied by a 285 ft. bore. Excellent, roofed service areas for water and waste disposal. Toilet facilities are very good with under floor heating, basins in curtained cubicles, free hot water, hand and hair dryers. Facilities for babies and the handicapped (unisex). Laundry room and dishwashing (H&C). A small toilet block at the furthest end completes the provision. Amenities include a large, comfortable bar area and á la carte restaurant, open some evenings and weekends. Patio area outside with barbecue. TV room, an information centre, table tennis, giant chess and mini library. The reception area shares with the shop. The children's play area is fenced, with bark surface. Telephone. Dogs accepted on leads and a dog walk is provided. A friendly, helpful atmosphere prevails and as the park is 8 miles from the coast, it is ideally situated to explore North Norfolk. Bed and breakfast also available on site. Gas barbecues and bicycles for hire. A member of the Best of British group.

Charges 1995:
-- Per unit, incl. 2 persons £7.75 - £9.75; child (3-15 yrs) £1.00 - £1.25, (0-3 yrs) 50p - 75p; extra adult £2.00; awning or pup tent 70p - £1.40; dog (max. 2) free; visitor £1.00; electricity £1.95.
-- VAT included.
-- Credit cards accepted.
Open:
1 March - 31 October.
Address:
Little Barney Lane, Barney, Fakenham, Norfolk NR21 0NL.
Tel:
(01328) 878305.
FAX: (01328) 878948.
Reservations:
Advisable for peak weeks and made with £10 deposit.

Directions: From Fakenham take A148 Cromer road. After 6 miles, fork right on B1354 Aylsham road and in 300 yds, turn right, signed Barney, then left on a narrow country lane with passing places, for ¾ mile. O.S.GR: TG004332.

143 Gatton Waters Lakeside Touring Site, Hillington, nr. Sandringham

Family owned park developed around two small lakes.

Conveniently situated for exploring north Norfolk, Gatton Waters has much potential, with pitches well spaced out around the 8-acre lake (coarse fishing is £2 per day - licence required). There is space for 70 units, all personally sited on level grass and there are now 40 electrical connections (10A). The main toilet block beside the reception/bar area is of good quality with free hot water. It is supplemented by two small units (4 showers and 4 WCs in each) and all are well maintained. Laundry and hairdrying facilities. The attractive bar/lounge is only for campers and arrangements can be made to order Sunday lunch. Papers and milk are delivered. Public phone. Reservation is advised for peak periods. Dogs welcome on a lead. B&B facilities. Sandringham House is 2½ miles, the nearest beach 8 miles.

Charges 1996:
-- Per unit incl. 2 persons £5.50 - £7.50; small tent incl. 1 person from £3.50; extra person £1.00; electricity £1.75.
-- VAT included.
Open:
1 April - 6 October.
Address:
Hillington, nr. Sandringham, Kings Lynn PE31 6BJ.
Tel:
(01485) 600643.
Reservations:
Min. 3 days at B.Hs. with £10 deposit.

Directions: From Kings Lynn follow A148 Cromer road. Park signed after sign to West Newton but before one to Sandringham and Hillington (all to left). O.S.GR: TF705255.

144 Highfield Farm Camping Park, Comberton, nr. Cambridge

Quiet, sheltered, well cared for touring park.

This park takes 60 caravans or motorcaravans and 60 tents following the addition of a large third meadow at the far end of the site. Pitches are all numbered and spaced out round the perimeters, backing on to tall hedges (50 with hardstanding) with the centre part left free, so there is no overcrowding. There are 100 electrical connections. Couples without children are usually put in a special part. Excellent facilities include a new toilet block, well fitted out with extra large showers and washbasins in cubicles, which has increased the provision to three blocks giving good coverage for the site. One of the original blocks has controllable hot showers on payment and washbasins with free hot water, shelf and mirror and there is another unisex shower block. All are kept very clean and well maintained, and can be heated. 10 covered washing-up sinks. Hair dryers. Laundry room with 2 washing machines, 2 tumble dryers, spin dryer, iron and board with baby bath. Basic provisions kept in reception; village shops and pub ¾ mile. Public phone and postbox. There is an extensive new dog walk and a children's play area with swings and tree house. No special on-site activities, but a kiosk provides information on what to see and where to go nearby. The owners also provide a very useful local guide for all visitors. This is a family run site with a friendly welcome, and it is popular with readers. A member of the Best of British group, it has developed and matured over the years, making an attractive park suitable for visiting the Cambridge area. Gates closed at night (midnight-7.30 am).

Directions: Park is 5 miles southwest of Cambridge town centre near eastern edge of Comberton village. From M11 take exit 12, the A603 towards Sandy and right after ½ mile on B1046 to Comberton. From A428 turn south at Hardwick roundabout to Comberton. O.S.GR: TL391571.

Charges 1995:
-- Per caravan/large tent incl. 2 persons £6.50 - £8.00, acc. to season; motorcaravan or small tent £6.25 - £7.75; m/cyclist tent £5.50 - £6.50; hiker/cyclist tent £5.00 - £6.00; extra adult £1.50 - £1.75; child (5-16 yrs) £1.00 - £1.25; awning or pup tent £1.00; porch awning 50p; electricity £1.90.
-- VAT included.
Open:
25 March - 31 October.
Address:
Long Road, Comberton, Cambridge CB3 7DG.
Tel:
Cambridge (01223) 262308.
FAX: as phone.
Reservations:
Made for any length with £10 deposit and 50p fee.

𝕳𝖎𝖌𝖍𝖋𝖎𝖊𝖑𝖉 𝕱𝖆𝖗𝖒
𝕮𝖆𝖒𝖕𝖎𝖓𝖌 𝕻𝖆𝖗𝖐

COMBERTON, CAMBRIDGE. CB3 7DG
Telephone: Cambridge (01223) 262308

A popular award winning park run by the proprietors (Brian & Loraine Chapman) which features 100 electrical hook-ups, small shop, public telephone, modern toilet and shower blocks, laundry room with automatic washing machines and tumble dryers, iron and washing up sinks. Camping Gaz/Calor Gas, battery charging and ice pack freezing facilities. Only five miles from the historic University City of Cambridge and ideally situated for touring East Anglia. Leave M11 exit 12, take A603 (Sandy) for ½ mile. Turn right on B1046 to Comberton.

A.A. Campsite of the Year (Midlands Winner 1991-92).
Calor 'Best Park England' (Runners-up 1991 & 1992).
Practical Caravan 'Regional Choice' Park, 1993.
Please write or telephone for colour brochure.

145 Stanford Park, Burwell, nr. Newmarket

Useful open all year site on the edge of the Fens.

Stanford Park, formally known as Barron Cove Caravan Park is a mature site, well signed from the village and tucked behind the owner's house. It consists of a number of open, level, hedged fields, of which two are for seasonal vans, and provides 75 places for touring units, including six hardstandings. There are 16A electrical hook-ups, with 30A available for winter use on a coin operated system. The modern toilet block can be heated and provides open, vanity-style wash-basins, curtained showers on payment (20p) and en-suite facilities for the handicapped. Separate chemical toilet disposal point. Children's play area. Purpose built reception, with some tourist information provided. On an outside wall is a useful map of the village, which is a 20 minute walk for shops, pubs, etc. and the Burwell Museum of `village life on the Fen edge'. Newmarket is 4-5 miles, Cambridge is 12.

Charges 1995:
-- Per unit £7.50, with electricity £8.50.
Open:
All year.
Address:
Weirs Road, Burwell, Cambridgeshire CB5 0BP.
Tel:
(01638) 741547.
Reservations:
Contact park.

Directions: Park is just south of Burwell village off the B1102 road and is well signed. O.S.GR: TL585674.

146 Park Lane Caravan and Camping Park, Godmanchester, Huntingdon

Neat, well organised, attractive town touring park.

Personally run by the owners, Alan and Kay Mills, and only 10 minutes walk from the historic town of Huntingdon, in the adjacent village of Godmanchester, Park Lane provides 50 marked pitches on a neat, level and well drained grass field, sheltered by the bank of the A14 Huntingdon - Cambridge dual carriage-way. This could be noisy, but I am told that after one night, you do not notice it. Electricity (10A) is available on 45 of the pitches. A circular, gravelled roadway, an orchard area for tents below the bank, a few mixed trees and a smaller beech hedge area for those seeking seclusion, create a very pleasant ambience, enhanced by the neat gravelled entrance (gates closed 11.30 pm.), with an attractive water feature manned by an army of gnomes. At present reception is in a static caravan but permission has been given to rebuild. Tourist information is provided. The toilet block, to one edge of the park, is operated on a security basis by card number. It is very well maintained and provides free hot water in open plan washbasins, on payment in the showers (complete with seat, duck boards, grab rail), baby bath, large deep basin for clothes washing (10p), washing machine, iron and board, hairdryers and under cover dishwashing. There are toilets for the disabled. Central waste disposal area (for all types of waste) and 4 water points are provided at the end of the block. Play area for up to 7 year olds on Astroturf, but no bicycles or ball games. Dog walk. Public telephone. The Black Bull is virtually at the bottom of the drive for food or drink, a shop is 200 yds. The river and boats are close and nearby St. Ives and St. Neots are also known for river and boating connections. Also near are Grafham Water for sailing and fishing, not to mention Cambridge and Ely for their political and religious connections. A useful and pleasant park to know.

Charges 1996:
-- Per caravan, tent or motorcaravan £3.00; adult £2.25; child (3-15 yrs) £1.00; awning £1.00; electricity £1.75.
Open:
Mid March - end October.
Address:
Godmanchester, Huntingdon, Cambridgeshire.
Tel:
(01480) 453740.
Reservations:
Advisable for B.Hs.

Alan Rogers' discount
Less 10% for stays 3 nights or more

Directions: From the A14 (was A604) northbound, take the Huntingdon exit and pick up signs for Godmanchester. O.S.GR: TL245709.

East Midland Tourist Board

Exchequergate, Lincoln, LN2 1PZ. Tel: (01522) 531521

Derbyshire, Leicestershire, Lincolnshire, Northamptonshire
and Nottinghamshire

This is a region offering much variety, including the Peak District, the Fens and
Sherwood Forest, as well as miles of coastline.

147 Bainland Country Park, Woodhall Spa, nr. Lincoln

Family park with many amenities including indoor pool.

Bainland, under its enthusiastic manager, has developed into a first class park, comparing favourably with European sites. There are now 150 spacious, level pitches in hedged bays, linked by circular roadways, forming circles and islands. Of these, 51 are 'superpitches' with hardstanding for car and caravan, honey-combed for awning, individual water, drainage and chemical toilet disposal point, hook-up and TV aerial. The rest of the pitches are on level grass and all have 16A electricity. There are 10 mobile homes and 25 bungalows to hire. Two excellent toilet blocks, not only well equipped for all basic necessities (except, perhaps, for showers in peak times), but in addition providing a baby care centre, unisex shower room for families, hair care room, family bathroom and a fully equipped unit for the disabled, a laundry room, undercover pot washing and separate hand washing sinks. The park is also well equipped with bins, water points, etc. and motorcaravan service points.

The efficient, friendly reception is housed in a pleasant Swiss style building adjacent to the shop (groceries, souvenirs and licensed) which is open 8 am. - 10 pm. March-Oct. It also houses the heated indoor pool and jacuzzi, etc. (children must be accompanied). This is overlooked by the bistro, open 10 am - 10 pm. and spacious bar area, which overlooks the golf course and new outdoor bowls area. A super children's adventure play area has been created in a large hollow area with a sand base in addition to a trampoline, crazy golf, croquet, TV and games room. For adults there is an 18 hole, par 3 golf course, a tennis club with a year round floodlit tennis dome with 3-4 courts including badminton (dome comes off in the summer). Note: the bar and bistro are open to the public; the great range of leisure activities, including the pool, are individually booked and paid for at reception. Barbecues, jazz, country and western, and medieval evenings are all organised! Bainland is 1½ miles from Woodhall Spa, with its old fashioned charm and Dambusters associations, yet deep in the heart of the Lincolnshire Wolds, surrounded by mature trees and with direct access to woods for walking dogs. An impressive park of a high standard, offering much yet still able to provide peace and quiet. A member of the Best of British group.

Charges 1996:
-- Per car/caravan incl. electricity and awning £7.50 - £18.00, acc. to season; super pitch £12.50 - £22.00; pup tent free - £2.00.
-- Discounts for senior citizens.
-- VAT included.
-- Credit cards accepted
Open:
All year (in winter, super pitches only).
Address:
Horncastle Road, Woodhall Spa, Lincolnshire LN10 6UX.
Tel:
Woodhall Spa (01526) 352903.
FAX: (01526) 353730.
Reservations:
Recommended and made for any length. Deposit at B.Hs. only (one night's fee).

Alan Rogers' discount
£1 off full rate excl. B.Hs.

Directions: Entrance to park is off the Horncastle road B1191 just outside Woodhall Spa by derestriction sign. O.S.GR: TF214637.

For travel further afield remember the other titles in the **ALAN ROGERS'** series

GOOD CAMPS GUIDE - FRANCE and GOOD CAMPS GUIDE - EUROPE

Available by mail order from the publishers - phone 01308 897809

LINCOLNSHIRE

148 Lakeside Holiday Park, North Somercotes, nr. Louth

Large family park near coast with comprehensive entertainment and very reasonable charges.

The 47 acres of pine forest forming Lakeside have been thoughtfully developed to provide two areas of privately owned holiday homes and a separate 15 acre touring field. This is reached by way of a tarmac access road leading from the security barrier at the entrance, with reception on the right. Around 300 touring units of all kinds can be accommodated on the neatly laid out, flat, grassy area, with numbered pitches and, at present, 235 electrical hook-ups (15A). There are several water and bin points around the area, which is quite open with some saplings growing. The first part of the touring area contains a modern, fenced children's adventure playground and a heated outdoor pool. The sanitary building to the right provides showers, washbasins and toilets, with a separate room for dishwashing and laundry. It is an adequate if not luxurious provision which may be a little hard pressed if the park is full, but new toilet facilities being added for 1996 at the pool are intended to alleviate any such problem. There are also two other sections of swings and slides on the touring area.

The entertainments area is about 100 m. back towards the entrance and pride of place goes to the impressive, ultra-modern 'Tropicana' pool complex which, for £1.95 for adults and £1.25 for children offers an indoor heated pool with jacuzzi and sauna in a tropical setting, with excellent changing and toilet facilities. A time limit is only imposed at the busiest periods and the pool is closed for cleaning from 12.30 to 1400. Both this and the outdoor pool are well staffed by a team of lifeguards. There is a large cabaret club and bar with a full entertainment programme every day in season and at weekends otherwise, a separate bar area and 4 pool tables in the entrance area. Another room provides lots of amusement machines and just opposite is a takeaway (open daily 12-2 and 6-10 except Sundays). Modern laundry. Well stocked, licensed supermarket. The Cabaret club and bars are programmed for complete rebuilding. Opposite this area is an attractive 7 acre freshwater fishing lake (free for campers). Mablethorpe beach is just 15 minutes away by car.

Directions: Park is on the A1031 road, 7 miles north of Mablethorpe towards Cleethorpes. O.S.GR: TF430960.

Charges 1995:
-- Per unit incl. up to 6 people £7.00 - £11.00; awning free; electricity £2.00; dog £1.25; extra car £1.50.
-- B.H. 'bargain weekend' offers.
-- VAT included.
-- Credit cards accepted.
Open: Easter - end October.
Address: North Somercotes, nr. Louth, Lincolnshire LN11 7RB.
Tel: (01507) 358315 or 358428.
Reservations: Advised for B.Hs and main summer season with deposit (£3 per night booked, min. 3 nights for electricity at B.Hs).

149 Cherry Tree Site, Sutton-on-Sea, nr. Mablethorpe

Small, unsophisticated, good value park.

Cherry Tree is being gradually and lovingly developed by its enthusiastic owners, the Bolton family. It is nice to see a small, tidy, grass site in this area where large holiday parks are the norm. In total there are 60 good sized pitches on well drained grass, in the main backing on to hedges (some still struggling to grow in the sea climate) and 44 have 10A electricity. A bright and cheerful, very well maintained toilet block has vanity style washbasins, controllable showers (20p) and dishwashing sinks (10p), but at present no laundry facilities. There are two water points and a waste disposal area. A neat reception, public telephone and a small children's play area complete this pleasant site from which it is possible to walk to the sea (via the road). Buses stop outside hourly and a shop and pub are within 10 minutes walk. Tennis, bowls and golf near. Mablethorpe beach is known for its sand yacht racing and Skegness with its attractions is just down the road. Dogs are welcome on leads if exercised off the park.

Directions: Park is 1½ miles south of Sutton-on-Sea on the A52 coast road to Skegness, with the entrance leading off a layby on the left. O.S.GR: TF518828.

Charges 1995:
-- Per unit incl. up to 4 persons £4.00 - £5.00; extra person 50p; electricity £1.65.
-- Min. stay 3 nights at B.Hs.
Open: March - end October
Address: Huttoft Road, Sutton-on-Sea, Lincolnshire LN12 2RU.
Tel: (01507) 441626.
Reservations: Made with £10 deposit (non-returnable).

150 Walesby Woodlands Caravan Park, nr. Market Rasen

Family owned, small, pleasant touring park near to the Wolds.

This park is surrounded by mature Forestry Commission woodland and is therefore very peaceful and sheltered. About 1½ miles distant is the small town of Market Rasen, but further afield and within easy driving distance, are Lincoln, the Wolds and the coast. There are 64 well spaced pitches, 61 with 16A electricity, marked out on a single mainly flat grassy field sectioned by double rows of young trees and divided by a central gravelled track. The one toilet block, operated by key, is exceptionally clean and modern with fully tiled surfaces and toilet facilities for the disabled. Hot water is free to the pre-set showers (curtain screen, seat, hook but no shelf), vanity-style washbasins and outside, covered, dishwashing sinks. The same block also houses a laundry room, sun room, and small shop with information section. Battery charging and gas. A thoughtful provision is a small, comfortably furnished room overlooking the park with facilities for making tea and coffee, where one can sit in peace and quiet. Children's play area on grass to one end of the site (no kite flying - overhead wires). Winter caravan storage. The Viking Way passes through Walesby and there are many other shorter walks in the forest.

Charges 1996:
-- Per unit incl. 2 persons £6.50; extra person £1.25; child (2-11 yrs) £1.00; awning £1.25; electricity £1.50.
Open:
1 March -- 31 October.
Address:
Walesby, Market Rasen, Lincolnshire LN8 3UN.
Tel:
Market Rasen (01673) 843285.
Reservations:
Any length, with deposit.

Directions: Park is northeast of, and signed from, the main approach roads to Market Rasen. O.S.GR: TF117907.

151 Limetree Park, Buxton

Neat, tidy park with views, close to the town.

Despite its proximity to Buxton, older parts of this park have a secluded setting with mature trees, amongst natural outcrops of rock. Newer parts too, on higher ground, see little housing and enjoy a panorama enhanced by a splendid railway viaduct just beyond the southern boundary of the site but may, however, be a little exposed due to their elevated position (trees and bushes have been planted). These comprise a caravan section for 35 units with unmarked pitches, but all with electricity (10A) and a tent section for 30 units at the northern end of the site on terraced levels above the older chalet, caravan holiday home and seasonal caravan section. A late arrivals area also has electric hook-ups. An older, well kept toilet block serves the northern parts of the park with a small new block in the caravan field (key system) with ramp, toilet and washbasin for the disabled. Both blocks have free hot water throughout. At peak times the provision for showers in particular could be under pressure. Laundry room. On-site amenities are few - a small shop has basic supplies but Buxton is close. Small, grass-based children's playground. Telephone. Dogs are permitted. The site's attraction is undoubtedly its central position within the Peak District and the range of possible activity around. Buxton is 15 minutes walk and Alton Towers, 22 miles.

Charges 1995:
-- Per large tent or caravan incl. 2 persons £6.50 - £7.50; tent (2 man) + car £5.50 - £6.50; tent (1 man) £3.00 - £4.00; motor caravan £6.00 - £7.00; awning £1.50; extra adult 75p; child 50p; dog 50p; electricity £1.50.
-- VAT included.
Open:
1 March -- 31 October.
Address:
Dukes Drive, Buxton, Derbyshire SK17 9RP
Tel:
Buxton (01298) 22988.
Reservations:
Any length with deposit of one night's charge (min. 3 nights at B.H.s with full payment).

Directions: From Buxton take the A515 (Ashbourne) road south, turning sharp left after the hospital on the outskirts of the town past the railway viaduct. From Bakewell on the A6, turn left (back on yourself) just before roundabout (beside new Safeway) at town outskirts. O.S.GR: SK069725.

152 Darwin Forest Country Park, Darley Moor, Two Dales, nr. Matlock

Well maintained park for caravans and motorhomes in the heart of the Derbyshire Dales.

Between Matlock and Bakewell, this park, as its name implies, is set amongst 44 acres of tall pines close to the Peak National Park. A large proportion of the park is given over to pine lodges for holiday letting but it also provides 56 touring pitches, all with hardstanding and electric hook-up (10A) in level grass bays amongst the pines - the unspoilt woodland is home to a variety of birds and wildlife. The modern toilet block is tiled and well equipped (including music) providing free hot showers, washbasins in cabins, hairdryers, a full unit for the disabled and a laundry room. The pleasant Forester's Inn provides meals. Small shop for basics and gas. Children's adventure play area and separate games room with pool table.   **continued overleaf**

Charges 1996:
-- Per unit (all persons) £10.00 - £12.00; awning £2.00; electricity £2.00.
-- VAT included.
-- Credit cards accepted.
Open:
1 March - 30 December.
Address:
Darley Moor, Two Dales, Matlock, Derbyshire DE4 5LN.

152 Darwin Forest Country Park, Darley Moor, Two Dales, nr. Matlock (continued)

Heated, indoor pool (40 x 20 ft.) with a railed off children's section, spectator area and terrace, with good changing and shower facilities (charge: adult £2.50, child £1.50). A useful park from which to explore the picturesque towns and villages of the Peak District - 4 miles from Chatsworth House, 40 mins. from Alton Towers. The Peak District Steam Railway currently operates a 2 mile section from Darley Dale to Matlock Riverside.

Tel: (01629) 732428. FAX: (01629) 735015. **Reservations:** Advised and made with deposit (details from park).

Directions: Park is best approached via the A632 Chesterfield - Matlock road. North of Matlock take the B5057 signed Darley Dale and park is on the right before descending into the village of Two Dales. O.S.GR: SK287633.

153 Highfields Camping and Caravan Park, nr. Ashbourne

Spacious park in Peak District National Park.

The Redfern family run Highfields which is set on high, flat ground in the Peak District National park with marvellous views. It takes 105 touring units, with 67 electrical connections (5A), in open, hedged fields accessed by tarmac roads, with an area for tents, another for vans with concrete slabs for jockey wheels and an area for adults only. Also a number of privately owned caravan holiday homes in separate fields. American motorhomes accepted. The main toilet block is kept locked (deposit for key) and is well maintained. Hot water is free to the washbasins, but metered to laundry and dishwashing sinks, and to the showers. A second smaller block is in the far static field, with both blocks heated when necessary. Readers report that facilities are busy and hard pressed in season. Shop for basics and gas, a children's playground, bicycle hire and a dog exercise field. Rally room. Public phone. An impressive indoor heated swimming pool is open all year (small charge). Pub and restaurant close. People are encouraged to venture off-site to enjoy the Peak District - Dovedale and Ilam are only a mile or two's distance by footpath and the Tissington Trail with access to the High Peak Trail passes by the park. The park can be very busy in peak times.

Charges 1995: -- Per unit incl. 2 persons £6.50; extra adult or child 50p; extra car or awning £1.00; pup tent £2.00; electricity (5A) £1.50; 1 person tent (no car) £4.50. -- VAT included. **Open:** 1 March - 31 October. **Address:** Fenny Bentley, nr Ashbourne, Derbyshire DE6 1LE. **Tel:** (01335) 350228. FAX: (01335) 350253. **Reservations:** Made with payment of one night's fee.

Directions: Park is west off A515 Buxton-Ashbourne road, just north of Fenny Bentley village (take care of a sharp turning to the site road when approaching from Ashbourne). O.S.GR: SK170510.

154 Greenhills Caravan Park, Ashford-in-the-Water, nr. Bakewell

Medium sized park in glorious landscape.

Set in the tranquil (A6 traffic noise notwithstanding) and beautiful Wye valley just west of Bakewell, this park has marvellous views and is ideally situated for the many attractions of the Peak District. The park is friendly and welcoming, probably at its best just off high season when there is less pressure on facilities - it does become very busy in high season. About 100 touring units are taken with caravans in a flat 'reserved' field with 55 electric hook-ups (5A). Ten pitches have hardstanding, with electricity, for winter use. Tents either go in the somewhat sloping entrance field, a small area of less sloping ground by the main buildings or, if reserved and space is available, in the caravan field. 65 caravan holiday homes are in a separate field. The one large, modern central sanitary block is partially tiled, the toilet sections being airy and spacious, but with only 3 showers per sex, is under pressure at peak seasons, when maintenance can be variable. Hot water is free to the controllable showers, the washbasins and the outside washing-up sinks. Most interest in amenities is likely to be off-site in the Peak District National Park, but the park does offer a tastefully converted barn bar and lounge with resident organist most Friday evenings in season and barbecues at weekends and the school holidays. There is an adjacent children's play area. Shop with limited takeaway food (April-Oct). Laundry room. Dogs accepted. Telephone. The park is within a mile of the Monsal Trail - part of the old Midland Railway line, now converted to 8 miles of superb, scenic walking.

Charges 1995: -- Per pitch incl. 2 persons, caravan or frame tent and car £8.50; motorcaravan or 2-man tent £7.50; 1-man tent £3.00; extra adult £2.50; child (5-15) £1.00; awning £1.50; porch awning £1.00; electricity (5A) £1.50; dog 70p. -- VAT included -- Club membership incl **Open:** All year. **Address:** Crow Hill Lane, Bakewell, Derbyshire DE4 1PX. **Tel:** Bakewell (01629) 813467 or 813052. FAX: (01629) 815131. **Reservations:** Made with deposit of first night's fee.

Directions: Park entrance is off Crowhill Lane which is south off the A6 main road just east of Ashford, 1 mile west of Bakewell town. O.S.GR: SK201693.

155 Sherwood Forest Caravan Park, Old Clipstone, nr. Mansfield

Country park between M1 and A1 roads.

A quiet country park, this is attractively landscaped in pleasant surroundings, and is close to many places of interest. Recently taken over by the Civil Service Club, non-members are also welcome. The touring areas stretch alongside the River Maun, each offering a slightly different aspect, some set aside for dog owners, others overlooking the lakes and river. Trees and shrubs enhance the rural atmosphere and wild life abounds (the park is popular with bird watchers). One small lake is especially for inflatables and canoes, the other for fishing (coarse fishing on permit). There are 200 numbered pitches on level grass, 137 with electricity. Four toilet blocks, with good, well maintained facilities, have free hot water in washbasins, on payment in the showers, under cover washing up, hair care room and laundry. Reception and the licensed shop with souvenirs and caravan accessories are housed in a central, ivy clad building. Behind this is the barn which provides a mother and toddlers room with toys, TV room and a large room for special events. Attractive children's play areas are around the park, but perhaps feeding the ducks is more enjoyable. A small wooden kiosk provides visitor information. Resident wardens on site. Sherwood Forest Visitor Centre is 5 minutes away by car, and a Rare Breeds Farm Park is close. The village is 1½ miles (no public transport) and there are walks from the site.

Charges 1995:
-- Per unit incl. 2 persons £9.00 - £9.75; walker or cyclist/tent £5.00 - £6.00; extra adult £1.50; child (5-15 yrs) £1.10; extra pup tent £1.50; dog 80p; electricity (10A) £2.50.
-- VAT included.
Open:
1 April -- 30 October.
Address:
Nr. Edwinstowe, Mansfield, Notts NG21 9HW.
Tel:
(01623) 823132.
Reservations:
Made with £5 deposit.

Directions: Best approach is via the Ollerton - Mansfield road A6075; turn south towards Old Clipstone opposite turning to Warsop and ½ mile to park. From M1 take exit 27 from south and 30 from north. O.S.GR: TG423145.

156 Glencote Caravan Park, Cheddleton, nr. Leek

Pleasant, family run park, 3 miles south of the market town of Leek, at the entrance to Churnet Valley.

A 6 acre park, Glencote has 40 numbered pitches set on flat grass with patio style hardstandings and all with electrical connections (10A), with a tarmac, curved central access road. In addition there is a small tenting area, 6 caravan holiday homes for hire and 2 privately owned. The fairly modern, tiled toilet block is centrally situated and has recently been extended. Facilities include free, controllable showers (a little on the small side), vanity style washbasins (1 private cabin for ladies), hair dryer, razor points and mirrors, a small laundry room and two dishwashing sinks under cover (free hot water). An attractive, sunken children's play area, on grass and bark with an abundance of shrubs and flowers, sits alongside the small (fenced in) coarse fishing pool. In the village of Cheddleton, ½ mile away, is a small supermarket and a post office. There is also a variety of inns within easy walking distance. Attractions nearby include a renovated Flint Mill powered by two giant water wheels and Cheddleton railway centre. A good park for relaxation, walking (being near the Staffordshire Way Walk and on the edge of the moorlands), or, for the more energetic, pony trekking, cycling, canoeing and hang gliding opportunities are close by. Also, just 10 miles away, is the famous Alton Towers leisure park. Dogs are accepted.

Charges 1995:
-- Per unit incl. 2 persons £6.50; awning £1.00; child (under 16 yrs) £1.50; extra adult £2.00; electricity £1.75.
-- For each 7 nights booked, one night free (except electricity).
-- VAT included.
Open:
Easter - end October.
Address:
Station Road, Cheddleton, nr. Leek, Staffs ST13 7EE.
Tel:
(01538) 360745.
FAX: (01538) 361788.
Reservations:
Made with deposit of £3 per night booked.

Directions: Park is signed off the A520 Leek-Stone road, 3½ miles south of Leek on the northern edge of Cheddleton Village. O.S.GR: SJ982524.

New to camping?

For a general guide to camping and outdoor life, we recommend:

'FAMILY CAMPING'

by Barbara Bignell, published by Cicerone Press, price £6.99 ISBN: 1 85284 176 1

Heart of England Tourist Board

Larkhill Road, Worcester WR5 2EF Tel: (01905) 763436. Fax: (01905) 763450

Gloucestershire, Herefordshire, Shropshire, Staffordshire, Warwickshire, Worcestershire, West Midlands and the districts of Cherwell and West Oxfordshire

1996 Events: Cheltenham Gold Cup Festival, 12-14 Mar: Crufts Dog Show, N.E.C. 14-17 March: Badminton Horse Trials, 2-5 May: National Dog Show, Perry Barr, 10-12 May: Ludlow Festival, 22 June-7 July: Warwick and Leamington Festival 29 June-14 July: Hereford Summer Festival, 5-14 July: Birmingham International Jazz Festival 5-14 July: Cheltenham Cricket Festival, 18-29 July: 8th Women's World Bowls Championships, Leamington Spa, 3-18 Aug: Walsall Illuminations, 14-27 Sept. (provisional): "Autumn in Malvern", 14-22 Sept: International British Motor Show, N.E.C. 18-29 Oct.

---

157 Clent Hills Camping and Caravanning Club Site, Romsley, Halesowen

Surprisingly pretty and tranquil site close to Birmingham and motorways.

This site, conveniently close to Birmingham and only a couple of miles or so off the M5/M42 intersection, is a real surprise in terms of being quiet and peaceful and very pretty with good views. Its only disadvantage is that it is on sloping ground, but the present, very helpful wardens are happy to assist in pitching anyone who has a problem in getting level (mainly motorcaravanners); in fact, there are some level pitches and these are all earmarked for motorcaravans. The 120 pitches are all of a good size, with electrical connections. The central sanitary block is new and provides the latest facilities, including hot showers, washbasins in cabins, hairdryers, baby room and a toilet and shower for the disabled. It was spotless when seen in high season. There is a new children's play area sited on bark for safety. Generally this is a well run and attractive site, very usefully situated.

Directions: From junction 4 on the M5 take the A491. Branch right to Romsley on the B4551 and watch for site signs. Site is on left. O.S.GR: SO955795.

Charges 1995:
-- Per adult £3.15 - £3.50; child £1.20 - £1.35; non-member pitch fee £3.00; backpacker £4.35 - £4.75; electricity £1.50.
Open:
27 March - 6 November.
Address:
Fieldhouse Lane, Romsley, Halesowen, W. Midlands B62 0NH.
Tel:
(01562) 710015.
Reservations:
Contact the wardens (not after 8 pm).

---

158 Poston Mill Caravan and Camping Park, Peterchurch, Golden Valley

Pleasant, neat park set in farmland, 1 mile from Peterchurch.

Poston Mill Park offers 92 pitches set on level grass with some very attractive pitches near the river Dore and mature trees and conifers surrounding the perimeter. Some 80 pitches have electrical hook-ups and some are `super' pitches with TV connections. There are 23 privately owned caravan holiday homes, plus 1 to rent. There is one central sanitary block with a smaller block near the holiday home area. They are of reasonably modern construction, tiled with controllable showers on payment (20p) and mainly open style washbasins. Unit for the disabled (toilet and basin only). A small laundry room houses a campers' fridge and a freezer for ice packs. Small children's play area. No on site shop but Peterchurch village is only 1 mile away. Next to the park is the Poston Mill restaurant. Dogs are permitted on a lead.

Directions: Park is 1 mile southeast of Peterchurch on the B4348 road. O.S.GR: SO354575.

Alan Rogers'
discount
Low seaseon:
stay 7 nights,
pay for 6.

Charges 1995:
-- Per caravan, motor caravan incl. 2 adults £6.50 - £7.50; trailer tent incl. up to 4 persons £6.50 - £7.50; tent £3.50 - £7.00, acc. to size; extra person (over 3 yrs) 50p; awning £1.50; electricity £1.75; TV hook-up 50p.
-- Min. charge at B.Hs.
Open:
All year.
Address:
Peterchurch, Golden Valley, Herefordshire HR2 0SF.
Tel:
(01584) 711280 or (01981) 550225.
FAX: (01981) 550885.
Reservations:
Made with £10 deposit, min. 3 nights for B.Hs.

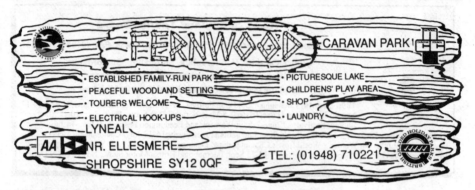

159 Ranch Caravan Park, Honeybourne, nr. Evesham

Popular touring park in 50 acres for caravans only, close to the Cotswolds.

In quiet country surroundings, Ranch lies not far from both Evesham and Broadway and is only half an hour's drive from Stratford-on-Avon. A free swimming pool (55 x 30 ft.), with chute, is open and heated June - Sept. The park takes 120 touring units - trailer or motorcaravans but not tents - on flat, hedged meadows with well mown grass and there is a spacious feeling. Pitches are not marked but the staff site units. There are 97 electrical connections and 8 new fully serviced pitches (electricity, TV, water and sewer connections). There are also 180 private caravan holiday homes in their own section. Reservation for peak weeks and B.Hs. is advisable. A very good, well appointed sanitary block has been built to replace the older of two previous ones making a good provision. Free hot water to washbasins and hot showers on payment. Self-service shop. The comfortable clubhouse (open weekends only in early and late season) offers a wide range of good value meals and entertainment is arranged at B.H. weekends and on Saturdays in school holidays. There is a small games room with TV (with Sky TV), video machines and pool table. Children's playground. Laundry room. Riding close. American motorhomes not accepted.

Directions: Park is west off the old Roman road (Ryknild Street) just north of Honeybourne village. O.S.GR: SP112444.

Charges 1995:
-- Per unit incl. 2 persons £5.00 - £10.50; extra person (over 5 yrs) or dog 75p - £1.00; awning free - £1.50; extra car free - £1.00; electricity £2.00; full services £2.00.
-- One free night for every 7 nights booked.
-- VAT included.
-- Credit cards accepted.
Open:
1 March - 30 November.
Address:
Honeybourne, Evesham, Worcs WR11 5QG.
Tel:
(01386) 830744.
FAX: (01386) 833503.
Reservations:
Made with £5 per night deposit and essential for B.Hs. (min. 3 days).

160 Fernwood Caravan Park, Lyneal, nr. Ellesmere

Quiet, pretty park in semi-woodland near Welsh border, for caravans and motorhomes.

The floral landscaping, the setting and the attention to detail at Fernwood are all of a very high standard and planted and natural vegetation blend harmoniously to provide a real oasis of calm and rural tranquillity. In addition to 165 caravan holiday homes, used normally only by their owners, the park takes 60 tourers and motorcaravans (no tents) on several well cut, grassy enclosures. Some are in light woodland, others in more open, but still relatively sheltered situations. There are 40 electrical connections (10A) at present. Siting is carried out by the management and there is always generous spacing, even when the site is full. The refurbished sanitary block for tourers has free hot water to washbasins (with good shelves) and to the pre-set hot showers, a unit for the disabled, but no dishwashing sinks. Water points around and new motorcaravan service point. Nicely tiled laundry room (open 8.30 am.-7 pm.) near shop, with two extra toilets and basins. Other facilities include a small shop, which doubles as reception (open daily, sometimes limited hours). Coarse fishing lake, 28 acres of woodland for walking. Grass children's play area. Public phone. Pets allowed.

Directions: Park is just northeast of Lyneal village, signed southwest off the B5063 Ellesmere to Wem road, about 1½ miles from junction of the B5063 with the A495. O.S.GR: SJ453338.

Charges 1995:
-- Per unit £5.00 - £9.25; awning £1.00 - £1.25; electricity £2.00; extra car £1.00.
--10% discount on every 7 nights booked in advance.
-- VAT included.
Open:
1 March - 30 November.
Address:
Lyneal, nr. Ellesmere, Shropshire SY12 0QF.
Tel:
(01948) 710221.
Reservations:
Necessary for peak season and B.Hs with deposit of £5 per night.

161 Briarfields Caravan and Camping Park, Cheltenham

New park close to M5 for night stop or for visiting the Cotswolds and local towns.

Newly planted saplings (in addition to the mature trees already here) and 3,000 rosewall bushes will mature to enhance the overall appearance and security of this developing park. Situated just a mile from the M5, a short entrance drive leads from the B4063 to the 72 flat, grassy pitches. These are set around the tarmac access road and in the central area and all have electrical connections and are well lit. The brand new heated sanitary building has excellent facilities for the disabled and a large laundry and dishwashing room. Just across the road, in the owner's holiday home park, is a well stocked, licensed mini market. A pub, a short walk away, offers meals and a children's garden. Other on site facilities, which should all be completed for spring 1996, will include a swimming pool, children's play area, reception and accommodation for wardens, plus Travel Lodge rooms. Cheltenham Racecourse is 4 miles away and there is a golf course open to all just a few minutes up the road. Possibly some road noise.

Directions: From the M5 take J11 exit onto A40 towards Cheltenham. In ½ mile turn left on B4063 Gloucester road, park is shortly on left. Via Cheltenham take signs for M5 and look for B4063 as above. O.S.GR: SO922220.

Charges 1996:
-- Per unit £5.00 - £6.00; tent £4.00 - £5.00; electricity £1.90.
Open:
All year.
Address:
Gloucester Road, Cheltenham, Glos. GL51 0SX.
Tel:
(01242) 235324.
Mobile: 0836-274440.
FAX: as phone.
Reservations:
Advisable at times of race meetings - contact park.

BRIARFIELDS
Caravan and Camping
Tents or Tourers
Just one mile from junction 11 M5 motorway
For Golfers - For Horseracing Enthusiasts - Cheltenham - The Cotswolds
Tel and Fax 01242 235324   Mobile 0836 274440

162 Stansby Caravan and Camping Park, Cheltenham

Small, neat park with easy access from the M5 motorway.

Stansby is an orchard park, set in a peaceful location even though it is within a residential area. It suffers from a little train noise but on the whole is quiet and secluded. You site yourself on the level grass amidst the fruit trees or on a hardstanding bay. This allows for 30 places, 12-14 of which can be on hardstanding. There are 24 electric hook-ups (10A). The central toilet block is scrupulously cleaned and is well equipped with free hot water, controllable hot showers (1M, 1F) with dressing area, vanity style washbasins and hair and hand dryers. There is one washing up sink, partially covered, a chemical toilet point and a 'dog loo' for poopscoop users. There are no other site facilities except tourist information and very helpful owners. A post office, pub and shop are within walking distance and it is 10 minutes drive to Gloucester, 5 minutes to Cheltenham. Possibly some road noise.

Directions: From M5 junction 11, follow signs A40, Cheltenham. At first round- about turn right, follow new road for approx. ½ mile and brown and white signs to park. O.S.GR: SO908208.

Charges 1996:
-- Per unit incl. 1 or 2 persons £6.00 - £7.00; extra adult £1.00; child (3-13 yrs) 50p; extra vehicle 50p; awning £1.50; electricity £2.00.
Open:
1 February - December.
Address:
The Reddings, Cheltenham GL51 6RS.
Tel:
(01452) 712168.
Reservations:
Necessary at B.H.s for electricity; min. 3 days with £10 deposit.

Alan Rogers' discount
Less 50p p/n per pitch

163 Cotswold Hoburne, South Cerney, Cirencester

Good touring park with holiday caravans and a variety of watersports amenities close by.

Since the park is adjacent to the Cotswold Water Park, those staying here will have easy access to the varied watersports there which include sailboarding and water ski-ing. On the park itself there is a lake with pedaloes and canoes for hire. Its wide range of other amenities include an outdoor (44 x 22 ft) heated swimming pool open from Easter (heated from May) and a new, large indoor leisure complex including pool with flume, spa bath, sauna, steam room and sun bed. There are 300 well marked touring pitches for any type of unit, all with hardstanding (only fairly level) and grass surround for awning or tent. Of good size but with nothing between them, all have electrical connections (some need long leads). Also 150 holiday units, mainly for letting. Six toilet blocks are all quite small and maintenance can be variable. Hot water is free in the washbasins and pre-set showers. Baby changing facilities. Basic facilities for the disabled are to be found in the clubhouse, but are locked at night. The site has heavy weekend trade. The large clubhouse has a big general lounge with giant TV screen, entertainment at times, full restaurant (or food bar in lounge), big games room and a lounge bar which overlooks the outdoor pool and lake with a patio. Supermarket. Football field. Tennis courts. Good quality adventure playground with bark base. Crazy golf. Launderette. Fishing lake (permits from reception). No dogs or pets accepted. Part of the Hoburne group.

Directions: Turn south off the A419 Cirencester-Swindon road 3 miles from Cirencester at camp sign, second right (Broadway Lane) and through to site. O.S.GR: SU055957.

Charges 1996:
-- Touring pitch incl.electricity £7.75 - £16.00; tent pitch £5.50 - £12.75, both acc. to season; pup tent £1.75.
-- Weekly rates and weekend breaks.
-- VAT included.
-- Credit cards accepted.
Open:
Easter - 28 October.
Address:
Broadway Lane, South Cerney, Cirencester, Glos. GL7 5UQ.
Tel:
(01285) 860216.
FAX: (01285) 862106.
Reservations:
Tents: 1-6 nights payable in full at time of booking; caravans with £50 deposit for min 4 days at B.Hs (3 days for May B.H).

All the parks in this guide are inspected regularly by our team of experienced site assessors, but we welcome your opinion too.
- See Readers Report on page 180 -

Yorkshire and Humberside Tourist Board

312 Tadcaster Road, York YO2 2HF Tel: (01904) 707961

North, South and West Yorkshire, Humberside

1996 Events (provisional): Bradford Film Festival 1-16 March: Harrogate Int. Youth Music Festival 5-12 Apr: Harrogate Spring Flower Show 25-28 Apr: Leeds Int. Music Festival 4-12 May: National Needlework Exhibition and Championships (Doncaster Exhibition Centre) 13-16 June: York Mystery Plays 13 June-7 July: Grimsby International Jazz Festival 5-7 July: Great Yorkshire Show, Harrogate 9-11 July: Great Autumn Flower Show, Harrogate 13-15 Sep: Fifth Otley Folk Festival 21-23 Sept: Leeds International Film Festival 10-26 Oct.

164 Waudby's Caravan and Camping Park, South Cave, nr. Hull

Small, neat park with excellent toilet block.

Don't let the actual situation of Waudby's - beside the road and overshadowed by the Caravan Centre and repair and storage area - deter you from trying this little site. It is suitable for visiting the Yorkshire Wolds or over-nighting on the way to the ferry (Hull is 12 miles). There are only 15 pitches on grass or hardstanding, most separated by grass banks or small fencing, all with electrical connections (10A). An excellent, recently built toilet block provides large, controllable, free hot showers, washbasins in cabins, tiled throughout. It can be used by the disabled and is very well maintained. A restaurant and bar are within walking distance and the historic town of Beverley is 12 miles. The park has a resident warden and is owned by the Waudbys who own the Caravan Centre. It is well worth consideration.

Directions: Park is south of the motorway at the exit for the village of South Cave; clearly signed. O.S.GR: SE914316.

Charges 1996:
-- Per unit incl. all persons £4.50; ridge tent £4.00; awning £1.20; drainage/hardstanding 50p; electricity £1.20.
-- Credit cards accepted.
Open:
1 April - 6 January.
Address:
Brough Road, South Cave, East Yorkshire HU15 2DB.
Tel:
(01430) 422523.
Reservations:
Advised for B.H.s and weekends and made with £1 deposit per night booked.

165 Thorpe Hall Caravan and Camping Park, Rudston, Bridlington

Pleasant touring park, west of Bridlington.

This small park in the grounds of Thorpe Hall just outside the village of Rudston and 4½ miles from the sea at Bridlington, is on flat grass, largely enclosed by the old kitchen garden wall. The 90 pitches are all numbered and well spaced out, with free area in centre, with 53 electrical connections, 46 with TV connection also. A separate area takes tents. There are no caravan holiday homes. The park is enthusiastically managed by Malcolm and Kathy Taylor. There is always a chance of finding space, though it is best to book for B.H.s and peak weeks. The central toilet block is of good quality, with free hot water in the washbasins, with shelf and mirror, and in the pre-set showers with turn-on tap. Ladies have 3 washbasins in private cabins and 1 bath. Hair washing and drying facilities. Well equipped unit for the disabled with bath. New dishwashing sinks. Small shop with essentials. Launderette. Public phone. Games room with 2 pool tables and table tennis, tourist information area and satellite TV room. 2 acre games field, short tennis net and children's play area on grass and sand. Dog walk. Information sheets on a range of local walks are available and Thorpe Hall Gardens are open to park visitors between 1 - 4 pm. There is a footpath to the village with a shop, post office, garage, a pub serving bar meals and a new restaurant. Twice weekly bus service to Bridlington.

Directions: Park is beside B1253 road on east side of Rudston 4½ miles from Bridlington. O.S.GR: TA105676.

Charges 1996:
-- Per unit, incl. all persons £6.00 - £8.00; extra car £1.00; electricity £1.50.
-- Less 10% for 7 days or longer.
-- Special rate for October.
-- VAT included.
Open:
1 March - 31 October.
Address:
Rudston, Driffield, East Yorks YO25 0JE.
Tel:
Kilham (01262) 420393 or 420394.
FAX: (01262) 420588.
Reservations:
Made with advance payment; (min. 3 nights at Spr. B.H).

Alan Rogers' discount
Less 50p-£1 p/n acc. to season

166 Flower of May Holiday Park, Lebberston, Scarborough

Large, family owned, pleasant park with indoor pools; for touring units and holiday caravans.

Flower of May is a mixed park with many amenities and evening activities and it is well worth your consideration for holidays in these parts. The park is on a cliff top about 4½ miles from the centre of Scarborough and 2½ miles from Filey in the other direction. There is a cliff walk down to the sea for the reasonably active or one mile away, by a car park, is a footpath giving easy access to the beach. A leisure centre and pool complex provide a large indoor leisure pool (steps divide adult and children's sections), water flume and jacuzzi, two squash courts, 10 pin bowling alley, full fitness gym and amusement machines. The leisure centre is open to the public (charge to campers as well) and staffed with trained attendants. A pay and play golf course will be added for 1996. The park is licensed for 276 touring caravans and 24 tents (motorcaravans also taken); there are 179 caravan holiday homes (50 for hire, others privately owned). Pitches are individual ones in wide avenues divided by trees, mainly on grassy ground. There are 210 with electricity (5A) including 31 'star pitches' with water and drainaway also. Reservations for the main season are advisable. The three toilet blocks are being refurbished and fully tiled to provide vanity style washbasins in cabins, pre-set showers (hot water free), baby room and facilities for the disabled. Fully enclosed washing-up sinks in all blocks and excellent laundry room in the main complex. Large shop. Two modern bar lounges, one suitable for families with children, and discos most nights in season. Games room with TV. Large children's adventure playground with rubber surface. Cafe and fish and chips. If this is not enough, the Plough Inn near the park entrance does a good bar meal. Treatment room. Dog exercise area but numbers limited (1 per pitch) and not allowed at all for B.Hs. or the 6 week summer holiday.

Charges 1995:
-- Per unit incl. up to 4 persons £6.25 - £9.95; awning £1.50; extra person (under 3 yrs) £1.50; extra car £1.50; dog £1.00 (limited); electricity £1.50; star pitch £3.00 extra.
-- 10% discount on pitch fee for weekly bookings.
-- VAT included.

Open:
Easter - late October.

Address:
Lebberston Cliff, Scarborough, N. Yorks YO11 3NU.

Tel:
Scarborough (01723) 584311 or 582324.

Reservations:
Made with £20 deposit per week and £1 booking fee (Sat.-Sat. only for Spr. B.H. and 16/7-27/8).

Directions: Park is signed from the roundabout at junction of A165 and B1261 from where it is 600 yds. O.S.GR: TA088836.

167 Northcliffe Holiday Park, High Hawsker, nr. Whitby

Peaceful family park with lovely sea views.

Within the North Yorkshire Moors National Park, this park for touring units and holiday caravan homes is modern, well planned and attractive with all building regulated by the Park authorities. The young and friendly owners continue to upgrade the facilities and it is now a first rate base from which to explore this lovely area. The touring area is on flat ground with 14 amply sized grassy pitches (10A electricity) and 16 new, individual fully serviced pitches with access from a tarmac road. Some trees have been planted but as yet there is little shade. The sanitary block, operated on a key system, was spotless when we visited, with free hot showers and good facilities for mothers with babies. Unit for the disabled. There is also a dishwashing room and a well equipped laundry. A fully stocked shop, most attractive tea room and a good range of reasonably priced meals and takeaway are available (8.30-8.00 in high season, 8.30-1.00 and 3.00-6.00 in low season). Excellent provision for children includes a play area, lots of grass, junior football pitch and an indoor room with pool and 2 amusement machines. No dogs allowed. American motorhomes up to 30 ft. are accepted by prior arrangement only. The park is situated on the Heritage Coast and one can walk along the Cleveland Way into Whitby or Robin Hood's Bay - the park has produced walks leaflets and a Countryside Notes leaflet (50p per pack). The surrounding area has a host of attractions - sports, cliff top walks, sandy beaches and quiet coves, the beauty of the moors and small and large resorts like Whitby and Scarborough are within easy reach. York is about an hour away and the Dales are a possible day excursion.

Charges 1996:
-- Per unit in1cl. up to 6 persons in 1 family £5.50 - £8.50, acc. to season; super pitch incl. electricity £8.00 - £13.00; backpacker (no car) £2.00 - £3.00 per person; extra car £2.00 - £3.00; electricity £1.75.
-- VAT included.
-- Credit cards accepted (2% surcharge).
Open:
3rd week in March - 31 October.
Address:
High Hawsker, nr. Whitby, N. Yorks YO22 4LL.
Tel:
(01947) 880477.
Reservations:
Made with deposit and fee, min. 3 nights in high season, 2 nights other times; contact park for details.

Directions: Three miles south of Whitby on the A171 (Scarborough) road turn left onto the B1447 signed High Hawsker and Robin Hood's Bay. Go through Hawsker village and continue on Robin Hood's Bay road. At top of hill turn left onto private road - go on ½ mile towards sea. O.S.GR: NZ936080.

168 St. Helens in the Park, Wykeham, nr. Scarborough

Spacious touring park with views across the Vale of Pickering.

St. Helens is 6 miles from the sea at Scarborough, on the edge of the North Yorkshire Moors National Park. Carefully planned and designed from 30 acres of parkland, the 250 level pitches for touring units have a spacious feel, 52 with gravelled hardstanding (useful in winter). 240 pitches have 10A electrical hook-ups; even the late arrivals area has electricity. Up to 40 tents can be taken and in high season a 28-day overflow field is available. The park is maintained to a very high standard, neat and well organised, and this is no doubt due to the hard work and enthusiasm of the wardens, Ann and John Ridley. Local stone has been used for all the park facilities, which blend into the rural landscape. The four strategically placed toilet blocks (heated in winter) are well equipped, with free hot water, individual, vanity style washbasins, some in private cabins, pre-set showers, 2 baths and ladies' hairwashing cabins. Babycare units in two blocks. Undercover dishwashing at all blocks. Excellent refurbished laundry room. Large, well provisioned shop, open March-Oct (mornings only in low seasons), as is the games room with amusement machines and pool table. A very comprehensive adventure playground is well set up on bark, as part of a 3 acre play area suitable for mountain bikes or games with goal posts. On certain evenings each week from March-Oct. a takeaway provides good value, simple meals, but a short walk can take you to the Downe Arms in the village, where you can indulge and be well fed. The telephone chalet has comprehensive tourist information. A large scale chess set forms a nice feature, noticeable after the formal drive from the main road.

Charges 1995:
-- Per unit incl. 2 persons £6.50 - £8.50, acc. to season; extra person (over 5 yrs) £1.00; awning £1.30; porch awning 80p; pup tent £5.50; dog free; electricity £1.95.
-- VAT included.
-- Credit cards accepted.
Open:
All year.
(Reduced facilities Nov-Feb).
Address:
Wykeham, Scarborough, N. Yorks YO13 9QD.
Tel:
Scarborough (01723) 862771.
FAX: (01723) 864329.
Reservations:
Made for any period with £10 deposit.

Directions: Park access road leads off the A170 (Pickering - Scarborough) road in Wykeham village 2 miles west of junction with B1262. O.S.GR: SE963835.

YORKSHIRE

169 Spiers House Campsite, Cropton, nr. Pickering

Secluded Forestry Commission site, set in the working forest of Cropton - taking all units.

Spiers House offers 100 pitches, 74 with electricity, and a further 50 for tents, set on flat, sloping grass. Pitching is informal but there must be at least 20 ft. left between each unit. Reception (including an information centre) and a small shop are at the entrance to the site in an attractive cobbled courtyard. In this area also is the toilet block, which is of a good standard if a little spartan, tiled with free hot showers (pre-set), vanity style washbasins and hairdryer. Dishwashing sinks are under cover and there is a small laundry. There is a unit with toilet and basin for use by the disabled. A large children's play area, of wooden construction and with a bark base, is set in a forest clearing. Clearly marked forest walks can be taken, and there are opportunities to join ranger organised walks during summer holiday and bank holiday periods. Dogs are accepted.

Directions: Site is 5 miles northwest of Pickering. Approach through Cropton village and along the minor road off the A170 between Pickering and Kirbymoorside. Turn right at the sign one mile north of Cropton on the road to Rosedale. O.S.GR: SE756918.

Charges 1995:
-- Per unit incl. 2 persons £6.00 - £7.00; extra person £1.00; electricity £1.60.
-- VAT included.
Open:
26 March - 2 October.
Address:
Cropton, Pickering, Yorkshire YO18 8ES.
Tel:
(01751) 417591.
Reservations:
Only for 7 days or more with £5 deposit (S.A.E. to warden at site).

170 Wombleton Caravan and Camping Park, Wombleton, Kirkbymoorside

Neat, well cared for park in popular area.

The Proctors bought Wombleton in 1990 and have they have worked hard to make a well cared for, family park. On open, level grass, 88 pitches are spaced and identified between separate trees. These are of a mixed variety and give an attractive appearance to the park which was formerly an old airfield, sheltered from the surrounding rural farmland by an edging of tall trees. A central toilet block, although of older design, is exceptionally well maintained. It has curtained showers (20p), open washbasins, washing machine and dryer and undercover dishwashing. A new, fenced adventure play area is in the top part of the park. Basic provisions are kept in reception, but a pub in the village is within walking distance. Helmsley and Kirkbymoorside are 4 miles each and all the other attractions of this area are at hand.

Directions: Near no. 172 Foxholme. From A170, follow signs for Wombleton village and then park signs. O.S.GR: SE670835.

Charges 1996:
-- Per unit incl. 2 persons £5.00 - £6.00 (B.H.s £8.00); extra person 50p; awning £1,50; electricity £1.75; extra car £1.00.
Open:
1 March - 31 October.
Address:
Wombleton, Kirkbymoorside, N. Yorks YO6 5RY.
Tel:
(01751) 431684.
Reservations:
Made with £10 deposit.

171 Vale of Pickering Caravan Park, Allerston, nr. Pickering

Well designed, neat, family owned park with good views.

Vale of Pickering has been carefully planned and neatly developed by its owners, who are local farmers, over 10 years and it is well placed to explore the North Yorkshire Moors and Wolds. On a level grass site, in places edged by soil banks now partly hidden by trees, foliage and attractive flower beds, 120 pitches are provided, all with electricity. The main circular site road is tarmac and lit at night. Rally field available also. There is a good children's playground (grass) and a separate dog walk is provided outside the park. The well maintained toilet block is tiled with some washbasins in cabins, coin-operated showers, with curtains, good supply of shelves, hooks and mirrors and a bath and unit for the disabled. 2 hairdryers. Launderette (2p for hot water in sinks and also for dishwashing sinks) and microwave oven. Well stocked, licensed shop with caravan accessories, open according to demand. Separate chalet with tourist information A fish and chip van calls twice weekly in main season. Occasional outdoor entertainment is organised.

Directions: Park is 1 mile off the main A170 (Scarborough - Helmsley) road at the village of Allerston. O.S.GR: SE879808.

Charges 1995:
-- Per unit incl. 2 adults and 2 children £5.50 - £8.00; extra adult £1.00; child (over 2 yrs) 50p; electricity £2.00; hardstanding 40p; 2 dogs free, extra dog £1.00; awning £1.50.
-- Early and late season discounts.
-- VAT included.
Open:
15 March - 31 October.
Address:
Carr House Farm, Allerston YO18 7PQ.
Tel:
(01723) 859280.
Reservations:
Made with £10 deposit (min. 3 nights at B.Hs with £20 deposit).

172 Foxholme Touring Caravan Park, Harome, Helmsley

Good quality touring park for caravans and a few tents.

This small park is of an unusual type for Britain, with nearly all the pitches being fully individual ones on clearings fashioned out of quite dense coniferous plantations and affording good privacy and lots of shade (manoeuvring may be difficult). There are 60 pitches, all with electricity and 40 on quick draining grass, where awnings are possible. The park is basically for caravans but a few tents can be taken. Some picnic tables are provided.

The toilet block is of excellent quality in local stone, with all washbasins in private cabins set in vanity type units with mirror and free hot water, and hot showers on payment. It is supplemented by three single units in other parts of park. Six washing-up sinks. Laundry room. Reception doubles as a shop, supplying basics and tourist information. A torch would be useful. The park is set in quiet countryside and makes a good touring base close to the North Yorkshire Moors National Park. There are no on-site activities but basic provisions are kept in reception and the village shops are 1 mile. Restaurants etc. at Helmsley (5 miles). Public telephone.

Charges 1996:
-- Per unit £5.00 - £6.50, acc. to season; awning £1.50; extra car 50p; electricity £2.00.
-- VAT included.

Open:
Mid March - 31 October.

Address:
Harome, Helmsley, North Yorkshire YO6 5JG.

Tel:
Helmsley (01439) 770416, 771241 or 771696.

Reservations:
Made for any dates with £10 deposit.

Directions: Turn south off the A170 between the adjoining villages of Beadlam (to west) and Nawton (to east) at sign to Ryedale School, then 1 mile to park on the left (passing another park on right). From east ignore the first camp sign at turning before Nawton. From west turn right ¼ mile east of Helmsley, signed Harome, turn left at church, go through the village and follow camp signs. O.S.GR: SE661831.

York's Finest Tourist Site. Licensed Club House,
Calor Gas and Full Facilities.

Rawcliffe
Caravan Company
Limited

MANOR LANE · SHIPTON ROAD · YORK YO3 6XJ
Telephone (01904) 624422

YORKSHIRE & HUMBERSIDE
TOURIST BOARD
WHITE ROSE AWARD
FOR TOURISM

WINNER
— 1994 —

Rawcliffe Caravan Park is situated ½ mile from the A19 on the York side at its junction with the A1237 (northern York bypass). The site is open all year with weekend entertainment, electric and satellite TV on all pitches with water and drainage on most. A very large supermarket, shopping complex, ten pin bowling alley and 10 screen cinema are very near to the site. York with all its tourist attractions, including the Minster and Yorvic Centre are only three miles away and are within walking distance. There is a new regular bus service to York from the site. The Yorkshire Moors, Dales and the seaside are within easy travelling distance.

173 Golden Square Caravan and Camping Park, Oswaldkirk, Helmsley

Family owned, quiet country touring park, south of Helmsley.

The area around Helmsley appears very popular, being in the North Yorkshire Moors National Park and around 20 miles from York. Mr and Mrs Armstrong, local farmers, have worked hard to develop the park around old quarry workings, providing a number of split level areas or bays with beautiful views over the surrounding countryside. The 130 pitches, although not separated, have markers set in the ground and back mainly on to grass banks and are on fairly flat grass. The underlying ground is a little hard - steel tent pegs needed. There are now 120 electrical connections (10A) and 24 pitches in the new extension have drainaway also. Four `all service' pithces (including waste water and sewage connections) are planned for 1996. The two toilet blocks are good tiled ones with washbasins set in flat surfaces with free hot water, shelf and mirror (some private cabins), showers with pre-set and timed hot water on payment, a heated bathroom with baby changing facilities and units for disabled. Mrs Armstrong takes a pride in them and pot plants and arrangements make them more homely. Covered washing-up sinks. Washing machine and dryer. Microwave. Tourist information. Self service shop with off licence and craft gifts. Play area and play field. Games room in top barn. Visitors may have cheap membership of nearby Ampleforth College sports centre with indoor swimming pool, tennis, gym etc. Public phone. Pony trekking nearby. The Ebor Way, Cleveland Way and Lyle Wake Walk are near for walkers. Pubs with meals at Ampleforth and Helmsley.

Charges 1996:
-- Per unit incl. 2
persons £6.00 - £8.00;
child under 10 yrs free,
extra person (over 10)
75p; full awning £1.20,
porch awning 90p; extra
car £1.00; electricity
£1.70; drainage 50p;
hikers/bikers £2.60 -
£3.30 per person.
-- VAT included.

Open:
1 March - 31 October.

Address:
Oswaldkirk, York
YO6 5YQ.

Tel:
Ampleforth (01439)
788269.

Reservations:
Essential for B.Hs and
made with £10 deposit.

Directions: Park is on the Helmsley-Ampleforth road close to the `caravan route' which avoids the banned Sutton Bank on the A170 Thirsk-Helmsley road. Turn off B1257 to west at camp sign by Golden Square Farm, 1 mile south of junction with A170. O.S.GR: SE605797.

Regional Loo winner 1989, 1989, 1990 & 1994

NORTH YORKS MOORS NATIONAL PARK

Helmsley 2 miles, Ampleforth 1 mile. Secluded position.
Magnificent views. Surrounded by open countryside and woodland
Luxury heated toilet block and bathroom. Many pitches with
electricity and some with drainaway also.. Launderette. Shop.
Covered washing up sinks. Play areas. Dogs welcome with fields
and woods for walking. Indoor sports centre nearby for swimming,
tennis, etc. Runner up - Calor Award for Most Improved Site 1992.

AA 4 pennants, RAC appointed, ETB

OSWALDKIRK, YORK. Tel: 01439 788269 *Owners: Mr. & Mrs. D. Armstrong*

174 Rawcliffe Manor Caravan Park, Rawcliffe, York

Neat touring park close to the city of York.

This park takes 120 touring units (caravans and tents) on flat, grassy ground with tarmac/concrete hardstandings and access roads built on the site of a former RAF station. As the surrounding area has become more built up and residential, the park has been updated and redesigned with numerous flowerbeds and hedge bays and all pitches becoming fully serviced. Caravan pitches have jockey wheel markers and all have electricity, satellite TV, water and drainaway connections. American motorhomes are accepted (contact park for length restriction). Now open all year, it has easy access to a range of amenities. A city site, it could become very busy.

There are two modern toilet blocks operated by security codes (heated in winter) with free hot water in the plentiful washbasins, set in flat surfaces, and in the controllable hot showers. Hair dryers and excellent facilities for the disabled. Washing machines and tumble dryers in both blocks. There is a clubhouse on site with a large bar lounge (with some bar meals and takeaway service) and separate restaurant also used by the general public (weekends only Nov-March). Games rooms for both adults and children with pool tables etc. and a well equipped children's play area outside. Entertainment is provided frequently in season. Petanque pitch. Large supermarket nearby. Picnic tables. 12 screen cinema and 10-pin bowling within walking distance. Public transport is available into York (2 buses a day call at the park). A park and ride service is near (every day except Sunday in Aug. and at B.Hs, Saturdays only at other times). Cycle route adjacent to site. Local nature park.

Directions: Park is ½ mile off the A19 York - Thirsk road at the A1237 junction (York side) with the new northern bypass. O.S.GR: SE583552.

Charges 1995:
-- Per unit incl. 2 persons and electricity £10.70 - £11.70; small tent incl. 2 persons £5.30 - £6.30, 1 person £3.80 - £4.80; extra adult £1.40; child (12-16 yrs) £1.00 - £1.20; awning £1.20; extra car £1.70; electricity £1.60; satellite TV 50p - £1.00 (free for 5+ nights); m/cycle £1.20; dog 80p.
-- 10% senior citizens low season discount.
-- VAT included.
-- Credit cards accepted.
Open:
All year.
Address:
Manor Lane, Shipton Road, York YO3 6TZ.
Tel:
York (01904) 624422.
Reservations:
Made for min. 3 nights with £25 deposit.

175 Goose Wood Caravan Park, Sutton-on-the-Forest, York

Family owned park in woodland setting 6 miles from York, for caravans and motorcaravans only.

Goose Wood provides a quiet, relaxed atmosphere from which to explore York itself or the surrounding Yorkshire Dales, Wolds or Moors. The park has a well kept air and rural atmosphere, with 75 well spaced and marked pitches on level grass, all with electrical hook-ups and 35 with paved hardstanding and patio pitch. No tents or trailer tents are accepted. The excellent toilet block, modern and well maintained, provides good facilities which include free showers (4 minute pushbutton which also operates the light and is located outside cubicle) and hairdryers. A separate unit provides 4 extra toilets and washbasins, and coin-operated washing up sinks. A laundry room, small shop and public telephone complete the practical facilities supporting the needs of the discerning visitor. For children, there is a 'super plus' adventure playground in the trees at one side of the site and, for adults, a small coarse fishing lake and extra woodland area for walking, plus a large scale chess set. Dogs welcome on a lead, to be exercised in nearby woodland. The park is popular with families in high season when it can be busy at weekends. A 'park and ride' scheme for York operates from nearby in the school holidays, but there is a local bus every 2 hours, six days a week. The park is 1¼ miles from Sutton village. A member of the Best of British group.

Directions: Park is 6 miles north of York. From A1237, York outer ring-road, take B1363 for Sutton-on-the-Forest and Stillington, taking the first right after the Haxby and Wigginton junction and follow camp signs. O.S.GR: SE595636.

Charges 1996:
-- Per unit (incl. up to 2 persons + car) £7.50 - £9.00; extra adult £1.00; child (2-14 yrs) 50p; awning (no ground-sheet) £1.00; extra pup tent (1 only) £1.00; extra car £1.00; electricity (10A) £2.00; hardstanding patio pitch + 50p.
-- VAT included.
Open:
24 March -- 31 October.
Address:
Sutton-on-the-Forest, York YO6 1ET,
Tel:
Easingwold (01347) 810829.
Reservations:
Made with deposit of one night's fee (min. 3 nights at B.Hs).

176 Ripley Caravan Park, Ripley

Family run touring park with heated indoor pool.

Peter and Valerie House are the resident owners of Ripley Park, an 18 acre grass site accommodating 100 units. Pitches are not marked but are carefully spaced (allowing the grass to recover) on fairly level grass, undulating in parts with 72 electrical connections and 10 hardstandings, all connected by circular gravelled roads. The park has a fairly open field like aspect, with trees beginning to grow and a small pond (lake) provides a pretty feature. The central, attractive toilet block provides pushbutton showers, washbasins in curtained cubicles, baby bath and a separate unit for the disabled with shower. Small laundry, washing up sinks under cover. The leisure block by the entrance with the reception and shop, offers a games room with TV, nursery play room and a heated indoor pool (50p pp), sauna and sunbed. Play area. Dog walk - dogs welcome (max. 2 per unit). The park is situated at the gateway to the Yorkshire Dales National Park and almost midway between the spa town of Harrogate and historic Knaresborough. The village of Ripley, dominated by its castle, is within walking distance.

Directions: About 4 miles north of Harrogate, entrance is 150 yds. down B6165 Knaresborough road from roundabout junction with A61. O.S.GR: SE291601.

Charges 1995:
-- Per unit incl. 2 persons £5.00 - £6.50; extra person (over 5 yrs) £1.00; pup tent £1.50; awning 75p; electricity £1.60.
-- Per family unit £9.00.
-- VAT included.
Open:
Easter - 31 October.
Address:
Ripley, Harrogate, Yorks HG3 3AU.
Tel:
(01423) 770050 or (01836) 562899.
Reservations:
Made with £10 deposit.

Ripley Caravan Park
where the country and enjoyment comes naturally...

This luxury touring caravan park in the beautiful North Yorkshire countryside, is within easy reach of Ripley Castle, village and only ten minutes north of Harrogate.

First class facilities include amenities for the disabled; there is a shop, laundry, games rooms, telephone, childrens playground and play area, electric hook-up points and an indoor heated swimming pool.

For further information:–
Peter & Valerie House, Ripley Caravan Park,
Ripley, Harrogate, HG3 3AU.
Tel: (01423) 770050   *Dogs permitted*

177 Rudding Holiday Park, Follifoot, Harrogate

Touring park set in quiet, mature parkland, with swimming pool and golf course.

Within the Rudding Park Estate where the extensive, part-wooded, part-open grounds are at campers' disposal, this park has an attractive, quiet, rural setting. It is principally a touring park with 141 pitches for units of any type, all with electrical connections, arranged in three parts. One is formed from the old kitchen garden with pitches on fairly flat grass, backing onto walls or hedges, another is beyond on more open, gently sloping parkland under mature trees with a further area for 17 fully serviced `super' pitches (including satellite TV) near 85 owner occupied caravan holiday homes and lodges in their own area. Two excellent, modern sanitary blocks are centrally heated and well maintained and equipped. They have free hot water in the washbasins, some in private cabins, pre-set showers (button beside door), babies' room, bathroom and well equipped launderette. Separate facilities for the disabled. A heated outdoor swimming pool, (43 x 20 ft.), with paddling pool, is open Spr. B.H. - early Sept and is charged for (closes 5 pm.). Self-service shop. Separate restaurant/bar (Inn on the Park) a little away from the other amenities near the new 18 hole golf course and driving range. Children's adventure playground on bark and games room, minigolf, mountain bikes for hire. Public phones. Hot air balloon trips are arranged on most summer evenings! A well run, quality site.

Directions: Park is 3 miles south of Harrogate clearly signed between the A658 and A661 roads. O.S.GR: SE333528.

Charges 1995:
-- Per pitch £9.30 - £11.80, with electricity £11.50 - £14.00; super pitch £13.00 - £18.00; 2-man tent £5.50 - £6.50; extra car £1.00; dogs (on leads) free.
-- Special offers - contact park.
-- VAT included.
-- Credit cards accepted.
Open:
15 March - 3 November.
Address:
Follifoot, Harrogate, N. Yorks HG3 1JH.
Tel:
Harrogate (01423) 870439.
Reservations:
Made with full advance payment (essential for B.H. w/ends).

Alan Rogers'
discount
Ask for details
at the park

178 Wood Nook Caravan Park, Threshfield, Skipton

Small, rural park, farm-owned, for touring units; popular for walking holidays in Wharfedale.

Wood Nook, within the Yorkshire Dales National Park, includes 6 acres of woodland, with wildlife and flora and views of the surrounding Dales. Do not be put off by the narrow access road but continue to the farmhouse and reception and meet the peacocks. There are two gently sloping, oval fields with gravelled roads, providing 25 pitches, mainly for caravans (some with hardstandings), and 24 for tents backing onto dry stone walls. All have electricity (long leads may be required) and there are water and chemical toilet points available. The sanitary blocks, with a key system, are contained within the farm buildings. Do not be deceived - the conversions provide modern facilities with washbasins in cabins, mirrors, shelves and hairdryers. The showers, with curtains, hooks and stools, are coin-operated, but in separate areas, all well maintained. Laundry and dishwashing facilities. A small shop beside reception, open for 2 hours in the morning, and 2 in the evening, provides basics; public telephone and new information area. Dogs are welcome on a lead and an exercise area is provided. The park has 10 static vans for hire and a holiday cottage, originally a coach-house and granary. An attractive children's play area is on top of a small hill, between the touring fields and farmhouse buildings. The farm produces beef cattle and is operated by the owners alongside the caravan/camping park. Food is available at the Old Hall Inn at Threshfield. There is direct access to the fells and the National Park from the top of the site - follow the gurgling stream.

Charges 1995:
-- Per adult £2.00; child (3-15 yrs) 50p, (16-17 yrs as part of a family unit) £1.00; pitch incl.car £3.00; awning £1.00; hiker/cyclist £2.50; electricity £1.50.
Open:
1 March - 31 October.
Address:
Skirethorns,
Threshfield, Skipton,
N. Yorks, BD23 5NU.
Tel:
Grassington (01756) 752412.
Reservations:
Necessary for high season and B.H.s with £10 deposit. American motorhomes by prior arrangement only.

Directions: From Skipton take the B6265 to Threshfield, then the B6160. After 50 yds turn left into Skirethorns Lane and follow signs for 600 yds, up narrow lane then 300 yds. O.S.GR: SD992517.

WOOD NOOK near GRASSINGTON

small secluded park in the heart of the YORKSHIRE DALES

ROSE AWARD CARAVAN HOLIDAY PARK

TEL/FAX 01756 752412

CARAVAN HOLIDAY HOMES for HIRE TOURING CARAVANS and TENTS

TOILETS, SHOWERS, ELECTRIC HOOK-UPS, SHOP, CHILDREN'S PLAY AREA, AA 3 PENNANTS

stamp for brochure to:

Mrs Thompson, Wood Nook Caravan Park, Skirethorns, Threshfield, Skipton, N. Yorks BD23 5NU

---

179 Scotch Corner Caravan Park, Scotch Corner, Richmond

Touring park with good toilet block at junction of main routes.

This park is most conveniently placed for overnight stops for north - south travellers but is also suitable for longer stays to explore the Yorkshire Dales and Moors. Part of the Caravan Club's 'managed under contract' scheme, non-members are also very welcome. It takes 75 units of any type with well spaced pitches on flat grass marked out by jockey-wheel plates. There are 44 electrical connections (10A). The single toilet block (on a key system) is of ample size with washbasins with free hot water and separators, free controllable hot showers with curtain screen and covered washing-up sinks. Washing machine and tumble dryer. The park has a shop (8-11 am and 4-6 pm) and there is an adjacent hotel for drinks and restaurant or bar meals. Gates closed 11 pm - 8 am.

Charges 1995:
-- Per unit incl. 2 persons £8.00 - £9.00; extra person £3.00; child (under 12) £1.10; awning free; extra car £1.00; electricity £1.25.
Open:
Easter - mid-October.
Address:
Scotch Corner,
Richmond, N. Yorks.
Tel:
Richmond (01748) 822530 or 824424.
Reservations:
Any length with one nights fee.

Directions: Park is 100 yds from the roundabout junction of A1 and A6108 with entrance off the Richmond road. O.S.GR: SD211050.

180 Constable Burton Hall Caravan Park, nr. Leyburn

Tranquil park in beautiful Wensleydale for caravans and motorcaravans only.

For those who require a relaxed and quiet environment - this is the site for you. It blends in very well with the surrounding countryside, being situated in what was the Hall's deer park and every effort has been made to make it as unobtrusive as possible. The laundry room and sanitary blocks, with ample showers and washbasins, are built with local stone and were very clean when visited. One has been adapted from the former deer barn and is consequently an unusual shape. The park is on lovely grass, part level, part sloping, and the 120 pitches are of a good size, all with electricity (10A). Ideally placed for visiting the Northern Dales, there are many interesting towns, villages and historical sites within a short drive as well as the beautiful countryside. There is no shop but all you should need is available in nearby Leyburn. Opposite the park entrance is the Wyvill Arms - well worth a visit! Dogs are permitted on leads. Public telephone. Gates closed 10 pm - 8 am.

Charges 1996:
-- Per unit incl. 2 persons £7.50; extra adult £2.00; child 70p; awning £1.50; extra car 50p; electricity £2.00.
-- Less £1 5/9-31/10.
-- VAT included.
Open:
Early April - end Oct.
Address:
Constable Burton Hall, nr. Leyburn, N. Yorks DL8 5LJ.
Tel:
(01677) 450428.
Reservations:
With deposit (£20 for B.Hs. £5 other times).

Directions: Park is by A684 between Bedale and Leyburn, ½ mile from the village of Constable Burton on the Leyburn side. O.S.GR: SE152907.

181 Holme Valley Camping and Caravan Park, nr. Holmfirth

Attractive, small park in heart of `summer wine' country.

There are 62 reasonably sized pitches situated around a well stocked former mill pond at Holme Valley (fishing available). The site is sheltered and bounded on two sides by the River Holme (the small lake and bridge have been featured in `The Last of the Summer Wine'). Many pitches enjoy good shade from mature trees and are naturally divided amongst the silver birch, all with access to electricity (16A). The heated sanitary block, built in local stone, is very clean, well decorated and gives more than adequate provision. There is a separate facility for handicapped visitors, a fully equipped laundry room and a `designer' chemical disposal unit! The park has a very reasonably priced, well stocked shop (licensed for off-sales) and at peak periods, there is a takeaway van which provides a range of meals from breakfasts and snacks to full Sunday lunches including Yorkshire pudding! There is a solarium, a children's play area (with bark surface and fencing) and an attractive terrace for relaxation. The park also has caravans (tourer type) for hire. The Holme Valley is very beautiful and there are lovely walks all around. Holmfirth with many leisure facilities and eating places is just over 1 mile away. This is a site ideally located for visiting the Pennines, the Peak District and, a little further away, the Dales, as well as the towns of West Yorkshire which have fascinating museums charting our industrial heritage. Dogs are permitted on leads.

Charges 1995:
-- Per large caravan or trailer tent incl. up to 4 persons and awning £7.00 - £8.00, caravan or small trailer tent incl. 4 persons £6.00 - £7.00, motorcaravan or tent incl. 2 persons £5.00 - £6.00; extra person (over 2 yrs) 50p; extra car £1.00; electricity £1.70.
-- VAT included.
Open:
All year.
Address:
Thongsbridge, Holmfirth, W. Yorks HD7 2TD.
Tel:
(01484) 665819.
Reservations:
Advised at peak periods, preferred other times; made with deposit (full cost of first night).

Directions: Park is a few miles south of Huddersfield, halfway between Honley and Holmfirth on the A6024 (signed from the main road) and approached by a reasonably steep, but easily negotiable, gravel road. O.S.GR: SE144102.

 Alan Rogers' discount
Ask at park for details

We would like to thank the parks which offer discounts to our readers.

Remember - you will need to show your 1996 discount card on arrival at the park

182 Nostell Priory Holiday Home Park, Nostell, nr. Wakefield

Very attractive quiet woodland park site.

Situated within the estate of Nostell Priory, this well cared for site provides an excellent base from which to explore the area's many attractions. The 60 tourist pitches, all with electrical connections (5A), are located in a grassy, flat and sheltered area separate from the 80 static holiday caravans. There are adequate water points and an area of hardstanding. Amenities blend into the environment in rustic wood, including the clean, well maintained sanitary block. There is a fully equipped laundry and a good children's play area. Milk and newspapers can be ordered but there is no shop (shops 1½ - 2 miles away in local villages and numerous supermarkets 5 miles in Wakefield). Nostell Priory with its attractive gardens and the Rose Centre are well worth a visit and the Dales, York, the Peak District and the East Coast are all within an hours drive. However there are many places of interest and leisure within 20 minutes of the park. A hardworking, friendly management are keen to help visitors make the most of their stay and also help the children to appreciate the abundance of wild life in the park. Dogs accepted on leads (max. 2 per unit).

Directions: There is excellent access from other parts of the country via M1, M62 or A1. The park entrance is off the A638 Wakefield - Doncaster road, 5 miles from Wakefield. O.S.GR: SE394181.

Charges 1996:
-- Per unit incl. 2 persons £7.50 - £8.50; extra person (over 5 yrs) 50p; extra vehicle 50p; awning £1.00; electricity (5A) £1.25; dog £1.00.
-- Reductions mid week for senior citizens.
-- VAT included.
Open:
1 April - 30 September.
Address:
Nostell, Wakefield, W. Yorks WF4 1QD.
Tel:
(01924) 863938.
Reservations:
Advisable and made with £5 deposit and 50p fee (min. 2 nights).

North West Tourist Board

Swan House, Swan Meadow Rd, Wigan Pier, Wigan, WN3 5BB
Tel: (01942) 821222. Fax: (01942) 820002

Lancashire, Cheshire, Greater Manchester, Merseyside
and the High Peaks of Derbyshire.

1996 Events: Grand National, Aintree, 28-30 March: 8th. Lancaster Easter Maritime Festival, 5-8 April: 32nd Buxton Annual Antiques Fair, 11-18 May: 3rd International Gilbert and Sullivan Festival, Buxton, 4-18 Aug: Southport Flower Show, 22-24 Aug: International Mersey Beatle Festival, Liverpool. 22-27 Aug: Blackpool Illuminations, 30 Aug-3 Nov.

---

183 Chester Southerly Caravan Park, Chester

Busy, satisfactory park convenient for visiting historic Chester.

On flat ground by the Chester southerly bypass and therefore attracting much international transit trade, this park takes 92 touring units (72 caravans and 20 tents). Caravan pitches are mainly on hardstandings and marked by flagstones, off large gravelled bays with 63 electrical connections available; tents go on an unmarked meadow. The single toilet block is bright and clean and of fair size, with free hot water in both washbasins (with shelf) and showers, and with facilities for handicapped. Coin operated hair dryers. 6 washing-up sinks and launderette. Food preparation/dishwashing room. There is a small shop with basics (order milk, bread and papers daily) open odd hours and evenings. Public telephone. Rustic type adventure playground on bark. Duck pond. This is a useful, partially landscaped park which usually has space available - no commercial vehicles (eg. vans) taken. Reception is only open certain hours, morning and evening. There may be some road noise.

Directions: Park is on the Dodleston/Kinnerton turn off from A483 and is signed from the junction of A55 and A483. O.S.GR: SJ385624.

Charges 1995:
-- Per unit incl. 2 adults £6.00 - £7.80; 1 adult £3.65 - £4.50; extra adult £2.35 - £3.30; child (5-16 yrs) £1.10 - £1.20; awning free - 50p; electricity £1.25 - £1.40 (low season).
Open:
1 March - 30 November.
Address:
Balderton Lane, Marlston-cum-Lache, Chester CH4 9LF.
Tel:
Farndon (01829) 270697 or 270791.
(Evenings and w/ends)
Reservations:
Accepted for B.Hs. Other times min. 5 days.

184 Royal Umpire Caravan Park, Croston, nr Preston

Good, spacious park near coast and M6 motorway for overnight stops or longer stays.

Much progress has been made in improving and updating this 58-acre park by its owners (a major local caravan dealer). It has 200 pitches, almost all with electricity (10A) and 4 super pitches. Pitches are given plenty of space in distinct bays, separated and sheltered by pleasant trees and shrubs, on level grass or hardstanding (with TV and water connections). The two, tiled toilet blocks, one beside reception, have been modernised to top standards with well equipped showers, free hot water, and kept spotlessly clean. Fully equipped laundry and dishwashing sinks. Special facilities for disabled visitors shared with baby facilities. Among the general facilities are a licensed shop, indoor recreation area with table tennis, pool and various games, a super adventure playground on bark and a leisure area consisting of an outdoor shuffle board, boules, chess and draughts overlooking a rather attractive garden/water grotto. First aid room. Outside information area. There is a separate field for rallies and a good choice of pubs serving bar or restaurant meals nearby. It is a tidy, well run site with a good welcome from the managers, Norman and Christine Roberts. Gates closed 11 pm. - 7 am. (outside parking provided). The first park to be awarded BS5750, this is reflected in the good management of the park. A member of the Best of British group.

Directions: If approaching from north use exit 28 from the M6 and join the A49 going south (parallel to M6) for 2 miles. Then turn right across M6 on A581 to Croston (approx. 4 miles). From the south use exit 27 from the M6 onto the A5209 but immediately take right turn on B5250 and follow in direction of Eccleston, joining the A581 at Newtown (approx. 5 miles). Park is clearly signed with wide entrance east of Croston. O.S.GR: SD505189.

Charges guide:
-- Per unit incl. 2 persons and awning £5.40 - £8.80; back packer/ cyclist £3.15 - 3.85; extra adult £3.15; extra child (5-17 yrs) £1.15 - £1.45; electricity £1.95 - £1.65; satellite TV £1.50; extra car, boat £1.20; `superpitch' plus £4.50 - £6.00.
-- VAT included.
Open:
All year except 7 Nov - 21 Dec.
Address:
Southport Road, Croston, nr. Preston, Lancs PR5 7HP.
Tel:
Preston (01772) 600257.
FAX: (01772) 600662.
Reservations:
Made with £2 per night deposit and £1 fee.

185 Bridge House Marina and Caravan Park, Nateby, Garstang

Small, friendly park on bank of Lancaster Canal, close to M6; for caravans, motorvans and trailer tents.

A nice little park making a good stopover close to the M6 and A6, Bridge House is also only 12 miles from Morecambe and 15 from Blackpool. Adjacent to the Marina (with joint reception/shop) and the Lancaster Canal, the park has 50 pitches on flat grass, all marked but with nothing between them; giving a pleasant open feel about the place. Caravans, motorcaravans and trailer tents are taken, but not other tents, with 25 hardstandings and 37 electrical connections (note: no groundsheets). It can become full, especially at B.Hs. The part-tiled toilet block has washbasins set in flat surfaces, well spaced out with free hot water, mirrors and well equipped hot showers. Laundry and dishwashing room (10p for hot water) in the same block. Shop at entrance with provisions and boat accessories. Some children's play equipment and large grass play area. No other on-site amenities but pub with meals and shops quite close. Dogs permitted (on leads) with a pleasant exercise area on the old railway line behind the site.

Directions: Garstang is on the A6 between exits 32 and 33 of the M6. Follow A6 Garstang bypass and turn off west by Chequered Flag pub, then right at once and park is 300 yds. O.S.GR: SD483458.

Charges 1995:
-- Per unit £6.20; awning 80p; porch awning 50p; electricity £1.20.
-- VAT included.
Open:
All year except 5 Jan - 28 Feb.
Address:
Nateby, Garstang, nr. Preston, Lancs PR3 0JJ.
Tel:
Garstang (01995) 603207.
FAX: (01995) 601612.
Reservations:
Made for any length without deposit.

Cumbria Tourist Board

Ashleigh, Holly Road, Windermere LA23 2AQ

Tel: (015394) 44444

Covering the county of Cumbria and the English Lake District, this region with its lakes, mountains and fells is unique. Visitors from all over the world are attracted by the scenic beauty of the Lake District, with its mountains, still lakes and villages which seem to have grown out of the rocky landscape. Stone walls can be seen stretching skywards over all but the highest hills in an area where beauty inspired Wordsworth, bringing walkers and climbers in droves.

186 Limefitt Park, Troutbeck, Windermere

see advertisement on inside front cover

Well managed Lake District park with outdoor activities.

Limefitt Park is centrally situated for the southern lakes and has fine views and walks, with the beck running alongside. It is a park with various active pursuits available and some evening entertainment and is basically for families or couples (no organised groups of young people). It is very well managed with excellent facilities. The pitches for touring caravans are good and flat, with hard-standing, electricity (10A) and water, with cars parked at an angle on further hardstanding. The remainder of the park is on flat or slightly sloping grass with some terracing and shade provided by trees with numbered pitches for tents or more caravans or motorcaravans. The ground by the beck has been developed for 45 log cabins (for private sale) and there is another field for 20 long stay caravans. The sanitary facilities consist of one large, central block for the tenting area and a smaller block for the caravan area, accessed by combination locks. Both are of excellent quality, well maintained and fully tiled with modern fittings including oval washbasins, with mixer taps, flat surfaces, mirrors and side lighting. Hot water is free. Toddler's room with half-size bath and changing facilities. Covered washing-up sinks. Well stocked supermarket and licensed bar lounge with real ales, bar meals and weekly entertainment, both open all season. Bistro restaurant. Takeaway. DIY camping kitchen (metered). Launderette. Sporting activities from park include walking, pony trekking (main season only), fishing. Bicycle hire. Games room with many machines. Play field and adventure playground on grass by the river and small beach area with picnic tables. American motorhomes not accepted. Only one dog allowed per touring pitch, none at all with tents. Boats not accepted. The park is full and very busy for a long season, reservation is advisable.

Directions: Limefitt is 2½ miles north up the A592 from its junction with the A591 north of Windermere. O.S.GR: NY416030.

Charges 1995:
-- Per unit incl. 2 persons and electricity £9.50 - £11.50; tent £9.00 - £11.00; extra adult £2.00 - £2.50; child (2-14 yrs) £1.00 - £1.25; awning, pup tent, trailer or 2nd car £1.75 - £2.25.
-- Max. charge 1 family pitch £11.50 - £14.00 (excl. supplements).
-- VAT included.
Open:
18 March - 29 October.
Address:
Windermere, Cumbria LA23 1PA.
Tel:
(015394) 32300.
FAX: (015394) 32848.
Reservations:
Made with full payment at time of booking.

Alan Rogers' discount
Ask for details at the park

This small, quiet and pleasant touring site overlooking the Bowland Hills is family owned and operated, ideally situated for Blackpool, Morecombe or the Lake District.

The Park caters for fifty tourers and is adjacent to our Boating Marina alongside the Lancaster Canal.

We are ideally placed for the holiday-maker wishing to spend a holiday in the country or a night halt for people travelling north or south.

★ Electric hook-up   ★ Dogs welcome on lead
★ Shop, Laundry room   ★ Fishing permits available
★ Childrens play area   ★ Pony treking by arrangement

Nateby, Garstang, Nr. Preston, Lancashire, PR3 0JJ.
Telephone Garstang 3207

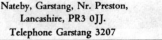

115

187 Fallbarrow Park, Bowness, Windermere

Park with Lake Windermere frontage, for caravans only; many caravan holiday homes.

Fallbarrow Park is most attractively situated alongside Lake Windermere with a lake frontage of about 600 m; one can stroll among the lawns, gardens and mature trees near the lake which are not occupied by caravans and swimming and boating are possible from the site. It is only a ¼ mile walk to the centre of the attractive resort of Bowness. The major part of the park is occupied by seasonal holiday homes - about 70 for letting and 180 private ones. However, there are also 72 marked touring pitches, regraded to provide more space, in two areas for caravans and motorcaravans only, the `Glade' and the `Lake'. All pitches have hardstanding, electricity and and water, with TV and waste water connections to some. Pitches are very heavily booked and reservations are essential June - Sept. American motorhomes accepted (max. 25 ft.) with prior booking. No vehicle entry to the park after 11.30 p.m.

Two toilet blocks serve the touring sections (access by combination locks). The one in the central building is of an excellent standard with smart, modern fittings and lighting (music also!). It provides washbasins in surfaces with mirrors, showers with controllable mixer tap, baby washroom and make-up/ hair-drying tables with stools. The other block has been refurbished to the same high standard. Both provide free hot water in washbasins and showers. The new `Boathouse' pub contains spacious and comfortable lounges with bar and hot snacks (said to be the best in Bowness). TV lounge with music or entertainment at times. Supermarket. Public phones. Dog exercise area (one dog only per booking). Launderette. Dishwashing. Takeaway. Large games room. Good, grass based, children's adventure play area. Boat park with winter boat-parking. Very smart, comfortable reception also providing tourist information. Sailing, watersports, fishing, pony trekking and numerous visitor attractions close.

Directions: Park is by the A592 road just north of Bowness town centre. O.S.GR: SD401971.

Charges 1995:
-- Per unit inclusive:
Glade pitch £9.95 - £13.85; Lake pitch £11.15 - £14.95; awning £2.90 - £3.70; boat (max 17 ft.) £9.30; sailboard or canoe £1.85; extra car £1.90 - £2.05.
-- VAT included.

Open:
Mid March - end October.

Address:
Rayrigg Road, Windermere, Cumbria LA23 3DL.

Tel:
Windermere (015394) 44428.
FAX: (015394) 88736.

Reservations:
Made for 3 nights min. (7 at Spring B.H). Payment in full at time of booking.

Alan Rogers'
discount
Ask for details
at the park

fallbarrow ♀ park
...more than just a picturesque lakeside location.

Set amidst this wooded parkland that borders the eastern shore of Lake Windermere — you may find your ideal holiday.
Lake and Glade touring sites with free electric hook-ups, individual hardstandings and grass surrounds. First class toilet and shower facilities. Friendly reception and information centre. Licensed bar with good food. Family lounge. Mini-market with off-licence. Children's playground — and of course boat launching facilities.
And — not 300 yards away there's the Lakeland village of Bowness with its restaurants, shops, local inns and lake cruises.

AA **acsi** **RAC** **Rose award park** **The Discerning Choice For Over 25 Years**

For full colour brochure write to Fallbarrow Park, Windermere, The Lake District LA23 3DL or telephone (015394) 44428

188 Skelwith Fold Caravan Park, Ambleside

Spacious, family owned park for caravans, motorhomes and trailer tents only in southern Lake District.

Skelwith Fold has been developed in the grounds of a country estate taking advantage of the wealth of mature trees and shrubs. The 300 privately owned caravan holiday homes and 150 touring pitches are absorbed into this unspoilt natural environment, sharing it with red squirrels and other wildlife in several discrete areas branching off the central, mile long main driveway. Touring pitches are on gravel hardstanding and metal pegs will be necessary for awnings. Electric hook-ups (10A) and basic amenities available in all areas. The owners have completed a programme of updating all eight toilet blocks, providing free hot showers and all usual facilities including laundry, drying and ironing rooms. There is a well stocked, licensed self-service shop, together with a store for gas, battery charging and caravan spares and accessories. Public phones. While there is an adventure playground, most youngsters and indeed their parents will find endless pleasure exploring over 50 acres of wild woodland and, if early risers, it is possible to see deer, foxes, etc. taking their breakfast in the almost hidden tarn deep in the woods. It is a fascinating site at any time of the year, but beautiful in the spring with wild daffodils, bluebells and later rhododendrons and azaleas. Family recreational area with picnic tables and goal posts. Reservation is essential for July, August and B.Hs. 1½ miles to Ambleside village.

Directions: From Ambleside take the A593 towards Coniston. Pass through Clappergate and on far outskirts watch for B5286 to Hawkshead on the left. Park is clearly signed 1 mile down this road on the right. O.S.GR: NY358028.

Charges 1995:
-- Per caravan or trailer tent £8.00; motor caravan £7.50 (both + £1.00 in August); awning £2.50; porch awning £1.20; extra car £1.50; boat £4.00; electricity £1.50.
-- Discounts for weekly or monthly stays.
-- VAT included.
Open:
1 March - 15 November.
Address:
Ambleside, Cumbria LA22 0HX.
Tel:
(015394) 32277 (site office) or 32327.
Reservations:
Essential for July/Aug and B.Hs;made for min. 3 days with £10 deposit.

189 Walls Caravan and Camping Park, Ravenglass

Small, neat, well equipped park in west Cumbria.

Set in 5 acres of existing woodland amongst mature trees, Walls was once part of the large Pennington Estate. It has space for 50 caravans or motorcaravans on hardstanding with a grass verge for awnings. A small grass area at the top and back of the park provides an attractive spot for tents. A circular gravel road provides access and all pitches have electrical hook-ups (10A). An attractively designed central courtyard complex includes the owner's home, reception with tourist information, `shop' (only a few basic necessities) and a good modern toilet block with all the usual amenities and H&C water throughout. This is very well kept and has a warm, comfortable feeling often missing in British campsite toilet blocks. There is also a laundry room, with baby bath, washing machine, spin dryer, iron and board and a separate room with dishwashing facilities. All is excellently maintained by Keith and Stephanie Bridges, who have used the site since it was first developed and now own it and provide a very warm welcome. Dogs are permitted but must be exercised off the park and poopscoops used. It is a useful site to explore the Cumbria coast with its Roman connections, the western Lake District or to enjoy the Ravenglass and Eskdale Miniature Railway. The small village of Ravenglass - a single, cottage lined street - is within walking distance and does provide a pub.

Directions: Park is just off the A595 (between Egremont and Millom) on the road into the village of Ravenglass. O.S.GR: SD096965.

Charges 1996:
-- Per caravan, frame or trailer tent incl. 2 adults £7.00, motorcaravan £6.50; ridge tent (2 persons) £6.00; small tent (1 person) £3.50; extra person 50p; child under 16 yrs free; awning 50p; electricity £1.50; dog 50p; extra car 50p.
Open:
1 March - 15 November.
Address:
Ravenglass, Cumbria CA18 1SR.
Tel:
Ravenglass (01229) 717250.
Reservations:
Are accepted - contact park.

Also published by Deneway Guides & Travel:

Directory of Camping and Caravanning ALL YEAR ROUND

Available by mail order from the publishers - phone 01308 897809

190 Wild Rose Park, Appleby-in-Westmorland

Well organised, family park in Eden Valley with holiday homes also.

In a peaceful, rural situation within reach of the Lake District and the Yorkshire Dales, Wild Rose is a well managed, attractively laid out park which deserves its excellent reputation. There are 180 tourist pitches in two distinct areas, one level with hardstanding, fully serviced pitches for trailer and motor caravans, the other a sloping field for 60 tents. There is a number of super pitches with all facilities, plus their own barbecue, picnic table, artificial turf and satellite TV connections (expect these to be booked well in advance). Owner-occupied holiday homes have their own areas.

The three very well maintained and modern toilet blocks are of excellent quality with washbasins, mainly in private cabins, with free hot water, mirror and light. Provision for babies includes baths, bottle warmers and other facilities and there are hair washing basins and dryers for ladies. The central block, near reception, has good, free hot showers (access by key). All have washing-up sinks with free hot water. Facilities for the disabled. A swimming pool (20 x 50 ft) is open 10 am. - 10 pm. and heated mid-May to mid-Sept with a paddling pool adjacent. Well stocked shop, attractive restaurant (both Easter - end Oct) and takeaway service. Two TV rooms and children's video shows. Games room including table tennis for older children and Postman Pat's room for the under-5s - marvellous for rainy days. Launderette and drying room. Telephones. Fly fishing. Pitch and putt and other outdoor games. BMX track and bikes for hire. Playgrounds with safety surfaces. Dogs (excluding dangerous breeds) are permitted on leads and a small exercise area is provided. Motorcaravan service station. American motorhomes are accepted but in season prior booking is essential. There are many good walks in the area and the Appleby Castle Conservation Centre (with Norman keep) and Rare Breeds Survival Trust are near; Appleby Horse Fair is in June. A well run, quality site and a member of the Best of British group.

Directions: Park is signed south off B6260 road 1½ miles southwest of Appleby. Follow signs to park, in the direction of Ormside. O.S.GR: NY697165.

Charges 1995:
-- Per unit incl. 2 persons: standard pitch £6.85 - £10.30; super pitch £12.50 - £24.20; walker or cyclist £2.50; extra person (over 4 yrs) £1.30; awning, extra car, toilet or pup tent £1.70; electricity summer £1.90, winter £2.50; first dog free, others £1.00.
-- 10% discount for 7 nights or more.
-- Special winter or long-stay rates.
-- VAT included.
-- Credit cards accepted.
Open:
All year.
Address:
Ormside, Appleby-in-Westmorland, Cumbria CA16 6EJ.
Tel:
Appleby (017683) 51077.
FAX: (017683) 52551.
Reservations:
Made with deposit of £5 per night + £1 fee, remainder on arrival. Min. 3 nights at B.Hs.

Excellence in Eden

Friendly family park in beautiful countryside with magnificent views of the Pennines. Ideal base for exploring the LAKE DISTRICT and YORKSHIRE DALES, or simply relax and enjoy the peace and tranquillity of the EDEN VALLEY.

Superb facilities for tourers and tents including super clean loo's, laundry, special play facilities for under five's, playground and sports areas for older children, heated outdoor swimming pools, TV rooms and games for all the family to enjoy.

Well stocked mini-market and licensed restaurant with take-away.

Seasonal and Monthly rates for tourers, also Luxury Holiday Homes for sale- Seasonal or all year use. Sorry No Letting, No Bar, No Club.

Brochure with pleasure- Telephone 017683 51077

Ormside,

Appleby-in-

Westmorland,

Cumbria

CA16 6EJ

191 Sykeside Camping Park, Patterdale, nr. Penrith

Touring park in attractive Lake District location for tents and a few motor caravans.

This small site, set in the northern lakes area, is ideal for active holidays with walking or climbing on high hills, and the small lake of Brotherswater ¼ mile away taking dinghies or canoes. It would also be useful for a touring holiday and is a little away from the busiest areas. It takes 100 tents which could include a few motorhomes, but no caravans, on flat grass in the valley floor. Pitches are not marked and campers arrange themselves. Reservations are advisable for peak times. 14 electrical connections. The stone-built, main block near the entrance (200 m. from the field) houses all the facilities, including the washing and toilet block which has washbasins with free hot water (1 private cubicle in ladies and make-up section), and hot showers (20p). Small launderette. Dishwashing room. Self-service shop doubling as reception, with camping equipment, boot hire and ice-pack service. Public telephone. An attractive, licensed bar and restaurant serves breakfast and evening meals. Bunkhouse accommodation is provided for 30 persons in various groupings. Fishing and pony trekking available nearby.

Charges 1995:
-- Per adult £1.60 - £2.10; child (3-14) 85p - £1.00; car or m/cycle £1.60 - £2.10; tent or awning £1.60 - £2.10; dog 50p..
-- VAT included.
Open:
All year.
Address:
Brotherswater, Patterdale, Penrith, Cumbria CA11 0NZ.
Tel:
(01768) 482239.
Reservations:
Made with £10 deposit; Easter & Spr. B.H. - min. 3 or 4 days.

Directions: On west side of A592 road about 2 miles south of Patterdale, which lies at the southwestern end of Ullswater. O.S.GR: NY396005.

192 The Larches Caravan Park, Mealsgate, nr. Carlisle

Peaceful, quality, family run park with excellent sanitary facilities.

Mealsgate and The Larches lie on the Carlisle - Cockermouth road, a little removed from the hectic centre of the Lakes, yet with easy access to it (and good views towards it) and to other attractions near - the Western Borders, North-umberland, etc. The park takes 73 touring units of any type with 100 privately owned holiday leisure homes. Touring pitches are in different grassy areas with tall, mature trees, shrubs and accompanying wildlife. Some are sloping and irregular, others on marked hardstandings, with electricity and water. The sanitary blocks are a feature of the site, particularly one of outstanding quality consisting of en-suite facilities for both sexes. The block also includes a purpose designed unit for disabled of either sex and can be heated. The second block is also fully tiled with the ladies' washbasins in cubicles and men's set in flat surfaces, with controllable hot showers. Well stocked shop with events in the surrounding district displayed prominently in the window. Games room. Table tennis. TV room in summerhouse. Camping kitchen with metered power to cooker, microwave and breakfast bar. Laundry room. Telephone. The Elliots provide a warm welcome at this very well organised, tranquil park, which is very suitable for couples. On arrival everyone is loaned very comprehensive tourist information brochures. Bus route to Carlisle and Keswick. Walks from the park.

Charges 1995:
-- Per unit (incl. 2 persons) £6.50 - £8.50; backpacker £3.50 - £4.50; m/cycle + 1 person £3.50 - £4.50; extra person, awning or car £1.00; electricity £1.80.
-- VAT included.
Open:
March - October incl.
Address:
Mealsgate, nr. Carlisle, Cumbria CA5 1LQ.
Tel:
(01697) 371379.
FAX: (01697) 371782.
Reservations:
Made with £1 per night deposit, balance on arrival.

Directions: Park entrance is south off the A595 (Carlisle-Cockermouth) road just southwest of Mealsgate. O.S.GR: NY206415.

193 The Quiet Site, Watermillock, Lake Ullswater

Peaceful, family site for tents and some caravans overlooking Lake Ullswater and fells.

This small, family run park, 1½ miles from the western shores of Ullswater, provides a friendly welcome in a situation ideal for enjoying the attractions of the Lake District with a touch of individualism aimed at children. Attractively laid out, with flowers and trees, the park provides sheltered pitches on sloping grass with terracing for motorcaravans and tents and tarmac access roads. It takes 50 tents and 10 tourers in separate areas - units are placed by the family. There are 23 holiday homes also. Reservation is essential for the small number of caravan pitches. Electricity and hardstandings are available. American motorhomes accepted by arrangement.

The amenities are housed in converted farm buildings, the main features being the bar with open fire, old furniture, wooden beams and balconies, with `no smoking area' and pool table (Americans just want to transport it lock, stock and barrel to the USA!). Shop/reception, games and TV rooms. The bar and shop open from the week before Easter. The toilet facilities are adjacent (a little way from the tent pitches) providing adequate facilities with free hot water to the washbasins, vanity style for ladies, the showers and the separate dishwashing sinks. Laundry facilities also. There is a `fort' adventure playground for children, with bark surface, an adjacent play field, pets area (including pot bellied pigs) with the possibility of helping at feeding time, and a wild flower area. Public telephone. Dogs are allowed on a lead but must be exercised off-site - there is a track leading up the hill for some distance behind the site and a `Short Walk' map and local information sheet is available. The Aira Falls may be reached on foot from the park.

Directions: From M6 exit J40 take A66 for Keswick. After 1 mile take A592 for Ullswater. After 7 miles turn right at T junction (still on A592) and after 1½ miles turn right at the Brackenrigg Hotel. Site is on **right** after 1½ miles. Book in at shop. O.S.GR: NY431236.

Charges 1995:
-- Per caravan incl. 2 persons and car £7.50 - £9.00; motorcaravan or tent £6.50 - £8.00; awning £1.50; extra person (over 4 yrs), pup tent, car or boat £1.00; dog 50p; electricity (10A) £1.75.
-- VAT included.
Open:
1 March - 31 October.
Address:
Watermillock, Penrith, Cumbria CA11 0LS.
Tel:
Pooley Bridge (01768) 486337.
Reservations:
Essential for caravans, min. 7 days for Easter and Spr. B.H. with £10 deposit.

194 Kielder Water Caravan Club Site, Falstone

Caravan Club site overlooking Kielder Water, welcoming non-members.

Situated in a high, woodland setting, above the shores of Kielder Lake there are superb views across the water from many of the 118 terraced pitches at this park. The pitches are individually marked, 99 for caravans with electrical connections (16A) and some separated by small trees and shrubs, with a choice of grass for tents or gravel hardstandings for vans. The central sanitary block, of good, modern construction and tiled, was very clean when we visited. Washbasins are in vanity style units with curtains, and hot showers are free. Larger unit for use by the disabled. Dishwashing facilities are under cover and there is also a small but well equipped laundry in the block, all operated by a key system. At the lower end of the site a gate gives access to the Leaplish Waterside Park where boats and canoes may be hired and launching facilities are available (for a fee). Motorboats and swimming are prohibited. The Border Forest Park offers a variety of activities including many forest drives with picnic areas. Dogs are allowed on a lead. The site has no shop but is situated midway between the villages of Kielder and Falstone (5 miles) which both have village stores. Falstone also has a pub serving food. **Note:** Midges can be troublesome mid-June - August.

Directions: From the east approach from Bellingham on B6320 in the direction of Kielder Water and Kielder. after the Visitor Centre, continue by the lake until Leaplish is signed. From the west using B6357 via Newcastleton, continue until Kielder is signed at Saughtree on unmarked road. Passing places are provided but are hardly necessary. Continue past Kielder village until Leaplish is signed. O.S.GR: NY626938.

Charges 1995:
-- Per caravan pitch (non-member) £4.00 - £4.50; adult £2.50 - £3.50; child (5-17 yrs) £1.10 - £1.20.
-- Per tent pitch with car £3.50, with m/cycle £2.50, cyclist or walker £2.00; adult £2.65; child £1.20; extra car or trailer £1.00;electricity £1.45 - £1.90.
Open:
March - 30 October
Address:
Leaplish Waterside Park, Falstone, Northumbria NE48 1AX.
Tel:
(01434) 250278.
Reservations:
Essential for B.Hs. Contact site.

Northumbria Tourist Board

Aykley Heads, Durham DH1 5UX

Tel: 0191 384 6905

This region includes the counties of Northumberland, Durham, Tyne and Wear and Cleveland - the scenery is wild and sometimes desolate, but has a romance of its own, with places such as Alnwick, Dunster, Hadrians Wall and Lindisfarne and the famous Geordie welcome.

195 Waren Caravan and Camping Park, Bamburgh

Spacious family park with good sea views, with touring area.

Northumberland has very few quality parks in proportion to its size but we have found Waren Park to provide a friendly, family atmosphere, with marvellous views. It has been developed from 100 acres of private heath and woodland and provides a static park (caravans for hire), a 4 acre, self contained touring area and a separate tenting area, enclosed by shelter banks and with its own on-site warden. There are 200 clearly marked pitches on level grass, 69 with electrical connections (10A). The toilet block is rather basic but an adequate provision, except perhaps in peak season when a second block supplements. It provides free hot water in washbasins (with shelves and mirrors) and showers, and baby changing facilities, a laundry room with washing, drying and ironing facilities and washing up sinks with free hot water. What the sanitary facilities lack in modern design is balanced by 'Nora'. Nora is the cleaner who not only does an excellent job, but also has an ongoing rapport with the children, evidence of which is the children's pictures covering the walls. Amenities include a licensed mini-market, pool table and well equipped children's play park. The reception/shop area has been rebuilt to include a coffee shop (licensed) with an attractive terrace overlooking the pool complex (small hexagonal pool and a deeper 9 x 6 m. pool). There is a play field and games for children are organised in season. Dog walks. Video transmission available. As well as the spacious grounds to wander in, there is much to see nearby from historic castles, the Farne Islands to the Cheviot Hills. Golf, birdwatching and riding all near. Holiday homes to let.

Directions: Follow B1342 from A1 to Waren Mill towards Bamburgh. After Budle Bay turn right and follow signs. O.S.GR: NU154342.

Charges 1996:
-- Per pitch with up to 4 persons £8.00 - £11.00; extra person 50p; 1 child under 7 free; boat or awning £1.50; dog £1.00; electricity £1.50.
-- Less 10% for 7 days or over.
-- VAT included.
Open:
Easter/1 April - end Oct.
Address:
Waren Mill, Bamburgh, Northumberland NE70 7EE.
Tel:
(01668) 214366.
FAX: (01668) 214224.
Reservations:
Early reservation advisable for high season. Deposit of one night's charge plus £1 fee.

Waren Caravan Park, Bamburgh, Northumberland

A beautiful landscaped park close to England's finest sands ideally situated for Northumbria National Park, Lindisfarne Nature Reserve, Farne Islands, and Bamburgh Castle. Excellent facilities - shop, games room, sunbed, solarium, restaurant and heated outdoor pool. Well equipped laundry, electric hook ups and children's play area. Luxury holiday homes (Rose Award), touring and tenting pitches. Free colour brochure and tariff.
Waren Caravan and Camping Park, Waren Mill, Bamburgh, Northumberland Tel: 01668 214366 Fax: 01668 214224

196 Percy Wood Caravan Park, Swarland, nr. Morpeth

Attractive, quality woodland site, open 11 months of the year.

Percy Wood provides excellent facilities but with a real feel of camping in the middle of a forest. A lot of thought and effort has gone into developing a park which blends with its natural surroundings. There are 40 level pitches, all with electricity (10A), of which 8 at least have hardstanding and are fully serviced. A grass tent field will be added for 1996. The central sanitary block is of wooden construction (heated) and in consequence blends in beautifully with the woodland surroundings. It is very well equipped with controllable showers, open, vanity style washbasins, free hot water, dishwashing under cover and a new laundry room. Reception provides basic necessities and tourist information, the village store is ½ mile, local pubs and a restaurant are within a mile. Children's play area and games room. A few caravan holiday homes for hire. Dogs accepted on leads (not dangerous breeds). On the boundary of the park is an 18 hole golf course, with bar and restaurant (membership can be arranged). This is an excellent area for rambling and for nature lovers generally. The park is only 4 miles from Throughton Wood and on the bus route for Alnwick and Rotherby. Druridge Bay Country Park is near (lake visitor centre, good for watersports).

Directions: Park is 2 miles west of the A1 (only signed northbound), 3 miles from A697 (12 mls north of Morpeth, 7 south of Alnwick). O.S.GR: NU160042.

Charges 1996:
-- Per unit incl. 2 persons and electricity Mon-Thurs incl. £7.00 - £8.50, Fri, Sat, Sun and B.Hs £7.00 - £9.50; extra person (over 5 yrs) 50p - £1.00; dog 50p; extra car £1.00.
-- Credit cards accepted.
Open:
All year except Feb.
Address:
Swarland, Morpeth, Northumberland NE65 9JW.
Tel:
(01670) 787649.
FAX: (01670) 787034.
Reservations:
Made with £10 deposit; min. 5 nights at B.Hs.

WALES

Wales Tourist Board, Brunel House, 2 Fitzalan Road, Cardiff CF2 1UY

Tel: (01222) 499909

The green hills and mountains of Wales are surprisingly easy to reach by road, as indeed is the coast. The scenery is often quite breathtaking, the activities varied and numerous, and the hospitality normally generous.

There are no less than 700 miles of coastline, three National Parks and five Areas of Outstanding Natural Beauty in Wales, and with relatively quiet roads, it makes ideal touring country. For simplicity we have used the following Welsh counties to divide our selected sites into areas:

1. Gwent 2. Powys 3. Dyfed 4. Gwynedd 5. Clwyd

---

197 Cwmcarn Forest Drive Campsite, Cwmcarn, nr. Risca

Small, council owned park in a beautiful setting.

Set in a narrow, sheltered valley with magnificent wooded slopes, this park is not only central for the many attractions of this part of Wales, but there is also much of the natural environment to enjoy. The 7 mile forest drive (open daily) shares its Visitor Centre with the camp reception and has much to offer - bird and badger watching, the Twmbarlwm ancient hill fort to visit with magnificent views across the Severn. Guided walks are available. The 40 well spaced, flat pitches (28 electric hook-ups, 3 concrete hardstandings with tarmac for the car) are spread over three fields between the Visitor Centre and a small lake (fishing permits available). The well equipped, heated toilet block (£5 deposit for key) includes toilet facilities for the disabled, laundry facilities and a kitchen with 2 washing up sinks, small cooker and fridge (hot water free). Telephone. The Visitor Centre has a coffee shop open at weekends from Easter. A variety of shops, a leisure centre, pubs and takeaway food are available in the village ¾ mile away. Pets welcome under control. Wardens are on hand daily and the Visitor Centre and reception are manned from 10 am.- 6 pm. all year. If arriving after then you will need to arrange for a toilet block key.

Directions: Cwmcarn is well signed from M4 J28. From Midlands and the Heads of the Valleys A465 road, take A467 south to Cwmcarn. O.S.GR: ST230935.

Charges 1995:
-- Per unit £4.40 - £5.40, acc. to season; small ridge tent £3.30 - £4.30; awning £1.60; electricity £1.80.
-- VAT included.
Open:
All year.
Address:
The Warden, Cwmcarn Forest Drive Campsite, Cwmcarn, nr. Newport, Gwent NP1 7FA.
Tel:
(01495) 272001.
Reservations:
No stated policy. 14 day max. stay.

198 Bridge Caravan Park and Camping Site, Dingestow, nr. Monmouth

Quiet, family run park in village 4 miles from Monmouth.

Bridge Caravan Park was established in 1979 and was a working farm until 6 years ago. Now, still in the hands of the Holmes family, it provides a peaceful haven bordered by the River Trothy and woodland on one side and by the farm buildings and church on the other. Well drained, level grass with tarmac access roads provides 56 pitches for caravans, some taken up by seasonal tourers in a discrete area and 25 for tents. Many hardstandings are available, 38 (5A) electrical hook-ups and 3 holiday caravans for hire. The purpose built, central toilet block is well maintained, with hot water to basins, metered for showers and hairdryers. New fully equipped laundry and dishwashing room with free hot water. The nearby village and Post Office is run by the family and there is a children's play area in the village also. Two local pubs offer good food - one a short walk, the other a long walk!

Charges 1995:
-- Per unit incl. 2 adults £6.00; extra adult £2.00; child (5-14 yrs) £1.50; electricity (5A) £1.30.
Open:
Easter -- 30 October.
Address:
Dingestow, Monmouth, Gwent NP5 4DY.
Tel:
Dingestow (01600) 740241.
Reservations:
Contact park.

Directions: Take the Abergavenny junction off the A449 and follow camp signs (in fact you pass park on the A449 but there is no exit). O.S.GR: SO458099.

199 Tredegar House Touring Park, Newport

Purpose built site in parkland with easy access form the M4.

Situated in the grounds of Tredegar House, home to the Lords of Tredegar for 500 years, the house and park are now in the care of the Borough of Newport. Mature pine trees, mixed with younger hardwoods and the edging wall provide secluded tenting areas and 29 hardstanding pitches with electricity for caravans and motorcaravans (not all are large enough for awnings) reached by two circular, tarmac roadways. A rustic, central toilet block provides hot showers with curtain but no seat or shelf, and washbasins including a smaller one for children. a room with a washing machine doubles for laundry and washing up and has a telephone. All these facilities are operated on a key system - it is therefore necessary to arrive before 9.45 pm. before the gates are closed (warden available 9 am.- 9 pm). Neatly fenced water and refuse points and an outside chemical disposal point. A very big plus factor for the site is the access to the grounds of the house, the lake, the farm, the craft centres and the Brewhouse restaurant. many special events are staged throughout the year. The house and craft workshops are also open to the public. A possible minus factor is the proximity of the M4, with accompanying noise but the advantage of easy access. Local shops are within easy walking distance.

Charges 1995:
-- Per large unit £6.00, small unit £4.00; electricity £2.00.
Open:
Easter -- end October.
Address:
Tredegar House and Country Park, Newport, Gwent NP1 9YW.
Tel:
Newport (01633) 816650.
Reservations:
Advisable for peak season - contact the Touring Site Warden.

Directions: Park is 2 miles west of Newport town centre. Use exit 28 from the M4 and follow signs for Tredegar House. O.S.GR: ST299855.

200 Riverside International Caravan Camping Park, Talgarth, Brecon

Attractive park with good views and adjacent, new Leisure Centre.

This park, in addition to providing good camping facilities in attractive surroundings, also has the benefit of a modern, on-site leisure complex with an indoor swimming pool, sauna, solarium and well equipped multi-gym, and a restaurant. The large pitches, many with electricity, are essentially in two well mown fields on two levels. The lower area is very attractively situated beside the river with views of the Brecon Beacons. There are some hardstandings. The sanitary block includes large, free hot showers with hooks (but without dividers), washbasins, dishwashing sinks under cover, laundry facilities (washing machine, dryer, iron and board) and even a bathroom. There is a good games/TV room, a putting green and a new adventure playground. No dogs are permitted.

Charges 1995:
-- Per unit incl. 2 persons £7.50 - £8.50; extra adult £2.00 - £2.50; child £1.00 - £1.20; electricity (10A) £1.00; extra car £1.00.
-- VAT included.
Open:
Easter - 31 October.
Address:
Bronllys, Talgarth, Brecon, Powys LD3 0HL.
Tel:
(01874) 711320.
Reservations:
Made with £10 deposit and £2 fee.

Directions: Park is just off the A479 road, mid-way between Bronllys and Talgarth, opposite Bronllys Castle. O.S.GR: SO148346.

201 Fforest Fields Caravan & Camping Park, Hundred House, Builth Wells

Secluded park in the heart of Radnorshire, only 4 miles from Builth Wells.

This rural park has glorious views of the surrounding hills and a distinctly family atmosphere. This is simple country camping and caravanning at its best, without man-made distractions or intrusions. The facilities include large pitches on level grass, with 16A electrical connections, on a spacious and peaceful, landscaped field by a stream. The well maintained sanitary facilities are good, if not especially luxurious, with free hot showers (with curtain and hook), open washbasins with mirrors, razor points, etc. and with laundry facilities including washing machines and dryer. There are few other on-site facilities, but the village of Hundred House, one mile away, has a pub, village stores and post office. The owners of the park are encouraging wildlife to the site with nesting boxes for owls, songbirds and bats and by leaving their field margins unmown to encourage small mammals.

Directions: Park is signed off the A481 Hundred House and Builth Wells road. O.S.GR: SO098535.

Charges 1996:
-- Per caravan or trailer tent £7.00; motor caravan £6.00; tent £4.50 - £6.00; electricity £1.50; awning free.
Open:
Easter/1 April - 31 October.
Address:
Hundred House, Builth Wells, Powys LD1 5RT.
Tel:
(01982) 570220.
Reservations:
Contact park.

202 Brynich Caravan Park, Brecon

Well kept, family run park with picturesque setting and super views towards the Brecon Beacons.

Brynich has been gradually developed by Colin and Maureen Jones to a very high standard. Originally farmland, there are two hedged camping fields, neatly mown and level with tarmac roadways and a mixture of hardwood trees and shrubs maturing nicely, providing for 130 touring units of all types. There are 78 (10A) electric points. Each field has a modern toilet block with free hot water throughout, well equipped showers, 15 washbasins in cubicles, washing up sinks and a laundry room. Two fully equipped units for the disabled are in one block, one providing left handed toilet facilities, the other right handed (operated by a key system) and a baby unit including bath. In total it is an excellent provision. A recent addition in a sloping field leading down to a stream is an extensive dog walk on one side of the stream and a children's adventure play area on the other. Mr Jones has the regular job of 'undamming' the stream which is shallow and super for children. Seats have also been provided. For smaller children there is some play equipment near reception. The reception includes a shop with basic food requirements plus hiking accessories, some souvenirs, papers and an off-licence. Telephone. Within the Brecon Beacons National Park, this is a good area for hill walking and climbing. There are also two golf courses and possibilities for watersports. The Brecon and Monmouthshire Canal crosses the River Usk 1½ km. from the park. Market days in Brecon on Tuesday and Friday. A member of the Best of British group.

Directions: Park is off the A470 (Builth Wells) road, 250 yds. from the junction with the A40 (Abergavenny) road, 1 mile east of Brecon. O.S.GR: SO069278.

Charges 1996:
-- Per unit incl. 2 persons £7.00 - £8.00; extra adult £1.50; child (4-16 yrs) £1.00; small tent + car (1 person) £3.25 - £3.75; backpacker £3.00 - £3.25; awning £1.25; dog 25p; electricity £1.75.
Open:
Easter - October.
Address:
Brecon, Powys LD3 7SH.
Tel:
Brecon (01874) 623325.
FAX: as phone.
Reservations:
Advisable for hook-ups at B.Hs. and made with £5 deposit.

BRYNICH CARAVAN PARK,
BRECON, POWYS, LD3 7SH.
Tel: 01874 623325

Ideally positioned for walking and touring Mid Wales, Brynich is a family run park which has easy access to a flat, closely mown site which values its reputation for cleanliness and has panoramic views of the Brecon Beacons. Two modern shower blocks which include 2 fully equipped disabled rooms and baby changing room with bath, ample dishwashing and laundry facilities with free hot water throughout. Adventure playground, picnic tables along picturesque brookside walk and dog exercise area.

WTB √√√√√ – A.A. 3 Pennant – R.A.C. Appointed – SAE for Brochure

203 Disserth Caravan Park, Disserth, nr. Llandrindod Wells

Small, family owned riverside park with some caravan holiday homes.

In a secluded situation between a church and the Ithon river and sheltered by a wooded cliff formed by river action, yet with handy access to many attractions in mid-Wales, Disserth provides a good base for families with an outdoor disposition. Up to 40 caravans, motorcaravans and tents are taken on one meadow adjacent to the river. The pitches are marked and spacing is generous with electrical hook-ups (10A) for all places. The pride of the park is the homely restaurant/coffee shop with an upstairs bar serving real ales. Small, yet nicely converted from an old barn, this provides a restful evening haven after a day out. Reasonably priced meals are served in the evenings (7.30 - 9.30 pm.) in the main season. A toilet block provides free hot showers (3M 3F) and for ladies, a hair drying cubicle and 3 washbasins in cubicles. Also provided are a laundry room and separate dishwashing sinks with hot water. Other amenities include a small shop, information kiosk, public telephone, and private fishing.

Charges 1996:
-- Per unit, incl. 2 adults £6.25 - £7.25; extra adult £1.75; child (3-15 yrs) 90p; awning 40p - 75p; electricity £1.75.
-- VAT included.
Open:
1 March - 27 October.
Address:
Disserth, Howey, Llandrindod Wells, Powys LD1 6NL.
Tel:
(01597) 860277.
FAX: as phone.
Reservations:
Made with £5 deposit.

Directions: Follow signs for Disserth and park, west off A483 at Howey, or east from B4358 around eastern edge of Newbridge-on-Wye. O.S.GR: SO035585.

Alan Rogers' discount
Less 50 p p/n
(max. 7 nights)

Graham and Audrey Houghton invite you to

DISSERTH CARAVAN PARK

DISSERTH, HOWEY, LLANDRINDOD WELLS LD1 6NL

Telephone: 01597-860277

DELIGHTFUL
INTIMATE
SMALL
SELECT
ENCHANTING
RELAXING
TRANQUIL
HIDDEN

IT ALL ADDS UP TO "DISSERTH"
A SECRET PLACE WORTH FINDING

Riverside camping, touring and holiday caravans. Peace and quiet with private fishing

MEMBER

---

204 Abermarlais Caravan Park, Llangadog, nr. Llandeilo

Sheltered park close to main holiday route, in natural setting.

Apart from the attractions of mid-Wales for a stay, this family run park could also double as a useful transit stop for those en-route to Pembrokeshire. Up to 88 touring units are accommodated in one flattish, tapering 5-acre grass field edged by mature trees and a stream. Pitches are numbered, and generously spaced around the perimeter or on either side of a central, hedged spine at the wider end, with 42 electrical hook-ups (10A) and some hardstanding. Backpackers have a small, separate area. The park is set in a sheltered valley. There is also an old walled garden, with some pitches and lawns for softball games, which screens the park, both audibly and visibly, from the A40 road. However, the most sought after pitches are beside the stream, loved by children and a haven for wildlife. The one small toilet block is clean and adequate with free hot water to washbasins (shelf and mirror) and controllable showers (ample space but no screen). There are two external, uncovered washing-up sinks (free hot water), but no laundry facilities - nearest about 5 miles away. A small shop doubles as reception and gas supplies are available. Play area with netball and play equipment. No other major on-site amenities and torch would be useful. Little Chef near and pubs, etc. at Llangadog. Winter caravan storage.

Charges 1996:
-- Per pitch £4.00; adult £1.50; child (over 5 yrs) £1.00; awning 60p; electricity £1.75.
-- VAT included.
Open:
March - November incl.
Address:
Llangadog, Dyfed SA19 9NG.
Tel:
(01550) 777868 or 777797.
Reservations:
Any length, with £5 deposit.

Directions: Park is on the western side of the A40, between Llandovery and Llandeilo. O.S.GR: SN685295.

205 Anchorage Caravan Park, Bronllys, Brecon

Friendly, simple park, with good views of the Black Mountains.

Anchorage was established over 30 years ago and is still in the hands of the Powell family. A well run site, it is in a good touring region close by the Brecon Beacons National Park. Also with 80 static caravans, it takes 110 tourist units, including quite a lot of long stay, seasonal ones, in two meadows. In one, 30 caravans go on individual pitches with jockey wheel markings on a slope with good views. The other (larger, either flat or with variable slopes) takes 80 mixed units (trailer or motor vans and tents) without marked pitches but with plenty of space, and a number of hardstandings now. Reservations are said to be only necessary for B.Hs. 64 electrical points (10A) for tourers. There are two toilet blocks, both near the entrance and providing an ample capacity. They have recently been modernised and are well kept, with free hot water in the individual basins set in flat surfaces and hot showers on payment. Covered washing-up sinks, bathroom/WC for the disabled and a baby room. Amenities include a well appointed launderette and a hairdresser on site, which also serve the village and are open all year. Shop. TV room (not in winter). Children's play area. Public phone. There is a pub in the village with meals. Leisure centre within 1½ miles.

Charges 1995:
-- Per unit incl. 2 persons £6.00, 1 person £3.50; extra person £1.00; child (under 5 yrs) free; awning 75p; electricity £1.75.
Open:
All year.
Address:
Bronllys, Brecon, Powys LD3 0LD.
Tel:
Talgarth (01874) 711246.
Reservations:
Accepted - write to site.

Alan Rogers' discount
7th night free when 6 booked

Directions: Park is signed north off the main Brecon-Hereford road in the centre of Bronllys village, the garage adjacent. O.S.GR: SO143350.

ANCHORAGE CARAVAN PARK

BRONLLYS BRECON POWYS LD3 0LD. TEL. TALGARTH (01874) 711246

A peaceful high standard park with panoramic views of the Brecon Beacons National Park. Ideal centre for touring and walking.

★ Tourers ★ Tents ★ Motor Caravans ★ Shop
★ 60 Electrical Hook Ups ★ Public Telephone
★ Hot & Cold Showers ★ Bath ★ Launderette ★ TV Room
★ W.C. for Disabled ★ Dogs allowed ★ Open all year
★ Bus stop at entrance ★ Pub in village ★ Baby bathroom

AA ▷▷▷   W.T.B. Q √√√√√   SAE FOR BROCHURE   PROPS: THE POWELL FAMILY

---

206 Moreton Farm Leisure Park, Saundersfoot

Well run park with modern facilities 4 miles from Tenby.

Moreton Farm has been developed in a secluded valley, a 10 - 20 minute walk from Saundersfoot. It provides 20 caravan and 40 tent pitches on two sloping, neatly cut grass fields, with 12 pine holiday lodges and 4 cottages for letting, occupying another field. The site is approached under a railway bridge (height 10'9", width across the top 6'6"). There are a few trains during the day, none at night. The new reception and toilet block (heated) is light and airy, providing some of the best facilities we have seen in Wales. There are preset hot showers (metered), vanity style washbasins (H&C) with soap and hand dryers, a ramp to a unit for the disabled, under cover dishwashing sinks (H&C) and laundry facilities with a fenced, outside clothes drying area. A small shop provides basics. Telephone. Children's playground on bark and grass. A fishing lake at the bottom of the valley is said to be well stocked (with ducks also), but is fenced for children's safety - `Henry' lives beside the lake. Pembroke and Carew castles and a variety of visitor attractions are close. This is a quiet family site.

Charges 1995:
-- Per caravan £8.00 - £9.00; trailer tent £7.00 - £8.00; tent £5.00 - £6.00; awning £1.00; electricity £1.50.
-- VAT included.
Open:
All year except 11 Jan - 28 Feb.
Address:
Moreton, Saundersfoot, Dyfed SA69 9EA.
Tel:
(01834) 812016.
Reservations:
Made with deposit (£20/week caravans, £15/week tents), balance 28 days before arrival.

Directions: From A477 Carmarthen - Pembroke road take the A478 for Tenby at Kilgelly. Park is signed on the left after 2-3 miles. Watch carefully for the sign. Site is ½ mile up poorly made-up road and under bridge. O.S.GR: SN122047.

207 Parciau Bach Caravan Park, St. Clears, nr. Carmarthen

Small, park in a peaceful, rural setting, which owner is continually seeking to improve.

There are some narrow lanes to be negotiated to get to Parciau Bach but it is worth it to enjoy the peaceful setting of this site. The 19 privately owned caravan holiday homes (and 2 site owned for letting) are hidden in the wooded slopes at the back of the park - a haven for wild flowers and squirrels. The open field for tents is sloping, but now has some individual terraced places with dividing shrub hedges (15 pitches) and a lower level, part terraced for caravans (25 pitches, with plans for a further 8). There are 20 electrical hook-ups and views across the valley. A wooded stream area unfortunately does not belong to the park but further up on the park is a small wild life pond with ducks. The owner's pine chalet home, sited on the slope between the touring field and the wooded area houses reception, a tourist information room and a small toilet unit for both sexes with a separate shower, toilet and washbasin with hairdryer for each. The main toilet block, open in the main season only, is in the wooded area reached by a steepish, hardcore path through the trees, lit at night. Free hot water is provided and the showers have the necessary seat, hook and curtain - not luxurious, but good and well maintained. There is also a laundry room and two washing up sinks, one beside reception, one near the tent area. There is an adventure play unit. Bar snacks and good breakfasts are available at the Parciau Bach Inn (separate ownership) situated above the site which also has a small shop for basics. Telephone. When you tire of the rural atmosphere, Tenby is only 18 miles away, with the 7 mile long Pendine sands 6 miles away or to the north, the Preseli mountains. Fishing and birdwatching opportunities abound.

Charges 1995:
-- Per unit £4.00 - £6.00; small tent £3.00 - £4.00; electricity £1.50; TV connection 50p; extra car (per person) £1.00.
Open:
All year except 11 Jan. - 28 Feb.
Address:
St. Clears, Carmarthen, Dyfed SA33 4LG.
Tel:
(01994) 230647.
Reservations:
Made with 20% deposit.

Alan Rogers' discount
10% discount

Directions: From St. Clears traffic lights, take the road to Llanboidy forking right after 100 yds. Follow this road for almost 2 miles and turn right. After less than a mile turn right at small crossroads and park is on left. O.S.GR: SN298184.

208 Afon Teifi Caravan and Camping Site, nr. Newcastle Emlyn

Small, friendly, family run park beside the River Teifi; some caravan holiday homes.

Situated 10 miles from the sea in the Afon Teifi valley, this is an ideal park for those interested in both coast and countryside accommodating 110 touring units in two well maintained grassy fields, separated by a low hedge, with a tarred perimeter road. 94 pitches have electrical hook-ups (6, 10 or 15A) and 20 are on hardstandings. Spacing is generous and there are 15 acres of land for walking dogs and children's play areas. The single, heated toilet block is clean, well maintained and thoughtfully designed. Hot water is free to the pre-set showers (push-button type) and washbasins and to the dishwashing sinks in the laundry room. Some basins are in cabins and there is also a bathroom (metered) and a toilet, shower and washroom for the disabled. The block is closed during the winter months. The owners are most helpful and other facilities include a good sized games room with tourist information, a small children's playground and a football field. A garage shop close to the entrance provides basic foodstuffs etc, and gas supplies are available on the site. There is a freezer for ice packs in the laundry room. Dogs are accepted but off-park walks for them along the river banks are sometimes restricted. Fishing permits available. A swimming pool and leisure centre and golf are within 2-4 miles and a restaurant/pub is within walking distance. Public phone in village. Day trips to Ireland are possible from Fishguard, or leave your unit on the site and spend a few days in Ireland.

Charges 1995:
-- Per pitch, incl. up to 4 persons £6.00 - £7.00; awning £1.00; extra person or car 75p; pup tent £2.00; small ridge tent incl. 2 persons £5.00 electricity £1.50.
Open:
All year, (reduced facilities Dec, Jan and Feb).
Address:
Pentrecagal, Newcastle Emlyn, Dyfed SA38 9HT.
Tel:
(01559) 370532.
Reservations:
Any length, with £10 deposit.

Directions: Park is on the north side of the A484 road, about 2 miles east of Newcastle Emlyn; entrance is by a garage on west side of Pentrecagal village. O.S.GR: SN340405.

209 Aeron Coast Caravan Park, Aberaeron

Family park with wide range of recreational facilities on west coast of Wales.

Although Aeron Coast has a high proportion of caravan holiday homes, it provides well for touring units in two fields separated from the beach and sea by a high bank (although the best beach is south of this pretty fishing village). Pitches are on level grass with units regularly spaced in lines (6 ft. spacing). Two toilet blocks, of older design but updated, provide clean, basic facilities with free hot water. Good laundry room. The main attraction of the park is its excellent recreational provision, both in and outdoors: a heated kidney shaped pool plus toddlers' pool and paved, walled area for sunbathing, tennis court and small half-court, 5-aside football and a sandpit. A new indoor leisure area provides an under-5s' room with slide, etc, teenagers' room with juke box, table tennis, pool and games machines, TV room with satellite. In high season these facilities are looked after by two students who arrange activities such as tennis tournaments, teenage discos or free films if the weather is poor. Club house and bar (open 12 -2 and from 7 pm) with bar meals and takeaway. Reception keeps tourist information. Shop at petrol station at entrance. Phone. Only one dog per unit. A steam railway, craft centre, woollen mills and potteries can be visited locally.

Charges 1996:
-- Per unit £5.50 - £8.50, acc. to season and type of unit; person (over 2 yrs) 50p; electricity £1.00.
Open:
Easter - end October.
Address:
North Road, Aberaeron, Dyfed SA46 0JF.
Tel:
(01545) 570349.
Reservations:
Made with £5 deposit.

Alan Rogers' discount
Less £1 p/n outside school and B.Hs.

Directions: Park is on northern outskirts of Aberaeron village with entrance on the right beside an Elf petrol station - not too easily seen. O.S.GR: SN461633.

210 Glan-y-Mor Leisure Park, Clarach Bay, Aberystwyth

Seafront, holiday-style park with many holiday homes and touring sections.

Glan-y-Mor has an enviable situation on this part of the Cambrian coast, on an attractive bay beside the beach, yet within easy reach of Aberystwyth. On a wet day you may not wish to go far with the comprehensive leisure centre on site (reduced entry for campers). Although the balance is very much in favour of caravan holiday homes which dominate the open park and bay, there are 75 touring pitches, 40 with electricity (10A) rather pressed together in two small sections on the lower part of the park. During high season you can opt for space and fine views (beware of winds) on a ridge of higher ground. The main toilet block is fairly good with free hot water, but is a good walk from the touring area, in the holiday caravan section. A second small `portaloo' type block (high season only) is on the ridge. Facilities for the disabled in one block and at the leisure centre (RADAR key). The centre has a heated pool, jacuzzi, solarium, sauna, steam room and gym. The complex includes reception, video and amusement room, bar, buffet bar and dance room (free entertainment nightly, Easter and May-Oct). Launderette, supermarket, play area and large sports field. Reduced rates available at local golf courses. Licensed restaurant and takeaway. Freezer pack service. Dogs only accepted outside B.H. and school summer holidays.

Charges guide:
-- Per unit, incl. 2 persons from £6.50 - £9.50; children free; extra person (over 18 yrs) £1.00; awning £3.00; electricity £1.50; dog £2.00.
-- Club membership incl (not Leisure complex).
-- VAT included.
Open:
March - October.
Address:
Clarach Bay, Aberystwyth, Dyfed SY23 3DT.
Tel:
(01970) 828900.
FAX: (01970) 828890.
Reservations:
Any length, with £20 deposit. Balance 28 days before arrival.

Directions: Clarach is signed west from the A487 (Aberystwyth - Machynlleth) in the village of Bow Street. Follow signs over crossroad to park. Access for caravans from Aberystwyth on B4572 is difficult. O.S.GR: SN580850.

211 Penybont Touring and Camping Park, Bala

Small North Wales park close to lake and mountains, under new ownership.

This is an unpretentious but well kept touring park in a scenic area, very close to Bala lake, which is a centre for various sailing and canoeing events during the season. There are only 35 caravan pitches, numbered and well spaced out, with wheelstrips on hardstanding for both car and van, and mainly flat, and 50 full tent pitches plus extra spaces for small hikers'/cyclists' tents on a slight slope. 22 electric hook-ups (10A). Reservations are needed for high season, especially for caravans. American motorhomes accepted up to 22 ft. The single toilet block, screened by tall trees, is neither modern nor large but is kept clean and well maintained. It has washbasins with free hot water and shelf, but only one hot shower (on payment) per sex. Hot water on payment for dishwashing outside. The owners have created a new entrance and plan new toilet facilities for 1996. Small shop with necessities - the town's amenities are under 1 mile. Space is left free for a play area. Public phone. Dogs permitted. Barbecues for hire. Winter caravan storage available. The site has a congenial atmosphere. The Welsh National White Water Centre is close.

Directions: Park is ½ mile southeast of Bala village on the B4391. Bala is between Dolgellau and Corwen on the A494. O.S.GR: SH931349.

Charges 1995:
-- Per unit incl. 2 persons £5.00 - £6.95, acc. to season and type of unit; backpacker £4.50 - £5.50; extra person (over 5 yrs), car, boat or trailer £1.00; full awning 50p - £1.00; electricity £1.60.
-- VAT included.
Open:
1 March - 31 October.
Address:
Llangynog Road, Bala, Gwynedd LL23 7PH.
Tel:
Bala (01678) 520549 or 520006.
Reservations:
Made for exact dates with £10 deposit.

LLANGYNOG ROAD
BALA LL23 7PH
TEL 01678 520549

The Lovely Little Park

TOURING & CAMPING PARK

Excellent, small, family park 1/2 mile from Bala town on the B4391 and 200 yards from Bala Lake in beautiful natural landscaped surroundings for 35 Touring Caravans on hard standing strips with electric and 50 Tent pitches.

★ SAILING ★ WINDSURFING ★ WHITE WATER RAFTING ★ CANOEING ★ SWIMMING ★ FISHING
★ PONY RIDES ★ SMALL GAUGE RAILWAY ★ CYCLING ★ GOLFING ★ SHOP ★ BBQ HIRE ★ LAUNDRY
★ CLEAN TOILETS & SHOWERS ★ DOG WALK ★ PAYPHONE

212 Pen-y-Garth Camping and Caravan Park, Bala

Family run, small touring park in Snowdonia National Park, a short walk from Bala Lake.

Pen-y-Garth is attractively set in 20 acres of undulating ground with views towards surrounding hills, amidst varied trees and shrubs. Ten acres take 35 touring caravans or motorvans, 28 tents on the main site and more in a 28-day field. Also 50 caravan holiday homes, 6 let by the park. There are 40 electrical connections (4/10A) and 8 pitches with water and drainage also. American motorhomes accepted depending on weather conditions. The central, modern toilet block and the smaller units with private facilities elsewhere, are a very adequate provision. Washbasins are set in flat surfaces and there is free hot water in these, as everywhere except in the new en-suite showers. Launderette. Two rooms for dishwashing, one at each end of the site. Amenities include a shop and a small, family run, licensed restaurant (w/ends only in low seasons) with a home cooked menu (takeaways cooked to order every evening), and an adjacent, lawned play area for children, with further play areas elsewhere. Games room, table tennis and croquet. Barbecue. Public telephone. Dogs permitted (3 acre dog walk area). There is a leisure centre in Bala, a water sports centre by the lake and the Snowdonia National Park offers climbing, walking, steam railways and slate, copper and gold mines. Golf, tennis, fishing and white water rafting near.

Directions: Park is close to B4391 road, southeast of Bala. Fork right off B4391 at camp sign. O.S.GR: SH940348.

Charges 1995:
-- Per unit incl. 2 persons £6.00 - £7.00; extra person (over 5 yrs) £1.50; electricity £1.50 per night, £8.00 per week; awning £1.00; backpacker/cyclist £2.50 per person.
Open:
1 March - 31 October.
Address:
Rhosygwaliau, Bala, Gwynedd LL23 7ES.
Tel:
Bala (01678) 520485.
Reservations:
Any length with 25% deposit.

213 Llanystumdwy Camping and Caravanning Club Site, nr. Criccieth

Small, well maintained park with good facilities, overlooking mountains and sea.

One of the oldest Camping and Caravanning Club sites, Llanystumdwy is on sloping grass, but the wardens are very helpful and know their site and can advise on the most suitable pitch and even have a supply of chocks. There are 70 pitches in total (20 ft. spacing), 46 with 10A electricity connections, spaced over two hedged fields with mainly caravans in the top field, motorhomes and tents lower down. A good, purpose built toilet block to one side provides excellent, full facilities for the disabled including access ramp. Tiled and nicely finished with green fittings, it has free hot water (you can set your own temperature in the showers), one washbasin each in a cubicle for male and female and extra large sinks. Facilities for babies, hairdryers and laundry (taps with fitting for the disabled). Chemical toilet, enclosed with bolt! Good, fenced refuse points are located about the park. A small dog walk is provided but main exercising should be off the park. Public phone. A small library and a good supply of tourist information are next to the small reception. A shop and pub are in the village and a bus leaves each half hour from outside the site to Pwllheli or Porthmadog. This is a good point from which to explore the Lleyn peninsular or Snowdonia National Park. Portmeiron with its Italianate village is near.

Directions: Follow the A487 from Porthmadog, pass through Criccieth and take the second sign to Llanystumdwy village. Site is on the left. O.S.GR: SH469384.

Charges 1995:
--Per adult £3.15 - £3.50; child £1.20 - £1.35; non-member pitch fee £3.00; non-member backpacker £4.35 - £4.75; electricity £1.70.
-- High season 27/5-1/9.
Open:
21 March - 31 October.
Address:
Tyddyn Sianel, Llanystumdwy, Criccieth, Gwynedd LL52 0LS.
Tel:
(01766) 522855.
(no calls after 8 pm).
Reservations:
Made with £5.60 deposit - contact park.

214 Bryn Gloch Caravan and Camping Park, Betws Garmon, Caernarfon

Well run and family owned touring park in the impressive Snowdonia area.

Bryn Gloch is a neat, well kept, quiet country park taking some 42 trailer caravans and 50 motorcaravans or tents on five flat, wide meadows, with 14 caravan holiday homes. There are tarmac roads and free areas are allowed in the middle for play. 100 electrical connections (10A) are available, some all weather pitches and 5 fully serviced super pitches. The sanitary arrangements have been extensively upgraded and the two blocks are now of very commendable standard. The far field has been equipped with a `portaloo' containing all facilities, for use in peak season. There is free hot water in the washbasins (some private cabins) and in the preset showers and indoor washing-up sinks. An excellent new building houses a family bathroom, baby changing room and complete facilities for the disabled. Fishing is possible on the river bordering the park with a barbeque and picnic area. Walks and pony trekking are available nearby and Caernarfon with its famous castle, only 5 miles. A shop, plus a restaurant and bar which are part of the guest house under the same ownership (all open 1/3-30/10). A well equipped laundry and separate drying room, TV and games rooms with pool tables, amusement machines and tourist information are located in one complex by the reception; this building also houses an extra shower and toilet per sex. Minigolf. Public phone. Dogs permitted. Car washing facility. Limited facilities 1 Nov. - 1 March.

Directions: Park is just beyond Waunfawr, 4½ miles southeast of Caernarfon on A4085 towards Beddgelert. Watch for signs and park entrance is opposite St Garmon church. O.S.GR: SH538578.

Charges 1995:
-- Per unit incl. 2 persons £7.80 (caravans over 18 ft. plus £1); extra person £1.80; child (2-14 yrs) £1.40; awning £1.10; dog 50p; electricity £2.20; `supersite' pitch plus £2.00.
-- VAT included.
Open:
All year.
Address:
Betws Garmon, nr. Caernarfon, Gwynedd LL54 7YY.
Tel:
Waunfawr (01286) 650216.
FAX: as phone.
Reservations:
Necessary for B.Hs. and made with deposit.

Wales Tourist Board

Brunel House, 2 Fitzalan Road, Cardiff, CF2 1UY Tel: (01222) 499909. Fax: (01222) 485031

1996 Events: Holyhead Arts Festival, 26 April-5 May: St. David's Cathedral Festival, 25 May-1 June: Urdd National Eisteddfod, Wrexham, 27 May-1 June: Barmouth - Fort William Three Peaks Yacht Race, 22-28 June (yachts assemble during previous week): Llangollen International Music Eisteddfod, 9-14 July: Royal Welsh Show, Builth Wells, 22-25 July: Royal National Eisteddfod of Wales, Llandeilo, 3-10 Aug: Conwy River Festival 4-10 Aug: Llandrindod Wells Victorian Festival, 17-25 Aug: Celtic Watersports, Milford Haven, 17-24 Aug:

215 Rhyd y Galen Caravan Park, Bethel, nr. Caernarfon

Small, family owned park with views of the mountains.

A friendly, small and quiet park, Rhyd y Galen has panoramic views of Snowdonia (they tell me that on a clear day you can even see the little train going up Snowdon!) and is situated 2 miles from Caernarfon. Developed on a sloping field, it provides 20 pitches for caravans, 5 for tents and one hardstanding for a motorcaravan. The toilet facilities, on the lower part of the site, comprise a tiled block each for male and females and provide full facilities with free hot water. The dishwashing room is at the back of the ladies block. Chemical toilet facilities, water, bins and fire points are clearly identified. A small children's play area completes this neat but unpretentious park. Pets are permitted. Ask what it means when `elephant mountain' goes pink.

Directions: Follow Caernarfon alternative tourist route onto the B4336. Continue through village of Bethel and park is on left. O.S.GR: SH512643.

Charges 1995:
-- Per unit £6.00; awning 50p; electricity £1.50.
Open: Easter -- October.
Address: Bethel, Caernarfon, Gwynedd.
Tel: (01248) 670110.
Reservations: Made with deposit of 1 nights fee.

216 Cadnant Valley Caravan Park, Caernarfon

Town park under new ownership, 10 minutes walk from Caernarfon centre.

This is an unusual, town centre park where the fairly steep road past reception leads you to a hidden, tree lined valley area with a little stream, complete with two bridges, which once fed the moat of the historic Caernarfon Castle. The shower and toilet blocks (with free hot water and kept very clean) are to one side of the site which has 60 marked, level and well spaced pitches (25 with 10-16A electricity and 5 hardstandings). You can choose a secluded area across the stream, a more open, central grass area or a terraced pitch, depending on your unit. Cadnant's natural environment has been thoughtfully enhanced with many plants, shrubs, picnic tables and stepping stone paths; even the new play area blends in and provides solid, rustic equipment on grass and an outdoor table tennis table. Well equipped laundry room, under cover dishwashing (with H&C), information area beside reception and small shop. Mini-supermarket 30 yds away but the main shops and restaurants are only a 5-6 minute walk and Caernarfon's leisure centre with swimming pool is ½ mile. Easily accessible by public transport are Bangor, Llanberis/Snowdon and Porthmadoc. It is unusual to find such an attractive site within town centre walking distance, never mind the added attractions of this historic area of Wales. The park is, however, within the town and in an urban area so there may be the odd extra noise. Dogs are welcome on a lead, small dog area provided.

Directions: Park is on the A4086 Llanberis road. From the town centre watch carefully for the park entrance after the 2nd roundabout, opposite a school and just before the fire station. O.S.GR: SH483626.

Charges 1995:
-- Per caravan incl. 2 persons £6.30 - £8.10, motorvan £6.10 - £7.70, tent £5.90 - £7.30; extra adult £1.30 - £1.50; child (6-16 yrs) £1.20 - £1.40; electricity £1.90; extra car or awning with non-aerotex groundsheet 50p.
-- Reductions for hikers/cyclists and over 60s.
Open: 14 March - 30 Sept.
Address: Llanberis Road, Caernarfon, Gwynedd LL55 2DF.
Tel: (01286) 673196.
Reservations: Recommended in high season and made with £10 deposit.

217 Nant Newydd Park, nr. Benllech, Anglesey (Ynys Mon)

Clean, well kept park with swimming pool; several caravan holiday homes.

A medium sized park taking 65 touring units in addition to 85 holiday homes, Nant Newydd is very long in shape, the lower, more sheltered parts closer to the entrance being used for the statics. The upper parts for tourers could be a little exposed. The park is neat, attractively landscaped and well maintained - most facilities are new and modern and there is an outdoor heated swimming pool with terraced patio and walled surround. The main touring field has well mown grass and spacious, flattish, marked pitches, all with electricity and some with water and drainage also, arranged around a perimeter gravelled track. Above this is a large over-spill/rally field with an additional 12 hook-up points and scattered bouldery outcrops. Two toilet blocks serve the park, one a fair distance from the touring area. Both are a credit to the park, being exceptionally clean and well appointed, even to the extent of timed air fresheners. Hot water is free to washbasins, preset pushbutton showers and for the main block, outside covered dishwashing sinks. The smaller block also has a good laundry room and full facilities for the disabled. Games room and pleasant shop and reception building with adjacent pool and fountain. The children's play area on the grassy slopes above the site is generous and safety tiles have been laid under and around the equipment. A play area for toddlers (up to 10 yrs) is opposite the reception area.

Charges guide:
-- Per caravan pitch £6.50 - £10.00, acc. to season; tent or motorcaravan £5.50 - £10.00; awning £1.00; electricity £1.50.
Open: Easter - end October.
Address: Brynteg, Benllech, Anglesey, Gwynedd.
Tel: (01248) 852842 or 852266.
Reservations: Advisable for peak season and B.H.s; £10 deposit.

Directions: Park is north off the B5110, about 3 miles west of Benllech. From there take the B5108 before turning left onto B5110, about 1 mile from park. O.S.GR: SH480820.

218 Rhos Caravan Park, Pentraeth, Ynys Mon (Anglesey)

Anglesey park on working farm with some holiday caravans.

For a busy, countryside, working farm the space given to camping at Rhos is very extensive, with three fair-sized fields for caravans, two mainly for caravan holiday homes, one all touring and three very large tent fields. It takes 52 touring caravans on grass plus 60 caravan holiday homes, some of which are let. For tents, there is no special limit and much more space. 50 electrical connections (10A). The two toilet blocks have free hot water in the washbasins (with shelf and mirror) and fully controllable hot showers on payment. There is a laundry room with a washing machine and dryer and a dishwashing room with free hot water. The blocks should suffice for normal numbers. A sandy beach (tide goes out a long way) is about 1½ miles away and the island offers a range of possible excursions. Shop (Easter - early Sept. w/ends only in early and late season), children's playground and public phone on site. Pub nearby. Dogs permitted with field provided.

Charges 1995:
-- Per caravan and car £6.00; electricity £1.50; awning £1.00; tent and car or motorcaravan incl. 2 persons £5.00; extra person 30p; extra car or boat 50p.
-- VAT included.
Open: 1 March - 31 October.
Address: Pentraeth, Anglesey, Gwynedd LL75 8DZ.
Tel: (01248) 450214.
Reservations: Any length, with deposit - caravan £10, tent £5.

Directions: Park is just north of Pentraeth on A5025, about 6 miles from the Britannia Bridge. O.S.GR: SH518794.

219 Hunter's Hamlet Touring Caravan Park, Betws-yn-Rhos, nr. Abergele

Small, family owned, quality park with beautiful rural views.

The design, layout and facilities of this purpose built site, now eight years old, are of a very high standard and the Hunter family are justifiably proud of the park. Situated on a gently sloping hillside, providing panoramic views, one area provides 15 well spaced hardstandings with 10A electric hook-ups and access from a circular, hard-core roadway. A new area has been developed next to this of a similar design but with 8 pitches fully serviced by new tourer 'super pitches' (water, waste water, sewerage, TV and electricity connections). Shrubs and bushes at various stages of growth complement both areas. An excellent purpose built, heated sanitary block has fully tiled facilities including showers en-suite with toilets for both sexes and vanity style washbasins. Also included is a 'kitchen' with basins for laundry and dishwashing (H&C), washing machine and dryer, iron and board, freezer and fridge. For 1996 there will be extra covered washing up sinks outside. Separated toilet/shower facilities for the disabled. Chemical toilet and central refuse points. A natural play area incorporating rustic adventure equipment set amongst mature beech trees with a small bubbling stream (supervised by the ducks) is a children's paradise. Table tennis and pool in a barn also. Milk and papers can be ordered and the Hunters will do their best to meet your needs. Only two dogs per unit allowed. The park is well situated to tour Snowdonia and Anglesey and is within easy reach of Llandudno and Rhyl.

Directions: From Abergele take the A548 south for 2¾ miles; turn onto the B5381 in the direction of Betws-yn-Rhos and park is on left after ½ mile. To date there are no local authority caravan signs so watch carefully for the farm after turning - it can be identified by a artistically painted sign with the house and farm name: 'Sirior Goch Farm' and Hunter's Hamlet. O.S.GR: SH929736.

Charges 1995:
-- Per unit incl. 2 adults and 2 children: basic pitch £8.00 - £10.00, super pitch £13.00 - £16.00; extra adult £1.50; awning £1.50; electricity (10A) £1.50.
-- Less £5 on weekly bookings.
Open:
21 March - 31 October.
Address:
Sirior Goch Farm,
Betws-yn-Rhos,
Abergele,
Clwyd LL22 8PL.
Tel:
(01745) 832237.
Reservations:
Made with £2 per night deposit - min. £10. B.H. Min. 4 nights Easter and Whit, May Day and Aug. B.H. min. 3 nights.

220 Ty Ucha Caravan Park, Llangollen

Quiet, family owned park in the Vale of Llangollen, for caravans and motorhomes only.

Only a mile from Llangollen, world famous for the Eisteddfod, Ty Ucha has a rather dramatic setting, nestling under its own mountain and with views across the valley to craggy Dinas Bran castle. It is a well ordered park, carefully managed by the owners, providing 40 pitches (30 with 10A electrical hook-up) well spaced round a large, grassy field with an open centre for a play area. One side slopes gently and is bounded by a stream and wood. A path leads from here for various mountain walks, depending on your energy and ability.

The single toilet block, although a 'portaloo', is clean and well maintained, providing 2 metered showers for each sex (a little cramped), small basins with free hot water, shelf and mirror, toilets and chemical toilet. A dishwashing sink with cold water is provided outside. There are no laundry facilities but there is a launderette in Llangollen. The small shop, providing only the bare necessities (papers can be ordered), is open 9.30-10.30 and 4.30-5.30 all season. A games room with table tennis is next to it. Because of overhead cables, kite flying is forbidden; no bike riding either. A small, separate hedged area provides for those who prefer to be without the company of children or dogs. Public phone. A late arrivals area completes the facilities and there is an hotel ½ mile away where reasonably priced meals are available. Eisteddfod is an international festival of music and dance held for six days in the first week of July every year - a very busy time for the area.

Directions: Park is signed off the A5 road, 1 mile east of Llangollen (250 yds). O.S.GR: SJ228411.

Charges 1996:
-- Per caravan incl. 2 persons £6.50,
motorcaravan £6.00;
extra person £1.00;
awning (environmental groundsheets) £1.00;
electricity £2.00.
-- Reductions for OAPs for weekly stays.
Open:
Easter - October.
Address:
Maesmawr Road,
Llangollen, Clwyd
LL20 7PP.
Tel:
Llangollen (01978)
860677.
Reservations:
Necessary for B.Hs. and Eisteddfod and made with £5 deposit; 3 days min. at B.H.s.

Alan Rogers' discount
Less £1 per party outside B.Hs and high season

221 The Plassey Touring and Leisure Park, Eyton, nr. Wrexham

Spacious, rural 250-acre park in the Dee Valley, offering many activities.

The Plassey is not just a touring park but is also a leisure and craft centre with a relaxed atmosphere and pleasant environment. The Edwardian farm buildings have recently been tastefully converted to provide a restaurant, coffee shop, health, beauty and hair studio, small garden centre and fifteen different craft units, open all year to the public. Other amenities include a 9 hole golf course, farm fishing pools and countryside footpaths. Unusually there is also a small brewery on site, producing its own unique Plassey Bitter!

The park itself is spacious with 120 pitches around the outer edges of a series of five fields forming circles, with 112 electrical connections (16A) and 10 hard-standings (some seasonal vans). The original toilet facilities beside the entrance and under the club house have been refurbished to a good standard and are supplemented by a neat `portaloo' block in the top field area with four extra showers - well maintained but possibly under pressure at B.Hs. Showers are metered, as are the two washing up sinks. Laundry room. The Tree Tops clubhouse, serving Plassey Bitter, overlooks the park and has a children's room. Good adventure playground beside a small wood with equipment for smaller children on bark chippings. Badminton courts including an indoor one can be booked. Indoor, heated swimming pool (50p per hour) with sunbed and sauna (open May - Sept). There is much to do and to look at in a rural setting at the Plassey but it is best enjoyed mid-week and avoiding Bank Holidays.

Directions: Park is clearly signed (brown and cream signs for The Plassey) from A483 Oswestry - Chester bypass and from the A528 Marchwiel-Overton road). O.S.GR: SJ349452.

Alan Rogers' discount
Ask at park
for details

Charges 1996:
-- Per unit incl. 2 adults, 2 children, electricity £8.50 - £10.50; extra person, dog or car £1.00; awning £1.00; pitch without electricity less £2.00.
-- Includes club member-ship, coarse fishing, badminton and table tennis (own racquets and bats).
-- B.H. supplement £1.
-- Discount for weekly booking £7.
-- VAT included.
-- Credit cards accepted.

Open:
1 March - 6 November.

Address:
Eyton, nr. Wrexham, Clwyd LL13 0SP.

Tel:
(01978) 780277.
FAX: (01978) 780019.

Reservations:
Necessary for w/ends, July/Aug for electricity; made with £15 deposit.

---

222 Hoddom Castle Caravan Park, Lockerbie

Pleasant, spacious park in partially wooded parkland.

Hoddom Castle is an example of the many Pele Towers which were a feature of the Borders, but the years have seen its destruction, rebuilding and adaptation from a Border keep to a fortified castle. The castle, as it stands now, was last occupied by the army during the Second World War and today the restaurant and bar have been developed in the courtyard area and former stables house an excellent toilet/shower block. The park has been well laid out in the parkland of the estate with a one-way system. There are 120 numbered individual pitches especially for caravans, well spaced out amongst mature trees and most with electricity (10A), plus 50 for any units on two meadows which are not marked. The main well appointed toilet block has 16 free hot showers, washbasins in cubicles and is supplemented by two smaller blocks - toilets and washbasins only - with washing up facilities under cover (all with free hot water). Good water and dustbin points. Other amenities include a shop, large bar lounge, restaurant, partly self service (limited opening). games room with pool table, TV room and launderette. There is a children's playground on grass, crazy golf and a public phone. The estate has its own 9 hole golf course (open to all) and salmon and brown trout fishing is available in the River Annan (trout and course fishing are also available elsewhere on the estate - rods limited). A countryside warden is employed by the estate who maintains well signed nature trails and also offers guided walks. Tennis nearby. A good, peaceful base from which to explore historic southwest Scotland.

Directions: From A/M74 take Ecclefechan exit, turn southwest in village on B725. Park entrance is signed at Hoddom Bridge, 2½ miles from Ecclefechan. O.S.GR: NY155725.

Charges 1996:
-- Per unit incl. 2 adults and 2 children £6.50 - £10.00, acc. to season; extra person £1.50; awning £2.00; electricity (10A) £2.00.
-- VAT included.

Open:
Easter/1 April - end October.

Address:
Hoddom, Lockerbie, Dumfriesshire DG11 1AS.

Tel:
Ecclefechan (01576) 300251.

Reservations:
Necessary for July/Aug and B.Hs. Any length with deductible £3 deposit.

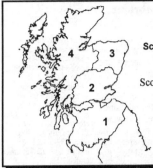

SCOTLAND

Scottish Tourist Board, 22 Ravelston Terrace, Edinburgh EH4 2EU

Tel: 0131-332-2433

Scotland is divided into 33 Area Tourist Boards - we considered this too complicated for our purposes and have therefore used the following Regional Tourist Areas to list our parks:

**1. South of Scotland   2. Heart of Scotland
3. Grampian   4. Highlands and Islands**

223 Park of Brandedleys, Crocketford, nr. Dumfries

Friendly, family owned park providing a range of facilities including swimming pools.

The McDonalds have worked hard to make Brandedleys a first class park providing pitches for some 80 caravans and a limited number of tents, plus 27 self-contained holiday homes (12 of which, with 2 cottages and 3 chalets, are let) in three or four flat and variably sloping fields with tarred access roads. It has excellent installations and amenities. Caravan pitches are on lawns or terraced hardstandings, many with a pleasant outlook across a loch. There are 80 with electricity (10A) and 21 with water and drainage also. The main toilet block has been extensively modernised with clean, well appointed cubicled showers with toilet and washbasin (just one for men), in addition to the normally provided showers, washbasins and toilets, full length mirror, hairdryers and a bathroom for the disabled with en-suite toilet. Laundry room, baby and hair care room, and covered dishwashing sinks. A second block of equal size and standard in the lower field has laundry and dishwashing facilities also. It is excellently equipped and maintained. A small free heated pool is open when the weather is suitable. An indoor pool adjacent to the bar/restaurant is open all season on payment with changing room and sauna. Well stocked shop (April-Oct). TV room. Bar and licensed restaurant (April-Oct) with full menu at reasonable prices, for lunch, supper and dinner, with patio overlooking Loch Auchenreoch. Takeaway to order (6.15-9.30 pm.). All-weather tennis courts, outdoor badminton and draught board. Games room. Table tennis, pool table and amusements. Football pitch. Putting course and golf driving net. Small playground with grass base. Dog exercise area. Public phone. Fishing, golf, riding and pony trekking all nearby. Walks on open moors or forest and beautiful sandy beaches 12 miles away. A popular, quality park and a member of the Best of British group.

Directions: Park is 9 miles from Dumfries on south side of the A75 Dumfries - Stranraer road, just west of the village of Crocketford. O.S.GR: NX830725.

Charges 1995:
-- Per unit incl. 2 persons £8.00 - £12.00; extra adult £2.00; child (5-14 yrs) £1.50; awning £2.00; extra small tent £3.00; extra car £1.00; electricity £2.00 - £2.20; individual water/ drainage £2.00; dog £1.00.
-- Less 5-10% for weekly bookings.
-- VAT included.
-- Credit cards accepted.

Open:
1 March - 31 October.

Address:
Crocketford, by Dumfries DG2 8RG.

Tel:
(0155) 669 0250.
FAX: (0155) 669 0681.

Reservations:
Recommended for peak dates and made for min. 3 days, £20 deposit per pitch.

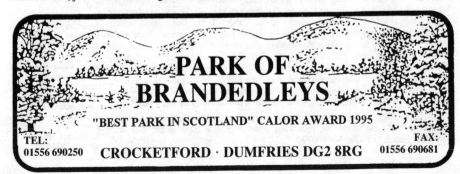

PARK OF BRANDEDLEYS

"BEST PARK IN SCOTLAND" CALOR AWARD 1995

TEL:
01556 690250

CROCKETFORD · DUMFRIES DG2 8RG

FAX:
01556 690681

224 Brighouse Bay Holiday Park, Borgue, Kirkcudbright

Seaside park with exceptional all weather facilities.

Hidden away within 700 acres, on a quiet, unspoilt peninsula, this spacious family park is only some 200 yards from a lovely sheltered bay on the Solway coast. It has 120 self-contained holiday caravans of which about 30 are let, the rest privately owned. Over 90% of the 120 touring caravan pitches have electricity, some have hardstanding and some are fully serviced (incl. TV aerial connections). The three tenting areas, with stone wall shelter, are on fairly flat, but undulating ground and some pitches have electricity. The well maintained main toilet block is large with ample washbasins with shelf and free hot water, free hot showers and en-suite bathrooms (one with spa-bath, one for the disabled). A second, newer and excellent block next to the tenting areas has en-suite shower rooms (one for the disabled), separate washing cubicles, hot showers, en-suite bathroom, baby room, clothes washing sinks, laundry and covered dishwashing sinks. One section is winterised for all year use.
On site facilities include an indoor complex (open all year) with a 16.5 m. pool, water features, jacuzzi, Turkish room, fitness room, sunbed, viewing bistro, members lounge bar and games room. Adjacent is a 9 hole, par 34 golf course. There is summer tuition in windsurfing, sailing, canoeing, jetski and waterski, plus a boating pond, mountain bike hire, playgrounds, pitch and putt, sea angling and all-tide slipway. Tours are taken by tractor and trailer around the park's Open Farm, which also has a BHS approved pony trekking centre (in summer only). Cottages, lodges and chalets to rent. Licensed supermarket. Takeaway. Advance booking advised. A well run park of high standard and a member of the Best of British group.

Directions: From Kirkcudbright turn south off A755 onto B727 (to Borgue). After 4 miles Brighouse Bay is signposted to south. From west take B727 to Borgue and beyond, turning south as above. O.S. GR: NX630455.

Charges 1996:
-- Per unit incl. 2 persons £8.25 - £10.95; extra adult £2.00; child (4-15) £1.25; full awning ££1.60; porch awning, extra car or small pup tent £1.00; electricity £2.50 - £2,00; electric/ TV £2.90 - £2.60; fully serviced pitch £3.90 - £3.60; trailed craft £2.75, other craft £1.50.
-- Up to 10% reduction for weekly bookings.
-- VAT included.
Open:
All year.
Address:
Brighouse Bay, Borgue, Kirkcudbright DG6 4TS.
Tel:
(01557) 870267.
FAX: (01557) 870319.
Reservations:
Made with £17 deposit plus £3 booking fee for each pitch booked.

225 Caldons Campsite, Galloway Forest Park, nr. Newton Stewart

Truly peaceful Forestry Commission site ideal for exploring vast Forest Park.

The drawbacks first - Scotland is known for its midges and they love the combination of water and trees here, so follow the warden's advice on where to pitch (away from the trees) and use repellents. Secondly, the sanitary facilities, with the notable exception of the expensively refurbished ladies' toilets, are adequate rather than luxurious. The site itself is mainly, though far from all, on sloping ground. The benefits are a wonderfully quiet and relaxing streamside site with mountain views and a perfect base for exploring this enormous 240 square mile Forest Park. Situated in the beautiful Glen Trool, the Loch Trool Trail oak and pinewoods are a naturalist's delight. The trail starts at the site and takes walkers on a 5 mile circuit of the Loch with spectacular loch views and passing Bruce's Stone, commemorating his first victory over the English in 1307 (this can also be reached by car). There are many other walks and drives into the moorland and rugged hills. At the site, children can play on the varied adventure equipment (on bark) or splash around in the Caldon Burn. Dogs are accepted. Neither boating nor fishing is permitted in Loch Trool, but permits (from £6.50 for adults, £1.50 for children) for fishing elsewhere in the park are cheap for Scotland. Picnic benches, games rooms with table tennis and pool, and a rest room with drinks machine are provided. There is a shop for basic supplies. The site has 160 pitches with 52 electrical hook-ups and 12 hardstandings. There is a launderette and dishwashing facilities. Access makes it unsuitable for very large units. The village of Glentrool is 4 miles, with a pub at Bargrennan, 5 miles.

Directions: From A714 Newton Stewart - Girvan road turn east at Bargrennan and right just past Glentrool, following signs on single track forest road with passing places. O.S.GR: NX400790.

Charges 1995:
-- Per family pitch £6.00 - £7.00, acc. to season; 1 person tent £3.00 - £3.50; electricity £1.75.
-- VAT included.
Open:
1 April or 2 wks before Easter - first w/e in Oct.
Address:
Galloway Forest Park, Glentrool, Dumfries and Galloway.
Tel:
Site: (01671) 840218. Reservations and enquiries : Forestry Commission (01671) 2420.
Reservations:
Recommended for hook-ups in peak season and made with at least 2 weeks notice and £10 deposit through the Forestry Commission, Creebridge, Newton Stewart DG8 6AJ.

BRIGHOUSE BAY

AA **Best Scottish Campsite 1994**
Scotland's only 5 pennant park

One of Scotland's finest family parks with its own sandy beach, slipway,
watersports, pony trekking, 9 hole golf course and all-weather Leisure Centre

Highest Quality Awards: Facilities : Recreation : Environment

British Grading Scheme   ADAC German Camping Fuhrer
Scottish Tourist Board   Automobile Association
Recommended **ANWB   ASCI   ANAC & Alan Rogers**

HOLIDAY HOMES FOR SALE   ALL TOURISTS WELCOME

BRIGHOUSE BAY HOLIDAY PARK   Kirkcudbright   Tel 01557 870267

226 Cressfield Caravan Park, Ecclefechan, Lockerbie

Purpose designed, modern park just north of the border, open all year.

Cressfield is close to main routes (A/M74/M6) for transit, yet very suitable to explore the Solway Firth, Dumfries and Galloway or visit Gretna Green! It has been developed in pleasant undulating countryside, next to the village of Ecclefechan, to a very high standard and is personally managed by the owner. The park provides 115 pitches of which half are taken up by holiday homes and seasonal vans and is pleasantly landscaped (trees growing well). The level pitches, mostly with hardstanding, are connected by gravel roadways and provided with 16A electric hook-ups. A good rally field is also fully equipped with electrical hook-ups. The modern, heated, central toilet block is operated on a key system and provides excellent facilities - free, well equipped showers, washbasins in cubicles, hairdryers (metered) and a bath is a welcome addition in the ladies (20p). Toilet and washbasin for the handicapped in both the male and female sections. Excellent laundry room and under cover washing up area and bin store. Large dog exercise field. Other amenities include a well equipped, fenced children's play area, 9 hole putting green (not in winter) and a sports field with goal posts, tennis and badminton nets and netball posts. Giant chess and draughts, plus boules. No shop but only ¼ mile to the village and adjacent to the park is an hotel for a drink or a meal. For the more active there are 7 golf courses nearby, opportunities for coarse or game fishing, cycling, walking, birdwatching and historical Solway to explore. Some road noise possible.

Directions: From south on A/M74 (10 miles north of Gretna) take Ecclefechan exit 19 and B7076 for ½ mile to south side of village. O.S.GR: NY196744.

Charges 1996:
-- Per unit incl. 3 adults or 2 adults and 2 children £6.00 - £7.50; car, small tent £6.00; awning, extra car or small tent £1.00; extra adult £1.00; child 50p; electricity £1.80 - £2.00.
-- £1 extra p/n at B.Hs..
-- VAT included.
Open:
All year.
Address:
Ecclefechan, Lockerbie, Dumfries and Galloway DG11 3RD.
Tel:
(01576) 300702.
Reservations:
Phone bookings accepted.

Alan Rogers' discount
Extra person or tent free

227 Crossburn Caravan Park, Peebles

Peaceful, friendly small park.

Just half a mile north of the town, the entrance to Crossburn takes you down a gentle slope towards the reception/shop building. Passing on via gravel and tarmac access roads, through the caravan holiday homes, you reach a pleasant, quiet and flat grassy area surrounded by trees and bushes. There are 50 fair sized pitches with a few hardstandings and 46 electrical connections (16A), with an area for tents at one end. The single sanitary block is at the entrance to the touring field and facilities provide vanity style washbasins and controllable showers, all free, clean and quite satisfactory. Other amenities include giant draughts, mountain bike hire, a large games room with table tennis and machines and a large 9 hole putting green. There is a dog walk by the burn where fishing is possible. The town facilities are quite close, with just basic food supplies kept in the park shop, but also many caravan accessories. Reservations advised for July/Aug.

Directions: Park is by the A703 road, about ½ mile north of Peebles. O.S.GR: NT248417.

Charges 1995:
-- Per person (over 5 yrs) 50p; caravan £7.00; motorcaravan £6.50; car and tent £4.50 - £7.00; awning £1.00 - £2.00; hiker or cyclist plus tent £3.65; electricity £2.00.
Open:
Easter/1 April - end Oct.
Address:
Edinburgh Road, Peebles EH45 8ED.
Tel/Fax:
(01721) 720501.
Reservations:
Made with £12 deposit including £2 fee.

228 The Monks' Muir, Haddington, nr. Edinburgh

Small, relaxed, 'individual' park, open all year and handy for visiting Edinburgh.

The Monks' Muir is just back from the A1, a few minutes from Haddington, East Lothian's county town and about 20 minutes by rail (P&D) or an hour by bus from Edinburgh from just outside the site (parking in Edinburgh itself is not to be advised). It therefore provides a base from which to explore the city, to enjoy the golden beaches of East Lothian, discover the border country or just play golf! The enthusiastic owners, Douglas and Deirdre Macfarlane, are continually improving The Monks' Muir, one of Scotland's oldest parks. They have created a continental style cafe cum delicatessen shop which provides the atmosphere which sets the style of the park. The stock in the shop is amongst the most wide ranging we have seen, with an excellent choice of coffee. Future plans include a new touring area, a plant centre and a restaurant. The atmosphere is very different here from most parks, with arrivals accepted very late. There are no marked pitches for the 60 units which are taken on fairly level grass beyond a line of 10 caravan holiday homes (7 for hire), which are broken up into groups by trellising. Finding your own place either side of the central gravelled roadway amongst the odd tree contributes to the friendly and relaxed atmosphere. Some hardstandings and 44 electrical connections (11A) are on an elongated strip of land between the fields, finishing with a natural play area for children. The main toilet block, a little dated but well maintained, provides toilets and washbasins with free hot water plus hand and hair dryers. The adjoining free hot showers with roomy changing area have a separate entrance. Outside washing-up sinks also have free hot water. A fully equipped laundry room doubles to provide tourist information. The second toilet block is only opened in the high season and should ensure adequate provision. Public telephone. Boules pitch.

Directions: Park is on the north side of the A1, halfway between East Linton and Haddington. O.S.GR: NT 559762.

Charges 1995:
-- Per unit incl. 1 person £7.00 - £8.80; m/cyclist and tent £6.50, cyclist and tent £4.00, hiker and tent £3.00; extra person (over 11 yrs) £1.00; awning or pup tent £1.00; electricity £1.60 - £2.20.
-- Various discounts: 10% for 7 day stays, 20% for 14 days, a further 30% for over 55s prebooked for over 7 days outside July/Aug.
-- VAT included

Open:
All year.

Address:
Haddington, East Lothian EH41 3SB.

Tel:
(01620) 860340. FAX: as phone.

Reservations:
Made with £7 deposit and £3 booking fee.

 Alan Rogers' discount Ask at park for details

229 Drum Mohr Caravan Park, Musselburgh, nr. Edinburgh

Family owned, attractively laid out touring park on east side of Edinburgh.

Although adjacent to built-up areas, this is a secluded, well kept modern park, conveniently situated for visits to Edinburgh, the Lothian and Borders regions. It has been carefully landscaped and there are many attractive plants, flowers and hedging. There are 120 individual pitches, 40 with hardstanding, for touring units of any type, well spaced out on gently sloping grass in groups of 12 or more, marked with white posts. There are electric hook-ups on 110 of them and. from 1996. 8 will be probably be fully serviced with water and waste water connections also. Free space is left for play and recreation. The two toilet blocks are clean, attractive and of ample size. They have washbasins set in flat surfaces with free hot water in these and in the 4 external washing-up sinks, but hot water is on payment for the showers and the laundry sinks. Laundry facilities in each toilet block. There is a well stocked shop (bread and papers to order) and a children's playground on sand. No other on-site activities but the town's amenities are quite close, as is a golf course. Musselburgh centre is 1½ miles and Edinburgh 7, with a frequent bus service to the latter. A well run park, managed personally by the owners, Mr and Mrs Melville. A member of the Best of British group.

Directions: From Edinburgh follow A1 signs for Berwick on Tweed for 6-7 miles. Turn off for Wallyford and follow camp and Mining Museum signs. From south follow A1 taking junction after Tranent village (A199 Musselburgh) and follow signs. O.S.GR: NT371732.

Charges 1996:
-- Per unit incl. 2 persons £7.50 - £8.50, acc. to season; extra person £1.00; additional pup tent or awning £1.00; electricity £2.00; fully serviced pitch + £4.00; extra car £1.00.
-- VAT included.

Open:
1 March - 31 October.

Address:
Levenhall, Musselburgh EH21 8JS.

Tel:
0131 665 6867. FAX: 0131 653 6859.

Reservations:
Made for any length with deposit of one night's fee.

230 Mortonhall Caravan Park, Edinburgh

Attractive, large touring park in the mature grounds of Mortonhall mansion.

The Mortonhall park makes a good base to see the historic city of Edinburgh. Although only 4 miles from the city centre, it is in quiet mature parkland, easy to find with access off the ring road. The park can accommodate 250 units; the majority of pitches are for caravans, mainly numbered ones on a slight slope with nothing to separate them but marked by jockey wheel points. There are also tent pitches on flat meadow. There are over 150 pitches with electricity and 16 with water and drainage as well. Holiday caravans are available to let. The park is very popular and reservation is advisable for July/Aug, though only part is reserved and tourists arriving early may find space. The three modern toilet blocks, which are well constructed and of sufficient size, have free hot water in the individual basins, in the showers and the outside, covered dishwashing sinks. Water points around site. Laundry room with washing machines and dryer. Self-service shop. An attractive courtyard development houses a lounge bar and restaurant, open to all. Games room. TV room. Table tennis, children's play area on grass. Golf courses and driving range very near.

Directions: Park is well signed south of the city, 5 minutes from A720 city by-pass. Take Mortonhall exit from the Straiton junction and follow camping signs. Entrance road is alongside the Klondyke Garden Centre. O.S.GR: NT262686.

Charges 1996:
-- Per unit with all persons £7.75 - £11.25; serviced pitch + £2.50; electricity £1.75; awning £2.00; dog £1.00.
-- VAT included.
Open:
Easter/1 April - 31 Oct.
Address:
38 Mortonhall Gate, Frogston Road East, Edinburgh EH16 6TJ.
Tel:
0131 664 1533/2104.
FAX: 0131 664 5387.
Reservations:
Made with 1 night's charge plus £1.50 fee.

231 Strathclyde Country Park Caravan Site, Bothwell, Motherwell

Good touring site near Glasgow in Country Park with many amenities.

The 2,000 acre Country Park is a big green area less than 8 miles from the centre of Glasgow and is suitable for both overnight or period stays (max. 14 days). The very well kept park, open to all, has a large water sports section offering sailing, water ski, windsurfing, canoeing, rowing (all with craft for hire), `bumper boats' and a water bus, plus a 9-hole golf course, pitch and putt, tennis courts, coarse fishing, bowls, nature trail, funfair and children's adventure play area. Charges are low. The site has some 100 numbered pitches for caravans, all with electricity and drainage. Arranged in semicircular groups on flat grass they are served by made-up access roads and the site is well lit. There is also a tent field which could take 50, or more, for special events. Four solidly built modern toilet blocks make a good provision, with free hot water to the close together washbasins (shelf and mirror) and the showers, which now have cubicles. Enclosed sinks for washing-up or food preparation and launderette (irons from reception). Block 4 has facilities for disabled. Children's play area. Basic food provision only - shop 1 mile. Cafe 1½ miles away on Park. Public phone. 24 hour security. American motorhomes accepted up to 22 ft. The site is close to the motorway so there may be some traffic noise.

Directions: Take exit 5 from M74 and follow sign for Strathclyde Country Park. Turn first left for site. O.S.GR: NS720584.

Charges 1995:
-- Per caravan pitch £6.80; awning £1.55; tent pitch £5.85; small ridge tent £3.10; electricity £1.85.
Open:
Easter - 31 October.
Address:
Information and enquiries: Strathclyde Country Park, 366 Hamilton Road, Motherwell ML1 4ED.
Tel:
Motherwell (01698) 266155.
FAX: (01698) 252925.
Reservations:
Made for any period with deposit of one night's fee.

232 Tullichewan Caravan Park, Balloch

Good touring park south of Loch Lomond, open all year.

Almost, but not quite, on the banks of Loch Lomond (10 mins. or ¼ mile), this family owned and well planned park is good for both transit or longer stays. It takes 135 touring units, including 30 tents, all on well spaced, numbered pitches. On flat or gently sloping rough grass, most have hardstandings, 106 have electricity (10A) and 8 are `all-service'. The single, large, heated toilet block is well maintained and clean with plenty of WCs and basins, hot showers, 2 baby baths, 2 en-suite wash rooms (ladies) and shower room for the disabled. Covered washing-up sinks. Launderette. Good water and rubbish points. Well stocked shop by reception. Games room/TV, table tennis, pool table. Mountain bike hire. Children's playground on grass and bark. A leisure suite provides a sauna, sun-beds and spa-bath. There are watersports activities and boat trips on Loch Lomond and good rail and road connections to Glasgow. Dog walks. Pine lodges to let. Public phone. Restaurants and bar meals in Balloch (5 mins). American motorhomes accepted with prior notice. Reduced facilities Dec-March. A well run park with very helpful management. A member of the Best of British group.

Directions: Turn off A82, 17 miles northwest of Glasgow, onto A811 Stirling road. Park is well signed in Balloch. O.S.GR: NS389816.

Charges 1995:
-- Per unit incl. up to 2 persons £8.50 - £10.90 (all persons in winter £6.90); extra adult £1.20; child (5-15) 60p; electricity £1.80.
-- Less 10% for 7 nights or over booked.
-- VAT included.
Open:
All year except Nov.
Address:
Balloch G83 8QP.
Tel:
(01389) 759475.
FAX: (01389) 755563.
Reservations:
Any length with deposit of first nights charge

233 Ardgartan Campsite, Arrochar, nr. Tarbet

Forestry Commission site on banks of Loch Long with mountains all around.

Ardgartan, in the Argyll Forest Park, is a most attractively positioned site for a relaxing and peaceful break (apart from the very busy school holidays when it will be noisy) with lots of sightseeing and activity opportunities. At the northern end of the Cowal Peninsula, it is on a promontory on the shores of Loch Long, where there is good sea fishing and facilities for launching small boats. The 160 touring pitches, most with hardstanding and marked by numbered posts, are accessed from hard surface roads; 46 have electricity There are additional grass areas for tents. The main sanitary block is opposite the reception and shop (2 small others are close by for the busiest periods). It is satisfactory, if not plush, with facilities for the disabled and a launderette. Play equipment is provided (with bark surfaces). Barbecues are allowed. Arrochar village (2 miles) has fuel, general stores and a restaurant. Pony trekking, walking and climbing, as well as sea and river fishing (permits obtainable locally), are all available nearby.

Directions: From A82 Glasgow-Crianlarich road take A83 at Tarbet to Arrochar. Site is 2 miles past Arrochar, entrance on a bend. O.S.GR: NN275030.

Charges 1995:
-- Per adult £2.65 - £3.25; child £1.20 - £1.50; electricity £1.75.
Open:
April - October.
Address:
Ardgartan, Arrochar, Dunbartonshire G83 7AL.
Tel:
(013012) 293.(when closed: (0136984) 666.
Reservations:
Advisable in peak season for electricity.

234 Trossachs Holiday Park, Aberfoyle

Well run, friendly family park, ideal for exploring the Trossachs and Loch Lomond.

Nestling on the side of a hill, 3 miles south of Aberfoyle, this is an excellent base for touring this famously beautiful area. Lochs Lomond, Ard, Venachar and others are within easy reach, as are the Queen Elizabeth Forest Park and, of course, the Trossachs. The park specialises in sales and hire of top class mountain bikes and offers a 'passport' scheme with the local Leisure Centre (swimming, sauna, solarium, badminton, tennis, windsurfing, etc). There are also fishing and golfing opportunities nearby. A very neat and tidy park, there are 45 well laid out and marked pitches arranged on three terraces. Most have hardstanding, all have electricity and TV connections, and some 'super pitches' have water and drainage. There are trees between the terraces and lovely views across the valley. A modern wooden building houses the sanitary facilities which offer a satisfactory supply of toilets, showers and washbasins, the ladies' area being rather larger, with two private cabins. The building also contains a laundry room and a large games room with TV and lots of seating. There are several items of play equipment on gravel. A well stocked shop and the bike shop are either side of reception, where you will receive a warm welcome from Joe and Hazel Norman. Luxury caravans (38) for hire in separate section.

Charges 1995:
-- Per unit incl. 2 persons £6.50 - £9.00; electricity/TV £2.00; all services £3.00; extra adult £1.00; child (2-15 yrs) 75p.
-- Less for weekly stays.
-- VAT included.
-- Credit cards accepted.
Open:
15 March - end October.
Address:
Aberfoyle, Perthshire FK8 3SA.
Tel:
(01877) 382614 (24 hr).
FAX: (01877) 382732.
Reservations:
Min. 3 days with £15 deposit.

Directions: Park is 3 miles south of Aberfoyle on A81 road. O.S.GR: NS544976.

235 Blair Castle Caravan Park, Blair Atholl

Well kept park in attractive setting with some holiday homes.

This is an attractive park, well laid out in part of the grounds of Blair Castle, home to the Duke of Atholl but open to the public. There is a feeling of spaciousness with a large central area left free for children to play and for general use. Separate areas for caravans, motorhomes or tents can accommodate 270 units, 140 pitches having electricity, some on hardstandings and some also with water and drainage. There are 105 holiday homes, of which 27 are for hire, and rallies are taken on a special field. Motorcaravan service point and American motorhomes accepted (max. 30 ft. or 5 tons). Reduced facilities in low season. The original sanitary building has been refurbished and now offers fewer (13) but better showers. It is supplemented by four newer buildings providing between them, showers (some en-suite), toilets, chemical disposal, dishwashing and facilities for the disabled, not all in each building. Some blocks can be heated. Laundrette and drying room. Large self-service shop and a coffee shop which provides home cooked food, with good value meals and snacks all day until 9 or 10 pm. in the main season (weekends only in low season). A modern recreation building has a pool table, table-tennis and TV room. Well placed for Central Highland tours, mountain bike hire, pony trekking, golf and fishing are also nearby, plus many walking trails with leaflets provided in reception. A quality park, quiet at night and well managed by Mr Crerar, a local man who is justifiably proud of the park and determined not only to maintain the facilities but also to upgrade them. A member of the Best of British group.

Charges 1995:
-- Per unit with all persons £9.00; small tent plus vehicle £7.00; small tent, no car £5.00; awning £1.50; dog 50p; electricity £1.50.
-- 10% discount for OAP's outside Juy/Aug.
-- VAT included.
-- Credit cards accepted.
Open:
Easter/1 April - late October.
Address:
Blair Atholl, Perthshire PH18 5SR.
Tel:
Blair Atholl (01796) 481263.
FAX: (01796) 481587.
Reservations:
Any length with deposit of 1 night's charge + £2 fee except 15/7-15/8 when min. 3 nights and payment in full.

Directions: From the A9 just north of Pitlochry take the B8079 into Blair Atholl. Park is in grounds of Blair Castle, well signed. O.S.GR: NN868659.

Scottish Tourist Board

23 Ravelston Terrace, Edinburgh, EH4 3EU. Tel: (0131) 3322433 Fax: (0131) 3154545

1996 International Burns Festival. Two hundred years after his death, the life and works of Robert Burns are to be celebrated in poetry, song and entertainment starting in January, continuing from May to October, finale season in December, closing with a Hogmanay party and fireworks. Information Tel/Fax: 01292-288080.
Battle of Britain Airshow, RAF Leuchars 14 Sept: Loch Lomond World Invitation Golf Championship, Luss, By Alexandria 19-22 Sept. There are also the many traditional Highland Games throughout Scotland and of course the Edinburgh International Festival, 11-31 August, as well as a long list of other attractions throughout the year.

236 Craigtoun Meadows Holiday Park, St. Andrews

Attractively laid out park with individual pitches and good installations; holiday homes available.

Though outnumbered by caravan holiday homes, the touring section on this park is an important subsidiary. The facilities offered are both well designed and comprehensive with 98 units taken on the fairly flat park. Caravans go on individual hardstandings with grass alongside for awnings on most pitches, mostly in a separate touring field, and tents on a grassy meadow at one end. All caravan pitches are equipped with electricity, water and drainage and have been redesigned to increase size (13 sq.m.). There are also 16 larger 'patio' pitches with summer house, barbecue patio, picnic table and chairs, individually screened. All groundsheets (tents and awnings) must be lifted daily. Reservation is required for main season. The 140-odd caravan holiday homes stand round the outer parts of the park; 34 are owned and let by the park. The two toilet blocks which can be heated are well equipped and of quite adequate size. They have individual washbasins with shelf or flat surface and mirror, free hand and hair dryers, free hot showers and some washing-up sinks. Unit for disabled. On site are a self-service shop (all season) and an attractive little licensed restaurant (open Easter-31 Oct, 8 am.- 9 pm. in main season) which also supplies takeaway food. Launderette. Games room and mini-gym. Well equipped children's playground and play field and 8 acres of woodland (some under development). Barbecue area. Public phone (card). All weather tennis court. Small information room. A well run park, 2 miles from St Andrews with its golf courses and sandy beaches, and within walking distance of Craigtoun park with boating pond and miniature railway, etc.

Charges 1996:
-- Per unit, incl. 2 persons and electricity £11.25 - £12.25, 3 persons £11.75 - £12.75, 4-6 persons £12.25 - £13.25; awning £2.00; patio pitches £3.00 extra.
-- VAT included.
-- Credit cards accepted.
Open:
1 March - 31 October.
Address:
Mount Melville,
St. Andrews, Fife
KY16 8PQ.
Tel:
St. Andrews (01334) 475959.
FAX: (01334) 476424.
Reservations:
Any length of stay with full payment at time of booking.

Directions: From M90 take junction 8 to St. Andrews on the A91. Just after the sign for Guardbridge (to left, A919), turn right at sign for 'Strathkinness, 1¼ miles'. Go through village, over crossroads at end of village, left at next crossroads, then ¾ mile to park. O.S.GR: NO482151.

237 Nether Craig Caravan Park, by Alyth, Blairgowrie

Very attractive, family run touring park in peaceful Glenisla.

Richard and June Nicoll farmed in Glenisla before developing Nether Craig which they are continually looking to improve (they have recently planted 7,000 trees). Attractively designed and landscaped with views across the Strathmore valley to the long range of the Sidlaw hills, the park is linked by a circular gravel road and provides 40 well spaced pitches. All have 10A electrical connections and 29 have hardstanding. The central, modern, purpose built toilet block provides free pre-set hot showers with dressing area, shelf and hooks, vanity style washbasins and free hairdryers for both male and female. A complete unit for the handicapped (entry by key) also includes a hairdryer. Separate sinks for dishwashing and clothes are provided in the laundry room with metered hot water, washing machine, dryer and iron, with a rotary clothes line outside near the dog walk. It is a good provision which is very well maintained. There is a personal welcome for all visitors at the attractive wooden chalet beside the entrance (with a slope for wheelchairs) which doubles as reception and shop providing the necessary essentials and tourist information. Children have swings and other play equipment. A one mile circular woodland walk from the park has picnic benches and a leaflet guide is provided. Otherwise you can just enjoy the peace of the Angus Glens by hill walking, birdwatching, fishing or pony trekking. Alyth with its Arthurian connections (and golf course) is only 4 miles away and Glamis Castle, the childhood home of the Queen Mother, is nearby, as is the beautiful Glenshee and Braemar with its castle.

Charges 1996:
-- Per unit incl. 2 persons £7.00 - £9.00; extra person 85p; electricity £1.50; tent £2.50 per person.
-- VAT included.
Open:
15 March - 31 October.
Address:
Alyth, Blairgowrie,
Perthshire PH11 8HN.
Tel:
(01575) 560204.
FAX: (01575) 560315.
Reservations:
Advisable for main season - contact park.

Directions: From the A926 Blairgowrie-Kirriemuir road, at roundabout south of Alyth join the B954 signed Glenisla. Follow caravan signs for 4 miles and turn right onto unclassified road signed Nether Craig. Park is on the left after ½ mile. O.S.GR: NO265528.

238 Auchterarder Caravan Park, Nether Coul, Auchterarder

Recently developed small family run park in sheltered position.

This is a charming small park, purpose designed and landscaped by the owners Stuart and Susie Robertson. It is conveniently situated for exploring central Scotland and the Highlands with many leisure activities close at hand, particularly golf, and within walking distance of the village (1 mile). The 21 pitches, all with electricity (5A at present) and hardstanding, 12 with drainage also, are well spaced around the edge of an elongated, level grass field. Marked pitches with grass frontage back on to raised banks which are tree planted. A tarmac hold-over area at the entrance for late arrivals (with electricity) ensures no one is disturbed. A modern pine chalet, blending with the environment, is also at the entrance housing reception, a small shop with basic items (milk delivered daily), small library and excellent sanitary facilities with a key system. These include roomy toilets, controllable hot showers and vanity style wash-basins. A toilet for disabled is provided in both the male and female units. Laundry room with sink and washing machine - iron and board can be provided as well. Under cover washing up with free hot water. Two secluded chalets (self catering) for hire and B&B. Public phones. Easy access from the A9 road.

Directions: Park is between the A9 and A824 roads east of Auchterarder village, only ½ mile from the main road. It is reached by turning on to the B8062 (Dunning) road from the A824. O.S.GR: NN946138.

Charges 1995:
-- Caravan, car and up to 4 persons £7.00; tent and vehicle £5.00 - £7.00; awning 50p - £1.00 electricity £1.50.
-- Less 10% for OAPs and registered disabled.
Open:
All year.
Address:
Nether Coul,
Auchterarder, Perthshire
PH3 1ET.
Tel:
(01764) 663119.
Reservations:
Advisable July/Aug. and made with deposit of one nights charge and booking fee (£1).
Bookings held until 5

239 Aberfeldy Caravan Park, Aberfeldy

Municipal park in attractive touring area.

On the banks of the River Tay and enjoying mountain views, this municipal park is on the edge of the town with all its shops and restaurants and a recreation centre with swimming pool, golf course and watersports activities. There are 121 pitches, all with electricity (16A), plus 30 seasonal places, mostly in the front field where the modern sanitary block (operated by key) is situated. There is a secondary overflow field by the river served by an old building. Pitches are clearly marked on level grass with tarmac, one-way access roads. Laundry room. Fenced children's play area. Tourist information provided in reception along with a microwave, a freezer for ice and a phone box. The park is very busy in high season.

Directions: Accessed directly from A827 on the eastern outskirts of Aberfeldy. O.S.GR: NN858495.

Charges 1995:
-- Per unit incl. 4 persons £8.20; extra person (over 10 yrs) £1.00; electricity £1.60.
Open:
1 April/Easter - end Oct.
Address:
Dunkeld Road,
Aberfeldy PH15 2AQ.
Tel:
(01887) 820662.
Reservations:
Contact park. Take up reservation by 6 pm.

240 Haughton Country Park Caravan Site, Alford

Good touring park situated west of Aberdeen, a pleasant base for visiting the eastern Highlands.

A surprisingly pleasant park to come across in a little town some 25 miles to the west of Aberdeen, Haughton is run by the district council. It adjoins an attractive 53-acre park which contains picnic and recreation areas and a large adventure playground. In a quiet sheltered situation, the camping ground is laid out in quite spacious individual pitches in mature park land with a good quota of free space, with a total capacity of 175 pitches. They are mainly on hardstandings with some on grass and 118 have electricity (16A); 40 are occupied by caravan holiday homes. Five flats, two caravans and a chalet are for rent. An area for tents is being developed in the walled garden. There is usually space. The central toilet block, with free hot water in good individual basins and hot showers is supplemented by two good new blocks in a newer area with baby baths (key system). Plentiful water points and dustbin units. Shop. Launderette. Children's playground and play area. Nature walks, putting green and 'trim track'. TV, games room. Flood lit dry ski slope in Alford (with ski hire and lessons), as well as a swimming pool, Transport Museum, miniature railway and Heritage Centre.

Directions: Turn north on road signed Haughton Park and Montgarrie in the village of Alford on A944; park entrance is ½ mile. O.S.GR: NJ583168.

Charges 1995:
-- Per unit incl. all persons £6.75 (week £40.50); awning £2.50; single person tent £3.50; electricity £1.65.
-- One night discount for 7 nights stayed
-- VAT included.
Open:
1 April - 3 October.
Address:
Alford, Aberdeenshire
AB33 8NA.
Tel:
Alford (019755) 62107.
Reservations:
No advance bookings accepted.

GRAMPIAN

241 Burnside Caravan Site, Fochabers

Speyside park for touring units and holiday homes, with swimming pool.

Fochabers enjoys a mild climate and is surrounded by farmland, forest and market gardens (the home of Baxters soups). Burnside is a pleasant little site in a semi-woodland setting with a heated, covered pool (60 x 19 ft.) which is open from May-Sept. to campers (90p charge) and outside visitors. The 100 tourist pitches here are mostly intended for trailer caravans, the majority numbered around the perimeter of a flat meadow, others marked by jockey wheel points, with a lesser number in wooded clearings. There are 40 electrical connections (10A). A small, sheltered tent area will open for 1996. 70 privately owned holiday caravans also. Reservations are made but otherwise arrive early in high season. The two good toilet blocks have free hot water in basins set in flat surfaces and in the large showers. The top ladies block has 2 large family showers. Two dishwashing sinks and washing machine and dryer. No shop, but the village is near. Children's play area on bark. Large recreation room with TV, table tennis, tables for sitting. Public phone. Forestry Commission walks. The park is 4 miles from the sea. Possibly some road noise from the adjacent A96.

Directions: Entrance is by A96, just south of A98 junction. O.S.GR: NJ345585.

Charges 1995:
-- Per unit £6.75; 1 man tent £4.25; electricity £1.50.
-- VAT included.
Open:
1 April - 31 October.
Address:
Keith Road, Fochabers, Moray.
Tel:
Fochabers (01343) 820362 or 820511.
Reservations:
Accepted with deposit of one night's fee (by cheque).

242 Turriff Caravan Park, Turriff

Small neatly landscaped municipal by Haughs Park.

This is one of the most neat, tidy and spacious parks we have seen, and is a credit to the warden Mrs Pirie. Owned by the local authority, the park is almost in the middle of the town and, although hedges and trees provide a degree of seclusion, there may be some traffic noise. There are 60 touring pitches, of which 57 have electrical connections. Sanitary facilities (with key on deposit) have good free hot showers and were spotlessly clean when visited. Unit for the disabled (no shower) and laundry and dishwashing facilities. Milk and bread are available from reception, with the local shops within a few minutes walk or by bus from outside the gate. Children's play area. Public phone. Nearby Haughs Park offers a variety of amenities including an indoor swimming pool, tennis courts, putting green and a boating pond and Turriff is an interesting old town.

Directions: Park is south of the town on the A947 Aberdeen Road and is well signed. O.S.GR: NJ725494.

Charges 1995:
-- Per unit £6.55; small tent £2.85; awning £1.50 - £2.85; electricity £1.50.
-- Reductions for OAPs out of season.
Open:
1 April - 30 September.
Address:
Station Road, Turriff, Aberdeenshire.
Tel:
(01888) 62205.
Reservations:
Advisable in season.

243 Aden Country Park Caravan Park, Mintlaw, nr. Aden

Attractive, landscaped park in large country park with many attractions.

Aden Country Park is owned by the local authority and is open to the public offering several attractions including an Agricultural Heritage Centre, wildlife centre, nature trail, restaurant and craft shops, as well as open and woodland areas, with a lake, for walking and recreation. The caravan and camping park is on one side. Beautifully landscaped and well laid out with trees, bushes and hedges, it is kept very neat and tidy. It provides 50 numbered pitches all with electricity (16A), plus 10 caravan holiday homes in a row as you enter. A modern, fully tiled sanitary block, with good facilities for the disabled, was very clean when we visited. It provides free, pre-set hot showers, with dressing area, and plenty of toilets and vanity type washbasins, with hairdryer for ladies and a baby bath. Dishwashing and laundry facilities are together. Large dog walk area. Good facilities for children include two games areas and various items of play equipment (with safety surfaces). Small shop in the reception area and the restaurant in the Heritage Centre is available for meals. The park is in a most attractive area and one could spend plenty of time enjoying all it has to offer.

Directions: Approaching Mintlaw from the west on A950 road, park is shortly after the sign for Mintlaw station. From the east, go to western outskirts of village and entrance is on left - `Aden Country Park and Farm Heritage Centre'. O.S.GR: NJ985484.

Charges 1995:
-- Per caravan or motorcaravan £6.55, with electricity £8.05; large tent £5.75; small tent or awning £2.85; porch awning £1.50.
-- Reductions for OAPs out of season.
Open:
1 April - 30 September.
Address:
Old Deer, Mintlaw, Aberdeenshire.
Tel:
(01771) 23460.
Reservations:
Advisable for weekends; write to park for details.

144

ALAN ROGERS GOOD CAMPS GUIDE, BRITAIN & IRELAND 1996

DISCOUNT CARD, Valid 1 Jan - 31 Dec 1996

ME: ....

DRESS: ....

NATURE: ....

THE ALAN ROGERS
Good camps guide

PART 1   CAMPSITE DISCOUNT VOUCHER, Valid 1st Jan - 31st Dec 1996

voucher entitles the holder to the discounts shown against the relevant individual Campsite Report in this Guide. This
ion of the voucher should be retained by the holder, but made available for inspection at the campsite(s) concerned when
king-in and/or on departure.

ME of voucher holder: ....

RESS: ....

SIGNATURE: ....

VOUCHER NUMBER

17571

B96

PART 2   Travel, Breakdown, Caravan & Motorcaravan Insurance Discount Voucher, Valid 1st Jan - 31st Dec 1996

portion entitles the holder to a discount of 10% on Travel & Breakdown Insurance arrangements made via this guide,
or a discount of 5% on the annual caravan or motorcaravan insurances arranged through Bakers of Cheltenham, and
ertised on pages 181/182 of this guide.

travel/breakdown insurance please contact Deneway Guides & Travel Ltd., 01308 897809, quote your card number and
for a Travel & Breakdown Insurance proposal form and details.

caravan or motorcaravan insurance, please complete the forms on pages 181/182 and send it to BAKERS OF
ELTENHAM at the address shown on pages 181/182, quoting this discount voucher number.

ME of voucher holder: ....

RESS: ....

SIGNATURE: ....

VOUCHER NUMBER

17571

B96

PART 3   IRISH FERRIES DISCOUNT VOUCHER

IRISH FERRIES

voucher entitles the holder to the following 50% reductions with Irish Ferries on all their routes between BRITAIN &
LAND (except as detailed below) between 1st January 1996 and 31st December 1996.

luctions: For caravans and trailer tents - a discount of 50% off the published brochure tariff for towed caravans or trailer
s when making a standard return fare booking for a car, caravan or trailer tent and up to five adults, excluding Easter
k-end, Whit week-end, Christmas week and Fridays & Saturdays during July and August. For motorcaravans no
height supplement will be charged.

ditions of use: (1) Travel must actually take place within the period 1st Jan - 31st Dec 1996. (2) Any application for a refund must be accompanied by
nused portion of the ticket, and made through the issuing office within six months of the expiry date of the ticket. No replacement discount voucher will
pplied, nor cash refunded against the value of the voucher. (3) Only one discount voucher per booking will be permitted, and the voucher may not be
anged for cash. (4) Irish Ferries reserves the right not to accept any discount voucher where fraudulent use is suspected. (5) All other conditions are as
shed in the Irish Ferries brochure at the time of booking.

w to book: For brochure requests only, telephone 01233 211911. For telephone bookings: Telephone 0345 171717
quote this voucher number AND the Brochure/Fare Code No. BGSPC96/ARC at the time of booking. Send this section
e voucher to Irish Ferries when paying for your tickets

ME of voucher holder: ....

RESS: ....

SIGNATURE: ....

VOUCHER NUMBER

17571

B96

244 Aberlour Gardens Caravan and Camping Park, Aberlour

Small pleasant park situated within the walled garden of the Aberlour Estate.

This sheltered, family run park on Speyside provides a very natural setting amidst spruce and Scots pines. Of the 46 level pitches, 26 are for holiday homes, leaving 20 for touring units, 18 with electrical connections (10/5A); reservation is recommended for these in season. American motorhomes are accepted up to 20 ft. The toilet block has individual basins with shelves and mirrors (soap and towels), 4 large unisex showers on payment and facilities for the disabled. Laundry facilities. A small shop has basics, information area and mini library. Children's play area. Public telephone. Dogs are welcome if kept under control. This is an ideal area for walking, birdwatching, fishing (salmon angling), pony trekking or for following the only Malt Whisky Trail in the world. Golf (3 miles), swimming (1 mile) and bowls (2 miles).

Directions: Park is north of Aberlour on the A95 before Craigellachie. O.S.GR: NJ282432.

Alan Rogers' discount
Less 20%
outside July/Aug.

Charges 1996:
-- Per caravan or motorhome £5.50; tent £4.50; person 60p; electricity £1.50; awning £1.00.
Open:
1 April - 31 October.
Address:
Aberlour-on-Spey, Moray AB3 9LD.
Tel:
(01340) 871586.
Reservations:
Only necessary for electricity in season.

245 Grantown-on-Spey Caravan Park, Grantown-on-Spey

Family run touring park with good sanitary facilities.

Bill and Sandra Gourly own and personally run this park, continually upgrading an already excellent provision. Quietly and peacefully situated on the edge of the little town with views of the mountains in the distance, it consists of well tended grassy lawns, terraced or slightly sloping with made-up access roads and where the rabbits allow, colourful flower beds. For tourers, there are 100 individual caravan pitches, plus 50 which may be occupied by seasonal vans (many on hardstandings) and room for perhaps 50 tents. There are 12 large pitches with water and drainage (from 1996) and 80 electrical connections (10A). Everyone is individually escorted to their pitch, shown the facilities and given any help necessary. Recent landscaping has included the planting of many trees which are growing well. Caravan holiday homes are mostly separated to either end of the park. Sanitary facilities, comprising two clean, modern blocks, are of excellent quality and beautifully maintained, with a small night unit at the opposite end. Facilities include free hot water in individual washbasins (with flat surface and mirror) and in controllable showers, hairdryers, covered dishwashing sinks behind each block and a laundry room with washing machines, spin dryers and irons. Games room with table tennis and pool table. Football pitch. 2 public phones. Dog exercise area with hill top view! The gates closed 10.30 pm. - 7.30 am. No shop but the town shops are close. Grantown is a pleasant touring base for the Cairngorms and for following the Malt Whisky Trail. Fishing, golf, riding, pony trekking and mountain bikes for hire nearby. A peaceful park with a warden on site at all times. A member of the Best of British group.

Directions: Park is signed from the town centre. O.S.GR: NJ028283.

Charges 1995:
-- Per pitch incl. 2 persons £7.00 - £8.50; 2 man tent and vehicle £5.50 - £6.25; 2 man tent & hikers £4.50 - £5.00; awning or extra pup tent £1.50; extra person 50p; electricity £1.50.
-- VAT included.
-- Credit cards accepted,
Open:
28 March - 30 Sept.
Address:
Seafield Avenue, Grantown on Spey, Moray PH26 3JQ.
Tel:
Grantown (01479) 872474.
FAX: (01479) 873696.
Reservations:
Made with £5 deposit.

246 Auchnahillin Caravan and Camping Centre, Daviot East, nr. Inverness

Pleasant, family run park with attractive views.

The Graham family provide a warm reception to visitors to this open, level park with pleasant views of the surrounding pine and heather covered hills. They took over in 1990 and are working hard to improve the facilities. There are 65 touring pitches, with 30 electrical connections (16A), a separate area for tents and 30 caravans for letting, all well lit. The sanitary block is very clean and well maintained and offers good facilities including hot showers (on payment) and sufficient toilets and washbasins (free hot water at all times) with razor points and hairdryer. The laundry and dishwashing room is part of the same block. Children's play area (on grass and sand). A pub/restaurant on the park provides home cooked meals which seem good value and there is a new shop/reception with local information. This is a centre for outdoor activities such as walking, fishing (sea, river and loch), pony trekking, climbing, cycling and birdwatching or for ski-ing. Inverness is close by, as is Aviemore.

Directions: Turn off the A9 south of Inverness onto the B9154. Park is just north of Moy. O.S.GR: NH723926.

Charges 1996:
-- Per unit incl. 2 persons £5.50 - £8.50; hiker or cyclist (1) £3.50 - £5.00; extra adult £1.20; child 50p; awning, tent or boat £2.00; electricity £1.85. -- Discounts for senior citizens or over 3 days. -- VAT included.
Open:
1 April - October.
Address:
Daviot East, Inverness-shire IV1 2XQ.
Tel/Fax:
(01463) 772286.
Reservations:
Contact park for details.

247 Spindrift Caravan and Camping Park, Little Kildrummie, Nairn

Delightful quiet small family run park near popular resort.

Careful landscaping by the resident owners Mr and Mrs Guillot helps to make this a little gem of a park, situated in an elevated position overlooking the River Nairn and distant Monadlaith mountains. The popular seaside resort of Nairn with its shops, restaurants, beach and harbour is some 2 miles away and it is said to take 30 minutes to walk via the riverside path. The park is surrounded by trees and is arranged on three terraces (very easy access), the lowest primarily for tents. With 45 pitches altogether, electricity (16A) is available on 20 of the 30 pitches on the highest terrace and, provided you have a long cable, on the second level too, although this is usually used for tents. There are two good, well equipped modern sanitary blocks with free hot showers, hair dryers and a new laundry/indoor washing-up room but no facilities in terms of shop or restaurant, etc. but these are readily available in Nairn. Salmon fishing permits available.

Directions: From the A96 just west of Nairn take the B9090 south towards Cawdor. Pass through the residential area out into the country for about 1½ miles and follow Little Kildrummie sign to right. O.S.GR: NH863537.

Charges 1996:
-- Per unit, all incl. £5.50 - £7.50; electricity £1.50.
Open:
1 April - 31 October.
Address:
Little Kildrummie, Nairn, Morayshire IV12 5QU.
Tel:
(01667) 453992.
Reservations:
Advisable for July/Aug. with £5 deposit.

Alan Rogers' discount
£1 off pitch fee

248 Torvean Caravan Park, Inverness

Small, select touring park for caravans only.

Torvean is situated on the outskirts of Inverness beside the Caledonian Canal and within easy reach of the town's amenities which include an ice rink, theatre and leisure sports centre. Excursions to the coast and highlands, including Loch Ness, are possible in several directions. The pitches on neat, level grass are well spaced out and clearly marked with a tarmac access road and street lighting giving a very neat appearance. There are 50 touring pitches, 45 with electrical connections (7A) and 11 holiday caravans for hire. Torvean offers a children's play area on bark, a well equipped launderette and public telephone. The two toilet blocks are of good quality with free hot water in basins, set in flat surface with shelves and mirrors - ladies now have 2 cubicles with washbasin and toilet and a special hair washing cubicle. Controllable hot showers on payment. Hand and hair dryers. Toilet suite for the disabled with shower. Dog walking area.

Directions: Park is off the main A82 road on the southwest outskirts of the town by the Tomnahurich Canal Bridge. O.S.GR: NH638438.

Charges 1995:
-- Per caravan and car incl. 2 persons £8.50; motorcaravan incl. 2 persons £9.00; extra adult £1.50; extra child (under 16) 75p; small dog £1.00; awning £3.00; electricity £2.00.
Open:
Easter - end-October.
Address:
Glenurquhart Road, Inverness IV3 6JL.
Tel:
(01463) 220582.
FAX: (01463) 233051.
Reservations:
Necessary for July and Aug. and made with first night's charge.

HIGHLANDS and ISLANDS

249 Glenmore Forest Camping and Caravan Park, Glenmore, Aviemore

Forestry Commission Site ideally situated for exploring the Cairngorms.

The Glenmore Forest site lies close to the sandy shore of Loch Morlich amidst conifer woods and surrounded on three sides by the impressive Cairngorm mountains. It is convenien for a range of activities, including skiing (extensive lifts), hill and mountain walking (way marked walks), fishing and non-motorized watersports on the Loch. The site itself is attractively laid out in a fairly informal style in several adjoining areas connected by narrow gravel/tarmac roadways with access to the lakeside. One of these areas, the Pinewood, is very popular and has a premium charge. Of the 220 marked pitches on fairly level grass, 122 have electricity (10A). There are two modern toilet blocks with free hot water to the washbasins, but only one shower/laundry block which is some distance from the majority of the pitches reached by an underpass. Opened by electronic key pad (you are given a number), it is a large heated block with free hot showers, providing adequate facilities. Separate unit for the disabled. Amenities, also open to the public, include a well stocked shop, cafe, visitor centre and souvenir shop. The Aviemore centre is 7 miles and there are several golf courses within a range of 15 miles, as well as fishing and boat trips. No night time supervision.

Directions: Immediately south of Aviemore on the B9152 (not A9 bypass) take the B970 for a short distance then follow sign for Cairngorm and Loch Morlich. Site entrance is on right past the loch. O.S.GR: NH975097.

Charges 1995:
– Per pitch/unit £6.50 - £7.50; surcharge for Pinewood site £1.30 per pitch; electricity £1.90; backpackers or groups £2.70 per person.
-- Credit cards accepted.
Open:
All year except Nov. and first week in Dec.
Address:
Glenmore, Aviemore, Inverness-shire PH22 1QU.
Tel:
(01479) 861271.
Reservations:
Necessary for high season. Min. 3 nights with deposit (3 nights charge) plus £2 fee.

250 Woodend Camping and Caravan Park, Achnairn, by Lairg

Delightful, peaceful and welcoming park overlooking Loch Shin.

Mr and Mrs Ross run this small. friendly park and provide a wonderfully warm Scottish welcome. On a hill with open, panoramic views across the Loch to the hills beyond, the large camping field is undulating and gently sloping with plenty of reasonably flat areas. Most of the 22 hook-ups (16A) are in a line near the top of the field, close to the large, fenced children's play area on grass. The modernised sanitary facilities are kept very clean and are quite satisfactory, with hot water for showers and dishwashing on small payment. A laundry room is just behind and a kitchen for tent campers is being prepared. Reception and a shop are at the house, where Sunday papers can be ordered, strawberries are on sale in season and daily milk and bread may be ordered. Fishing licences for the Loch available (your catch will be frozen for you). Opportunities for hill walking, mountain bike hire in Lairg (5 miles). Several scenic golf courses within 20-30 miles. The famous Falls of Shin are 10 miles. Caravan holiday homes (5) to rent.

Directions: Achnairn is near the southern end of Loch Shin. Turn off the A838 single track road at signs for Woodend. From the A9 coming north take the A836 at Bonar Bridge, 11 miles northwest of Tain. O.S.GR: NC558127.

Charges 1995:
-- Per unit (all) £5.00; electricity £1.00.
Open:
1 April - 30 September.
Address:
Achnairn, Lairg, Sutherland IV27 4DN.
Tel:
(01549) 402248.
Reservations:
Not considered necessary.

251 Ardmair Point Caravan Park, Ardmair Point, nr. Ullapool

Spectacularly situated park on bay at Loch Kanaird.

Just 3 miles north of Ullapool and overlooking the little Loch Kanaird, this park has splendid views all round. The 45 touring pitches are arranged mainly on grass around the edge of the bay. Electrical hook-ups (10A) available. Some gravel hardstanding is provided on the other side of the access road, just past the new, well equipped second sanitary block. This block, with wonderful views from the windows in the launderette and dishwashing rooms, provides good facilities including hot showers (20p) and washbasins set in flat surfaces, plus en-suite rooms for the disabled. Tent pitches, together with cheaper pitches for tourers are in a large field behind the other sanitary facilities (also good). The reception and shop are housed in the same building and upstairs is a pleasant cafe (open 9.00-2130). Rowing and motorboats for hire and fishing trips. Seals are regularly seen in the bay and the whole area is full of interest, including visits to Inverewe Gardens and the Isle Martin bird and seal colonies.

Directions: Off the A835 road, 3 miles north of Ullapool. O.S.GR: NH109983.

Charges 1995:
-- Per unit incl. two persons £7.00; electricity £2.00.
Open:
1 May - late September, depending on weather, if in doubt phone.
Address:
Ardmair Point, Ullapool Ross-shire, IV26 2TN.
Tel:
(01854) 612054.
FAX: (01854) 612757.
Reservations:
Recommended for July/Aug.

252 Scourie Caravan and Camping Park, Scourie, nr. Handa Island

Family park with own restaurant, close to ferries for Handa Island Bird Sanctuary.

Mr Mackenzie has carefully nurtured this park over many years, developing a number of firm terraces with 60 pitches which gives it an attractive layout. Perched on the edge of the bay in an elevated position, there are pleasant views all around with a sandy beach close (young children would need to be supervised if you were in one area). The park has gravel access roads and some hardstandings with 5 or 10A electric hook-ups available. A modern building houses the reception, with lots of local tourist information, a launderette and the satisfactory sanitary facilities. Hot water is free to the vanity style washbasins and controllable showers (no divider or seat). The Anchorage restaurant is large and well appointed, with meals at very reasonable prices all cooked to order, or for just a coffee and scone. It is claimed that this is the only caravan park in the world from where, depending on the season, you can see palm trees, Highland cattle and Great Northern divers from your pitch. Red throated divers have also been seen and the corncrake has reappeared. Trips to Handa Island (a protected area for seabird colonies) from Tarbet. It is a short walk down to a safe sandy beach with very clear water - the area is ideal for skin-diving. Fishing permits (brown trout) arranged. The village has a well stocked shop with post office, gas available from local petrol station and mobile banks visit regularly.

Charges 1995:
-- Per unit incl. 3 persons £8.00; child (3-16 yrs) 50p; electricity £2.00.
Open:
Easter - end September.
Address:
Harbour Road, Scourie, By Lairg, Sutherland IV27 4TG.
Tel:
(01971) 2060.
Reservations:
Not made.

Directions: Park is by the village of Scourie on the A894 road in northwest Sutherland. O.S.GR: NC153446.

253 Reraig Caravan Site, Balmacara, Kyle of Lochalsh

Small, quiet, friendly park with views of the hills and loch; no large tents or awnings accepted.

This small park has a wooded backdrop and views across to Loch Alsh towards Skye from nearby. On mainly flat grass, it is sheltered by trees and provides just 45 numbered pitches. There are 28 with electricity (10A), 11 with hardstanding. Large tents, trailer tents and awnings are not accepted and small tents only at the discretion of the owner so it would be advisable to phone first if this affects you. A motorcaravan service point and chemical disposal are provided. American motorhomes are generally too big and heavy for this site. The single sanitary block, with a degree of individuality in its decor, is kept clean and provides controllable hot showers on payment (30p), hairdryers and razor points. Hot water to washbasins, dishwashing and clothes sinks is free, all under cover. Adjacent is an hotel with bar and restaurant, a grocery shop with off-licence and post office, and a petrol station. There are forest walks near and it is possible to launch small boats into the sea loch. This attractive park makes a good base for exploring the Isle of Skye and Wester Ross. Reservations are not normally considered necessary, but it is best to arrive before mid-afternoon in July/Aug.

Charges 1996:
-- Per unit incl. up to 4 persons £6.20; extra person 50p; extra tent or car £1.30; electricity £1.20.
-- Credit cards accepted.
Open:
1 May - 30 September.
Address:
Balmacara, Kyle of Lochalsh, Ross-shire IV40 8DH.
Tel:
(01599) 566215.
Reservations:
Not accepted by phone; if considered necessary, taken by letter with one night's fee as deposit.

Directions: Take A87 towards Kyle of Lochalsh. Park is signed very soon after Balmacara, on the right just before hotel and petrol station. O.S.GR: NG815272.

254 Loch Greshornish Camping Site, Edinbane, Isle of Skye

Simple, large lochside site in northwest Skye.

Peacefully situated on a mainly gently sloping field leading down to the loch, this site has pleasant views across to the low hills in the northwest of Skye. There are 30 reasonably flat touring pitches for motorhomes and caravans and places for up to 100 tents (although there are usually far fewer on site). There are no electrical hook-ups, hardstandings or a shop here. However, the sanitary facilities are satisfactory, positioned quite near the entrance to the long site. They provide free hot water to the washbasins with shelf and hook, and the showers with hooks, seat and curtain divider, and the dishwashing sink in each section. Hairdryer on payment and outside, but covered, is a tumble dryer, water points and bins. There are hotels for drinks and meals in the village close by.

Charges 1995:
-- Per any unit incl. 2 persons £5.50.
Open:
Easter/1 April - 15 Oct.
Address:
Arnisort, Edinbane, Isle of Skye IV51 9PS.
Tel:
(01470) 582230.
Reservations:
Advised for high season - contact site.

Directions: Site is 15 miles west of Portree on the A850 Dunvegan road by Edinbane (all two-lane road apart from last mile). O.S.GR: NG343524.

255 Staffin Caravan and Camping Site, Staffin, Isle of Skye

Hillside site with wonderful views in northeast Skye.

The holiday attractions of this area of Skye include fascinating geology, history, fauna and flora as well as activities such as walking, water sports, cycling and fishing. The camping site is on the side of a hill just outside Staffin, where the broad sweep of the bay is dotted with working crofts, with a marked walk leading to the seashore. It is a sloping field with gravel roads but there are reasonably flat places with 18 hardstandings and 14 electrical hook-ups (16A) and splendid views across to the hills behind the village. The new sanitary block, fully tiled with pine ceilings, is a fine facility with large controllable showers (no divider), vanity style washbasins, all with free hot water. An old, very basic block at the top is kept for use during cleaning and for tourers at that end should the weather turn nasty. Open, but separate, chemical disposal point and large hardstanding area for motorhome service. Cottages and 2 mobile homes for hire. Facilities in Staffin (400 yds) include a shop, restaurant, launderette and phone.

Directions: Site is 15 miles north of Portree on the A855 (2 miles of single track at the start), just before Staffin on the right and up a slope. O.S.GR: NG496668.

Charges 1995:
-- Per unit (all) incl. 2 persons £6.00; electricity £1.50.
Open:
April - September (maybe into October if weather fine).
Address:
Staffin, Isle of Skye IV51 9JS.
Tel:
(01470) 562213.
Reservations:
Maybe necessary for peak periods, but will always try to fit you in.

256 Faichem Park, Faichem, Invergarry

Small unspoilt site near Loch Ness with beautiful views.

Faichem Park, as yet, offers no electric hook-ups and is not the easiest site for large units to negotiate but, for those who manage, it is a beautiful setting overlooking Ben Tee (2,955 ft.) on a hillside. For the children there is the attraction of helping to feed the animals - goats, sheep and lambs, chickens, many types of ducks and strange marvellous looking types of pheasants (Mr Wilson's hobby), the pony and the three white pilot ducks which march around the park and farm. There are 30 unmarked pitches with 20 ft. spacing - 15 for tents, 15 for caravans. Motor homes may have some difficulty but there are a few level areas suitable. A log type cabin houses the sanitary facilities with controllable hot showers (on meter) and operated on a key system with deposit. Covered washing up sink (metered) behind the block. Pine lodges to let. Milk, free range eggs and fresh vegetables in season available from the farm house but there are shops, hotel, etc. in the village (½ mile). Fishing, hill walking, climbing, pony trekking, boating, golfing, much to do and maybe even the possibility of spotting Nessie!

Directions: From A82 at Invergarry take A87 towards Kyle of Lochalsh and continue for 1 mile. Turn right at Faichem sign and bear left up hill, farmhouse is the first entrance on the right, the site is second. O.S.GR: NH285023.

Charges 1995:
-- Per unit incl. 2 persons £5.50 - £6.00; extra adult 50p; extra child 25p.
Open:
15 April - 15 October.
Address:
Ardgarry Farm, Faichem, Invergarry, Inverness-shire
Tel:
(018093) 226.
Reservations:
Advisable in main season and made with small deposit.

257 Resipole Farm Caravan and Camping Park, Loch Sunart, Acharacle

Beautifully situated park on the loch shores, with good facilities.

This quiet, open park is marvellously set on the banks of Loch Sunart, 8 miles from Strontian, in the Ardnamurchan peninsular, with views across the water. It is a good base for exploring this scenic area or for fishing, boating or walking. There are 45 pitches, 28 with hardstanding of which 4 have all services and 20 have hook-ups. Tents are sited by the hedges. Some caravans and cabins for hire. The central, modern sanitary block provides free, pre-set showers, washbasins in rows, shaver points and hair dryers. The facilities are good and were very clean when seen. Dishwashing facilities in separate, enclosed rooms are also good. Excellent provision for the disabled. Games room. Adjoining the farmhouse are a bunk house and a nicely equipped bar/restaurant offering reasonably priced home made food in the evenings (vegetarians catered for). Well stocked, licensed shop (May - Sept, with hours according to demand). Drying room and laundry facilities. Public phone. The park is well located for day trips to Mull via the Lochaline ferry. A 9 hole golf course is under construction for 1996.

Directions: From A82 Fort William road, take the Corran ferry 5 miles north of Ballachulish, 8 miles south of Fort William. On leaving ferry, turn south along the A861. Park is on the north bank of Loch Sunart, 8 miles west of Strontian. Note: single track for 8 miles approaching Resipole. O.S.GR: NM676740.

Charges 1996:
-- Per unit, incl. 2 persons £8.50; electricity £1.50; extra person £1.50; awning or extra tent free.
-- VAT included.
-- Credit cards accepted.
Open:
Easter/1 April - mid-October.
Address:
Loch Sunart, Acharacle, Argyll PH36 4HX.
Tel:
(0196785) 617.
Reservations:
Advisable for hook-ups and made for any period with 1 night's fee.

258 Glen Dochart Caravan Park, Luib, Crianlarich

Small, neat park in beautiful Highland Glen setting.

The mountains and river which flows through the Glen to Loch Tay provide a dramatic setting to this park which is located on the site of the former Luib railway station on part of the line which used to connect east and west Scotland. The Falls of Dochart at the delightful village of Killin, 7 miles away are well worth a visit. It is a quiet site, just off the A85 Perth - Oban road, ideal for hill walking or fishing holidays, with a watersports centre close by. It is personally supervised by the Donaldson family. With 42 holiday homes at one end, there is space for 45 tourers on a mix of level grass or hardstanding pitches with 16 electrical points. A well renovated `portaloo' building provides satisfactory sanitary facilities with well equipped, free hot showers. Full laundry and dishwashing facilities are next to reception with an extra toilet. Reception and the shop are in the former station house with the platform providing some of the hardstanding. A phone and some children's play equipment complete the facilities. Dogs are permitted on short leads to be exercised away from touring and play areas - the old railway track provides a pleasant walk. Fishing permits for Loch Lubhair and the river are available from reception. A licensed hotel within walking distance provides meals and bar snacks.

Charges 1995:
-- Per unit incl. 2 persons £6.50 - £7.50; extra adult £1.00; child 50p; extra car, boat or awning 50p; electricity £1.00.
-- VAT included.
Open:
Mid March - end October.
Address:
Luib, Crianlarich, Perthshire FK20 8QT.
Tel:
Killin (01567) 820637.
Reservations:
Made with £5 deposit per pitch.

Directions: Park is mid-way between Killin and Crianlarich on the A85 road. O.S.GR: NN467278.

259 Invercoe Caravans, Invercoe, Glencoe

Family owned site in magnificent historical setting.

On the edge of Loch Leven, surrounded by mountains and forest, Iain and Lynn Brown are continually developing this attractively located park. It provides places for 60 caravans and 60 tents on level grass with gravel access roads and 4 hardstandings. You choose your own marked pitch, those at the Loch side being very popular, but the 36 with electricity are to the back of the park. The nicely refurbished toilet block adjoining the large shop near the entrance has free hot showers (the shower room is locked 10 pm. - 7 am.) and vanity style washbasins. Under cover dishwashing and excellent laundry facilities are provided, with a drying room. Five caravan holiday homes for hire. Public phone. Play area with swings. The village with pub and restaurant is within walking distance. There is much to do for the active with hill walking, climbing, boating. pony riding and sea loch or fresh water fishing in this area of outstanding natural beauty, with the Visitor's Centre at Glencoe just a couple of miles away.

Charges 1995:
-- Per unit incl. 2 persons £8.00; extra person 50p; extra car, boat or trailer £1.00; awning £1.50; electricity £1.50.
-- VAT included.
Open:
Easter/1 April - end October.
Address:
Invercoe, Glencoe, Argyll PA39 4HP.
Tel:
(01855) 811210.
Reservations:
Recommended in peak season for electricity.

Directions: Follow the A82 Crianlarich - Fort William road to Glencoe village and turn onto the B863; park is ½ mile along, well signed. O.S.GR: NN098594.

260 Linnhe Caravan and Chalet Park, Corpach, nr. Fort William

Quiet, well run park in a fine setting for caravans, motorcaravans and small tents only.

This park has a very peaceful situation overlooking Loch Eil, with good views around and boating on the loch is possible. There are pitches for 65 touring units on hardstandings in terraces leading down to the edge of the loch. They include 30 special ones with electricity, water and drainaway plus 26 with electricity only. The others are marked out in rows on the terraces. A separate area takes 15 small tents (unreserved). Also 75 holiday letting caravans and from 1996, 6 new, centrally heated chalets for hire. The toilet block for tourists is of very fair standard and size with free hot showers, baths on payment (£1) and a toddlers room. There are 2 washing-up sinks and a laundry plus separate drying room, charged per night. Self-service, licensed shop (Easter-end Sept). Well equipped children's play area on safe standing. Barbecue area. Public phones. American motorhomes accepted but book first. About 5 miles from Fort William, the park is well placed for touring the Western Highlands. Easily accessible are the Ben Nevis range (cable car to 2,000 ft.), a Geological Museum, distillery visits and the Caledonian Canal Fishing from the shore of Loch Eil at the park is free and you may bring your own boat and use the park's launching slip and dinghy park. Up to 2 dogs per pitch accepted. A member of the Best of British group.

Charges 1996:
-- Per unit with all persons £7.50 - £9.50; electricity £1.00 - £2.00; all service pitch £1.50 - £2.50; awning, extra tent or car 50p - £1.50; tent pitch £6.00 - £7.50.
-- VAT included.
-- Creidt cards accepted.

Open:
All year except 1 Nov - 14 Dec.

Address:
Corpach, Fort William, Inverness-shire PH33 7NL.

Tel:
(01397) 772376.
FAX: (01397) 772007.

Reservations:
Min. 3 nights with £13

Directions: Entrance is off A830 Fort William-Mallaig road, 1 mile west of Corpach. O.S.GR: NN072772.

Alan Rogers' discount
No per person charge

THE BEST IN THE WEST *Where Relaxing is Easy*

*Mains serviced pitches for touring caravans on this beautiful lochside park. Magnificent views. Ideally situated for all outdoor activities or simply relaxing in peaceful surroundings. Graded **Excellent**, our park includes a licenced shop, launderette, drying room, playground, toddlers room, private beach and slipway.*

Caravan holiday-homes for hire and sale. Pets welcome.

Colour brochure upon request.
Dept. AR, Corpach, Fort William,
PH33 7NL Tel: 01397-772376

261 Oban Divers Caravan Park, Oban

Scenic, peaceful and friendly park close to Oban.

Set most attractively in a 4 acre valley, yet close to Oban's facilities and local attractions this park has been thoughtfully developed as an extension to the garden of the owner's home and diving business which is run alongside the park. A small stream runs through the park, with several types of young eucalyptus and bamboo growing and fuchsias planted along one side. Tons of stone have been used to enhance its appearance. There are only 45 pitches with 15 hardstandings, 30 electrical connections and plenty of space, with tents placed mainly on a higher back terrace. Adequate sanitary facilities are provided in two chalets, the smaller one near the tent pitches. The main chalet is being replaced for 1996 and will include facilities for the disabled. Dishwashing sinks are under cover. Large drying room with tumble dryer. Other facilities include a small shop at reception, a divers' shop with drinks machine, picnic area and covered barbecue. An open fronted room is provided for tenters to rest and eat. Children's play items on gravel (those with children can pitch near). Definitely no dogs accepted. Access is unsuitable for the largest units. Log cabins for groups.

Charges 1995:
-- Per unit £5.00; person 50p; electricity £1.50; awning 80p; extra car £1.00.

Open:
Mid March - mid Nov.

Address:
Glenshellach Road, Oban, Argyll PA34 4QJ.

Tel:
(01631) 562755.
FAX: as phone.

Reservations:
Made with £5 deposit.

Directions: From north follow A85 one way system through town to traffic island; take 2nd exit via police station following signs to Glenshellach Camping. From south go into town to traffic island, then as above. O.S.GR: NM841277.

262 Glen Nevis Caravan and Camping Park, Fort William

Spacious touring park in wonderful situation by Ben Nevis range.

Just outside Fort William in a most attractive and quiet situation with views of Ben Nevis, this park is used by those on active pursuits as well as sightseeing tourists. It comprises 7 quite spacious fields, divided between caravans and tents (steel pegs required). It is licensed for 250 touring caravans but with no special tent limits. Pitches are marked with wooden fence dividers, 174 with electricity and a further 100 with water and drainage also. The park becomes full in the peak months but there are vacancies each day. If reception is closed (possible in low season) you site yourself. There are regular security patrols at night in busy periods. Motorcaravan service point. Holiday caravans and cottages are for hire at the adjacent site owned holiday park. The four modern toilet blocks make a good provision with plentiful WCs, washbasins with free hot water and hot showers on payment, with extra showers in two blocks; free hairdryers. Units for the disabled. An excellent new block has washbasins in cubicles, showers, a second large laundry room and further facilities for the disabled. Washing-up sinks and ample water points around. Amenities include a self-service shop (Easter - mid Oct), barbecue area and snack bar (May - mid-Sept). The park's own modern restaurant and bar with good value bar meals is a short stroll from the park, open to all. Public phones. Children's play area on bark. Pony trekking, golf and fishing near. A well managed park with bustling, but pleasing ambience, watched over by Ben Nevis.

Directions: Turn off A82 to east at roundabout just north of Fort William following camp sign. O.S.GR: NN124723.

Charges 1995:
-- Per caravan £5.10 - £6.50; motorcaravan or tent £4.80 - £6.20; small tent £4.30 - £5.70; backpacker's tent: 1 person £2.80 - £3.90, 2 persons £3.40 - 4.70; person 90p - £1.30; awning 80p - £1.20; fully serviced pitch extra £1.40 - £1.90.
-- VAT included.
-- Credit cards accepted.
Open:
15 March - 31 October.
Address:
Glen Nevis, Fort William, Inverness-shire PH33 6SX.
Tel:
(01397) 702191.
FAX: (01397) 703904.
Reservations:
Not normally necessary.

Beautifully situated in one of Scotland's most famous glens, close to mighty Ben Nevis, the highest mountain in Britain, yet only 2½ miles from the historic town of Fort William. The park has separate spacious areas for tourers and tents and offers modern, clean and well equipped facilities. Many pitches are fully serviced with electricity, water and drainage. Showers, laundry, scullery, well stocked shop, gas and play areas, are all situated on park and our spacious restaurant and lounge is only a few minutes walk. Excellent tour centre for the Western Highlands.

AA
RAC

Brochure from: Glen Nevis Caravan and Camping Park, Glen Nevis, Fort William, Inverness-shire PH33 6SX. Telephone: (01397) 702191

T5

263 Barcaldine Camping and Caravanning Club Oban Site, Barcaldine

Pleasantly situated, well kept park north of Oban.

Owned by the Camping and Caravanning Club, this park takes 75 units (under 25 ft.) on a flat, square and well kept grassy area, originally the walled garden belonging to Barcaldine House, which provides some shelter from any wind. There are some hardstandings, particularly for motorcaravans, and 40 electrical connections. A quiet, family park, it has a peaceful situation, with many miles of walks from the park available in Barcaldine Forest. The central, modern toilet block is very well maintained and has free hot water to the washbasins (with rails and hooks) and 4 showers, plus plentiful WCs. Laundry facilities. Shop for basic supplies and gaz (8-11 am. and 4-6 pm.) and attractive lounge bar, where bar meals may be served if staffed. Children's play area. Boats for hire nearby. Freshwater fishing on permit. Public phone. Gates shut 11 pm. - 7 am.

Directions: Park entrance is off the A828 road on south side of Loch Creran, 6 miles north of Connel Bridge. O.S.GR: NM966420.

Charges 1995:
-- Per adult £3.15 - £3.50; child £1.20 - £1.35; pitch £3.00; electricity £1.60.
-- VAT included.
-- Credit cards accepted.
Open:
25 March - 4 November.
Address:
Barcaldine, By Connel, Argyll PA37 1SG.
Tel:
Ledaig (0163172) 348, no calls after 8 pm.
Reservations:
Any length over 1 night with £5 deposit.

264 North Ledaig Caravan Park, Connel, by Oban

Friendly park with splendid views, many local amenities and immediate access to beach.

You are shown to your pitch at this friendly, well run park which has splendid views over the Sound of Mull. A member of the Caravan Club's 'managed under contract' scheme, non-members are also very welcome. Divided into three areas, one of which is for members only, there are 260 pitches, 230 with electricity. Some 140 are available for non-members with caravans, motorcaravans or trailer tents only, with 70 level hardstandings for motorcaravans (there is a service point). The new sanitary block is centrally located - you may have a bit of a walk depending on your pitch. It offers excellent facilities including full facilities for the disabled and for mothers and babies, both with access by key. There are free hot showers, washbasins in private cabins for ladies, (with one for men) and excellent laundry facilities, with irons for hire, and for dishwashing. Further, well renovated sanitary facilities are behind the reception block, which also provides a well stocked, licensed shop. A dog walk is provided with special hooks conveniently sited for dog leads (eg. outside the shop and toilet block). Being well organised and run, this is a quiet park. It should provide a pleasant holiday, either relaxing or participating in sailing, gliding, fishing, walking or pony trekking, all available close by. Boat hire available and a slipway for small boats. Suitable for American motorhomes.

Charges 1995:
-- Non members: Per pitch £2.00 - £3.00; adult £2.50 - £3.50; child (5-17 yrs) £1.10 - £1.20; electricity £1.25 - £2.00; extra car, trailer or m/cycle £1.00..
-- VAT included.
Open:
31 March - 31 October.
Address:
Connel, by Oban, Argyll PA37 1RT.
Tel:
(01631) 710291.
FAX: as phone.
Reservations:
Any length, with £10 deposit incl. £1 non-returnable fee.

Directions: The park is about 1 mile north of Connel Bridge, on the A828 Oban - Fort William road, 7 miles from Oban. O.S.GR: NM913456.

265 Glendaruel Caravan Park, Glendaruel, Kyles of Bute

Peaceful family park set in former wooded gardens surrounded by the Cowal hills.

Glendaruel is set in South Argyll, the area of Scotland bounded by the Kyles of Bute and Loch Fyne, yet is less than 2 hours by road from Glasgow and serviced by ferries from Gourock and the Isles of Bute, with a new summer service between Tarbert and Portavadie opening up the Mull of Kintyre. The park itself is set in the wooded gardens of the former Glendaruel House in a secluded glen surrounded by the Cowal hills. It makes an ideal centre for touring this beautiful area of Scotland. The park takes 34 units on numbered hardstandings with electrical connections (10A), plus 10 tents, on flat oval meadows bordered by mature trees. There are also some 30 privately owned holiday homes in a separate area. The toilet block is ageing but is kept very neat and tidy and has a good supply of toilets, washbasins and showers (2M, 2F), hair and hand dryers and a washing machine and dryer.

The stables of the original house have been converted to provide an attractive little shop selling basics and some tourist gifts and a games room with pool table, table tennis and amusement machines. Children's play area. Fishing (river, loch and sea) available. Adventure centre (assault courses, abseiling and rafting), golf and sailing school close. Dogs accepted by prior arrangement. Glendaruel is a park for families with young children or for older couples to relax and to enjoy the beautiful views across the Sound of Bute from Tighnabruaich or the botanical gardens which flourish in the climate. The owners, Quin and Anne Craig, provide a warm welcome and will advise you where to eat and what to do - they are justifiably proud of their park and its beautiful environment. A member of the Best of British group.

Charges 1995:
-- Per unit incl. 2 persons £7.50 - £9.00; awning or extra tent £1.00 - £1.50; extra adult £1.00; child (5-16 yrs) or senior citizen 50p; extra car, trailer or boat £1.00; electricity £2.00.
-- VAT included.
-- Credit cards accepted.
Open:
29 March - 27 October.
Address:
Glendaruel, Argyll PA22 3AB.
Tel:
Glendaruel (01369) 820267.
FAX: as phone.
Reservations:
Any length, with £15 deposit.

Alan Rogers' discount
Ask at park for details

Directions: Park entrance is off the A886 road 13 miles south of Strachur. Alternatively there are two ferry services from Gourock to Dunoon, then on the B386 which joins the A886 about 4 miles south of the park - this route is not recommended for touring caravans. Note: park has discount arrangements with Western Ferries: contact them before making arrangements. O.S.GR: NS001865.

NORTHERN IRELAND

Northern Ireland Tourist Board

11 Berkeley Street, London W1X 5AD Tel: 0171-355-5040

IRISH REPUBLIC

Irish Tourist Office

105 New Bond Street, London W1Y 0AQ Tel: 0171-493-3201

`You're welcome' is not said lightly to the visitor who sets foot in Ireland, it is said with sincerity. On this `Emerald Isle' you will find friendly and hospitable people, spectacular scenery and a selection of good campsites, both north and south of the country, to suit your particular needs. Whether you choose to be sited by a lough shore, at the foothills of a mountain range or close by golden sands and mysterious rock formations, the scenery is stunning and the pace of life slow. With the help of information and maps available from both Tourist Offices you discover for yourself, not only the beauty spots but many historic and interesting routes to follow. In such areas we have endeavoured to locate well run sites that range from family parks where children can find day long amusement, to the more basic site offering total relaxation.

The following ferry services are expected to operate between the UK mainland and Ireland in 1996. We particularly welcome the special offers provided by **Irish Ferries** to readers of this guide - see our Discount Voucher for details.

Irish Ferries

(01233) 211911

Holyhead - Dublin (3½ hrs)

Pembroke - Rosslare (4¼ hrs)

See colour advertisement and Discount Vouchers

Stena Sealink

(01233) 647047

Fishguard - Rosslare Ferry (3½ hrs)

Holyhead - Dun Laoghaire

Ferry (3½ hrs) Sea Linx (99 mins)

P&O European Ferries

(01581) 200276

Cairnryan - Larne (2¼ hrs)

Sea Cat Scotland

(0345) 523523

Stranraer - Belfast (90 mins)

Swansea Cork Ferries *See advertisement*

(01792) 456116

Swansea - Cork (10 hrs) - March-December

Norse Irish Ferries

(01232) 779090

Liverpool - Belfast (11 hrs)

266 Curran Caravan Park, Larne

Well kept site convenient for ferry terminal or local exploring.

Attractive garden areas add to the charm of this small, neat site which is very convenient for the ferry terminal and only a few minutes walk from the sea. The 28 pitches with hardstandings give adequate space off the gravel road and there is a separate tent area of 1½ acres. Like many sites in Northern Ireland, it is run by the local borough council. The warden can usually find room for tourists so reservations are not usually necessary. Only four electrical hook-ups at present. The sanitary block is clean and adequate, with free controllable hot showers (2 for men, 1 for ladies). There is a laundry room with dishwashing facilities. Children's play area with good equipment and safety surfaces. Bowls and putting are available on site and many other amenities are very close including a shop (100 yds), hotel for food and drink (next door), tennis and a swimming pool (300 yds). Larne market is on Wednesdays. You may consider using this site as a short term base for discovering the area as well as an ideal overnight stop.

Directions: Immediately after leaving the ferry terminal, turn right and follow camp signs. Site is just ¼ mile on the left.

Charges guide:
-- Per caravan or motorcaravan £5.45; tent £3.30; electricity £1.15.
Open:
Easter - 30 September.
Address:
Larne, Co. Antrim.
(Information: Larne Borough Council, Victoria Road, Larne).
Tel:
Larne (01574) 273797.
Reservations:
Not normally considered necessary.

267 Portballintrae Caravan Park, Portballintrae

Good base for visiting Giant's Causeway, close to beaches and watersports on popular north coast.

Portballintrae is close to Bushmills (of distillery fame) on the popular north coast of Antrim, under a mile from a sandy beach and ½ mile from a bay which offers water-skiing, windsurfing and sailing facilities. It is just 4 miles by road or a 2½ mile walk from the famous Giant's Causeway and 2 km. from Dunluce Castle. Other facilities close at hand are, sea, river and lake fishing, also several golf courses. The site is maintained to a high standard and is well run. There are 150 privately owned static holiday caravans here and provision for 40 touring units; 35 pitches have electrical hook-ups. These are situated to the rear of the site and around the perimeter. There are also 10 pitches for tents. The main sanitary block for tourers (access by key) is clean and offers free hot water for showers and dishwashing. There are private cabins in the ladies' washroom and an additional `portacabin' facility (better than many) is provided with further WCs and washbasins. There is a laundry room with washing machine, spin and tumble dryers and iron with clothes lines at the rear. Two hotels and two bars are located in the village of Portballintrae.

Directions: From B17 road take the B145 to Portballintrae and park is left on entering the village (International camping sign).

Charges 1995:
-- Per unit £9.00, with electricity £10.00; awning or extra small tent £1.00; 2-man tent £5.00.
Open:
Easter -- 7 October.
Address:
Ballaghmore Avenue, Portballintrae, Bushmills, Co. Antrim BT57 8RX.
Tel:
(012657) 31478.
FAX: as phone.
Reservations:
Desirable for July/Aug. and made for any length with full payment.

268 Carnfunnock Country Park Caravan Site, Drain's Bay, Larne

Modern park in a magnificent parkland setting overlooking the sea.

In exceptional scenic surroundings, 2 miles north of the market town of Larne on the famed Antrim Coast Road this is a caravanner's delight. The 28 numbered, level `super' pitches have hardstanding, water, electricity (15A), drainage and individual pitch lighting, with ample space for an awning and car parking. The site has a well laid out and neat appearance with a tarmac roadway following through to the rear where a number of pitches are placed in a circular position. There is allocated space for tents. A small, modern building beside the entrance houses the sanitary facilities (entry by key). There are two shower units, washbasins, shaver points, WCs, facilities for the disabled, dishwashing sinks and chemical disposal point. Run by the Borough Council, everything in this parkland is immaculately kept. The Visitor Centre is spacious with exhibits of arts and crafts plus information about local attractions. The restaurant/coffee shop is pleasant and looks towards the sea. Spending time around the parkland, you find a walled time garden with historic sundials, a maze, forest walk, open recreation area, children's adventure park and putting green.

Directions: From the ferry terminal in Larne, follow signs for Coast Road and Carnfunnock Country Park. Well signposted.

Charges 1995:
-- Per caravan or motorcaravan incl. electricity £10.00; tent £5.50.
Open:
Easter - 30 September.
Address:
Coast Road, Drain's Bay, Larne, Co. Antrim BT40 2QZ.
Tel:
Larne (01574) 270541.
Reservations:
Said to be necessary at all times.

269 Drumaheglis Marina and Caravan Park, Ballymoney

Well kept park on the banks of the River Bann, convenient for the Causeway coast.

A caravan park which continually maintains a high standard, Drumaheglis is popular throughout the season. Situated on the banks of the lower Bann, approximately 4 miles from the town of Ballymoney, it appeals to watersports enthusiasts or makes an ideal base for exploring this scenic corner of Northern Ireland. The marina offers superb facilities for water-skiing, cruising, canoeing or fishing, whilst getting out and about can take you to the Giant's Causeway, seaside resorts such as Portrush or Portstewart, the sands of Whitepark Bay, the Glens of Antrim or the picturesque villages of the Antrim coast road.

For tourers only, this site instantly appeals, for it is well laid out with trees, shrubs, flower beds and tarmac roadways. The 35 hardstanding pitches have electrical connections (5A) and 25 have water points. The toilet blocks are modern and were spotlessly clean when we visited. They house showers which are free, individual wash cubicles, toilets and facilities for the disabled. There are razor points, hand dryers, dishwashing sinks, washing machine, dryer and chemical disposal point. A children's play area, barbecue and picnic areas are added facilities. Ballymoney is a popular shopping town and the Riada Centre is a leading leisure establishment with a health suite which incorporates a high-tech fitness studio, sports hall, etc. There is much to see and do within this Borough and of interest is the Heritage Centre in Charlotte Street.

Directions: From the A26/B62 Portrush - Ballymoney roundabout continue for approx. 1 mile on the A26 in the direction of Coleraine. Site is clearly signed - follow International camping signs.

Charges guide:
-- Per unit incl. electricity £7.00, per 7 days £42.00; tent with electricity £6.00, per 7 days £36.00.
Open:
Easter - end-September.
Address:
36 Glenstall Road, Ballymoney, Co. Antrim BT53 7QN.
Tel:
(012656) 66466 (site) or (012656) 62280 (Ballymoney Borough Council).
Reservations:
Essential for peak periods and weekends.

270 Tullans Farm Caravan Park, Coleraine

Well run family park in rural setting convenient for the Causeway Coast.

This excellent park, opened in 1995, is set to become one of the most popular in the area. Its peaceful and quiet surroundings suggest that it is in the heart of the country, yet the University town of Coleraine is only 1 mile away, the seaside resorts of Portrush and Portstewart are within 5 miles and a shopping centre a 2 minute drive. Tucked in from the busy roads that lead to the coast, Tullans Farm is already earning a reputation for its spotlessly clean toilet block and its well cared for appearance. In a central position in the park, fronted by a large parking space, stands a long white building housing the sanitary facilities, reception, TV lounge and barn which is used for indoor recreation. The toilet and shower rooms are spacious, modern and have facilities for the handicapped. There are washbasins set in marble top units, mirrors, soap dispensers, hand and hair dryers, even flower arrangements. Next to the toilet area is the laundry and washing up room with sinks, washing machine, dryers and a fridge for campers to use. Around the park roadways are gravel and 20 of the 32 pitches have hardstanding, all have electric hook-ups (15A). Trees and shrubs have been planted and will eventually give a more mature look. Chemical disposal, water points, rubbish bins and receptacles for cans and plastic bottles are provided. An outdoor children's play area is another attraction.

Directions: From the Lodge Road roundabout (south end of Coleraine) turn east onto the A29 Portrush ring road and proceed for 1 mile. Turn right at sign for park and Windy Hall and park is clearly signed on left.

Charges 1995:
-- Per unit incl. all persons and electricity £8.00; awning £1.00; family tent £7.00; 2 man tent £5.00.
Open:
All year.
Address:
46 Newmills Road, Coleraine, Co. Londonderry BT52 2JB.
Tel:
(01265) 42309.
Reservations:
Advisable at peak times - contact park.

Alan Rogers' discount
Ask at park for details

Remember - to claim your discount you will need to show your 1996 discount card

271 Tollymore Forest Caravan Park, Newcastle

Well run site in forest setting at foot of Mourne mountains.

This park, for tourers only, is located within the parkland of Tollymore Forest. It is discretely situated away from the public footpaths and is noted for its scenic surroundings. The forest park, which is approached by way of an ornate gateway and majestic avenue of Himalayan cedars, covers an area of almost 500 hectares. It is backed by the Mourne mountains and situated two miles from the beaches and resort of Newcastle. The site is attractively laid out with hard- standing pitches, 33 of which have electric hook-ups. Toilet blocks are timbered in keeping with the setting, and are clean, modern and tastefully decorated. They include free hot showers with benches and hooks, wash cubicles, facilities for the disabled, dishwashing and laundry area. The toilet facilities and site have adequate night lighting. Added amenities are a confectionery shop and tea room within close proximity. A small grocery shop is located a few yards from the exit gate of the park and gas is also available here. The Head Ranger at Tollymore is helpful and ensures that the caravan site is efficiently run and quiet, even when full. Exploring the forest park is part of the pleasure of staying here. Of note are the stone follies, bridges and entrance gates. The Shimna and Spinkwee rivers flow through the park adding a refreshing touch and tree lovers appreciate the arboretum with its many rare species.

Charges guide:
-- Per unit incl. car and occupants £5.00 - £8.50, acc. to season; electricity £1.50.
Open:
All year.
Address:
Tollymore Forest Park (Administration), 176 Tullybrannigan Road, Newcastle, Co. Down BT33 0PW.
Tel:
Newcastle (013967) 22428.
Reservations:
Advisable in high season and for B.Hs. and made with £10 deposit.

Directions: Approach Newcastle on the A24 road. Before entering the town, at roundabout, turn right on to A50 signed Castlewellan and follow signs for Tollymore Forest Park.

272 Banbridge Gateway Amenity Area and Touring Caravan Park

Conveniently sited touring park on main A1 Belfast - Newry road.

Banbridge is in an ideal place for a stopover if travelling between Southern and Northern Ireland, is within easy towing distance of the main ports or makes an ideal base for discovering many tourist attractions such as the Bronte Homeland or the Linen Trail. A small site, with 8 handstanding pitches and electric connections (6A), it is part of the Banbridge Gateway Tourist Information Centre complex. The centre is an attractive building of modern design surrounded by a well maintained garden area and car park. Housed inside, apart from the offices of the centre and display areas for Irish crafts, are excellent sanitary facilities. These are ultra modern, spotlessly clean and key operated. They include 2 showers, 6 washbasins, WCs, good facilities for the disabled and an outside, covered dishwashing area. There is also a chemical disposal unit and an extensive children's play area with a safety base. The restaurant/coffee shop within the complex opens daily (9 am-5 pm.) and serves lunch specials between 12.30-2.30 pm, otherwise scones, cakes, etc. The touring park is located in the far left hand corner of the complex and is enclosed with ranch fencing, plus a security gate and barrier. The town of Banbridge is within 1 mile, with shops, restaurants, pubs and all services.

Charges 1995:
-- Per pitch £7.00;
electricity £1.00.
Open:
All year.
Address:
200 Newry Road, Banbridge, Co. Down BT32 3NB.
Tel:
(08206) 233322.
FAX: (08206) 23114.
Reservations:
Contact centre during office hours (summer: Mon-Sat 9 am - 7 pm, Sun. 2 pm - 6 pm; winter: Mon-Sat 10 am - 5 pm, Sun. closed). It is essential to arrive during opening hours for key.

Directions: Site is signed (as Gateway Amenity Area) off the A1 Belfast-Newry dual carriageway, 1 mile south of Banbridge.

see advert in next colour section

Northern Ireland Tourist Board
59 North St, Belfast BT1 1NB Tel: (01232) 231221 Fax: (01232) 240960

1996 Events: Opera: Northern Ireland Spring Festival, Belfast, 2-9 March: Belfast Spring Flower Festival 27-28 April: Belfast Civic Festival, 4-24 May: International Jazz and Blues Festival. Londonderry, 23-27 May: Proms '96, Belfast, 14-22 June: Oul' Lammas Fair, Ballycastle, 26-27 Aug. (Ireland's oldest traditional fair-1606).

FERMANAGH

273 Share Holiday Village, Smiths Strand, Lisnaskea

Caravan park in a village environment, offering a package deal.

Immediately you drive into this 30 acre site in its quiet and beautiful location on the shores of Upper Lough Erne, you want to get involved in the host of attractions on offer. The 5 acre touring park is separate, yet part of, this complex, which offers all the benefits and self contained aspects of caravanning, plus the opportunity to enjoy all the sports facilities of the village. The pitches are hardstanding with electricity and space for awnings. The sanitary blocks, which are kept very clean, have washbasins, showers, washing up and laundry facilities, including a drying room with tumble dryers, and a chemical disposal point. An important factor here is that Share is committed to the provision of facilities and opportunities for both the able bodied and the disabled. What makes the Share Village attractive for caravanners is that the charges include the use of the indoor leisure pool, massage pool, sauna steam room, fitness suite, tennis court, children's pool, jetties slipway, playground and TV room. If wanting to participate in the outdoor activities, an Activity Pass can be purchased (£4). It covers sailing, canoeing, windsurfing, banana-ski, archery, mountain bikes, or you may prefer a Viking longship cruise. A 2½ hour session costs £4 per person and includes all equipment and instruction, with a reduction if 10 or more passes are purchased. This centre is an approved British Canoe Union and Royal Yachting Association teaching school. A 30 berth marina has been added.

Directions: From Lisnaskea village, take B127 sign to Derrylin and Smiths Strand and proceed for 3 miles. Site is clearly signed on the right.

Charges 1995:
-- Per caravan or tent £9.00; 2 man tent £6.00.
-- Touring caravan and campsite packages available.
Open: All year.
Address: Smiths Strand, Lisnaskea, Co. Fermanagh BT92 0EQ
Tel: Lisnaskea (013657) 22122.
FAX: (013657) 21893.
Reservations: Advisable in peak season and for B.H.s and with deposit (weekend or midweek £20, 7 days £50; activity passes 50% of total cost per person).

274 LoanEden Caravan Park, Muckross Bay, Kesh

Friendly, family owned park by the shores of Lower Lough Erne.

All caravanners who enter this exceptional park are immediately made welcome and receive the attention of the owners, Noelle and Austyn Loane. Although this site has only been in existence since spring 1993, its reputation is already widespread. An overall neat and tidy appearance is a first impression, with 70 static caravan holiday homes occupying the centre and left hand side of the park, whilst to the right and separated by a tarmac roadway, stand the touring pitches. Flower beds, trees and shrubs are well maintained and an ornamental draw-well and illuminated barbecue give added effect. What makes LoanEden special to tourers is that their needs are thoughtfully catered for and not secondary to the static owners. The 26 touring pitches are level with hardstanding and water, electricity and drainage connections; also a dividing grass area on which to erect an awning. Good night lighting. Cleanliness is utmost and the immaculate, ultra modern toilet block is completely tiled inside and houses WCs, facilities for the disabled, showers, washbasins, washing machines, dryers and sinks for dishwashing or handwashing. Nothing has been forgotten - there are soap dispensers, hand dryers, paper towels, clothes hooks and points for hairdryers and razors. A small shop stocks basic foods, confectionery, freshly baked cakes and gas. Children have two play areas and a games room, whilst young and old can enjoy pony and horse riding tuition under the supervision of the owners' daughter Victoria, a BHAI. instructor.

Directions: Travelling northwest on the A35 Enniskillen-Kesh road, enter village of Kesh. At end of main street, cross over bridge and immediately turn left; park is signposted. Continue for ½ mile and site is on right.

Charges 1996:
-- Per caravan or motorcaravan incl. awning and electricity £9.00; tent £6.00; electricity £1.00.
Open: All year.
Address: Muckross Bay, Kesh, Co. Fermanagh.
Tel: Kesh (013656) 31603.
Reservations: Advisable for high season and B.Hs.

275 Táin Holiday Village, Omeath

Fun packed holiday village, scenically set on Carlingford Lough.

This holiday complex is one of the most extensive in Ireland and is exactly what a family seeking non-stop entertainment might want. The touring park is within the 10-acre village, overlooking Carlingford Lough with views towards the Mourne mountains, whilst nestling at the foot of the Cooley mountains. The area for tourers is situated to the far right of the main buildings, entrance through a security gate is by key (deposit required). There are 87 pitches with hardstanding and electrical hook-ups, plus 10 pitches for tents. Young trees are planted and will eventually add more detail to this well laid out, but open, site. The sanitary block is kept clean and houses WCs, hot showers, washbasins in cubicles with mirrors, etc. and facilities for the disabled. Dishwashing and laundry sinks with hot water, plus washing machines and iron.

Included in the site charges is the use of the 40,000 sq.ft. of indoor leisure facilities. These include a heated swimming pool with slides, flumes and rafts, an indoor play area with free fall, ball pool, climbing room and nets, also a games room. Not least at The Táin is a hands-on Science Interactive Centre. Jacuzzi, steam room and sun beds. The licensed restaurant offers varied menus. Outdoor activities include two adventure playgrounds, tennis courts, trim track and watersports, not forgetting the pleasant grounds with neat flower beds.

Charges 1995:
-- Per unit incl. 2 persons and electricity IR£15.00 - 17.50; tent on grass area IR£12.00 - 14.50.
-- Less 10% for 7 nights or more.
Open: All year.
Address: Omeath, Co. Louth.
Tel: (041) 75385.
FAX: (041) 75417.
Reservations: Made with deposit (caravan IR£15, tent IR£10).

Directions: From Newry take B79/R173 road signed Omeath. Site is 1.6 km. south of Omeath village, on the left.

276 Assaroe Lakeside Centre Caravan and Camping Park, Ballyshannon

Lakeside touring park at the head of the Erne estuary on Donegal Bay.

This is a small select park in an idyllic situation overlooking Assaroe lake and part of a lakeside centre. The complex is the northwest's newest attraction and the caravan park is everything many caravanners want. Apart from its location and facilities offered it is well run and constantly being monitored by the manager to ensure that the high standards set are being maintained. The neat appearance at present will further be enhanced by shrubs and trees which are already planted. Roadways are tarmac and the 28 pitches all have hardstanding and electric hook-ups. A tent area is on the grass alongside the caravan pitches. Toilet facilities are kept very clean and are housed in the centre which is a modern, attractive building. Apart from the ample WCs, washbasins and showers (token operated) allocated to the caravan site, there are a further 18 showers within the centre which may be used. Added amenities include a washing up and laundry sink, washing machine, dryer and facilities for the disabled.

There is a coffee shop and upstairs restaurant/bar which is tastefully decorated and offers panoramic views across the lake. Barbecue. Outdoor activities provided include an extensive adventure playground, football/rugby pitches, jogging track and watersports such as fishing, water-skiing, canoeing (tuition optional). There are water bus trips, lakeside walks or the appealing town of Ballyshannon is within walking distance of the site.

Charges 1995:
-- Per unit incl. electricity IR£9.00.
Open: All year.
Address: Belleek Road, Ballyshannon, Co. Donegal.
Tel: (072) 52436.
FAX: as phone.
Reservations: Advisable for peak periods.

Directions: From Ballyshannon travel east in the direction of Kesh. Site is 800 m. outside town immediately past electricity power station, on left.

To telephone the Irish Republic from the UK, replace the first `0' given in the number with the country code: 00 353.

eg. (094) 88100 becomes 00 353 94 88100.

277 Strandhill Caravan and Camping Park, Strandhill

Situated in the beautiful Yeats Country and an ideal touring base.

The northwest coast of Ireland is very scenic and this clean, comfortable park is set just back from the beach and dunes in an open position offering splendid views. This is a typical sand based site that tends to have a less than neat appearance. Nevertheless it is a friendly park with attentive management. A spacious park, it has caravan holiday homes, but also provides some 20 pitches with hardstanding and electricity for touring caravans or motorcaravans, with 28 others on mainly flat, grassy areas around the site. A further 40 pitches for tents are in a separate area. The sanitary block is kept spotlessly clean and offers hot showers on payment and adequate washbasin and toilet facilities, together with dishwashing and laundry sinks, and also a washing machine and dryer. The reception block also contains a TV room and pool table. Shops, restaurants and takeaway service are available in the village, just 200 m. away. It is possible to swim from the beach here when lifeguards are in attendance. The nearby beach at Culleenamore is safe for swimming, surfing, etc. An 18 hole golf course is across the road from the park, an equestrian centre is 3 km. away and the city of Sligo only a few minutes by car.

Charges 1996:
-- Per unit IR£6.00; person 50p; hikers/cyclists (all season) IR£5.50; electricity IR£1.00.
Open:
Easter - 15 September.
Address:
Strandhill, Co. Sligo.
Tel:
Sligo (071) 68120.
Reservations:
Accepted for any length.

Alan Rogers' discount
Less 10% in low seasons

Directions: From the centre of Sligo turn west on R292 towards Strandhill; park is signed to the right just before the village. Alternatively, follow signs for the airport - park is 300 m. off the airport road.

278 Greenlands Caravan and Camping Park, Rosses Point

Park with excellent facilities in the sandhills adjoining a championship golf course.

This is a well run park at Rosses Point, just off the N15 road and 8 km. from Sligo town. It is thoughtfully laid out with small tents placed to the front of reception and the hardstanding touring pitches separated from the trailer tent and caravan holiday home pitches which occupy the rear. The ground is undulating and adds interest to the overall appearance. Your view depends on where you are pitched - look towards Coney Island and the Blackrock lighthouse which guards the bay, take in the sight of Benbulben Mountain or appreciate the seascape and the water lapping the resort's two bathing beaches. The sanitary and laundry facilities are modern and kept exceptionally clean, with tiled walls and floors, WCs, washbasins, hot showers (50p tokens), razor and hairdryer points, mirrors and hand-dryers. Also dishwashing and laundry sinks, washing machine, dryer and iron. Electric hook-ups are available. Motorcaravan service point. The gate is locked at night. An information point and a TV room are located beside reception. There is a sand pit for children and a ground chess set; a mini market, restaurant and evening entertainment can be found in the village. This is an excellent base from which to explore the `Yeats Country' and discover the beauty spots immortalised in the poems of W B Yeats, such places as Lissadell, Dooney Rock, the Isle of Innisfree and the poet's burial place at Drumcliffe.

Charges 1995:
-- Per unit high season: IR£6.25 plus 50p per person, low season IR£6.25, per person nil; all season hiker/cyclist IR£5.25; electricity IR£1.00.
Open:
20 May - 20 September.
Address:
Rosses Point, Co. Sligo.
Tel:
(071) 77113 or 45618.
FAX: (071) 45618.
Reservations:
Contact park.

Directions: From Sligo city travel approx. 800 m. north on N15 road, turn left onto R291 signed Rosses Point for 6.5 km. and park is on right after village.

Speed limits in the Irish Republic

Motorways	112 kph	70 mph
Outside built up areas	96 kph	60 mph
Built up areas	48 kph	30 mph
Other roads as marked	64-80 kph	40-50 mph

The above limits also apply to vehicles towing a trailer and were correct as at September 1995)

Sláinte!

With our low fares there's always cause for celebration.

Raise your glass and with it the toast of "Sláinte" or "Cheers" as they say across the water.

Because with Irish Ferries you can celebrate the lowest fares to Ireland. Especially as we're offering you a 50% saving on the cost of bringing your caravan or trailer, when you buy a standard return fare. This offer in association with the Alan Rogers Good Camps Guide is available from 1st January to 31st December 1996. Just look out for the special discount voucher in this guide for full details.

Whether you choose Pembroke to Rosslare or Holyhead to the heart of Dublin, your trip to the Emerald Isle starts the moment you step aboard. A grand array of cosy bars, spacious lounges and restaurants await your pleasure.

And of course no trip would be complete without a visit to the tax and duty free supermarket, where a vast selection of bargains on wine, whiskies, cigars, perfumes and traditional Irish Crafts are laid out before you.

To book your ticket to the warmest of Irish welcomes, call Irish Ferries as soon as you can.

IRISH FERRIES

PEMBROKE ~ ROSSLARE · HOLYHEAD ~ DUBLIN

You'll enjoy our Irish ways.

For bookings: 0345 17 17 17

FOUR OF THE BEST

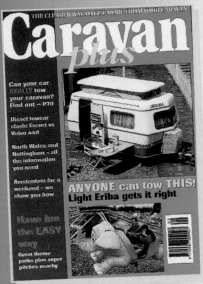

THE CLEVERER WAY WE GET MORE FROM YOUR CARAVAN

Caravan *plus*

Can your car **REALLY** tow your caravan? Find out ~ P70

Diesel towcar clash: Escort vs Volvo 440

North Wales and Nottingham - all the information you need

Amsterdam for a weekend - we show you how

Have fun the **EASY** way

Great theme parks plus super pitches nearby

ANYONE cau tow THIS!
Light Eriba gets it right

CARAVAN LIFE

FREE!
Haven
TOURING DISCOUNT VOUCHERS IN THIS ISSUE

200 OF MARKS & SPENCER ₤ft VOUCHERS TO BE WON!

- LIVE-IN TEST ~ AVONDALE LAND RANGER 5900
- TESTED: LUNAR METEOR & RANGE ROVER 2.5DT
- EIRE SITES SPECIAL ☐ WHICH SITES GUIDE IS BEST?
- SUSSEX COASTLINE ☐ BARCELONA – A DREAM CITY
- TAKE TO WATER – UPGRADING TO A HOT/COLD SYSTEM

MMM
MOTORCARAVAN MOTORHOME MONTHLY

FTEEN MANUAL OOD PROCESSORS O BE WON!

OMPETITION EXTRA! teen international Air attoo family tickets to be won!

- TESTED: PILOTE GALAXY 24 ON MWB PEUGEOT T/D ● TOURING
- 1988 AUTOHOMES HIGHWAYMAN ● TRAFIC TRANSFORMATION
- OWNER REPORT: BEDFORD PIONEER 1004 ● SITES FOR ALL
- DIY: MORE HELP - HINTS – TIPS ● BUYERS' GUIDE

BEST SELLING MOTORCARAVAN MAGAZINE FOR 29 YEARS

WHICH motorcaravan

1996

ALSO TESTED
● Pilote Galaxy
  2000 ~ A-Class luxury liner
● Mandinave Concerto II
  Nissan-based camper
● Glenwood/Dolphin
  Opulence from the USA

PLUS
KNOW YOUR MOTORCARAVAN:
Rainwear

PLUS
JOLLY
Exclusive readers' offers

PLUS
GREAT
TOURS:
Torbay

N 838 ASL

AMETHYST –
Auto-Sleepers' jewel, First test

on sale every month at your local newsagent

279 Belleek Caravan and Camping Park, Ballina

Family owned park in a quiet woodland setting, minutes from Ballina, a famed salmon fishing centre.

This is a park with excellent pitches, a luxury toilet block and family owners committed to ensuring that it is immaculate at all times. From the entrance gate the park is approached by a roadway, passing reception and leading to well spaced out pitches where an overall neat appearance abounds. There are 58 pitches, 32 with hardstanding, 35 with electric hook-ups, and you have a free choice of pitch. The spotlessly clean toilet block is tastefully decorated with tiled floors, cream coloured, rough cast walls, pine ceilings and trimmings and pot plants to complement the modern washbasins, showers (50p token), WCs and baby sink. There are also razor points, hand dryers, facilities for the disabled, washing up/laundry sink, washing machine and dryer. In a separate building is a TV and games room with table tennis and football game. A campers' kitchen is also located in this building and has a sink, free hot water, bench table and open fire. The reception area includes a shop and tea room serving delicious, home baked scones and fruit cake. If required, a cooked or light breakfast, omelettes, sandwiches or salads can be ordered. There is no specific children's playground, but a ball area and plenty of scope to play freely. Sports facilities within a short distance of the park include fishing, pitch and putt, golf, swimming pool, tennis and horse riding. Other local attractions are the Blue Flag beach at Ross, Ceide Fields (Neolithic farm), Down Patrick Head, Mayo North Heritage Centre or a Seaweed bath at Kilcullen's Bath House, Enniscrone.

Charges 1995:
-- Per unit IR£5.00; person IR£1.00; hiker or cyclist and tent IR£3.00; electricity (10A) IR£1.00.
Open:
1 March - 31 October.
Address:
Ballina, Co. Mayo.
Tel:
(096) 71533.
Reservations:
Contact park.

Alan Rogers' discount
7 nights for the price of 6 in low season

Directions: Take R314 Ballina-Killala road; park is on right after approx. 3 km.

280 Sandybanks Caravan and Camping Park, Achill Island

Busy park with direct access to a Blue Flag beach on Achill Island.

This is a park offering a taste of island life and the opportunity to relax in dramatic, scenic surroundings. Achill, Ireland's largest island, is 24 km. long and 20 km. wide and is connected to the mainland by a bridge. The site is situated beside Keel village and approached by the R319 from the swivel bridge at Achill Sound. Although there are static holiday caravans on this site, the 42 pitches for caravans and 42 for tents are kept separate. Some with hardstanding are located at the perimeter fence overlooking the beach. Being sandy based, the ground is firm and level. Roadways are tarmac and there is direct access to the beach which is supervised by lifeguards. Two modern and very clean toilet blocks serve the site, one at the entrance gate beside reception and the other in a central position. Facilities include WCs (one for the disabled), washbasins, hot showers (50p token), adequate razor points, mirrors, shelves, hooks, hair and hand dryers, dishwashing and laundry sinks and chemical disposal facilities. A barrier on site is closed between 1 am. and 8 am. For children there is a play area with safety base and a TV room. Water sports enthusiasts can enjoy surfing, canoeing and board sailing on Keel Strand and Lough. Fishing trips can also be arranged. In the village there is a food shop, takeaway, restaurants and music at night in the pubs. Occasionally a traditional music evening is organised on the site. Whilst a treat in store is the natural beauty on Achill, worth seeing is Kildownet Castle, the Slievemore deserted village and the Seal Caves.

Charges 1995:
-- Per caravan or motorcaravan IR£5.50 - 7.00; tent IR£4.00 - 5.50; electricity IR£1.00.
Open:
End May - mid-September.
Address:
Keel, Achill Island, Co. Mayo.
Tel:
(094) 32054 or (098) 43211.
Reservations:
Contact site.

Directions: From Achill Sound follow the R319 for 16 km. Site is on the left before Keel village.

Irish Tourist Board

150 New Bond St. London W1Y 0AQ Tel: (0171) 4933201 Fax: (0171) 4939065.

1996 Events: Cork International Choral Festival, 2-5 May: Co. Wicklow Gardens Festival, 17-23 June: Dundalk International Drama and Maytime Festival, 24 May-2 June: Castletown-Bristol 1996 International Sailing Regatta, 31 May-9 June: Galway Arts Festival, 10-21 June: Festival of West Cork, Clonakilty, 30 June-10 July: Irish Open Golf Championships, Portmarnock, 4-7 July: Blarney International Three Day Horse Trials, 13-16 July: Rose of Tralee International Festival, 23-29 Aug: Dublin Theatre Festival, 7-19 Oct.

281 Parkland Caravan and Camping Park, Westport

Popular park, enjoying the attractions of Westport House Country Estate.

Located in the grounds of an elegant country estate, this park offers the choice of a `pitch only' booking, or a `special' deal (min. stay 3 nights) which includes free admission to Westport House and Children's Zoo plus other activities, such as boating and fishing on the lake and river, pitch and putt, `slippery dip', ball pond and `supabounce'. Stay one week or more and all the above are free, plus tennis, children's pony riding (under 12s), hillside and miniature train rides. From Westport Quay, you enter the grounds of the estate by way of a tree lined roadway that crosses the river and leads to the site. In an attractive, sheltered area of the parkland, set in the trees are 55 pitches, 30 with hardstanding. There are 46 electric hook-ups, night lighting around the site and the gate is closed 11.30 pm.- 9 am. If late, vehicles must be parked in the car park. Toilet facilities, some at various points on the site, plus a `super-loo' located in the farmyard buildings. Hot showers are free and there are facilities for the disabled. Also included are dishwashing and laundry sinks, washing machines and dryers plus free ironing facilities. A well stocked shop is incorporated in the farmyard reception area and the Horse and Wagon bar offers bar food and musical entertainment. Within 5 km. of the estate are an 18 hole golf course and deep sea angling on Clew Bay. Westport is an attractive town with splendid Georgian houses and traditional shop fronts. There are many good restaurants and pubs. No dogs are accepted.

Charges 1996:
-- Per unit, pitch only IR£10.00 - 16.00 (weekly IR£70 - 112), 3 night `special': IR£77); hiker IR£8.00; electricity IR£10 per week.
Open:
1 June - 8 September.
Address:
Westport, Co. Mayo.
Tel:
(098) 27766.
FAX: (096) 25206.
Reservations:
Contact park.

Directions: Take T39 Westport-Louisburgh road and follow signs for Westport Quay, then turn right into Westport House Country Estate.

282 Camp Carrowkeel, Ballyvary, nr. Castlebar

Family run park in vale of Clydagh river, ideally situated for touring northwest Mayo.

A well laid out park for tourers, with a welcoming atmosphere and modern amenities, Carrowkeel is located off the main road and is approached by a short, narrow unclassified road leading to a setting that guarantees peace and relaxation. The park is maintained to a high standard with the grass and shrub areas neatly kept. There are 28 fully serviced hardstanding pitches with electric hook-ups (6A) and water point, and space for 30 tents. The toilet block continues to be upgraded and is kept exceptionally clean with WCs, washbasins, hot showers (50p), razor points, hand dryers and facilities for the disabled. Added facilities include dishwashing and laundry sinks, chemical disposal, washing machine, tumble dryer and clothes lines. Within the reception area is a shop and beside it is an attractive canteen with takeaway service serving scampi, chips, etc. Tourist information is available. For children there is a play area with safety base, games room and a field for ball games. Two self catering apartments for hire. There is river fishing on the Clydagh river which bounds three sides of the park and for which Camp Carrowkeel holds the fishing rights. For lake fishing, Loughs Conn and Cullin are a short distance away. Apart from the scenic and historic attractions in the area, swimming, tennis, horse riding, shops, and much, much more can be found within 12 km. at Castlebar.

Charges 1996:
-- Per unit incl. 2 adults and 2 children IR£10.00; awning IR£1.00; electricity IR£1.50; small tent for 1 or 2 persons IR£3.00.
-- Credit cards accepted.
Open:
1 February - 31 October.
Address:
Ballyvary, Co. Mayo.
Tel:
(094) 31264.
Reservations:
Adviseable for July, especially middle 2 weeks. Group bookings made with 10% deposit.

Alan Rogers'
discount
7 nights for the price of 6 if pre-booked

Directions: From Castlebar follow N5 Dublin signs; park is signed to left before Ballyvary village.

To telephone the Irish Republic from the UK, replace the first `0' given in the number with the country code: 00 353.

---

283 Knock Caravan and Camping Park, Knock

Clean, friendly park with many local attractions including religious shrine.

This park is situated immediately south of the world famous shrine, which receives many visitors. The site is kept very neat and is comfortable and clean. One enters on the tarmac roads to see a square shaped site surrounded by clipped trees. The pitches are of a decent size accommodating 30 caravans or motorcaravans, 20 tents and 14 holiday caravans (for hire). All pitches have hardstandings (5 doubles) and there are 26 electrical connections (13A), with an adequate number of water points. There is also an overflow field. The modern sanitary block, with good facilities for the disabled and a nice sized rest room attached, has 4 controllable hot showers (on payment) and adequate washing and toilet facilities. A laundry and dishwashing room is also part of this building. A children's playground is provided in the centre of the site. Because of the religious connections of the area, the site is very busy in August and indeed there are unlikely to be any vacancies at all for 14 -16 August. Besides visiting the shrine and Knock Folk Museum, local activities include golf, riding and fishing. This is also a good centre for exploring scenic Co. Mayo.

Directions: Take the N17 to the Knock site which is just south of the village. Camp site is well signed.

Charges 1996:
-- Per unit IR£5.00 - 5.50 plus 25p per person (weekly IR£30 plus IR£1 per person); hiker or cyclist and tent IR£3.50 - 4.00; electricity IR£1.50.
Open: 1 March - 31 October.
Address: Claremorris Road, Knock, Co. Mayo.
Tel: (094) 88100 or 88223.
FAX: (094) 88295.
Reservations: Any length, no deposit, but see above for Aug.

284 Hodson Bay Caravan and Camping Park, Kiltoom, Athlone

Peaceful, scenic park on shores of Lough Ree, in central Ireland.

This picturesque park is in a tranquil, wooded setting on the shores of Lough Ree on the River Shannon. Part of a 100 acre working farm, the site offers 20 pitches, with electricity for caravans and motorcaravans and 15 for tents, on flat grass. There are 2 holiday caravans for hire. The central sanitary block, with good facilities for the disabled, was exceptionally clean when we visited and offers hot showers on payment 8-12 in the morning and 4-9 in the evening, plus sufficient washing and toilet facilities. A dishwashing room at the rear of the block has 2 sinks and hot water for 10p. The spin and tumble dryers provided are available for use after you take your laundry to reception where it is put through an industrial machine for you. The reception block also provides a lounge area, campers' kitchen, a children's play room, TV, pool, table tennis and board games. No shop but a mini-market at the top of the road. Hotel serving bar snacks and a carvery close. You may fish, swim, go boating or just walk along the parks own path by the lough shore. Barbecues permitted on site and by the lough. Horse riding and golf are available nearby. No dogs allowed.

Directions: Leave the N6 at the Roscommon/Sligo junction to join the A61. Travel 4 km. and turn right onto minor road. Site is clearly signed. Continue to site at the end of this road (2.4 km).

Charges 1995:
-- Per unit IR£5.50, plus IR£1.00 per adult or child; small tent (1 or 2 man) IR£3.00 per person; hiker/cyclist IR£3.00 per person; extra car, awning or tent IR£1.00; electricity IR£1.50.
Open: 9 May - 15 September.
Address: Kiltoom, Athlone, Co. Roscommon.
Tel: Athlone (0902) 92448.
Reservations: Made for high season with IR£5 deposit.

285 Lough Ree (East) Caravan and Camping Park, Ballykeeran, Athlone

Touring park alongside a river, screened by trees and reaching the water's edge.

Drive into the small village of Ballykeeran and this park is discretely located behind the main street. The top half of the site is in a woodland situation. After the reception and sanitary block, Lough Ree comes into view and the remaining pitches run down to the shoreline. There are 40 pitches, 14 with hardstanding and 25 with electricity. The toilet block, with brightly tiled walls, is clean without being luxurious. It houses WCs, washbasins, razor and hairdryer points, mirrors and hot showers (50p). Dishwashing sinks are outside. A wooden chalet with accommodation and campers' kitchen is available for the use of campers and fishermen. A restaurant and singing pub are close. With fishing right on the doorstep there are boats for hire and the site has its own private mooring buoys, plus a dinghy slip and harbour.

Directions: From Athlone take the N55 in the direction of Longford for 4.8 km. Park is in the village of Ballykeeran, clearly signed.

Charges 1995:
-- Per adult IR£2.50; child IR£1.00; caravan IR£1.00; motorcaravan IR£1.50; car IR£1.00; electricity IR£1.00.
Open: 1 April -- 30 September.
Address: Ballykeeran, Athlone, Co. Westmeath.
Tel: (0902) 78561.
Reservations: Contact park for details.

KILDARE / LAOIS / WICKLOW

286 Carasalí Caravan and Camping Park, Rathangan, nr. Kildare

Caring, family run park in quiet village alongside the Grand Canal.

This is a peaceful and delightful little caravan park. Tall conifers and neat hedges enclose the site to the left and around as far as the gateway leading to the canal bank. A large grass area for tents is the centre piece, looking like a well cared for lawn, with several trees and picnic benches. Hardstanding pitches for caravans and motorcaravans are placed along the right hand perimeter where there is a view across an adjoining field. The small sanitary block looks fresh and is adorned with climbing plants and shrubs. It houses 2 WCs, 2 showers and 2 washbasins, which are kept very clean. There are three bays with caravan holiday homes for hire, with the family home secluded behind, with more high shrubbery. The owners, Rose and John Joseph Conway, are always available to offer a friendly welcome and help with any queries. In fact, these exceptional people make all their guests feel like lifelong friends. Carasalí is a fisherman's paradise with fishing on the clear waters of the Grand Canal and River Slate free for campers. It also makes a good base for exploring the area's many attractions which include the Peatland Museum and the Japanese Gardens.

Charges 1995:
-- Per unit IR£5.00; person 50p; awning IR£1.00; electricity (13A) IR£1.00; hiker, cyclist or m/cyclist incl. tent IR£4.00 plus 50p per person.
Open:
Easter - 31 October.
Address:
Tobarban, Rathangan, Co. Kildare.
Tel:
(045) 524331.
Reservations:
Contact park.

Directions: Take the R401 from Kildare centre signed Rathangan. Site is on the right at Jet filling station, just before the village.

287 Kirwans Caravan and Camping Park, Portlaoise

Friendly, peaceful park, ideal for exploring inland, rural Ireland.

One receives a warm welcome at this small 'homely' park, located on the edge of Portlaoise and surrounded by trees. The pitches are around the edges of a flat, firm grassy meadow and you site yourself sensibly, choosing morning or afternoon sun. The site offers 16 pitches with electricity for caravans or motorcaravans and another 14 for tents. There are a couple of static vans and mobile homes for hire. Adequate water facilities with a long hose available. The sanitary block, near the entrance, is very clean and is adequate, without being luxurious and offers hot showers on payment with additional facilities added in 1995. There are dishwashing facilities and a laundry with washing machine, spin and tumble dryers - the laundry is not to be used on Sundays. A TV and video room is provided and a rest room where one can make tea and coffee, plus a children's playground, barbecue and picnic area are on site. Shops, supermarkets, etc. are close by in Portlaoise, where there is a market on Thursdays. Laois is a beautiful inland county of Ireland, with picturesque small towns and many historical connections well worth exploring.

Charges 1995:
-- Per unit, incl. up to 4 persons IR£6.00; m/cycle and tent IR£3.00 per person; backpacker or cyclist IR£2.00 per person; tent, extra person, electricity, dog, awning or boat all IR£1.00.
Open:
1 April -- 15 October.
Address:
N7 Limerick Road, Portlaoise, Co. Laois.
Tel:
Portlaoise (0502) 21688.
Reservations:
Made for any length, with no deposit.

Directions: Site is on western outskirts of Portlaoise, on N7 Limerick road. Watch carefully for sign immediately by the entrance, going out of town.

288 Valley Motorcaravan Stopover and Caravan Park, Kilmacanogue

Small, family run park located in quiet, idyllic setting and convenient for Dublin ferries.

This neat and attractive ¾ acre park situated in the picturesque Rockey Valley could be used either as a transit site or for a longer stay. It has instant appeal for those who prefer the more basic 'CL' type site. There are 15 grassy pitches, 10 with electric hook-ups, 2 water points, night lighting and a security gate. Toilet facilities, which were spotlessly clean when we visited, are housed in one unit and consist of 2 WCs with washbasins, mirrors, etc. and a shower (50p). There is a dishwashing/laundry sink, a spin dryer, chemical disposal point, a campers' kitchen and hot water is constantly available. Staying put here you are only minutes from Enniskerry which lies in the glen of the Glencullen river. Here you can enjoy a delight of forest walks, or visit Powerscourt, one of the loveliest gardens in Ireland. If wanting to be at the sea, travel 6 km. to Bray and you are in one of the oldest seaside resorts in the country.

Charges guide:
-- Per caravan or tent with car IR£5.00; tent with bike IR£3.00; electricity 50p; awning IR£1.00.
Open:
4 April -- end-October.
Address:
Valleyview, Killough, Kilmacanogue, Co. Wicklow.
Tel:
Dublin (01) 2829565.
Reservations:
Contact park.

Directions: Turn off Dublin-Wexford N11 road at Kilmacanogue - follow signs for Glendalough. Continue for 1.6 km and take right fork signed 'Waterfall'. Park is first opening on the left in approx. 200 m.

289 Roundwood Caravan and Camping Park, Roundwood

Excellent park in the heart of the Wicklow mountains and convenient for ferries.

This park is neatly laid out with several rows of trees dividing different areas and giving some shade and an attractive appearance. There are 37 pitches, all with electricity and 12 with hardstanding, for caravans and motorcaravans and 42 for tents, arranged off tarmac access roads. The modern sanitary block was spotless when we visited, with adequate washing and toilet facilities and spacious showers. The block also houses 2 dishwashing sinks with free hot water and good laundry facilities (ask for assistance at reception as machines are not self use). The main toilets are locked from midnight to 6 am. but there are 3 children's toilets available during this time. Bicycles may be hired and there is a children's adventure playground, a TV room, a campers' kitchen and dining room. In the village of Roundwood you can find shops, pubs, restaurants and takeaway food and there is a Sunday market. There are excellent walks in the immediate area, around the Varty Lakes and a daily bus service to Dublin City. You should enjoy this excellent park, which is set in an area of mountains, lakes, rivers and forests.

Charges 1995:
-- Per unit IR£5.00 - 6.00; adult IR£1.50; child (under 14 yrs) £1.00.
-- 7 nights for the price of 6 if pre-paid.
-- Eurocheques accepted.
Open:
5 April- 29 September.
Address:
Roundwood, Co. Wicklow.
Tel:
Dublin (01) 2818163.
Reservations:
Accepted without deposit and are advisable for July/Aug.

Directions: Turn off the Dublin - Wexford N11 road at Kilmacanogue in the direction of Glendalough and then 15 km. to Roundwood.

290 River Valley Caravan and Camping Park, Redcross Village

Friendly, family run park in small village in the heart of Co. Wicklow.

In the small country village of Redcross, which abounds with character and atmosphere, is where you will find this well run park. Although only 58 km. from Dublin, being based here you are in the heart of the countryside with beauty spots such as the Vale of Avoca, Glendalough and Powerscourt within driving distance, plus the safe beach of Brittas Bay 6 km. away. Although there are many caravan holiday homes on this park, the touring pitches are together in a separate area. There are 50 with electrical connections (6A) and with a choice of hardstanding or grass, you select your pitch. Toilet blocks are clean, modern and well maintained with showers operated by token (50p), washbasins, razor and hairdryer points, mirrors, hand dryers and facilities for the disabled. Hot water is available for dishwashing and there is a laundry area and chemical disposal points. Within this 12 acre `award for excellence' site children can find day long amusement, whether it be `Fort Apache' the children's adventure playground, or at the natural mountain stream where it is safe to paddle. They may, however, prefer to get to know the farm animals and birds in the pets corner. Other amenities include TV, games room, a tennis court, par-3 golf course and bowling green. An attractive wine and coffee bar/conservatory is an inviting asset. Try a River Valley punch and get in the mood for a sing-a-long. An alternative may be the cosy atmosphere of the restaurant where `Beef and Guinness' is the speciality.

Charges guide:
-- Per caravan or tent IR£4.00 - 5.00; adult IR£1.00; electricity IR£1.00.
-- 7 nights for the price of 6.
Open:
17 March - 23 Sept.
Address:
Redcross Village, Co. Wicklow.
Tel:
(0404) 41647.
Reservations:
Made with IR£10 deposit.

Directions: From Dublin follow the N11 Wexford road. Turn right in Rathnew and then left (under railway bridge) onto the Wexlow-Arklow road. Continue for 11 km. and turn right at Doyle's Pub. Park is in Redcross Village, under 5 km.

To telephone the Irish Republic from the UK, replace the first `0' given in the number with the country code: **00 353**.

eg. (094) 88100 becomes 00 353 94 88100.

291 Nore Valley Park, Annamult, Bennettsbridge

Small working farm site, set in picturesque and peaceful surroundings.

This lovely site is set on a grassy hillock overlooking the valley and the river Nore, with a woodland setting behind. Situated on a working farm this site offers 70 pitches, 35 for caravans and motorhomes with electrical hook-up and some with hardstanding, and 35 for tents. The owners pride themselves on their home baking and farm produce and during high season cooked breakfasts are available in the small cafe. The reception area at the site entrance is in an attractive court yard and basic items such as milk, bread, camping gaz are available. A new sanitary block houses modern facilites which are kept spotlessly clean. These include free hot showers, WCs, washbasins and two units suitable for the disabled. There are dishwashing sinks with hot water and a laundry room with washing machine and dryer. The original sanitary block in the courtyard is for use mainly in the low season. A comfortable lounge is to be found next to the reception area, plus a games room with pool table. Crazy golf is a feature. Other facilities within the courtyard include a sand pit and straw loft playing area for wet weather and at the front of the park is a children's play area on gently sloping grass and fenced.

This is an ideal park for families, offering children and adults alike the opportunity to feed the animals, (goats, lambs, ducks, chickens, and donkey). The park is 11 km. from Kilkenny, renowned for its castle, history and crafts, and 5 km. from the village of Bennettsbridge, where there are shops and eating places. There is plenty of scope nearby for outdoor pursuits such as canoeing, pony trekking, walking and fishing.

Directions: From Kilkenny take the R700 to Bennettsbridge. Just before the bridge turn right at sign for Stoneyford and after approx. 3 km, site is signed Nore Valley Park.

Charges 1995:
-- Per person 50p; caravan IR£7.00; trailer or chalet tent IR£7.00; dormobile IR£6.00; 3-4 person tent IR£6.00, 2 person tent IR£5.00; backpacker IR£3.00; awning or extra small tent IR£1.50; electricity IR£1.00.
Open: 1 March - 31 October.
Address: Annamult, Bennettsbridge, Co. Kilkenny.
Tel: (056) 27229. FAX: (Tourist Office) (056) 63955.
Reservations: Contact park.

292 Newtown Cove Camping and Caravan Park, Tramore

Small, well run, friendly park, 5 minutes walk from the beautiful Newtown Cove.

This park offers views of the famous and historic Metal Man and is situated 2.5 km. from Tramore beach and 11 km. from Waterford. Neatly set out on gently sloping grass with an abundance of shrubs and bushes, there are 40 pitches. All have electrical connections, some with hardstanding also, with access by well lit tarmac roads. There are 50 privately owned caravan holiday homes. A new building at the entrance houses reception, a small shop (high season only), TV room, games room and further sanitary facilities. The village of Tramore, with a wide range of shops and eating houses, is close. The main sanitary block is situated at the bottom end of the site and offers good facilities which include a bathroom. Showers are on payment (50p for a token from reception). The block also provides a campers' kitchen with cooking facilities (20p), lounge and a washing up room and small laundry, with free hot water. A small children's play area set on sand is conveniently positioned in the centre of the park. A golf course is opposite and the choice of many delightful cliff walks in the immediate vicinity. Dogs are allowed if kept on a lead. No bookings are taken and the park does not accept single sex groups.

Directions: Park is on the R675 Tramore-Dungarven coast road, well signed from Tramore town.

Charges 1996:
-- Per car and caravan or family tent incl. 2 adults and 2 children IR£7.00 - 9.00; 1 or 2 man tent IR£7.00 - 8.00; hiker, cyclist or motorcyclist IR£2.50 - 3.00 per person; awning IR£1.00 - 2.00; electricity IR£1.50.
Open: Easter - 30 September.
Address: Tramore, Co. Waterford
Tel: (051) 381979 or 381121.
Reservations: Not necessary but for information contact park.

Alan Rogers' discount 3 nights for the price of 2 in May, June or Sept

293 Casey's Caravan Park, Clonea, Dungarvan

Family run site with direct access to the beach.

Set on 15 acres of flat grass, edged by mature trees, this park offers 70 touring pitches, 50 have electrical hook-ups and 24 hardstanding. There are also 100 caravan holiday homes. The central sanitary block (on a key system) has good facilities kept spotlessly clean with showers on payment (40p), free hot water to open style basins and washing up sinks (20p). Also in this block is a small laundry with machine and dryer. There is direct access to a sandy, blue flag beach with a lifeguard during July/Aug. Facilities on the site include a large children's adventure play area with bark surface, in its own field. Games room with pool table, table tennis and amusements, crazy golf and TV lounge. No shop, but two village stores are near the beach. The park is 5.5 km. from Dungarvan, popular for deep sea angling, from which charter boats can be hired and 9 and 18 hole golf courses are within easy distance. Recommended drives include the scenic Vee, the Comeragh Drive and the coast road to Tramore..

Charges 1996:
-- Per unit IR£9.00 - 9.50; hiker or cyclist IR£3.25 - 3.50; electricity IR£1.00.
Open:
11 May - 15 September.
Address:
Clonea, Dungarvan, Co. Waterford.
Tel:
(058) 41919.
Reservations:
Contact park.

Directions: From Dungarvan centre follow R675 east for 3.5 km. Look for signs on the right to Clonea Bay and site. Site is approx. 1.5 km.

294 Carrick-on-Suir Caravan and Camping Park, Carrick-on-Suir

Small, family run, town site in quiet and tranquil setting.

This memorable little site is not only conveniently situated off the main N24 between Waterford and Clonmel, but its owner, Frank O'Dwyer, is an excellent ambassador for his county. Campers are guaranteed the finest example of 'Cead Mile Ftrue' it is possible to encounter - personal attention and advice on where to go in the area is all part of the service. The entrance to the park is immediately past the O'Dwyer's shop, through a gate closed at 11 pm. The gravel driveway leads past tall hedges and well kept shrubs to the right and several caravan holiday homes (for hire) to the left. The touring park lies to the rear with scenic views to the wooded hills. At the moment there are 20 level pitches, several with hardstanding (likely to be extended). There are 12 electrical connections. What makes this little site distinctive is its excellent sanitary block which is well designed and sparkling clean. Facilities include WCs, showers, washbasins with mirrors, electric points, hand dryers and plenty of hot water each morning. Laundry room with washing machine and a dishwashing area also. A camper's kitchen is planned for 1996. Carrick town centre is a five minute walk away where there are all services, plus a castle open to the public. Within a short drive is the 'magic road', the Mahon Falls, a slate quarry or a romantic river walk.

Charges 1995:
-- Per unit incl. 2 persons IR£6.00 - 7.00; extra adult IR£1.00; child 50p; electricity IR£1.00; hiker or cyclist IR£2.00 - 3.00.
Open:
All year.
Address:
Ballyrichard, Carrick-on-Suir, Co. Tipperary.
Tel:
(051) 640461.
Reservations:
Contact site.

Directions: Approaching town on N24 road, follow signs for R690 Kilkenny. Site is north of town, clearly signed at junction with R697.

295 Parsons Green Caravan and Camping Park, Clogheen

Small, family run park with excellent on site facilities.

In a tranquil and scenic location, this open style site commands panoramic views toward the Vee Gap and Knockmealdown Mountains. It is surrounded by low ranch fencing, with 20 pitches for caravans or motorcaravans with hardstanding and electricity (10A) and 20 pitches for tents. Sanitary facilities, close to reception, are kept clean and include WCs, washbasins with mirrors, electric points, etc, free hot showers and good facilities for the disabled (shower and toilet), plus a laundry area with washing machines, dryer and sinks, and three dishwashing sinks. The village is within 500 m. with shops, pubs, bank, post office, etc. The range of amenities on site includes a coffee shop, garden area, river walks, picnic area, an extensive farm museum, a pet field with selection of domestic and rare animals and birds, playground, pony and trap rides, boating on the small lake and trout fishing river. TV/games room, campers' kitchen and function room. If not sitting back enjoying the scenic surroundings or participating in the many activities, there is much to see and do in this area.

Charges 1995:
-- Per caravan or motorcaravan IR£8.00; tent IR£5.00; electricity IR£1.00.
Open:
All year.
Address:
Clogheen, Co. Tipperary.
Tel:
(052) 65290.
Reservations:
Contact site.

Directions: Park is in the village of Clogheen, 200 m. off the R665 road, 24 km. west of Clonmel, 19 km. east of Mitchelstown.

296 Ballinacourty House Camping and Caravan Park, Glen of Aherlow

Family run, good quality site in the grounds of historic 16th century country estate near Tipperary.

The Ballinacourty estate enjoys a magnificent, secluded setting in the Glen of Aherlow, between the Galtee mountains and the wooded Slievenamuck Hills, yet is within 11 km, of Tipperary town. The reception and a shop are part of the beautifully restored 18th century courtyard buildings which were originally used as stables (Ballinacourty House itself was destroyed during the troubles of 1922). A coach-house and hay lofts form a surround for the courtyard with its cobblestone, well tended flower beds and patio. Within the old buildings is a Courtyard Restaurant serving top class cuisine and if required, a takeaway service, also a wine bar with extensive wine list and where regular music sessions are held. The sanitary facilities, housed to the outside, are kept exceptionally clean and include WCs, washbasins with H&C, mirrors, electric points, etc. Hot showers are free and there are dishwashing sinks, washing machine, tumble dryer and iron. Campers' kitchen, ice packs, TV/games room and chemical disposal point.

The touring pitches are to the right of reception and are spread over a large open area interspersed by trees and shrubs. The 26 pitches for caravans or motor-caravans have hardstanding and 6A electrical connections and there are 24 tent pitches. The site commands extensive views of the surrounding countryside and of interest to the rear is a walled Victorian kitchen garden. Apart from the tourist information available at reception, the owner and his family are happy to share with campers their knowledge of the area and give advice on top attractions.

Directions: From Tipperary town take N24 road towards Cahir (or Caher) for 8 km. to Bansha village. Branch west onto R663 Galbally road and follow signs for approx. 11 km. to park on left.

Charges 1995:
-- Per adult IR£1.00; child (under 12 yrs) 50p (charge for 3 only); caravan or tent IR£5.25 - 6.25; 1 person tent IR£4.00; awning or small extra tent IR£1.25 - 1.50; electricity IR£1.00.
Open:
Easter - 30 September.
Address:
Glen of Aherlow, Co. Tipperary.
Tel:
(062) 56230.
FAX: as phone.
Reservations:
Contact site.

297 The Apple Camping and Caravan Park, Cahir

Fruit farm and campsite combination offering an idyllic country holiday venue.

In one of the most delightful situations imaginable, this small farm site for tourers only is located off the N24, midway between Clonmel and Cahir. Entrance is by way of a 300 m. driveway which follows straight through the heart of the farm. Apple trees guard the route, as do various non-fruit tree species, which are named and of interest to guests, who are free to spend time walking the pathways around the farm. When we visited, strawberries were being gathered, the best we had tasted all season. Reception is housed with the other site facilities in a large farmyard barn. Although a rather unusual arrangement, it is very effective. Showers, WCs and washbasins with mirrors, electric points, etc. are in functional units and occupy two corners of the large floor space. They are kept very clean and are quite modern in design. There are simple extra touches such as green curtains and green coloured concrete floor which blend with the fittings to give an attractive well maintained appearance. Also in the barn are dishwashing sinks with hot water, bench seating and a fridge/freezer for the use of campers.

Pitches are in a secluded situation behind the barns and are mostly grass with a few hardstandings. There are electricity connections to 25 pitches, but some may require long cables. Amenities include a tennis court, a basketball/football pitch and children's play area. No dogs accepted. The towns of Cahir and Clonmel are of historic interest and the countryside around boasts rivers, mountains, Celtic culture and scenic drives.

Directions: Park is 300 m. off the main N24 road, 9.6 km. northwest of Clonmel, 6.4 km. southeast of Cahir.

Charges 1995:
-- Per person IR£2.75 - 3.25; child (0-12 yrs) IR£1.75; electricity IR£1.00 (no charge per unit).
Open:
1 May - 30 September.
Address:
Moorstown, Cahir, Co. Tipperary.
Tel:
(052) 41459.
Reservations:
Contact site.

CLARE / LIMERICK / CORK

298 Lahinch Camping and Caravan Park, Lahinch

Attractively situated park with superb views, 200 metres from the beach with life guard.

This park has 115 pitches set on gently sloping grass, of which 37 have electrical connections and 55 hardstanding. There are also 45 caravan holiday homes but these are sited in one area only and do not overlook the tourers. The three tiled sanitary blocks are of oldish construction with pre-set showers and open washbasins. Hot water is free throughout and dishwashing is under cover. Also included is a campers' hall for shelter in wet weather. Although there is no on-site shop, the village of Lahinch is just 200 m. away with a good range of shops, eating houses and new indoor swimming pool. However, the close proximity to the village does mean that parts of the site are overlooked by private residences. On site facilities include a children's play area on sand, a games room and bicycle hire. The park is an ideal touring centre for the Cliffs of Moher and the Burren. Ennistimon market town and Liscannor fishing village are near. Security gates are locked between midnight and 7 am. and a night watchman is on duty during the months of July and August.

Directions: Park is 200 m. south of Lahinch on the Milltown Malbay road.

Charges 1996:
-- Per caravan or family tent IR£5.50 - 6.60; motorhome IR£5.00 - £5.50; adult IR£1.00; child 50p; tent incl. 1 or 2 persons IR£5.50; electricity IR£1.50.
Open: 1 April - 30 September.
Address: Lahinch, Co. Clare.
Tel: (065) 81424.
FAX: (065) 81194.
Reservations: Advisable for July/Aug; made with IR£5 deposit.

299 Curraghchase Caravan and Camping Park, Kilcornan, Pallaskenry

Beautiful, tranquil park set in Curraghchase Forest.

This 39 acre park is set in 600 acres of beech forest, 21 km. from Limerick City. Touring pitches have hardstandings with drainage and electric hook-ups, plus a separate grassy area allocated for tents. One large amentities building houses a well stocked shop (including local, hand made crafts), TV lounge, a games room with table tennis and seating for an excellent campers' kitchen. Also within this building are the sanitary facilities which are basic, but very clean and hot water is free. Showers are separated by a partition, sharing a large base with single drain and a communal dressing area with hooks and benches. Washing up sinks are available in the campers' kitchen and a small laundry with washing machines, dryers and iron. Behind the main block is a small `sun trap' picnic area. Children's play area with a bark safety base. Card telephone on site. Barbecues are allowed. There are many lovely forest walks, a nature trail and a number of rare orchids can be found. Within the forest are the ruins of Curragh (or Currah) Chase House, which was once the home of the poet Aubrey de Vere. Fishing and golf facilities are within easy reach and Adare village, with its interesting historical buildings and shopping facilities are within 10 km.

Directions: From Limerick city take the N69 Foynes road; the park entrance is at Kilcornan. Park also signed from Adare on the N20.

Charges 1995:
-- Per unit IR£4.00; adult IR£2.00; child IR£1.00; electricity IR£1.00.
Open: Easter - 15 September.
Address: Kilcornan, Pallaskenry, Co. Limerick.
Tel: (061) 396349.
Reservations: Advisable in high season - contact site.

300 Sextons Caravan and Camping Park, Timoleague, Bandon, nr. Cork

Unpretentious, but atmospheric farm park within easy driving distance of Cork city.

This charming small park, although on the main Cork-Kinsale tourist route, offers a tranquil countryside setting. The flat, 3 acre park divided by hedging and trees, is approached by a roadway which runs from the entrance to the reception and family home. Pitches are placed to either side and a farming atmosphere is evident. Spotlessly clean, old, white farm buildings house the sanitary facilities, which have been extended. Also a launderette, shop, free freezer facilities, TV/games room, facilities for the disabled and a children's play area. Electric hook-ups are available and hot showers are free. The Sexton family run an unofficial tourist information centre and apart from offering their guests first hand knowledge of this locality, friendly conversation and advice is always available. Attractions near include the Lisnagun Ring Fort, Timoleague Abbey, Clonakilty model railway village and many sporting activities. It is 3 km. from many sandy beaches and 48 km. to Cork city and the ferries

Directions: Park is on the main Cork-Kinsale R600 tourist route or off the R602 Bandon, Clonakilty road mid-way between Timoleague (3 km) and Clonakilty (5 km). Park is signed from both the Clonakilty and Timoleague roads.

Charges 1995:
-- Per unit incl. 2 persons IR£6.00; extra person £1.00; awning IR£1.00; electricity IR£1.00.
Open: All year.
Address: Timoleague, Bandon, Co. Cork.
Tel: (023) 46347.
Reservations: Booking is advisable but not essential.

301 The Meadow Camping Park, Glandore

Small, mature garden park on Ireland's garden route; for tents and motorcaravans only.

The stretch of coast from Cork to Skibbereen reminds British visitors of Devon before the era of mass tourism. This is rich dairy country, the green of the meadows matching the emerald colours of the travel posters. Thanks to the warm and wet Gulf Stream climate, it is also a county of gardens - and keen gardeners. The Meadows is best described not as a site, but as a 1-acre garden surrounded - appropriately - by lush meadows. It lies 1.5 km. east of the fishing village of Glandore. A further 5 km. west is the regional centre, Skibbereen, beyond which the landscape moves from unspoilt Devon to unspoilt Cornwall. The owners, who live on the park, have cunningly arranged accommodation for 20 pitches among the flowerbeds and shrubberies of their extended garden. Space is rather tight and towed caravans are therefore not encouraged. There are 6 hardstandings for motorcaravans with 5A electric hook-ups. Facilities are limited but are well designed and immaculately maintained. Among the homely features are a sitting room and a well equipped kitchen and breakfast is available on request. Washing machine and dryer. American motorhomes are accepted with an additional charge according to length. No dogs accepted. Golf driving range, horse riding (5 km.), fishing, swimming and sailing at Glandore.

Charges 1996:
-- Per motorcaravan or tent IR£3.00; small tent IR£2.00; person IR£2.00; child (under 12) IR£1.00; car IR£1.00; electricity IR£1.00.
Open:
15 March - 30 Sept.
Address:
Glandore, Co. Cork.
Tel:
(028) 33280.
Reservations:
Please phone for details.

Alan Rogers' discount
4 nights for the price of 3

Directions: Park is 1.5 km. east of Glandore, off N71 road, on R597 road midway between Leap and Rosscarbery (coast road).

302 Eagle Point Caravan and Camping Park, Ballylickey, Bantry Bay

Spacious, well run park on a spectacular peninsular jutting into Bantry Bay.

Midway between the towns of Bantry and Glengarriff, the peninsula of Eagle Point juts into the bay. The first impression is of a country park rather than a camp site. As far as the eye can see this 20 acre, part-terraced park, with its vast grass areas separated by mature trees, shrubs and hedges, runs parallel with the shoreline. This is a park devoted to tourers, with campers pitched mostly towards the shore. It provides 125 pitches (60 caravans, 65 tents) thus avoiding overcrowding during peak periods. There are three toilet block with free hot showers, all maintained and designed well above expected standards. Other facilities include electric hook-ups, bin area, laundry and dishwashing facilities, a children's play area, tennis courts, a football field to the far right, well away from the pitches, plus a supermarket at the park entrance. A wet weather timbered building towards the water's edge houses a TV room and play room with books and toys. The brightly decorated interior is guaranteed to brighten the dullest of days. No dogs are accepted. Eagle Point makes an excellent base for watersports enthusiasts - swimming is safe and a slipway for small craft.

Charges 1996:
-- Per unit family rate IR£10.50 - 11.50, acc. to unit; per unit incl. 2 persons IR£8.50 - 9.00; extra adult IR£2.00; child 50p; m/cyclist, hiker or cyclist IR£3.50 per person; extra car IR£2.00; electricity IR£1.00.
Open:
26 April - 30 Sept.
Address:
Ballylickey, Bantry, Co. Cork.
Tel:
(027) 50630.
Reservations:
Bookings not essential.

Directions: On the coast side of the N71, 6 km. north of Bantry, 11 km. east of Glengariff. Park entrance is opposite Burmah petrol station.

303 Creveen Lodge Caravan and Camping Park, Healy Pass

Immaculately run, small hill farm park, overlooking Kenmare Bay.

The address of this park is rather confusing, but Healy Pass is the well known scenic summit of the road (R574) crossing the Beara Peninsula, which lies between Kenmare Bay to the north and Bantry Bay to the south. Several kilometres inland from the north coast road (R571), the R574 starts to climb steeply southward towards the Healy Pass. Here, on the mountain foothills, is Creveen Lodge, a working hill farm. Although not so famed as the Iveragh Peninsula, around which runs the Ring of Kerry, the northern Beara is a scenically striking area of County Kerry. Creveen Lodge, commanding views across Kenmare Bay, is divided among three gently sloping fields separated by trees. Reception is in the farmhouse which also offers guests a comfortable sitting room.

Charges 1996:
-- Per unit IR£5.00; person IR£1.00; hiker or cyclist IR£3.00 per person; electricity £1.00; extra tent IR£1.00.
Open:
Easter - 31 October.
Address:
Healy Pass, Lauragh, Co. Kerry.
Tel:
(064) 83131.

continued overleaf

303 Creveen Lodge Caravan and Camping Park (continued)

A small separate block is well appointed and immaculately maintained, with toilets and showers, plus a communal room with a fridge, freezer, TV, ironing board, fireplace, tables and chairs. Full Irish breakfast is served on request. This park is carefully tended with neat bins and rustic picnic tables informally placed, plus a children's play area with slides and swings. To allow easy access, the steep farm track is divided into a simple one-way system. There are 20 pitches in total, 16 for tents and 4 for caravans with an area of hardstanding for motor-caravans, and electrical connections are available. This is walking and climbing countryside or of interest close by is Derreen Gardens.

Reservations: Write to site with S.A.E.

Directions: Park is on the Healy Pass road (R574) 1½ km south east of Lauragh.

304 Ring of Kerry Caravan and Camping Park, Reen, Kenmare

Mature park overlooking Kenmare Bay.

On the Kenmare stretch of the Ring of Kerry route, located just off the N70, this peaceful park offers a 'far from the madding crowd' atmosphere. A narrow approach road leads to the entrance where 'welcome' is written in different languages. Then a well cared for garden area, interrupted by a small trickling stream and the children's play areas, stretches to the forecourt. It is evident that the owners are keen gardeners, their flair extending to hanging flower baskets to adorn the main building and flowers a feature in the toilet block. Beyond reception, shop and sanitary area are the elevated pitches which have electric hook-ups and are separated by high conifers. This is an organised park with a marker board indicating that caravan pitches have a red disc and tent pitches a green disc. The toilet block, whilst not ultra modern, is kept clean and facilities include washbasins, unisex showers (20p), laundry room and covered dish-washing area. There is also a campers' kitchen and dining room which is bright and colourful. Night lighting, security gate (locked 11 pm.- 8 am.) and chemical disposal. Scenic walks, fishing, boating, swimming and the town of Kenmare, with its many restaurants and shops, are only minutes away.

Charges 1995: -- Per unit IR£6.00; adult IR£1.50; child 75p; cyclist or hiker IR£3.50; extra tent or awning IR£2.00; electricity IR£1.00. **Open:** Easter - 31 October. **Address:** Reen, Kenmare, Co. Kerry. **Tel:** (064) 41366. **Reservations:** Advisable for peak periods; write for a booking form.

Directions: Park is off N70 Ring of Kerry-Sneem road, 4 km. west of Kenmare; park is signed.

305 Wave Crest Caravan and Camping Park, Caherdaniel

Dramatically located hillside park running down to Kenmare Bay.

It would be difficult to imagine a more dramatic location than Wave Crest's. Huge boulders and rocky outcrops tumble from the park entrance on the N70 down to the seashore which forms the most southern promontory on the Ring of Kerry. There are spectacular southward views from the park across Kenmare Bay to the Beara peninsula. Sheltering on grass patches in small coves that nestle between the rocks and shrubbery, are 45 hardstanding pitches offering seclusion. Two toilet blocks house the sanitary facilities and include hot showers (50p), toilet for the handicapped and dishwashing sinks. There is also a laundry service, central rubbish point, shop (open 1/5-7/9) and children's play area. A unique feature is the TV room, an old stone farm building with thatched roof. Its comfortable interior includes a stone fireplace heated by a converted cast iron marker buoy. Beside the park is a small beach or there is Derrynane Hotel with its swimming pool and tennis court. Caherdaniel is known for its cheerful little pubs and distinguished restaurant. The Derrynane National Park Nature Reserve is only a few km. away, as is Derrynane Cove and Bay.

Charges 1996: -- Per unit IR£6.50; adult IR£1.00; child 50p; hiker or cyclist incl. tent IR£3.00 per person; m/cyclist incl. tent £3.50; awning, extra small tent or car IR£1.00; electricity IR£1.00. **Open:** 1 April - 30 September. (off season by arrangement). **Address:** Caherdaniel, Co. Kerry. **Tel:** (066) 75188. **Reservations:** Write for details.

Directions: Park is on the N70 (Ring of Kerry) road, 1½ km. east of Caherdaniel.

306 Waterville Caravan and Camping Park, Waterville

Family run park in scenic location overlooking Ballinskelligs Bay.

Drive into Waterville and immediately feel welcome - the Horgan family place emphasis on being hospitable and attentive to their guests. The touring pitches, many with hardstanding, are located in three areas. Some are convenient to reception, whilst others are pitched to the middle and rear. There is also a sheltered corner allocated to campers with caravan holiday homes for hire, unobtrusively placed around the perimeter and centre, giving the park a spacious, neatly laid out appearance. Sitting high above the bay, the view in all directions is magnificent and the well tended grounds with plants, shrubs and cordyline trees gives a tropical appearance, especially on a fine sunny day. There are three sanitary blocks, all well maintained and kept clean, the newest tastefully decorated with white tiles, relieved with rows of decorative black. There are hot showers (50p token), facilities for the disabled, washing up and laundry areas, drying room, quiet room and chemical disposal. Other on site facilities include a campers' kitchen, shop and TV room. As well as an outdoor children's play area and above ground swimming pool, there is a play room in an old horse drawn caravan and a timber house with toys and upstairs, downstairs. Waterville is on the 'Ring of Kerry', convenient for all the scenic grandeur and attractions for which the area is famed.

Directions: Travelling south on the N70, park is 1 km. north of Waterville, 270 m. off the main road.

Charges 1995:
-- Per unit IR£5.50 - 6.50; adult IR£1.00; child 50p; hiker or cyclist incl. tent IR£3.25, plus per m/cycle 50p; electricity IR£1.00; awning IR£1.00 - 1.50; hardstanding IR£1.00; extra car IR£1.00; extra tent IR£1.00.
Open:
Easter - 23 September.
Address:
Waterville, Co. Kerry.
Tel:
(066) 74191.
FAX: (066) 74538.
Reservations:
Made with fee IR£5 plus IR£15 deposit.

307 Glenross Caravan and Camping Park, Glenbeigh, Ring of Kerry

Immaculate small park on the edge of Glenbeigh Village.

Being situated on the spectacular Ring of Kerry gives this park an immediate advantage and scenic grandeur around every bend of the road is guaranteed as Glenbeigh is approached. Quietly located before entering the village, its situation commands a fine view of Rossbeigh Strand, which is within walking distance. On arrival, a good impression is instantly created with the park well screened from the road and with a heavy ranch style gateway. Beyond the entrance stands a well maintained modern sanitary block which includes showers, and facilities for laundry and dishwashing. On site facilities include a games room and TV, a shelter for campers, also a sun lounge and barbecue patio. There are hardstanding pitches with electricity and although there are caravan holiday homes, the park is attractively laid out. There is no catering on site but the Glenbeigh Hotel is a popular venue. Watersports, tennis, fishing, golf and bicycle hire are all nearby, and not least is the Kerry Bog Village where you can go back in time in this reconstructed pre-famine village.

Directions: Park is on the N70 Killorglin-Glenbeigh road, on the right just before entering the village.

Charges 1995:
-- Per unit IR£2.50 - 3.50; adult IR£2.50; child 50p; electricity IR£1.20; awning IR£1.00; extra car IR£1.00; hiker or cyclist, incl. tent IR£3.00 - 3.50.
Open:
12 May - 10 September.
Address:
Glenbeigh, Co. Kerry.
Tel:
Killarney (064) 31590.
Reservations:
Write to site with IR£10 deposit (incl. IR£2 fee).

308 Mannix Point Camping and Caravan Park, Cahirciveen

Quiet and peaceful, beautifully located seashore park.

It is no exaggeration to describe Mannix Point as a nature lover's paradise. It is situated in one of the most spectacular parts of the Ring of Kerry, overlooking the Portmagee Channel towards Valencia Island. Whilst the park is flat and open, it commands splendid views, it is right on marshland which teems with wildlife (2 acre nature reserve) and it has immediate access to the beach and seashore. The owner has planted around 500 plants with plans for around 1,000 more. There are 41 pitches, 15 for tourers and 26 for tents, with electricity. A charming old fisherman's cottage has been converted to provide reception, a cosy sitting room with turf fire and emergency dormitory for campers. Toilet facilities are simple but immaculate, with well designed showers and free hot water. Also campers' kitchen and laundry. This park retains a wonderful air of Irish charm aided by occasional impromptu musical evenings. Watersports, bird watching, walking and photography can all be pursued here, but it should be noted dogs are not allowed on site. Local cruises to Skelligs Rock with free transport to and from the port for walkers and cyclists. This is also an ideal resting place for people walking the Kerry Way.

Directions: Park is 250 m. off the N70 Ring of Kerry road, 800 m. southwest of Cahirciveen (or Cahersiveen).

Charges 1995:
-- Per caravan or motorcaravan IR£1.50; adult IR£3.00; child IR£1.50; electricity IR£1.50; hiker or cyclist, incl. tent IR£3.00; m/cyclist incl. tent IR£3.50; 2 adults, car and tent IR£6.50.
Open:
15 March - 15 October, the rest of the year also, if you write first.
Address:
Cahirciveen, Co. Kerry.
Tel:
(066) 72806.
Reservations:
Made with deposit of one night's fee.

309 White Villa Farm Caravan and Camping Park, Killarney

Welcoming park in scenic surroundings for tourers only.

This is a very pleasing touring park on the N22 Killarney-Cork road. It is set in a 100 acre family operated dairy farm which stretches as far as the River Flesk, yet is only minutes away from Killarney town. Trees and shrubs surround the park but dominant is a magnificent view of the MacGillicuddy's Reeks. There are 25 pitches for caravans and tents, 8 with hardstanding with a grass area for awning, 22 electrical connections, 5 water points, rubbish disposal and night lighting. The toilet block, a sandstone coloured building to the rear of the park, is basic but clean. It houses showers (50p), a good toilet/shower room for the disabled, laundry area and dishwashing sinks. Chemical disposal and clothes lines. In a central position is a children's play area, areas for basketball and a novelty is old school desks placed around, plus an antique green telephone box. Walking through the oak wood, fishing on the Flesk or visiting White Villa's Vintage Farm Museum are on site attractions.

Directions: Travel 3 km. east from Killarney town on the N22 Cork road. Park entrance is 300 m. east of the N22/N72 junction.

Charges 1995:
-- Per unit IR£2.00 - 2.50; adult IR£1.50 - 2.00; child 25p; hiker or cyclist incl. tent IR£2.25 - 2.75; electricity IR£1.00; awning IR£1.00.
Open:
1 April - 31 October.
Address:
Cork Road (N22), Killarney, Co. Kerry.
Tel:
(064) 32456.
Reservations:
Made with IR£10 deposit; write for form.

310 Fossa Caravan and Camping Park, Killarney

Mature, well equipped park in scenic location, 5½ km. from Killarney.

A 10 minute drive from the town centre brings you to this well laid out park which is instantly recognisable by its forecourt on which stands a distinctive building housing a Roof Top Restaurant, reception area, shop and petrol pumps. The park is divided in two - the touring area lies to the right, tucked behind the main building, and to the left is an open grass area mainly for campers. Touring pitches, with electricity and drainage, have hardstanding and are angled between shrubs and trees in a tranquil, well cared for garden setting. To the rear at a higher level are a number of caravan holiday homes. These are unobtrusive and sheltered by the thick foliage of the wooded slopes which climb high behind the park. The toilet facilities are modern and kept spotlessly clean. A second amenities block is placed to the far left of the grass area beside the tennis courts. Other facilities, apart from a shop (all season), takeaway and restaurant (June-Aug), include a TV lounge, campers' kitchen, laundry room, washing up area, children's play area, games room, night lighting and security patrol.

Directions: Park is to the right on the R562, 5½ km. from Killarney on the road to Killorglin.

Charges 1996:
-- Per unit IR£3.00 - 3.50; adult IR£2.50; child 50p; electricity IR£1.00; hiker or cyclist per person IR£3.00 - 3.50; awning IR£1.50; extra car IR£1.50.
-- Credit cards accepted.
Open:
Mid-March - 31 Oct.
Address:
Killarney, Co. Kerry.
Tel:
(064) 31497.
FAX: (064) 34459.
Reservations:
Made for min. 7 nights with IR£10 deposit.

311 Fleming's Whitebridge Caravan Park, Ballycasheen, Killarney

Family run, 6 acre, woodland park on eastern outskirts of Killarney.

Once past the county border, the main road from Cork to Killarney (N22) runs down the valley of the Flesk river. On the final approach to Killarney, the river veers away from the road to enter the Lower Lake. On this prime rural position, between the road and the river, and within comfortable walking distance of the town, is Whitebridge. A new fence and entrance to the park were under construction when we visited. The ground is flat, landscaped and generously adorned with flowers, shrubs and trees. There are now 92 pitches (46 caravans and 46 tents) which extend beyond a wooden bridge to an area surrounded by mature trees and where a new toilet block, one of three, is sited. Facilities include a shop (June-Sept), TV room, games room, campers' shelter for wet weather, and a laundry, all housed in the main reception block. Hot water is free and there are dishwashing sinks. This is obviously a park of which the owners are very proud. The family personally supervise the reception and grounds, maintaining high standards. Although affiliated to the Caravan Club, all visitors are very welcome. There are 6 holiday caravans for hire, fishing (advice and permits provided), canoeing (own canoes), bicycle hire and woodland walks.

Directions: From Cork and Mallow: at the N72/N22 junction continue towards Killarney and take next turn left (signed). Proceed for 300 m. to archway entrance on left. From Limerick: follow the N22 Cork road. After passing the Castleheights Hotel take the first right (signed) and continue as above.

Charges 1996:
-- Per unit IR£2.50 - 3.50; adult IR£2.50; child 50p; awning IR£1.50; electricity IR£1.20; m/cyclist and tent IR£3.25 - IR£3.75; hiker or cyclist and tent IR£3.00 - IR£3.50.
Open:
15 March - 31 October.
Address:
Ballycasheen, Killarney, Co. Kerry.
Tel:
(064) 31590.
Reservations:
Adviseable in peak season; with IR£5 non-refundable fee.

Alan Rogers' discount
Ask at park for details

312 The Flesk Caravan and Camping Park, Killarney

Seven acre park at gateway to National Park and Lakes, near Killarney town.

This family run park is undergoing development and offers high quality standards. Housed in one of Europe's most modern toilet blocks are well designed shower and toilet areas, decorated in coordinating colours. Details include soap dispensers, hand dryers, vanity area with mirror and hair dryer, also a baby bath/changing room. Pitches are well spaced and have water, electric and drainage connections; 21 also have hardstanding with a grass area for awnings. Although there are several caravan holiday homes, the owners define The Flesk as a 'touring park'. Other facilities include a shop, laundry room, kitchen with dishwashing sinks, a games room and chemical disposal point. Night lighting and security checks. The grounds are being cultivated with further shrubs, plants and an attractive barbecue and patio area. This is situated to the left of the sanitary block and is paved and sunk beneath the level roadway. Surrounded by a garden border, it has tables and chairs, making a pleasant communal meeting place which commands excellent views of Killarny's mountains.

Directions: From Killarney town centre follow the N71 and signs for Killarney National Park. Site is 1½ km on the left beside the Gleneagle Hotel.

Charges 1995:
-- Per unit IR£3.00 - 3.50; adult IR£2.00; child 50p; extra car 50p; tent incl. 1 or 2 persons IR£2.50 - 3.00; hiker or cyclist incl. tent IR£3.00 - 3.25; awning IR£1.00; electricity IR£1.00.
Open:
16 March - 31 October.
Address:
Muckross Road, Killarney, Co. Kerry.
Tel:
(064) 31704
Reservations:
Advisable in peak periods, write to park.

FLESK

CARAVAN & CAMPING PARK △

Family run, 7 acre park, situated at the gateway to 25,000 acres of National Park and lakes.
AA award winning sanitation facilities 1994/5
Just 1 mile (1.5 km) from Killarney town on the N71 south of Kenmare,
adjacent to Gleneagle Hotel and leisure centre

MUCKROSS, KILLARNEY

CO. KERRY, IRELAND   Prop: Johnny & Sinead Courtney

Phone: 064-31704

Fax: 064-35439

JERSEY
Jersey Tourism
Weighbridge, St. Helier, Jersey C.I.
Tel: (01534) 78000

SARK
Sark Tourism Office
Sark (via Guernsey), C.I.
Tel: (01481) 832345.

GUERNSEY and HERM
States of Guernsey Tourist Board
PO Box 13, White Rock, Guernsey, C.I.
Tel: (014581) 26611

A visit to the Channel Islands offers a holiday in part of the British Isles, but in an area which has a definitely continental flavour. Of course, you don't need a passport or to change your money, although the proximity of the islands to the French coast might tempt one to take a day trip. All the islands have beautiful beaches and coves, pretty scenery and fascinating histories. Jersey is probably more commercially orientated, with more entertainment provided, while Guernsey will suit those who prefer a quieter, more peaceful holiday. For total relaxation, one of the smaller islands, such as Sark or Herm, where no cars are allowed, might appeal. Shopping in all the islands has the advantage of no mainland VAT - particularly useful for buying cameras, watches, jewellery and clothes.

Camping holidays on the islands are limited to **TENTS** only - caravans and motorcaravans are not permitted due to the narrow and sometimes crowded nature of the roads. Trailer tents (with canvas roof and walls) are permitted but on Jersey advance reservations must be made. Contact the Island Tourism authorities for more detailed information. Some of the parks we feature offer tents and camping equipment for hire, which may prove a popular option for some, and cars are also easily rented on the main islands.

Travel between mainland Britain and the Channel Islands is not cheap, particularly if you take your car. However the Condor wave-piercing catamaran service between Weymouth and Guernsey has made travelling to the Channel Islands a very easy and much quicker proposition than ever before. We used this service, which now carries cars, and were most impressed, in respect of the speed (Guernsey is only some 2 hours travelling time by this route), the comfort and the onboard service. These craft are surprisingly spacious with room to walk around (and even to go outside), a bar and snack bar and duty-free shopping facilities. Condor offer a range of fares, including a Family Saver deal. For further information contact:

Condor Ltd., The Quay, Weymouth, Dorset DT4 8DX Tel: (01305) 761551.

It is of course also possible to travel by traditional ferry, and the service provided by British Channel Island Ferries (BCIF) on their sailings from Poole is both friendly and efficient. The crossings are relatively long but cabins are available and, particularly on the larger of the two vessels, there is plenty to do. There is a full restaurant service, which is excellent value for money, as well as a self service lounge and bar, and of course the usual duty free shops. BCIF offer good `Saver Return' fares and `Island Camping' packages (with fully equipped tents). For further information contact:

British Channel Island Ferries, PO Box 315, Poole, Dorset BH15.

313 Rozel Camping Park, St. Martin

Rurally situated park in quieter northeast of island, close to picturesque harbour.

This family owned park is within walking distance of the famous Jersey Zoo and it is not much further to the pretty harbour and fishing village of Rozel where the north coast cliff path commences. The surrounding countryside is quieter than many areas of the island. A car is probably necessary to reach the main island beaches, although a bus service does run to St Helier from close by. The park itself is part of a working farm, quietly situated at the top of a valley and is surrounded by trees providing shelter. There are two main camping areas providing 70 pitches of which some 40 are for campers with their own tents. Some pitches, mainly for smaller tents are arranged on terraced areas. The remainder are on a higher, flat field where pitches are arranged in bays with hedges growing to separate them into groups. Free parking is permitted by the tents and electrical connections available. The clean, bright sanitary facilities are in a block between the two areas (access by steps from the lower part) and provide roomy, controllable hot showers and washbasins in pairs with mirror and shelf, with 2 in private cabins; hand dryers and heater for cooler weather. Dishwashing facilities are under cover. Hot water is free throughout. Laundry and make up room. The park reports a new sanitary block on the lower area with facilities for the disabled and babies. For entertainment there is a good play field with play equipment, an attractive, sheltered swimming pool with child's pool and grass and terrace sunbathing areas, crazy golf, games room, reading room and TV and bicycle hire. A torch would be useful. Public telephone. Breakfast, evening meals and possibly takeaway are offered in high season (closed Mondays) and there is a shop. In addition to package deals for tent hire and travel, the site offers a good range of camping equipment for hire on a daily basis. Boats are only accepted on site by prior arrangement. No dogs accepted.

Charges 1996:
-- Per person £3.50 - £5.40, acc. to season; child (3-11 yrs) half price; electricity £1.40.
-- Tent hire and travel packages.
Open: 1 May - 14 September.
Address: Rozel, St. Martin, Jersey, Channel Islands JE3 6AX.
Tel: (01534) 856797. FAX: (01534) 856127.
Reservations: Made for any length with £20 deposit; balance due 14 days before arrival.

Directions: From St. Helier take the A6 through tunnel, northeast to St. Martin's church and on towards Rozel Bay. Park is signed on the right.

314 Rose Farm Camping Site, St Brelade

Peaceful, well kept site in sheltered valley, but close to good beach.

Attractively situated in a sheltered valley with mature trees and lots of flowers, Rose Farm is a relatively peaceful place to stay, while still being within easy reach of St. Brelade's Bay, the village and harbour of St. Aubin and St. Helier. The site is arranged around an old farmhouse and outbuildings on the slopes of the valley and is divided into three main areas giving about 150 pitches, 100 of which are taken by tour operators. The top fields are divided into areas by bushes and trees, with electricity available and easy access for cars (allowed next to pitches). These pitches are part tour operator, part independent. The lower field is mainly used by tour operators and smaller tents and a few others are placed in an attractive, small, sloping meadow with small terraces around the good, fenced children's play area. The main sanitary facilities, near the house, provide free hot water to good, tiled showers with shelf and hook and to washbasins in rows, with some set in flat surfaces and two in private cabins. In a separate building are dishwashing facilities, a well equipped laundry room; separate hand laundry room and games and TV rooms. A further small block on the top field offers toilets and a couple of washbasins to save walking down the hill. The park has a heated pool with paved sunbathing area and there is a small snack bar for breakfasts and evening meals (high season). A well stocked shop provides an ice pack service (on deposit). Public phones. Torch useful. No dogs allowed in July or August.

Charges 1996:
-- Per person £3.50 - £5.00, acc. to season; child (3-11 yrs) £1.50 - £2.50; electricity (lighting only) 50p.
Open: May - September incl.
Address: St. Brelade, Jersey, Channel Islands JE3 8DF.
Tel: (01534) 41231. FAX: (01534) 490178.
Reservations: Necessary for July/Aug. and accepted in writing only for any length, with £10 deposit per adult. Balance payable on arrival.

Directions: From St. Helier, take the A13 west to St. Aubin and up winding hill towards St. Brelade. Park is signed to right 200 yds past Portelet turning.

315 Vaugrat Camping, St Sampson's

Neat, well tended site, close to beach, in northwest of island.

Vaugrat Camping is centred around attractive and interesting old granite farm buildings dating back to the 15th century, with a gravelled courtyard and colourful flowerbeds. Owned by the Laine family, Vaugrat provides 150 pitches on flat grassy meadows, which are mostly surrounded by trees, banks and hedges to provide shelter. Tents are arranged around the edges of the fields, giving open space in the centre, and while pitches are not marked, there is sufficient room. Cars may be parked next to tents. Only couples and families are accepted and the site is well run and welcoming, with 30 fully equipped tents for hire. Housed in the old farmhouse, now a listed building, are the reception area, shop (with ice pack hire) and upstairs 'Coffee Barn', with views to the sea, where breakfast and evening meals (to order in the morning) are served. One can also sit here in the evenings. Small games room with TV in the cider room complete with the ancient presses. Small adventure play area among trees for children. The sanitary facilities are in two buildings, one of which is in the courtyard, with hot showers on payment, washbasins and hairdryers (on payment). A laundry room here has a washing machine, dryer and iron. The other block is situated near the camping fields and provides toilets and washbasins in a row, set in a flat surface, plus one private cabin for ladies. The dishwashing facilities are housed in a room in this block with free hot water, with further sinks under cover outside. All these facilities are well kept and clean. There is a bus service within easy reach and car and bicycle hire are arranged. Hotel/bar nearby. No dogs. A torch may be useful.

Charges 1995:
-- Per adult £3.70; child (under 14 yrs) £2.75; car 80p; boat or extra tent 80p.
-- Fully equipped tents to hire.
Open:
May - September incl.
Address:
St Sampson's, Guernsey, Channel Islands.
Tel:
(01481) 57468.
Reservations:
Made for independent campers for any length, with £10 deposit and balance on arrival. Hire details from site.

Directions: On leaving St Peter Port harbour, turn right onto coast road for 1½ miles. At traffic lights, before 'filter in turn' turn left (Vale Road) towards L'Islet. After Craft Centre on right, straight over traffic lights, and through L'Islet to coast road. Follow road past hotel and Hourmet Tavern and site is signed to left.

316 Fauxquets Valley Farm Campsite, Castel

Attractive, rural site with good facilities in quiet, sheltered valley.

In the rural centre of the island, Fauxquets is in a pretty valley, hidden down narrow lanes away from busy roads and is run by the Guille family. A car would be useful to reach the beaches, St Peter Port and other attractions, although there is a bus service each day (20 mins walk). Once a dairy farm, there are still a few animals and hens for children to visit but the valley side has been developed into an attractive camp site, with the old farm buildings as its centre. Plenty of trees, bushes and flowers have been planted to separate pitches and to provide shelter around the various fields which are well terraced. The 90 pitches are of a good size, most marked and numbered and there is lots of open space. There are also a few smaller places for back-packers. The site has some tents for hire. The sanitary facilities are of very good quality, with modern, free, controllable hot showers, some washbasins set in flat surfaces, with others in private cabins and with a shower and baby bath for children. Hairdryers and irons are free. Dishwashing facilities are under cover, with free hot water and a tap to take away hot water. Laundry room with washing machine, dryer and free iron. In converted buildings around the farmhouse are a small shop with ice-pack hire, a 'Farmhouse Kitchen' providing (in high season, and for limited hours) breakfasts and evening meals and in an old hay barn, a good games room. TV room, a further table tennis room, small children's play area and play field, plus bicycle hire. A heated swimming pool (20 x 45 ft.) was added in 1995, with a paddling pool and a shallow end. There is plenty of room to sit around the pool, including a large grassy terrace with sunbeds provided. A torch would be useful.

Charges 1996:
-- Per adult £3.70 - £4.20, acc. to season; child (at school) £1.85 - £2.00.
-- Fully equipped tents for hire.
-- Credit cards accepted.
Open:
1 May - mid September.
Address:
Castel, Guernsey, Channel Islands.
Tel:
(01481) 55460.
FAX: (01481) 51797.
Reservations:
Made for independent campers for any length, with £30 deposit. Tent hire details from site.

 Alan Rogers' discount Less 5-10% acc. to season

Directions: From St Peter Port harbour follow sign for Catel - St Andrew's. At top of hill, turn left at 'filter in turn' into Queens Avenue, then right at another 'filter in turn'. Follow road through traffic lights and down hill past hospital, through pedestrian lights and straight on at lights at top of hill. Continue for 1 mile, then turn right at sign for German Underground Hospital, then 4th left.

317 Seagull Campsite, Herm Island

Small site on beautiful, peaceful island with no cars.

This tiny site, and indeed the island of Herm, will appeal to those who are looking for complete tranquillity and calm. Reached by boat (20 mins and approx. £6 return fare) from Guernsey, the 500 acre island allows only tractors on its narrow roads and paths (no bicycles either). One is free to stroll around the many paths, through farmland, heathland and around the coast, where there are beautiful beaches. The campsite, in the middle of the island, consists of two small fields offering just 60 pitches on flat grass. There is just a small, modern, but open, toilet block on site with WCs, hot showers (50p payment - there is a shortage of water on Herm) and washbasins, plus shaver points, with a freezer for ice-packs. One may bring one's own tent and equipment (luggage will be carried up to the site for you) or hire a tent and equipment (but not bedding, crockery and lighting) from the site. The harbour village is about ten minutes walk down the hill, where there is a small provisions shop, a post office, pub, restaurants and cafe. No animals or pets allowed. Herm is definitely not for those who like entertainment and plenty of facilities, but for total relaxation, with the absence of any bustle and noise it takes some beating!

Directions: Reached by boat from St Peter Port - report to Administration Office on arrival. Do not take your car as it is unlikely you will be able to park long term in St Peter Port.

Charges 1995:
-- Fixed site charge (irrespective of length of stay) incl. transportation of luggage £5.00.
-- Per adult £3.90; child (under 14 yrs) £2.00.
-- Equipped tents for hire (from £19.16 pp. per week).
Open:
May - September incl.
Address:
Seagull Campsite, The Administration Office, Herm Island, Channel Islands.
Tel:
(01481) 722377.
Reservations:
Made for any length with £10 deposit. Details of hire tents from above address.

318 Pomme de Chien Campsite, Sark

Tiny, family oriented site in superb 'away from it all' setting.

The 'island where time stands still' is an apt description of Sark, one of the smallest inhabited Channel Islands, some 45 minutes from Guernsey by boat. There is no airport, no cars or motorcycles and (apart from a tractor-drawn 'train' up Harbour Hill) the only transport is by bicycle or horse-drawn carriage. However everything you are likely to need for a tranquil holiday is provided with several small shops, pubs, hotels, restaurants, a Tourist Office and even two banks!

Situated some five minutes from the shops and ten minutes from the beach, the Pomme de Chien campsite on Sark is tiny in terms of the number of pitches, totalling only a dozen or so, of which six are occupied by large very fully equipped frame tents (of excellent quality) available for rent. The remainder are for campers with their own tents (no caravans, motorcaravans or trailer tents of course). The pitches themselves are large, on fairly level ground and the sanitary facilities, although small, are modern and well equipped, with free hot showers, washbasins, a baby bath, a clothes line and dishwashing facilities (open air, cold water only). Although you cannot take your car to Sark, transport by the Condor service via Guernsey means you can get there from Weymouth in a little over three hours either with your own small tent or of course you could hire one of the site's own fully equipped ones (equipment includes everything you're likely to need except bedding and a torch). Baggage can be transferred from the Harbour right to the site by tractor trailer, at a cost of 50p per item.

Directions: At the top of Harbour Hill turn left, first right, and follow the lane to the site entrance.

Charges 1996:
-- Contact site (hire tents from £130 per week).
Open:
All year - independent campers, June-Sept. for hire tents.
Address:
Sark, Channel Islands.
Tel:
(01481) 832316.
Reservations:
Write to site.

Alan Rogers' discount
Ask at park for details

We would like to thank the parks which offer discounts to our readers.

Remember - you will need to show your 1996 discount card on arrival at the park

OPEN ALL YEAR

The following parks are understood to accept caravanners and campers all year round, although the list *also includes some parks open for at least 10 months*.
For parks marked * please check our report for dates and other restrictions.
In any case, it is always wise to phone as, for example, facilities available may be reduced.

2	Broadhembury	117	Quantock Orchard	196	Percy Wood *
3	Pine Lodge	119	Southfork	197	Cwmcarn Forest
5	Black Horse Farm	120	Newbridge	205	Anchorage
7	Tanner Farm	122	Alderbury	206	Moreton Farm *
8	Canterbury C&C Club	123	Oxford International	207	Parciau Bach *
9	Thriftwood *	126	Diamond Farm	208	Afon Teifi *
14	White Rose *	128	Chertsey C&C Club	214	Bryn Gloch
17	Southsea	130	Abbey Wood	224	Brighouse Bay
23	Village Holidays *	133	The Grange *	226	Cressfield
24	New Forest Holidays	134	Low Housee	228	The Monks' Muir
33	Merley Court *	138	Rose Farm	232	Tullichewan
38	Wareham Forest	139	Two Mills *	238	Auchterarder
39	Moreton Glade *	140	Long Furlong *	249	Glenmore Forest *
42	Binghams Farm	145	Stanford	260	Linnhe *
51	Minnows *	147	Bainland	270	Tullans Farm
52	Kennford *	154	Greenhills	271	Tollymore Forest
55	Finlake *	158	Poston Mill	272	Banbridge Gateway
59	Ross Park *	161	Briarfields	273	Share
66	Grange Court *	168	St. Helens *	274	LoanEden
70	Higher Longford	174	Rawcliffe Manor	275	Táin
73	Riverside	181	Holme Valley	276	Assaroe Lakeside
87	River Valley *	184	Royal Umpire *	294	Carrick-on-Suir
95	Leverton Place	185	Bridge House *	295	Parsons Green
105	Budemeadows	190	Wild Rose	300	Sextons
115	Isle of Avalon	191	Sykeside	308	Mannix Point *
				318	Pomme de Chien

NO DOGS !

For the benefit of those who want to take their dogs with them and for those who do not like dogs on the parks they visit, we list here the parks which have indicated to us that they do not accept dogs. If you are planning to take your dog we do, however, advise that you phone the park first to check - there may be limits on numbers, breeds, etc. or times of the year when they are excluded.

3	Pine Lodge	66	Grange Court	163	Cotswold Hob.	297	The Apple
11	Woodland View	80	Pentewan	167	Northcliffe	301	The Meadow
30	Hoburne Park	100	Newquay	200	Riverside Int.	302	Eagle Point
32	Sandford	108	Twitchen	261	Oban Divers	308	Mannix Point
64	Beverley	114	Blue Anchor	281	Parkland	313	Rozel
				284	Hodson Bay	315	Vaugrat

Parks where we are aware that restrictions apply:

10	**Horam Manor** max. 2 per pitch	67	**Galmpton** not school holidays	139	**Two Mills** prior arrangement	208	**Afon Teifi** not in peak season
19	**Ashurst** only after 20 Sept.	75	**Whitsand Bay** prior arrangement	176	**Ripley** max. 2 per pitch	209	**Aeron Coast** one dog per pitch
22	**Bashley Park** max. 1 per unit	94	**Chacewater** prioe arrangement	182	**Nostell Priory** max. 2 per unit	210	**Glan-y-Mor** not B.H. or school holidays
33	**Merley Court** not high season	106	**Wooda Farm** not certain breeds	186	**Limefitt** one dog per pitch	219	**Hunter's Hamlet** max. 1 per unit
34	**Manor Farm** at owner's discretion	107	**Easewell Farm** one dog per pitch	187	**Falbarrow** one dog per pitch	260	**Linnhe** max. 2 per pitch
57	**River Dart** max.2, not certain breeds	133	**The Grange** max. 2 per pitch	190	**Wild Rose** not certain breeds	265	**Glendaruel** prior arrangement
58	**Ashburton** not certain breeds	138	**Rose Farm** prior arrangement	196	**Percy Wood** not certain breeds	314	**Rose Farm** not July or August
65	**Ramslade** not peak six weeks						

REPORTS BY READERS

We always welcome reports from readers concerning parks which they have visited. These provide invaluable feedback on parks already featured in the Guide or, in the case of those not featured in our Guide, they provide information which we can follow up with a view to adding them in future editions. Please make your comments either on this form or on plain paper. It would be appreciated if you would indicate the approximate dates when you visited the park and, in the case of potential new parks, provide the correct name and address and, if possible, include a park brochure.
Send your reports to:

Deneway Guides & Travel Ltd

Chesil Lodge, West Bexington, Dorchester, Dorset DT2 9DG

Name of Park and Ref. No. (or address for new recommendations):

....

....

Dates of Visit: ....

Comments:

Reader's Name and Address: ....

....

....

Caravan Insurance - it's not compulsory but it's a very good idea.

Unfortunately touring caravans are extremely vulnerable to all sorts of damage and can be relied upon to lose arguments with gate posts, walls, overhanging trees and people with crowbars! The following quotations taken from recently submitted claim forms are proof, if proof is needed, that caravan insurance is a <u>must.</u>

"Turned too tight an angle coming out of driveway catching side of van on brick pillar"

"The caravan was in storage and was broken into with 37 others"

"Caravan door damaged, twisted and levered, lock smashed"

"The rear window of the caravan was blown out due to high winds"

"My wife and I were pushing the caravan onto the drive when we misjudged how close to the gate post we were"

CLAIM YOUR ALAN ROGERS READERS DISCOUNT

All of these situations and many others are catered for by the specialist policies of 'The Caravan Insurance Centre'. For full details, including a copy of the 'Guide to Caravan Insurance', complete and return the coupon below. By utilising this coupon you will benefit from a special discount for readers of an 'Alan Rogers' publication.

Please send me by return your 'FREE Guide to Caravan Insurance' and proposal forms

AR

Name ....

Address ....

....

....

Postcode ....

THE CARAVAN INSURANCE CENTRE

THE QUADRANGLE
IMPERIAL SQUARE
CHELTENHAM GL50 1PZ

BAKERS
OF CHELTENHAM

PARK BROCHURE SERVICE

The following parks have supplied us with a quantity of their brochures. These leaflets are interesting and useful supplements to the editorial reports in this Guide. If you would like any of these simply cut out or copy this page, tick the relevant boxes and post it to us. Please enclose a large envelope (at least 9" x 6") addressed to yourself and stamped (some leaflets are heavier than others but, on average, 5 will weigh 50 gms). Send your requests to:

Deneway Guides & Travel Ltd, Chesil Lodge, West Bexington, Dorchester DT2 9DG

England

23	Village Holidays	☐
74	Polborder House	☐
79	Carlyon Bay	☐
81	Penhaven	☐
83	Tretheake Manor	☐
86	Calloose	☐
95	Leverton Place	☐
106	Wooda Farm	☐
118	Broadway House	☐
125	Cotswold View	☐
136	The Dower House	☐
144	Highfield Farm	☐
156	Glencote	☐
173	Golden Square	☐
	Countryside Discovery Group	☐

Wales

201	Fforest Fields	☐
205	Anchorage	☐
212	Pen-y-Garth	☐
219	Hunter's Hamlet	☐

Scotland

226	Cressfield	☐
237	Nether Craig	☐
246	Auchnahillin	☐

Northern Ireland

274	LoanEden	☐

Irish Republic

306	Waterville	☐
308	Mannix Point	☐
	Irish Caravan Council	☐

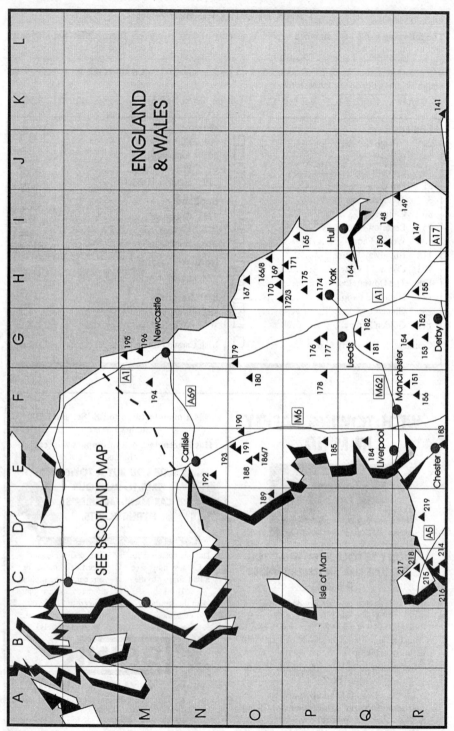

ENGLAND
& WALES

SEE SCOTLAND MAP

Newcastle

Carlisle

Isle of Man

Liverpool

Manchester

Leeds

York

Hull

Derby

Chester

195
196
194
179
176
177
180
178
167
166/8
169
170
171
172/3
175
174
165
164
155
150
148
149
147
190
193
191
186/7
188
192
185
184
189
182
181
154
152
153
151
156
183
217
218
215
216
214
219

A1
A69
M6
M62
A1
A17
A5

184

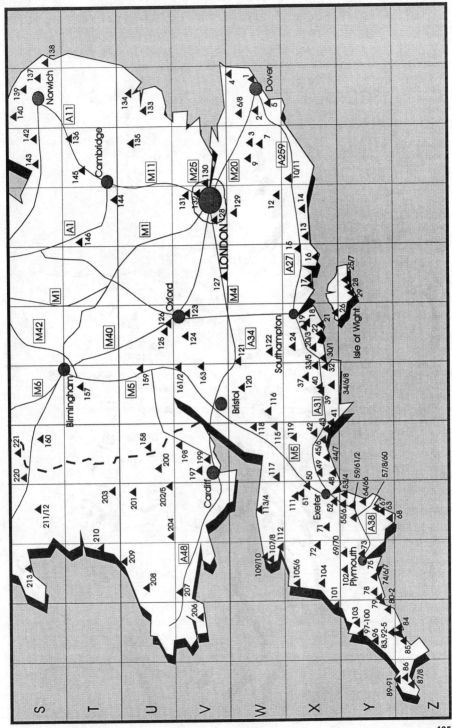

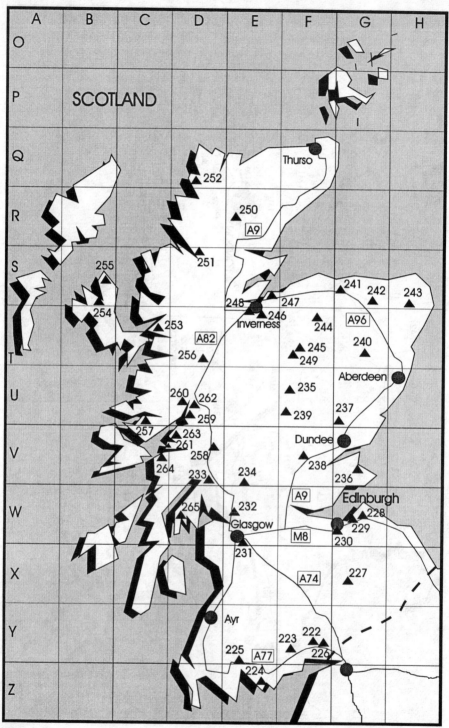

SCOTLAND

A B C D E F G H

O

P

Q   Thurso
    ▲ 252

R   ▲ 250
    A9

S   ▲ 251
    ▲ 255
    ▲ 254   ▲ 253
            A82   ▲ 246   ▲ 247   ▲ 241   ▲ 242   ▲ 243
            ▲ 248   Inverness   ▲ 244   A96
T   ▲ 256   ▲ 245   ▲ 240
            ▲ 249   Aberdeen
U   ▲ 260   ▲ 262   ▲ 235   ▲ 237
    ▲ 259   ▲ 239
    ▲ 257   ▲ 263   Dundee
    ▲ 261   ▲ 238
V   ▲ 258   ▲ 236
    ▲ 264   ▲ 233   ▲ 234
                    A9   Edinburgh
W   ▲ 265   ▲ 232   ▲ 228
            Glasgow   ▲ 229
            M8   ▲ 230
    ▲ 231
X   A74   ▲ 227
Y   Ayr   ▲ 223   ▲ 222
    ▲ 225   A77   ▲ 226
Z   ▲ 224

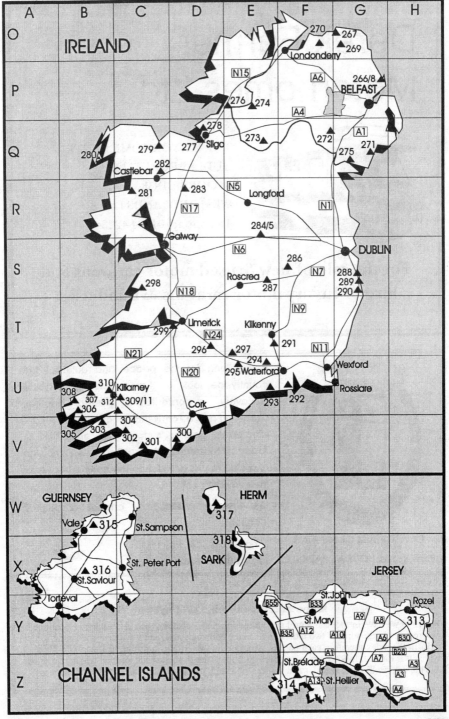

	A	B	C	D	E	F	G	H
O		IRELAND				270	267	
						Londonderry	269	
P				N15		A6	266/8	
							BELFAST	
				276	274	A4	A1	
Q	280	279	277	278	273	272	275 271	
		Castlebar	282	Sligo				
R		281	283	N17	N5	Longford	N1	
			Galway		284/5		DUBLIN	
S		298	N18	N6	Roscrea 287	286 N7	288 289 290	
T			299	Limerick N24 296 297	Kilkenny 291	N9 N11		
		N21		N20 295	294 Waterford		Wexford	
U	308 307 306	310 Killarney 312 309/11	304	Cork 300	293 292		Rosslare	
V	305 303 302 301							
W	GUERNSEY		Vale 315	St.Sampson	HERM 317			
X			316 St.Saviour St. Peter Port	318 SARK		JERSEY	Rozel	
	Torteval				St.John	B55 B33	A9 A8 313	
Y					St.Mary B35 A12 A10	A6 A7	B30 B28 A3	
Z	CHANNEL ISLANDS			314 A13 St.Helier	St.Brelade A1	A3 A4		

187

Maps and Index - new grid system

For 1996 we have introduced a grid system for our maps, whereby each grid square is identified by co-ordinates in the form of two letters - one on the horizontal axis, and a different one on the vertical axis. In the index therefore each park is identified by two letters, indicating the map grid square in which it is located, followed by a number which identifies the actual site location within that square. We hope this will make it easier and quicker to identify the location of parks in unfamiliar areas.

INDEX

INDEX

INDEX